THE ANSWERS LIE BELOW

Essays in Honor of
Lawrence Edmund Toombs

Edited by
Henry O. Thompson

UNIVERSITY
PRESS OF
AMERICA

LANHAM • NEW YORK • LONDON

Copyright © 1984 by

University Press of America,™ Inc.

4720 Boston Way
Lanham, MD 20706

3 Henrietta Street
London WC2E 8LU England

Library of Congress Cataloging in Publication Data
Main entry under title:

The Answers lie below.

1. Bible–Criticism, interpretation, etc.–Addresses,
essays, lectures. 2. Bible–Antiquities–Addresses,
essays, lectures. 3. Near East–Antiquities–Addresses,
essays, lectures. 4. Excavations (Archaeology)–Near East
– Addresses, essays, lectures. 5. Archaeological surveying
– Near East–Addresses, essays, lectures. I. Thompson,
Henry O. II. Toombs, Lawrence E.
BS540.A63   1984   220.9'3   83–23376
ISBN 0–8191–3745–6 (alk. paper)
ISBN 0–8191–3746–4 (pbk. : alk. paper))

All University Press of America books are produced on acid-free
paper which exceeds the minimum standards set by the National
Historical Publications and Records Commission.

LAWRENCE EDMUND TOOMBS

iii

iv

TABLE OF CONTENTS

LET US NOW PRAISE FAMOUS PEOPLE: By Way of Preface

A preface is a time of acknowledgement and it is a great pleasure
to recognize the help of many people on the way to the completion
of this delightful project. Obviously the contributors of the essays are the first of the great people to be praised. Without the
content they have provided, the text would not be, or at least it
would be entirely different. The help and moral support Carolyn
Toombs has been deeply appreciated. Background material has come
from Kevin O'Connell, Jeff Blakely, and Bob Bull among others and
their assistance has been most welcome. The enthusiasm that has
greeted this project, even among those who could not contribute because of other commitments, has been a source of much satisfaction.
While I have had this dream for several decades, the encouragement
of others makes it clear that I am but one among many who would
praise famous people. It is a joy to acknowledge here the truly
great assistance of Margaret Wilder whose typing of the manuscripts
went beyond the call of duty in corrections and care.

At an earlier stage of this project, I was told that festschrif-
ten do not sell well these days. That is unfortunate for there are
many good things published therein, so much so that they are now
being indexed. But the purpose of a festschrift is not to make
money in the first place, though one could hardly object if we had
a best seller on our hands! It is rather to praise the famous person for whom the festschrift is written. For that purpose, it is
an honor and a privilege to "write in celebration" of the 65th
birthday of Lawrence Edmund Toombs, or simply Larry to friends, or
"El Hakam," "the Wise One," to admirers. Surely here is one of the
Wise of biblical fame as in Jeremiah 18:18, or in Ecclesiasticus
or Ben Sirach or Qoheleth the Preacher who was himself one of the
Wise Ones and who called us all, saying: "Let us now praise famous people" (Sirach 44:1).

At one point in the preparation of this volume, the question of
a name or title came into the discussion. "What's in a Name?"
someone asked. There may be little or nothing, accident or chance.
But in the biblical tradition, among the ancient Hebrews and to
some extent the Semites in general and other peoples as well, the
name means something. It signifies something of the person so designated. Thus this text, in keeping with that tradition, has a
name or needed one that reflected not simply the contents but the
person whom it intends to honor in this small way. His achievements and his life speak loud and clear so there is no point in
"gilding the lily" for it already has the beauty of the Creator.
Thus this book is not intended as "gilding" but as an expression
of affection and respect for one we appreciate. One suggestion
for a title was "Dig We Must," borrowing from a sign often seen a-
round the larger holes in New York City. Larry has certainly dug
often enough and the writers of these essays have not only dug into the dirt of the Near East and elsewhere, they have dug into the
past in general and into the biblical text as well. And there is

no doubt that many or at least some of us work with an element of
compulsion. There is a sense in which we "must" dig. The curios-
ty, the challenge, the quest for some holy grail, whatever it is
that takes us into the depths of the past, is in some sense a driv-
ing force for some kind of answer or answers. The proposed title
would seem singularly appropriate for LET and for many of the students and colleagues he has led in the quest or in whose quest he
has shared.

The title chosen, however, is both distinctly reflective of the
man who has said it on many occasions and reflective of the above
"quest." While he has a great fund of answers, he has often as
not pointed the way to the answers, the way in which others, the
rest of us, any who chose to do so, might continue the quest. Given with great good humor and sometimes positive glee, Larry's a-
phorism carries a yet deeper meaning as humor often does. There
is hope in his dictum that the answers lie below. There are many
problems in life as well as in archaeology or the Bible but there
is hope, for "The answers lie below." Keep on digging!

Henry O. Thompson
Philadelphia, PA

LAWRENCE EDMUND TOOMBS

Lawrence Edmund Toombs was born April 1, 1919. In some cultures, that day is known as April Fool's Day. It is typical of the Lord God of Hosts that he turns upside down the usual expectations of people. According to I Samuel 16, the Lord sent Samuel to Bethlehem to anoint a king out of the sons of Jesse. The sons of Jesse passed before Samuel but not one of them was chosen. Finally Samuel said (vs. 11), "Are all of your sons here?" And he said, "There remains yet the youngest, but behold, he is keeping the sheep." Samuel would not take no for an answer and so David was brought to him. "And the Lord said, 'Arise, anoint him for this is he.'" It was not the oldest or biggest who was chosen but the youngest and the least. But the teen-ager became the great King David, builder of an empire, sweet singer of psalms, inspirer of loyalty and devotion (II Samuel 23:13-17).[1]

So April Fool's Day arrived in 1919, but instead of foolishness, God sent Wisdom! Colleagues at Tell el Hesi call him El Hakam! The Wise One!

The blessed event took place in the home of Edmund and Amelia Elizabeth (Luther) Toombs in Charlottetown, the largest city and the capital of Prince Edward Island, Canada. Charlottetown boasts a population of over 25,000. The island is just over 2,000 square miles though the island itself is anything but square. It is the smallest of the Canadian provinces and the birthplace (1864) of the Canadian Confederation of 1867. Its entire population is just over 100,000. The people are mainly of British extraction; also Acadian and Mimac Native Americans.[2] They make their living primarily from farm, sea and tourists. The island lies in the Gulf of St. Lawrence, east of New Brunswick, north of Nova Scotia and southwest of Newfoundland. Collectively, these are known as the Atlantic Provinces of Canada.

Larry's interest in science led him to Prince of Wales College (then a junior college, now part of UPEI) and Acadia University in Wolfville, Nova Scotia. He received a Bachelor of Arts (English) in 1940 and a Bachelor of Science in 1941, with Honors in Chemistry. Post-graduate work in Chemistry followed at the University of Toronto where he did research in explosives. These studies were interrupted to serve (1943-1945) as a meteorologist with the Canadian Department of Transport and the Royal Canadian Air Force during World War II.

This work ended in 1945, as did his bachelorhood. On June 25, he married Carol Millicent West. In due time, they had two children, Millicent Ann and Edmund Mark.

The year 1945 also saw a major career change. Larry entered Pine Hill Divinity Hall in Halifax, Nova Scotia. He received the Bachelor of Divinity degree there in 1948. He graduated with Honors in New Testament.

In 1948, he went to The Theological School of Drew University in Madison, N.J., U.S.A. Here he studied the Old Testament with Dr. John Paterson (1887-1967), a Scot noted for his ability to quote great lengths of the Bible from memory, and for the clarity and insights and common sense of his interpretations of the sacred texts. Larry's tribute to him came 20 years later in his article, "The Scholar as Preacher: John Paterson," published in the Drew Gateway 38, Nos. 1-2 (1967-1968), 7-10.[3]

Larry's dissertation bears the title, "Human Nature in the Old Testament." The Ph.D. was awarded in 1951. By this time, he had already been teaching at St. Stephen's College in Edmonton, Alberta, Canada for a year, as Associate Professor of Old Testament. He continued there for another two years, as Professor of Old Testament Language and Literature. He was already known for the excellence of his preaching and did a great deal of it for the United Church of Canada congregations of Edmonton and the province. He was also well along in his fascinating ability to take the results of biblical scholarship and translate them into prose as well as the spoken word. Out of his association with the National Young People of Canada came his first major publication, A Year with the Bible (United Church of Canada, 1953). It was used for years across the Dominion. He has continued over the years to make an extensive contribution to the church in his writings for church school, both pupils and teachers. Through his pen the Scriptures have come alive and make a living contribution to the lives of both throughout the United Methodist Church in the United States and wherever their publications are used. A look at the bibliography shows him ranging the length and breadth and depth of the Bible. Someone once sneered about wasting time writing "Sunday School stuff." Larry responded with characteristic candor that if we expect the church to read and use the Bible with intelligent awareness of scholarship, it was up to the scholars to let the church know what was going on. That down to earth wisdom has been extended to the small and great, the learned and unlearned. Wisdom held captive in the Ivory Tower or collecting dust in the library stacks, is perhaps the real foolishness, not only of April first, but for all time. Toombs' contribution to the young and to the teachers of the church is beyond calculation!

In 1953, Larry was enticed back to Drew as Assistant Professor and heir apprent to "Dr. John" who retired in 1957. Toombs spent the next 15 years of his life at Drew, rising through Associate Professor (1956-61) to Professor of Old Testament (1961-68). They were fruitful years as a glance at his bibliography will show. What that does not show, at least in cold print, is the masterful teaching that was done in those years, in The Theological School, but also in The Graduate School of Drew University. The Graduate School was formed in 1955 as a separate entity, though the University has been granting graduate degrees for most of its history. He further extended his mastery in the classroom in the College of Liberal Arts, originally called Brothers College. That mastery was shared in the public arena in untold numbers of talks, lectures, presentations and sermons throughout the area. His well known preaching ability had abundant opportunities during these years. His sermon on Hosea, "Love in a Slave Market," was published in Best Sermons, ed. G. Paul Butler; NY: T. Y. Crowell, 1959. To that one must add "The Law in English," Pulpit Digest (March 63), 11-15. Sunday after Sunday, the early service at Madison Methodist Church showed he had "the power of sustaining interest." His sermons respect the mind of his audience even as they reach for the heart.

Part of the marvel of the bearer of Wisdom was apparent in all of this. It has been said that those who can, do. Those who can't, teach. That did not apply to L. Toombs for he can teach extremely well! It has also been said that those who can, do. Those who can't preach. That does not apply to L. Toombs for he can preach extremely well! It has been said that those

who can, do. Those who can't, write! That does not
apply to L. Toombs, for he writes extremely well! To
put it mildly, he was endowed by his Creator with various and sundry gifts, all of which he cherished and
nourished and honed to sharpness of insight, clarity
of thought, articulate expression, and to quote
Socrates, a humble awareness of his own ignorance. It
was the latter you may recall which led the Oracle of
Delphi to proclaim Socrates the wisest man in all
Greece. This paean to our present subject will not go
quite that far! The writer <u>has</u> been accused of worshipping the ground his mentor walked upon but it is
not quite true. That would be to obscure the humanness
of the man which is as great as his scholarship. But
the old adage remains that unto whom much is given,
much is required (Luke 12:48). Toombs has been an
excellent steward of his gifts, returning 60 and 100-
fold.

One notable aspect of the scholarship, which appears in much of what he does in the pulpit, at the
lectern, in writing, and in field work, is what learning theorists call "insight." In Toombs, this appears
in his ability to cut through vast amounts of data to
get at the heart or core of a matter. It is not unusual that he does this with verve and humor which can
be a bit unsettling. A reviewer took him to task for
describing the intertestamental literature as a great
tapeworm! I thought it quite apt myself. I do not
see the analogy as a put-down at all. My background in
biology reminds me that a tapeworm is a long segmented
creature. The parts are loosely connected. They not
uncommonly break apart and exist independently of the
original. His professorial address was criticized as
being all about the obvious. Since I thought it was
well done, I pushed the critic a bit and found that the
"obvious" was only so, now that Toombs had pointed it
out.

The Drew years also saw a major move into archaeology. In December, 1955, the American Schools of
Oriental Research awarded him a fellowship. He spent
the 1956-57 academic year in Jerusalem, as a Fellow of
the ASOR in Jerusalem. He worked at Jericho in the
British School of Archaeology excavations directed by
the late Dame Kathleen Mary Kenyon (1906-1978). In the
summer before and the summer after, he shared in the
beginnings of the Drew-McCormick (later Joint) Expedition to Shechem, directed by George Ernest Wright

(1909-1974), then of McCormick Theological Seminary in Chicago, later Parkman Professor of Divinity at Harvard Divinity School in Cambridge, Massachusetts. His 1956 work at Shechem only lasted a week before the illness of his father caused a halt to that participation. However, he made a full season in 1957.

Larry began as a field supervisor and then became Assistant Director at Shechem in 1960 and Associate Director in 1962. His first article on Shechem was published in the Drew Gateway while the second article on Shechem (with Howard C. Kee, then of Drew, and now at Boston) was in 1957. Publications on Shechem have continued and he is currently at work on the final or definitive reports for Shechem covering Late Bronze Pottery and the city's fortification system. Several of his Shechem reports were co-authored with Director Wright; others were co-authored with Drew colleague, James F. Ross (now at Virginia Theological Seminary) others were with R. J. Bull of Drew and Edward F. Campbell, Jr. of McCormick.

Larry's organizational ability is implied in the above roles at Shechem. That ability has made a contribution to his professions through his work and membership in the usual professional societies. He has been national secretary for the Society of Biblical Literature and has been a member of the American Academy of Religion, The Biblical Colloquium, the National Association of Professors of Hebrew, and of course the American Schools of Oriental Research. He has been Secretary-Treasurer for the Jerusalem School and a member of ASOR's Committee on Archaeological Policy, the Committee on Computer Archaeology and the Committee on Archaeological Standards and Evaluation.

A second sabbatical in 1961-1962 saw him in London at the University of London's Institute of Archaeology, founded by the indomitable Sir Robert Eric Mortimer Wheeler (1890-1976). Wheeler's famous pupil, Kathleen Kenyon, was teaching there. Her tutelage of Toombs thus went from the field in Jericho to the classroom in London. Perhaps it is no accident that in archaeology, Larry is noted for many abilities but as a stratigraphist, he is simply superb. The Wheeler-Kenyon method, sometimes known as the Pitt-Rivers-Wheeler-Kenyon method, or the Wheeler-Kenyon-Albright or the Wheeler-Kenyon-Wright method has had virtually world wide acceptance though there remain many hold-outs and

modifiers, and it is often more preached than practiced.
Some devotees have out Kenyoned Kenyon in their worship
of the sacred baulk. Toombs, however, with his continuing insight, balance and common sense has read the
writing (graphe) of the strata and translated the story
told into the language of humankind, without pausing to
worship either past or present stratigraphers. A recent
publication, "The Development of Palestinian Archaeology
as a Discipline" (BA 45, No. 2 [Spr 82], 89-91) notes
again the importance of the horizontal in excavation as
Pitt-Rivers and Wheeler intended. Among his writings
on Shechem, not surprisingly, several are on its stratigraphy: "Appendix V. The Stratification of the Temple
Forecourt," pp. 214-228 in Shechem, ed. G. Ernest
Wright; NY: McGraw-Hill, 1965, The Annual of the Department of Antiquities of Jordan XVII (1972), 99-111,
and, The Bulletin of the American Schools of Oriental
Research No. 223 (Oct 76), 57-58. More recent work
involved Caesarea and is published as "The Stratigraphy
of Caesarea Maritima," pp. 223-232 in Archaeology in
the Levant: Essays for Kathleen Kenyon, ed. P.R.S.
Moorey and Peter Parr; Warminster: Aris and Phillips,
1978. The stratigraphy of Hesi is presented in Tell
el Hesi   published by Wake Forest University.

     While still working on Shechem, he became a part
of the staff of the College of Wooster expedition at
Pella (Tabaqat Fahl) directed by Robert Houston Smith
in the Jordan Valley. He wrote the Excavation Manual
but never made it to the dig himself. The work there
was interrupted by the 1967 Arab - Israeli war. Back
on the homefront, another kind of war erupted between
the president of Drew University and the faculty of
Drew's Theological School. The details remain obscure
with a good deal of speculation and little hard data.
Perhaps the full story will be known in the Afterlife
though one suspects that by that time it won't matter!
Suffice it to say, that Larry left Drew and Madison,
NJ in the U.S.A. to return to his native Canada. He
took the position of Professor of Old Testament at
Union College of British Columbia in Vancouver for one
year, 1968-1969.

     From the far west of the Dominion, he retraced his
steps to the midlands. Since 1969, he has been Professor of Religion and Culture at Wilfrid Laurier University in Waterloo, Ontario. The school was earlier
known as Waterloo Lutheran University until 1973. They
changed their name but not their initials. The changing

of schools and names did not change the quality of the
wise one born on April Fool's Day. In 1980, WLU named
Larry the "Outstanding Teacher of the Year" upon the
recommendation of students, alumni and faculty. He
became chairperson of the Department in May 1982.

Other changes have taken place. In May 1970, he
was Field Archaeologist at the Moyer site near New
Dundee, Ontario. This work led to the publication,
with Norman E. Wagner and Eduard R. Riegert, of The
Moyer Site: A Pre-Historic Village in Waterloo County;
Waterloo, Ontario: Wilfrid Laurier Press, 1973. In
1972, he became Senior Archaeologist to the Joint Expedition to Caesarea Maritima, directed by his old Drew
colleague, and fellow Shechemite, Robert J. Bull, who
also worked at Pella. Reports on Caesarea were published in the Israel Exploration Journal 22 (1972),
178-180, and in Revue Biblique 80, No. 4 (1973), 582-
585 both co-authored with Bob Bull.

In 1970, Larry also joined the staff, as Senior
Archaeologist and later Archaeological Director (until
1981), of the Joint Expedition to Tell el-Hesi. At
this writing, his work at Hesi continues as his publications on the site have continued since 1970. Several
of these were co-authored with Davis Glenn Rose (1928-
1981) to whom he paid tribute in ASOR Newsletter No. 4
(Jan 82), 1-3, and, Kevin G. O'Connell, S.J., whose
contribution in this volume is a tribute to Larry. In
addition to the several excavation reports, he co-
authored with Jeffrey A. Blakely, one of his students
at WLU, The Tell el-Hesi Field Manual: The Joint
Archaeological Expedition to Tell el-Hesi, I; Cambridge:
ASOR, 1980. The work is part of the ASOR Excavation
Report series edited by David Noel Freedman. Hesi II
is Tell el-Hesi: Modern Military Trenching and Muslim
Cemetery in Field I (Strata I - II); Waterloo, Ontario:
Wilfrid Laurier Press, 1984. It is also an ASOR excavation report. Publication of this volume is covered
by a grant from Aid to Scholarly Publication, a Canadian agency whose funds come from The Social Sciences
and Humanities Research Council of Canada (SSHRC). The
latter has also provided a three-year grant to process
Iron II material from Hesi. The publication will be an
additional volume in the Hesi series, co-authored this
time with Jeff Blakely and Ralph Doermann. Kevin G.
O'Connell, S.J., serves as editor for the Hesi volumes.

The year 1970 saw a major change in family with

the end of his first marriage. In 1974, he remarried.
Frances Carolyn (Wilson) Hicks has been a student of
Semitic languages. She toured the Near East in 1965
and worked at Ai (Director Joseph Calloway's article
is in this volume; he worked with us at Shechem for
several seasons) in 1968 and '69. She received her
M.A. from WLU in 1975. This marriage gave Larry four
more children: Angela, Christina, John and Kellie. It
also made Larry an instant grandfather through Frances
Carolyn's daughter Angela (Mrs. S. A. Nellis) and her
children, Leslie and Philip. There are five grand-
children as we go to press.

The year 1975 saw Millicent or Millie graduate
from WLU with a B.A. in English. She worked for seven
years as an accountant for the Waterloo County Board of
Education before moving to Calgary. Ed graduated from
WLU in 1978 as a gold-medal winner in philosophy, married Anne Fleming, another WLU grad, in Aug 78. In
1981, both earned L.L.S. degrees from Western Ontario
in London. They now live in Ottawa, employed by the
National Library. Ed is pursuing a Ph.D. in philosophy
at the University of Ottawa.

The academic year, 1975-1976 saw him once again in
Jerusalem, this time as Annual Professor at the American School of Oriental Research in Jerusalem, now re-
named the William Foxwell Albright Institute for Archaeological Research. Albright (1891-1971) was the "Dean"
of American biblical and Near Eastern archaeologists,
the mentor of G. Ernest Wright and by extension, the
mentor, or "grand-mentor" of Wright's students and
trainees in archaeology. Through his long association
with G. Ernest Wright, in field archaeology and interpretation, Toombs falls heir to the Albright tradition.
Through both field work and classroom, he is heir to
the Wheeler-Kenyon tradition. In his person, he thus
combines all the best we know of that fascinating
artistic science or scientific art known as archaeology,
the study of the old newly brought to light. However,
Larry himself would be the first to say that he by no
means knows it all. In fact, one of his more memorable
aphorisms in the field came regularly in response to
the frequent query, "What do you think was happening
here?" Often enough, he knew, or had a good idea. But
there not unusually would come a point in the conversation, when with his continuing proverbial and prophetic
wisdom, L. Toombs would proclaim, "The answers lie
below!"

On the occasion of his 65th birthday, the future is rich with uncertainty. We can expect a continuing flow of publication and insight but I do not predict all the details thereof. He taught a lesson on Jeremiah the prophet. Jeremiah was squared off against Hananiah (Jeremiah 28). In the vernacular, Hananiah was saying that the troops will be home by Christmas, or in that context, the Exiles would be back for Passover. Jeremiah wished it were true but his word from the Lord differed. How could people tell which prophet was right? Larry offered a Ph.D. to anyone who could determine with complete accuracy the answer to that question -- in advance. Jeremiah said time will tell and we look forward to many years of time for Lawrence Edmund Toombs, born on April Fool's Day - but filled with wisdom. Or, as another old friend is fond of saying, "The story is to be continued."

Henry O. Thompson

FOOTNOTES

1. Larry's students will recognize the source for this interpretation. For comments on "foolishness," readers will find of interest his "The Foolishness of Preaching," Drew Gateway (DG) 52, No. 1 (Fall 81), 14-20. This is the Michalson Society Lecture for 1981.
2. The Acadians are well known. The Micmac Indians are found in Nova Scotia, Cape Breton Island, Prince Edward Island, Newfoundland and New Brunswick. Their language is part of the Algonquin tradition. French missionaries were in touch with them in the early part of the 17th century. They are mainly Roman Catholic today. Expert canoeists, once centered on fishing and hunting, they are now primarily agriculturalists. The New Columbia Encyclopedia; NY: Columbia University Press, 1975, p. 1770.
3. In that same issue of DG is R. Benjamin Garrison's "John Paterson," pp. 11-12, and, an excerpt, pp. 1-6 of "The Church, The Bible, and The Preacher," Paterson's Matriculation Address. He came to Drew in 1931 and retired in 1957. His address was printed in full in the Drew University Bulletin XX, No. 2 (Nov 31), 3-19. A complete record of Paterson's publications are in Lawrence D. McIntosh and Francis S. Lee, "A Bibliography of the Writings of John Paterson," DG XXXIX, No. 3 (Spr 69), 140-149. He wrote many book reviews and made numerous contributions to books, journals and Christian Education Curricula. His books include:
The Goodly Fellowship of the Prophets; NY: Scribner's, 1948.
The Praises of Israel; NY: Scribner's, 1950.
The Book That is Alive: Studies in Old Testament Life and Thought as Set Forth by the Hebrew Sages; NY: Scribner's, 1954.

The Evangelistic Message of the Bible; Nashville: Tidings, 1955.
The Meaning of the Bible for Protestants; Nashville: Tidings, n.d.
The Wisdom of Israel: Job and Proverbs; NY: Abingdon, 1961.

Sources
Archaeological Discoveries in the Holy Land, compiled by the AIA;
NY: Crowell, 1967, p. 213.
Contemporary Authors, Vols. 5-8, rev.; Detroit: Gale, 1969, p.
1154.
Public Relations Office, Drew University, Madison, NJ.
Office of Information and Special Events, Wilfrid Laurier Univer-
sity, Waterloo, Ontario, Canada. Special thanks to Director Rich-
ard K. Taylor, who also supplied the picture for the frontispiece.
"Word about the Writer," Bible Lives Student Book 1 (Wint 79-80),
p. 4.
Family, Friends, Colleagues, Students

LAWRENCE EDMUND TOOMBS

A Partial Bibliography

1948
The Prologue to the Fourth Gospel; Halifax: Pine Hill Divinity
Hall. B.D. Thesis, unpublished. Degree conferred, 1948.

1950
with Phillip C. Hammond, Jr., "The Drew Samaritan," Drew Gateway (hereafter DG) XX, No. 4 (Sum 50), 9-12.

1951
Human Nature in the Old Testament; Madison, NJ: Drew University. Ph.D. Dissertation, unpublished. Degree conferred, 1951.

1953
A Year with the Bible; Toronto: United Church Publishing House.

1954
"The Temple of Baal," DG XXIV, No. 4 (Sum 54), 195-200.

Reviews
Donald G. Miller, Fire in Thy Mouth; NY: Abingdon, 1954.
Rev: DG XXIV, No. 3 (Sp 54), 163.
Virginia G. Millikin, Jeremiah, Prophet of Disaster; NY: Asso-
ciation, 1954. Laura Long, Queen Esther, Star in Judea's
Crown; NY: Association, 1954. Albert N. Williams, Paul, The
World's First Missionary; NY: Association, 1954.
Rev: DG XXIV, No. 3 (Sp 54), 162-163.
Edward P. Blair, The Bible and You; NY: Abingdon-Cokesbury,
1953. Moses Hadas, The Third and Fourth Books of Maccabees;
Harper, 1953.
Rev: DG XXIV, No. 4 (Sum 54), 223-224.
Edward Nielsen, Oral Tradition; Chicago: Allenson, 1954.
Rev: DG XXV, No. 1 (Aut 54), 47-8.
Julius A. Bewer, The Book of Ezekiel; NY: Harper, 1954.
Rev: DG XXV, No. 1 (Aut 54), 48.
James S. Stewart, A Faith to Proclaim; Scribner's, 1953.
Rev: DG XXV, No. 2 (Wint 54), 119.

1955
"Old Testament Theology and the Wisdom Literature," Journal of
Bible and Religion (hereafter JBR) 23, No. 3 (July 55), 193-6.

Reviews
Norman K. Gottwald, Studies in the Book of Lamentations; Chi-
cago: Allenson, 1954.
Rev: DG XXV, No. 3 (Sp 55), 172-3.
Joy Davidson, Smoke on the Mountain; Philadelphia: Westmin-
ster, 1954.
Rev: DG XXV, No. 3 (Sp 55), 173-4.
B. David Napier, From Faith to Faith; NY: Harper, 1955.
Rev: DG XXVI, No. 1 (Aut 55), 47-8.

Harry M. Orlinsky, Ancient Israel; Ithaca: Cornell, 1954.
Louis Wallis, Young People's Hebrew History; NY: Philosophi-
cal Library, 1953.
Rev: DG XXVI, No. 1 (Aut 55), 58-9.
Herbert F. Hahn, The Old Testament in Modern Research; Phila-
delphia: Muhlenburg Press, 1954.
Rev: DG XXVI, No. 1 (Aut 55), 59-60.
Elmer A. Leslie, Jeremiah; NY: Abingdon, 1954.
Rev: DG XXVI, No. 2 (Wint 55), 105-6.

1956
"Drew at Shechem," DG XXVI, No. 4 (Sum 56), 195-203.
"The Early History of the Qumran Sect," Journal of Semitic
Studies 1, No. 4 (Oct 56), 367-381.

Reviews
Ben Kimpel, Moral Principles of the Bible; NY: Philosophical
Library, 1956.
Rev: DG XXVI, No. 4 (Sum 56), 210-212.

1957
"Barcosiba and Qumran," New Testament Studies 4 (1957), 65-71.
with Howard C. Kee, "The Second Season of Excavation at Biblical Shechem," Biblical Archaeologist (hereafter BA) 20, No. 4
(Dec 57), 82-105.

1959
"The Doctrine of Resurrection in Intertestamental Judaism," DG
XXIV, No. 3 (Sp 59), 147-159.
"Love in a Slave Market," pp. 217-222 in Best Sermons VIII, ed.
G. Paul Butler; NY: Crowell, 1959.
"Recent Continental Old Testament Studies: A Review Article,"
DG XXX, No. 1 (Aut 59), 22-29.
"Worship in the Psalter," Religion in Life 29, No. 1 (Wint 59-
60), 118-127.

1960
The Threshhold of Christianity; Philadelphia: Westminster.

Reviews
Cecil Roth, The Historical Background of the Dead Sea Scrolls;
NY: Philosophical Library, 1959.
Rev: DG XXXI, No. 1 (Aut 60), 48-9.
Sigmund Mowinckel, The Old Testament as Word of God; NY: Ab-
ingdon, 1959.
Rev: DG XXXI, No. 1 (Aut 60), 49-50.

1961
The Old Testament in Christian Preaching; Philadelphia: Westminster.

"Archaeology and Theological Studies," DG XXXII, No. 1 (Aut 61),
26-34.
"The Formation of Myth Patterns in the Old Testament," JBR 29,
No. 2 (Ap 61), 108-112.

"History and History Writing in the Old Testament," DG XXXI,
No. 3 (Sp 61), 135-146.
with G. Ernest Wright, "The Third Campaign at Balatah (Shechem),"
Bulletin of the American Schools of Oriental Research (hereafter
BASOR) 161 (Feb 61), 11-54.
with James F. Ross, "Three Campaigns at Biblical Shechem," Arch-
aeology 14 (1961), 171-9.
"We Believe: The Bible - The Word of God for Man," Together V,
No. 12 (Dec 61), 45-6.

1962
  Nation Making; NY and London: Abingdon and Lutterworth.

  "The Bible: Word of God for Man," Ch. 4 in We Believe; NY:
  Abingdon.
  "Clean and Unclean," "Crown," "Knife," "Throne," "Traps and
  Snares," and several brief entries in The Interpreter's Dictionary of the Bible; NY: Abingdon, pp. 641-8, etc.
  "Daily Life in Ancient Shechem," DG XXXII, No. 3 (Sp 62), 166-
  172.
  with James F. Ross, "Les découvertes effectuies au cour des der-
  nières campagne de fouilles à Sichem," Bible et Terre Sainte
  44 (Fevr 62), 6-10.
  with G. Ernest Wright, "Sichem," Revue Biblique (hereafter RB)
  69 (1962), 257-266.

1963
  God's People Among the Nations; NY and London: Association and
  Lutterworth.
  Reader's Guide for Leviticus, Bible Reader's Service Guide 3;
  Nashville: Board of Education, The Methodist Church.

  "Encounter with God," Adult Student (hereafter AS) 22 (Aug 63),
  60+.
  "Encounter with God," AS 22 (Sep 63), 40+.
  "Faith in the Life of Men," AS 22 (Sep 63), 60+.
  with G. Ernest Wright, "The Fourth Campaign at Balatah (She-
  chem)," BASOR 169 (Feb 63), 1-60.
  "Joseph, Instrument of God's Will," AS 22 (Sep 63), 45+.
  "The Law in English," Pulpit Digest (Mar 63), 11-15.
  "Sichem," RB 70 (1963), 425-433.

  Reviews
    John Juxtable, The Bible Says; Richmond: John Knox, 1962.
    Rev: DG XXXIII, No. 2 (Wint 63), 105.
    Arthur Gabriel Hebert, The Old Testament from Within; London:
    Oxford University Press, 1962.
    Rev: DG XXXIII, No. 2 (Wint 63), 106-7.
    Bernhard W. Anderson and Walter Harrelson, eds., Israel's
    Prophetic Heritage; NY: Harper, 1962.
    Rev: DG XXXIV, No. 1 (Aut 63), 58-60.

1964
  "The Heart of the Old Testament," Adult Teacher XVII, No. 7

(July 64), 12-13.

"What Do You Mean?," W.O.R. Radio. Guest Author, Ap 64.

Review

John Gray, Archaeology and the Old Testament World; NY: Nelson, 1963.
Rev: DG XXXIV, No. 2 (Wint 64), 106-7.

1965

"Appendix I. Principles of Field Technique," pp. 185-190 in Shechem by G. Ernest Wright; NY: McGraw-Hill.
"Appendix V: The Stratification of the Temple Forecourt," pp. 214-228 in Shechem, op. cit.
"Lent - Preparation for Easter," The Methodist Teacher 1, No. 3 (Sp 65), 50,52,102,108,110. Pages are different grade levels.
"Love and Justice in Deuteronomy: A Third Approach to the Law," Interpretation 19, No. 4 (Oct 65), 399-411.
"The Old Testament," 52 study sessions in AS.
"Old Testament Biographies," International Lesson Annual, 4th Quarter; Nashville: Abingdon, 1965.
"The Way of Israel: No Balm in Gilead, Exposition," Adult Bible Course (hereafter ABC) 12 (Dec-Feb 65-6), 1+.
"The Way of Israel: Troublers of Israel, Exposition," ABC 12 (Sep-Nov 65), 1+.

Reviews

Willy Corswant, A Dictionary of Life in Bible Times; London: Hodder & Stoughton, 1960.
Rev: Methodist Teacher 5/6 1 (Sp 65), 4.
G. Ernest Wright, Shechem; NY: McGraw-Hill, 1965.
Rev: DG XXXV, No. 3 (Sp 65), 177-8.
John Gray, I and II Kings: A Commentary; Philadelphia: Westminster, 1963.
Rev: Interpretation 19 (Oct 65), 461-2.

1966

Excavation Manual; Wooster, Ohio: Wooster College.

"The Anchor Bible: A Review Article," DG XXXVI, Nos. 1-2 (Aut-Wint 65-6), 36-43.
"Social Teachings of the Bible," Workers with Youth 19 (Feb 66), 40.
"The Way of Israel: The Beginnings of Wisdom, Exposition," ABC 12 (June-Aug 66), 1+.
"The Way of Israel: A Light to the Nations, Exposition," ABC 12 (Mar-May 66), 1+.

1967

with James F. Ross, "Five Seasons at Biblical Shechem," Archaeological Discoveries in the Holy Land; NY: Crowell, 1967.

Reviews

Claus Westermann, The Praises of God in the Psalms; Richmond: John Knox, 1965. Cyril S. Rodd, Psalms 1-72; London: Epworth, 1963.

Rev: DG XXXVII, Nos. 1-2 (Aut-Wint 66-7), 52-4.

1968

"The Old Testament in the Christian Pulpit," The Hartford Quarterly 8, No. 2 (Wint 68), 7-14.

"The Scholar as Preacher," DG XXXVIII, Nos. 1-2 (Aut-Wint 67-8), 7-10.

with Robert J. Bull and Edward F. Campbell, Jr., "The Sixth Campaign at Balatah (Shechem)," BASOR 190 (Ap 68), 3-4, f.n. 4.

1969

"Guide for Leviticus," United Methodist Teacher (hereafter UMT) 2 (Fall 69), 107+. Ibid., UMT Kindergarten 2 (Fall 69), 111+. Ibid., UMT [Grades] I-II 2 (Fall 69), 101+. Ibid., UMT I-III 2 (Fall 69), 63+. Ibid., UMT III-IV 2 (Fall 69), 107+. Ibid., UMT IV-VI 2 (Fall 69), 61+. Ibid., UMT V-VI 2 (Fall 69), 105+.

"How to Study the Bible and Understand the Bible," Adult Bible Study (hereafter ABS) 1 (June-Aug 69), 1+.

"The Problematic of Preaching from the Old Testament," Interpretation 23, No. 3 (July 69), 302-314.

"Significance of the Bible for Faith," ABS 1 (June-Aug 69), 11+.

1971

with Norman E. Wagner, Pottery Coding Handbook; Waterloo: Waterloo Lutheran University Press.

"The Psalms," pp. 253-303 in The Interpreter's One Volume Commentary on the Bible ed. C. M. Laymon; Nashville: Abingdon.

with Edward F. Campbell, Jr., and James F. Ross, "The Eighth Campaign at Balatah (Shechem)," BASOR 204 (Dec 71), 2-17.

"Tell el-Hesi," Israel Exploration Journal (hereafter IEJ) 21, Nos. 2-3 (L971), 177-8.

with John E. Worrell, "Tell el-Hesi," IEJ 21, No. 4:232-3.

"Appendix: Coding Pottery in the Field," pp. 25-28 in Coding and Clustering Pottery by Computer by Norman E. Wagner; Waterloo, Ontario: Waterloo Lutheran University Press.

1972

with R. J. Bull, "Caesarea," IEJ 22, No. 4 (1972), 178-180.

"The Stratigraphy of Tell Balatah (Shechem)," Annual of the Department of Antiquities of Jordan XVII:99-111.

with John E. Worrell, "Tell el-Hesi," RB 79:585-588.

1973

with Norman E. Wagner and Eduard R. Riegert, The Moyer Site: A Pre-Historic Village in Waterloo County; Waterloo, Ontario: Wilfrid Laurier Press.

with Robert J. Bull, "Césarée Maritime," RB 80:582-585.

1974

"Correlating the Testaments," Adult Leader (AL) 7 (S-N 74), 22+.

"God's Purpose for Man," ABS 7 (S-N 74), 4+.

"Hopes for the Future," ABS 7:80+.

"How Archaeology Enriches Old Testament Study," AL 7:4+.

"In the Midst of Human Affairs," ABS 7:38+.
"Studying with Maps," AL 7:17+.
"Tell el-Hesi, 1970-1971," Palestine Exploration Quarterly (PEQ) 106 (1974), 19-31.
"Using Bible Translations," AL 7:20+.
"Using a Time Line," AL 7:24+.
"Writing a Covenant," AL 7:18+

1975
"Genesis: Quest for Identity," Mature Years (MY) 8 (S-N 75), 38-63.
with D. Glenn Rose, "Tell el-Hesi, 1975," IEJ 25:172-4.

1976
"The Life and Ministry of Jesus," MY 9 (D-F 76-7), 37-63.
"The Stratification of Tell Balatah (Shechem)," BASOR 223 (Oct 76), 57-9.
with D. Glenn Rose, "Tell el-Hesi, 1973 and 1975," PEQ 108:41-54.
with D. Glenn Rose, "Tell el-Hesi," RB 83:257-260.

1977
"Exploring the Past," ABS 9 (Sum 77), 2+.
"The Life and Ministry of Jesus," MY 9 (Mar-May 77), 37-63.
with Kevin G. O'Connell, S.J. and D. Glenn Rose, "Tell el-Hesi, 1977," IEJ 27, No. 4 (1977), 246-250.
with Kevin G. O'Connell, S.J. and D. Glenn Rose, "Tell el-Hesi, 1977," Hadashot Arkheologiot (in Hebrew).

1978
with D. Glenn Rose and Kevin G. O'Connell, S.J., "Four Seasons of Excavation at Tell el-Hesi: A Preliminary Report," pp. 109-149 in Preliminary Excavation Reports ed. D.N. Freedman, Annual (AASOR) 43.
"The Stratigraphy of Caesarea Maritime," pp. 223-232 in Archaeology in the Levant: Essays for Kathleen Kenyon ed. P.R.S. Moorey and Peter Parr; Warminster: Aris and Phillips.
with Kevin G. O'Connell, S.J. and D. Glenn Rose, "Tell el-Hesi (1977)," RB 85:84-9.
with Kevin G. O'Connell, S.J. and D. Glenn Rose, "Tell el-Hesi 1977," PEQ 110:75-90.

Review
Will Herberg, Faith Enacted as History; Philadelphia: Westminster, 1976.
Rev: Interpretation 33, No. 1 (1979), 84-6.

1979
"Appeals to Recommitment Rejected," MY 11 (Sum 79), 56+.
"Decisions that Shaped the Nation's Future," MY 11:46+.
"Major Decisions in a Nation's Beginning," MY 11:46+.
"Moses," Bible Lives of Faith Series; Nashville: United Methodist Publishing House.
"Shechem: Problems of the Early Israelite Era," pp. 69-83 in Symposia ed. Frank M. Cross; Cambridge: ASOR.

1980

with Jeffrey A. Blakely, ed. Kevin G. O'Connell, S.J., The Tell el-Hesi Field Manual: The Joint Archaeological Expedition to Tell el-Hesi I. ASOR Excavation Reports ed. David Noel Freedman; Cambridge: ASOR.

1981

"The Foolishness of Preaching," (The Carl Michalson Society Annual Lecture, Drew University, 5 May 81), DG 52, No. 1 (Fall 81), 14-20.

1982

"Davis Glenn Rose (1928-1981)," ASOR Newsletter 4 (Jan 82), 1-3.

"The Development of Palestinian Archaeology as a Discipline," BA 45, No. 2 (Sp 82), 89-91.

"Tell el-Hesi, 1981," IEJ 32, No. 1 (1982), 67-9.

Stratum VIId (Late Iron II) at Tell el-Hesi; Waterloo: WLU.

1983

"Tell el-Hesi, 1981," PEQ 115:25-46.

with Jeffrey A. Blakely, "Tell el-Hesi in Retrospect," ASOR Newsletter 2 (Nov 83).

IN PRESS

"Ba'al, Lord of the Earth: The Ugaritic Ba'al Epic," in the Festschrift for David Noel Freedman; Cambridge: ASOR.

"Tell el-Hesi, 1981," RB.

Tell el-Hesi Excavation Reports II: Strata I and II. The Military Trenching and the Muslim Cemetery; Waterloo: WLU, 1984. ASOR Excavation Reports II. Kevin G. O'Connell, S.J., general editor.

IN PREPARATION

Tell el-Hesi Excavation Reports IV: Strata VI and VII. The Iron II Remains with Jeffrey A. Blakely and Ralph W. Doermann, ed. Bruce Dahlberg; Waterloo: WLU, 1984.

"The Stratigraphy of the Site," Ch. 7 in Tell el-Hesi: The Site and the Expedition ed. Bruce T. Dahlberg and Kevin G. O'Connell, S.J.; Winston Salem: Wake Forest University, 1984. ASOR Excavation Reports IV.

Sources

Indices: Index to Periodical Literature; Religion Index 2; United Methodist Index; Christian Periodical Index; Religion and Theological Abstracts; Elenchus Biblica.

Contemporary Authors, 5-8; Detroit: Gale Research, 1969.

Archaeological Discoveries in the Holy Land, pp. 213-4, compiled by the AIA; NY: Crowell, 1967.

Richard K. Taylor, Director, Information and Special Events, WLU, Waterloo, Ontario, Canada N2L 3C5.

Public Relations Office, Drew University.

Family and Friends

Section

A

ARCHAEOLOGY

A STRATIGRAPHICALLY DETERMINED DATE FOR THE INNER

FORTIFICATION WALL AT CAESAREA MARITIMA*

Jeffrey A. Blakely

> (Herod) noticed on the coast a town called
> Strato's Tower, in a state of decay, but
> thanks to its admirable situation capable of
> benefiting by his generosity. He rebuilt
> it entirely with limestone and adorned it
> with a most splendid palace. Nowhere did he
> show more clearly the liveliness of his
> imagination. (Josephus, Jewish War I.408)

With the founding and dedication of Caesarea
Maritima (hereafter Caesarea) by King Herod, the
history and location of Caesarea and Straton's Tower
became intertwined and obscured. Likewise the archaeology of the two becomes inter-related and clouded.
Almost any finding of Hellenistic remains at Caesarea
automatically becomes evidence for Straton's Tower and
the distinctions between Hellenistic and Herodian remains are argued extensively. Such is the case for the
inner fortification wall at Caesarea. At various times
it has been called the Herodian wall, the walls of
Straton's Tower, and the G Field wall (by the Joint
Expedition to Caesarea Maritima). From what was known
up to 1980, no absolute date could be attributed to it
with any degree of certainty.

A determination of the date of construction for
Caesarea's inner fortification wall was attainable
through careful, controlled, stratigraphic excavation.
It is fitting that this study appear in a volume honoring Lawrence E. Toombs, a man who has demanded thorough
stratigraphic control, recording, and reasoning in all
of his archaeological endeavors. It is an application
of his logic and method, which was taught to the author
at Tell el-Hesi, Caesarea, and Wilfrid Laurier University, that were used to gather and interpret the material presented here.

The Question

In 1959 the Missione Archaeologica Italiana (hereafter the Missione) discovered a city wall located
about 250 m north of the Crusader city of Caesarea (see
fig. 1). Excavation along both sides of this wall was

completed in 1964 so that about 120 m of it were exposed. The wall was constructed of rectangular, lime
stone blocks dressed with marginal-drafting and moderate rustication. The individual blocks, which averaged
1.30 x 0.60 x 0.45 m in size, were laid in header-
stretcher fashion to create a wall about 2.30 m thick.
In addition to the wall, two round towers and a pentagonal tower were uncovered as part of it. Both round
towers had a diameter of 12 m and were constructed in
the same manner as the wall, although the tower walls
were only 1.70 m thick. These towers were about 14 m
apart, with the space between them being filled with a
wall which was about 3.00 m thick. The pentagonal
tower was placed where the wall turned about 40° towards
the south. The Missione dated the wall to the Herodian
period on the basis of the cultural remains collected
along the wall faces and on the style of construction
(Scavi, 247-92). The ceramic material, however, was
not reported in a manner which allowed stratigraphic or
chronological review. The aqueducts, which are so
often pictured in print, passed over the preserved top
course of the wall at a point between the pentagonal
tower and the eastern round tower. The Missione dated
them to the second century CE and used this date to
support a date in the Herodian period for the wall
system (Scavi, 274-5).

Negev contested this dating of the wall system
(Negev 1966a, 343-4; 1966b, 142-3). He suspected an
earlier date for the wall system because of the second
and third centuries BCE remains he had excavated near
where the Missione discovered the inner fortification
wall. Negev found fault with the results presented by
the Missione; he isolated three problems. First, since
the base of the high aqueducts, which he seems to assume
to have been Herodian in date, was set at the level of
the top course of the inner fortification wall, then
this wall, Negev reasoned, must have been out of use
when Herod built the aqueducts. According to Negev,
therefore, the wall was Hellenistic. Second, he saw a
similarity in the construction techniques used in the
round towers and those used in the Hellenistic towers
of Samaria. This similarity, therefore, implied a
Hellenistic date for the towers of Caesarea. Third,
Negev reasoned that the two round towers were part of
a gate which was blocked by the 3 m wide wall. Since
the Missione had dated this wall to the Herodian Period
and it was found blocking the gate, then the gate
towers and the thinner inner fortification wall must

4

date from the Hellenistic period. With all reasoning
pointing to the same conclusion, Negev argued a
Hellenistic date both for the towers and for the inner
fortification wall. In doing so he identified them as
the walls of Hellenistic Straton's Tower.

Starting from the views of the Missione and Negev,
others have attempted to solve the aforementioned architectural and chronological problems. On stylistic
grounds, Hodges, in his Ph.D. dissertation of 1970,
declared the architecture of the inner fortification
wall and its towers to be of Herodian date, which was
in accord with the artifactually determined date of the
Missione (Hodges, 189). Concerning the 3 m thick wall
which ran between the round towers, however, Hodges
suggested that the Missione missed its true stratigraphic context and he dated this wall to the Hadrianic
period (Hodges, 189). Ringel found Negev's arguments
far from conclusive and he commented that the similarity of the round towers of Caesarea to those of Samaria
was only superficial. Ringel supported the Herodian
date for the wall system, but he did admit the possibility of an earlier Hellenistic date (Ringel, 76-7).
Lee Levine reviewed these problems and then supported a
Herodian date for the wall system and towers. In doing
so he dismissed the 3 m thick wall as a later addition
(Levine 1975, 9-13). Also Levine pointed to the possible existence of an earlier gate below the Herodian
gate, as suggested by Frova (Levine 1975, 11 n 53). He
also suggested that Herod could have incorporated the
walls of the earlier Straton's Tower into his own.

Recent work has been conducted by the Caesarea
Ancient Harbor Excavation Project under the direction
of Avner Raban. The primary discovery from this project relates to Herod's harbor, Sebastos, which is located west of the Crusader city. Additional anchorages
may also have been located both north and south of the
main harbor (Raban, 80-8; Raban and Hohlfelder, 56-60).
Elsewhere other harbor remains were discovered which
were dated to the Hellenistic period. A third round
tower was found in the Crusader harbor. It was similar
to those found on land and was tentatively dated to the
second century BCE on the basis of a cooking pot found
smashed against its foundations (Raban and Linder,
241-3; Raban and Hohlfelder, 59-60). Raban found a
Hellenistic quay on the coastline between the Crusader
city and the inner fortification wall. In the vicinity
of the quay, which had been rebuilt in the Roman period,

Raban reported finding, "'basket-handles' from Persian store jars and sherds from Hellenistic wine amphorae from Rhodes, Knidos, and Kos (translated from Raban, 88)." He also found the remains of an older harbor in the same area. As part of this harbor he suggested that the inner fortification wall continued into the sea to form its northern wall (Raban and Hohlfelder, 59-60). Raban dated the construction of this harbor to the Hellenistic period and he identified it as the harbor of Straton's Tower (Raban, 87-8). He also suggested, "Perhaps it (the two large towers of the inner fortification wall) and even the harbor itself may have been incorporated into the master plan of the city (of Herod) (Raban and Hohlfelder, 60)." These conclusions, therefore, add to the controversy concerning the date of the inner fortification wall.

Literary Evidence

Ancient literary evidence concerning the fortification systems of Straton's Tower and Herodian Caesarea is scant. Specific mention of "the wall of Straton's Tower at Caesarea" is found in the Tosefta Shevi'it, a source which was a third century CE compilation of earlier materials (Zuckermandel, 66; Levine 1975, 12). This reference could imply either the re-usage of the wall system of Straton's Tower as part of the walls of Caesarea or a continued independent existence for those walls. At the end of the first century CE, Josephus noted that King Herod had constructed the fortress of Caesarea at Straton's Tower (Josephus, Antiquities XV.293). No other specific written documentation is known of the fortifications of this site. However, a general chronological outline of its early occupation can be obtained from various literary sources. Levine presented the evidence for the fourth century BCE founding of the site. He preferred the Sidonian King Straton I (375-361 BCE) as the founder, but Straton II (346-332) would have been possible (Levine 1973, 75-81). By the mid-third century BCE, Straton's Tower was important enough to be the landing point for Zenon and his companions during their tour of Palestine (Abel, 410-1). The writings of Josephus show that the site was well known in Hasmonaean times, and Levine, again, has shown that Straton's Tower may have been captured by Alexander Jannaeus soon after 103 BCE (Levine 1974, 62-9). This could have led to the demise of the city, for by 22 BCE the city was described as a polis kamnousa (delapidated city) when Herod initiated

the construction of Caesarea (Josephus, _Jewish War_
I.408; Roller forthcoming). Literary evidence, therefore, seems to confirm the presence of fortification
walls at Straton's Tower and Caesarea. These sources
also imply that Straton's Tower was founded in the
fourth century BCE, that it flourished in the third and
second centuries BCE, and that it was in a state of
decay in the first century BCE prior to the founding of
Caesarea by Herod the Great.

Masonry

The style of masonry is another factor which has
entered in the debate concerning the date of the inner
fortification wall. The masonry of this wall was considered to be Herodian by some and to be Hellenistic by
others (see above). Little specialized study of this
topic, however, has taken place. Laperrousaz cata-
logued the existence of marginal-drafting and rustication at various sites in Palestine where it has been
found in Iron Age and Persian period contexts
(Laperrousaz, 105-28). The dissertation of Hodges was
concerned with constructions of Herod the Great. Hodges
showed that this style of masonry existed both during
the third/second centuries BCE and during the time of
Herod the Great. He argued that the Herodian style of
masonry constitutes a resurgence of an earlier Palestinian style and that this resurgence was at least partially inspired by contemporary Roman constructions
(Hodges, 274-86). Hodges' general argument concerning
Herodian masonry is applicable here and thus, on a
structural stylistic basis, the inner fortification
wall could be either Hellenistic or Herodian in date.

Stratigraphic Argumentation

Conflicting archaeological interpretation, obscure
literary evidence, and imprecise structural dating have
not allowed the inner fortification wall to be dated
with any precision. The Joint Expedition to Caesarea
Maritima initiated new excavation along the wall system
in 1978. A new area of excavation, Area G 8, was placed
over the wall system in order to obtain firm stratigraphic control along its outer face (see fig. 1). At
the end of the 1980 season virgin sand had been reached
and a new section of the wall face had been exposed.
Here a tight stratigraphic sequence had been isolated
along the wall.

This new excavation along the wall was located between the eastern limit of the work of the Missione and the small probe that they had placed south of their main areas (see figs. 1 and 2). In Area G 8, four foundation courses and at least six, probably seven, original courses of the wall's superstructure were found (see fig. 3 and plate 1). The four foundation courses were constructed of an assortment of ashlar and field stones packed together in red humra. Since only the eastern face of the wall has been excavated, the total width of the foundation courses is unknown. In the east the foundations are wider than the superstructure, extending out 0.35 to 0.70 m from the vertical face of the superstructure. In Area G 8 the absolute elevation of of the top and bottom of the foundation courses does not vary by more than 0.04 m, as the total height of the foundation courses ranges from 1.52 to 1.54 m.

The bottom six courses of the inner fortification wall's superstructure are constructed of marginal-drafted, limestone blocks which were set in header-stretcher fashion. The wall seems to maintain a width of 2.30 m over its entire height since, wherever it has been exposed, both faces of the wall are vertical. These six courses of regular header-stretcher construction are dry-laid and rise 3.90 m over the top of its foundations. The current excavation has not penetrated the wall in order to determine its inner construction technique. A comparison of the inner fortification wall both where it was uncovered by the Missione and in Area G 8 strongly suggest that they are part of one unified construction. No evidence of a later reconstruction chronologically separates one part of the wall from any other.

A seventh course of superstructure was visible above the six courses of marginal-drafted, header-stretcher construction. The top course consisted of a series of headers set with two headers across in order to create a total width of 2.30 m (see fig. 2). Since this course was dry-laid, there was no stratigraphic way to tie the top course to the rest of the wall system prior to the Byzantine period when another wall, G 8083, was cemented to it. At that time the top course of this later concrete and stone structure was cemented to the top course of headers on the dry-laid, inner fortification wall. It is hypothesized that this course of headers is original to the inner fortification wall. It is also possible that this course of headers either

8

was the top course of the wall or was a course directly
below the top course.

Figure 4 shows the stratigraphic section against
the inner fortification wall, Wall G 8001. Above
Virgin Sand G 8122, three layers of sand were found,
G 8124, G 8123, and G 8119. These layers were cut by
Trench G 8125 which ran along the outer face of the
inner fortification wall, G 8001. Except for this wall,
all of these layers ultimately were covered by Sand
G 8118. In Virgin Sand G 8122 no evidence of human
occupation was found. Sand G 8124, which was directly
above the virgin sand, contained only small amounts of
pottery and no numismatic evidence. Only three indicator sherds were found in this layer and they are
shown in fig. 5.1-3. This small collection probably
dates to the second century BCE with 5.1 being paralleled at French Hill in Jerusalem (Strange, pl. 15.2)
and 5.2 in P. Lapp's <u>Palestinian Ceramic Chronology</u>
type 151.1-3. <u>Palestinian Ceramic Chronology</u> and N.
Lapp's <u>The Third Campaign at Tell el-Ful: The Excavations of 1964</u> provide comprehensive discussions of the
pottery of this period. The typology and absolute dating presented in these works will be referred to for
the dating of much of the following material. The Late
Hellenistic and Roman pottery from Area G 8 will be the
subject of a forthcoming article by J. A. Blakely,
W. D. Glanzman, and L. J. Tiede.

Sand Layer G 8123 rested directly upon Sand Layer
G 8124. Significant evidence of human activity was
found in this layer, a layer for which all indicator
sherds are illustrated in fig. 5.4-20. As in Sand Layer
G 8124, the ceramic evidence points to a second century
BCE date for this layer: note particularly cup 5.4
(P. Lapp Type 151.4A), bowl 5.6 (Crowfoot <u>et al</u>, pl. 40
#7), cooking pots 5.10-13 (N. Lapp, 104), and jars 5.16
and 5.20 (N. Lapp, 102). In addition, a badly corroded
imitation Seleucid coin of the 3rd to 1st centuries BCE
was found. This evidence supports the ceramic evidence
and suggests a second century BCE date for Sand Layer
G 8123.

A large corpus of pottery was found in Sand Layer
G 8119, the layer which covered Sand Layer G 8123. A
selection of this pottery is presented in figs. 6 and 7.
Taken as a whole the pottery suggests a late second cen-
tury or early first century BCE date: note especially
"Megarian" bowls 6.1-4, 21 (P. Lapp, 158; Rotroff, 32-4,

107-10), bowls 6.5, 7, 10 (P. Lapp 151.1), bowl 6.6
(Roller 1980, 36-7 #2), fish plates 6.9, 11 (P. Lapp
153.1), grooved bowls 6.12-13 (Grose, 54-9; Crowfoot
et al, 259-60) bowl 6.15-16 (P. Lapp 53F), jugs 6.18,
19, 22 (N. Lapp, 102-3), jars 6.20 and 7.1-6 (N. Lapp,
102), casseroles 7.7-8 (P. Lapp, 72.1), cooking pots
7.9-11 (N. Lapp, 104), and flask 7.10. Two Eastern
Terra Sigillata A bases are present, figs. 7.13, 16,
as well as fragments of a spouted lamp 7.17-18. Six
coins were found in addition to the pottery: one from
Alexander III (128-123 BCE), one from Antiochus III
(222-187 BCE), and four badly corroded examples whose
forms suggest a third to first century BCE date. Again
ceramic and numismatic evidence support each other and
suggest a late second century or early first century
BCE date for Sand Layer G 8119. All ceramic and numismatic evidence could, in fact, be comfortably placed
around 100 BCE.

Sand Layers G 8124, G 8123, and G 8119 were cut by
Trench G 8125 in order to erect inner fortification
wall G 8001. A small deposit of material was found
under Wall G 8001 and above virgin sand. This layer,
G 8126, contained some ceramic remains, all of which
are shown in fig. 8.1-10. Indicator sherds are few and
seem to date to the second century BCE. Fish plate
8.1, bowls 8.2-3, jar 8.4, jug 8.5, and casserole 8.6
are forms which were seen in earlier levels. Body
sherd 8.10 is a highly glossy, red-slipped sherd which
is probably an example of Eastern Terra Sigillata A.
Body sherd 8.10 is the only piece that may date after
the second century BCE, but this sherd is so small that
no clear date can be assigned to it.

The foundation trench, G 8125, contained large
quantities of pottery, a corpus from which all indicator sherds have been shown in fig. 8.11-21 and fig. 9.
Bowl forms 8.11-21 and 9.1, 3 are similar to second
century and early first century forms which were encountered earlier. Likewise, jars 9.7-11 and casserole
9.5 are similar to second century BCE forms which were
seen before. Jugs 9.2, 6 are similar to second and
first century BCE jugs described by N. Lapp (102).
Cooking pot 9.4 is an example of Strange's Type 1.2A
cooking pot which was found at French Hill. Strange
dated this form to the first centuries BCE/CE (Strange,
52 and fig. 13.18-21). Trench G 8125, therefore, is
composed of second century BCE material, but with a
possibly recognizable later component.

10

Both Sand Layer G 8119 and Foundation Trench G 8125 were covered by Sand Layer G 8118. Large quantities of pottery were found from which a selection is presented in figs. 10 and 11. Some of the earlier types are still present in identical or very similar forms, but they are probably residual material churned up during the excavation for the wall. Examples of these types are 10.1, 4-7, 9-17 and 11.3. Many new types are present in the collection, however. Eastern Terra Sigillata bowl 10.2 is a form from the early first century CE (Riley, 45 #78), and bowl 10.18 is another example of Eastern Sigillata. Bowl 10.8 is a different, glossy fine ware of the early first century CE. Early first century CE forms are also seen in cup 10.2 which is paralleled at Herodian Jericho (Netzer and Meyers, figs. 6.4, 12) and also in the Imperial style lamp 10.19 (Hayes, #215-21, #373). Flask 11.4 has good parallels at 'En el-Ghuweir (Bar-Adon, fig. 15) and krater 11.2 is another Early Roman type which was first described by P. Lapp (Type 45.2). Cooking pot 11.1, which is the only complete vessel in this corpus, is Sauer's Early Roman form and it has close parallels at Meiron Stratum II (Sauer, 18; Meyers, Strange, and Meyers, pl. 8.16). This form should date to the end of the first century BCE. Cooking pot 11.5 is yet another example of Sauer's Early Roman type (Sauer, 18). The Koan amphora handle, fig. 11.6, is so fragmentary that it is impossible to date it closely. The pottery of Sand Layer G 8118, therefore, shows a different character than the foregoing layers and is probably representative of the pottery from the end of the early first century BCE and the early first century CE. The numismatic evidence from this deposit is limited with the only identifiable coin dating from the reign of Antiochus III, hence the stratigraphic and ceramic evidence alone must date this layer.

The final figure of pottery is a selection of sherds found during balk trimming and clean-up work. These examples in fig. 12 all have parallels in the earlier stratified material with the exception of bowl base 12.15. This example is earlier than the rest of the material presented here and probably dates to the third century BCE, a unique form for this collection.

This stratified material provides a firm basis for dating the inner fortification wall. Prior to the construction of the inner fortification wall, occupation of the second century BCE or the early first century

BCE was present in the vicinity of Area G 8. At some time later in the first century BCE the inner fortification wall was built in a foundation trench which had cut all previous occupational layers. With the completion of the wall, the first layer to be used in conjunction with it was build up. This layer, G 8118, seems to date to the end of the first century BCE and the early first century CE. The inner fortification wall, therefore, probably dates to the mid or late first century BCE when one bases the chronological interpretation solely on stratigraphic argumentation.

Conclusions

The purpose of this article was to establish a stratigraphically determined date for the inner fortification wall at Caesarea. The stratigraphic evidence presented above establishes a first century BCE date for this wall system as it is seen in Area G 8. This date is far too late to correlate the inner fortification wall with Straton's Tower. Ancient literary evidence would imply, therefore, that this wall is part of the city walls of Caesarea Maritima which were established by Herod the Great when he founded the city. This conclusion is based on the limited stratigraphic evidence of one area of excavation, but on evidence which is conclusive for that area. It has been noted that no break in the construction technique of the wall is visible over the entire area excavated by the Missione and by the Joint Expedition. This implies that the entire inner fortification wall should be viewed as dating from the Herodian period.

The excavation of Area G 8 established the existence of three layers of stratified Late Hellenistic material, and nothing earlier. Since the inception of the Joint Expedition in 1971 only two sherds which definitely predate the second century BCE have been found in stratified contexts: one third century BCE base has been noted above, fig. 12.15, and one fourth century BCE cyma kantharos rim fragment was found in Area G 6, halfway between Area G 8 and the sea (fig. 1 and Roller 1980, 36 #1). Through the 1982 field season, the Joint Expedition has found no evidence for fourth and third century BCE Straton's Tower. If the Caesarea Ancient Harbor Excavation Project has found a quay dating from this earlier time period on the coastline directly west of Area G 8, then it was certainly part of a very limited occupational area whose identification (rightly or wrongly) as Straton's Tower would seem premature. On the other hand, stratified second century remains, which may continue into the early first century BCE, testify to some sort of occupation here. If these remains do represent part of Straton's Tower or some small settlement in its vicinity, then they add a certain circumstantial evidence in support of Levine's theory of the destruction of Straton's Tower by Alexander Jannaeus soon after 103 BCE. None of the remains in these layers must date after 100 BCE, thus the remains fit such a destruction. After this point, there is no evidence of occupation until the construction of the wall in the time of Herod the Great.

Excavation along the inner fortification wall at Caesarea has shown the existence of second century BCE occupation which probably ended at the end of that century, and which predates the construction of the wall. Late in the first century BCE, the earlier occupational remains were cut for the erection of the Herodian city wall at Caesarea. Further excavations will be needed to determine the exact course of the wall as it heads south to enclose the city. It is hoped that such work will be carried out and that such work will support the conclusions arrived at here.

*The author wishes to thank Dr. Robert Bull of Drew University and Dr. Olin Storvick of Concordia College for their help and encouragement while the author worked with this material. For the technical preparation, the author wishes to thank Mr. William Glanzman of the University of Pennsylvania for drawing the pottery, Ms. Mary Linda Govaars of Drew University for drawing the plans, and Mr. Peter Lampham of Drew University for cleaning and identifying the numismatic material. Dr. Duane Roller of Wilfrid Laurier University discussed this topic with the author and supplied him with unpublished material. Dr. Nancy Lapp was kind enough to go over the pottery with the author. Editorial and proofreading assistance was provided by Ms. Martha Risser of the University of Pennsylvania. Dr. James Sauer gave immeasurable amounts of advice as he supervised the author in writing this article. Finally, the volunteers of the Joint Expedition to Caesarea Maritima who were assigned to Area G 8 must be thanked for their careful and hard labor. More than anything else, this article reflects their efforts.

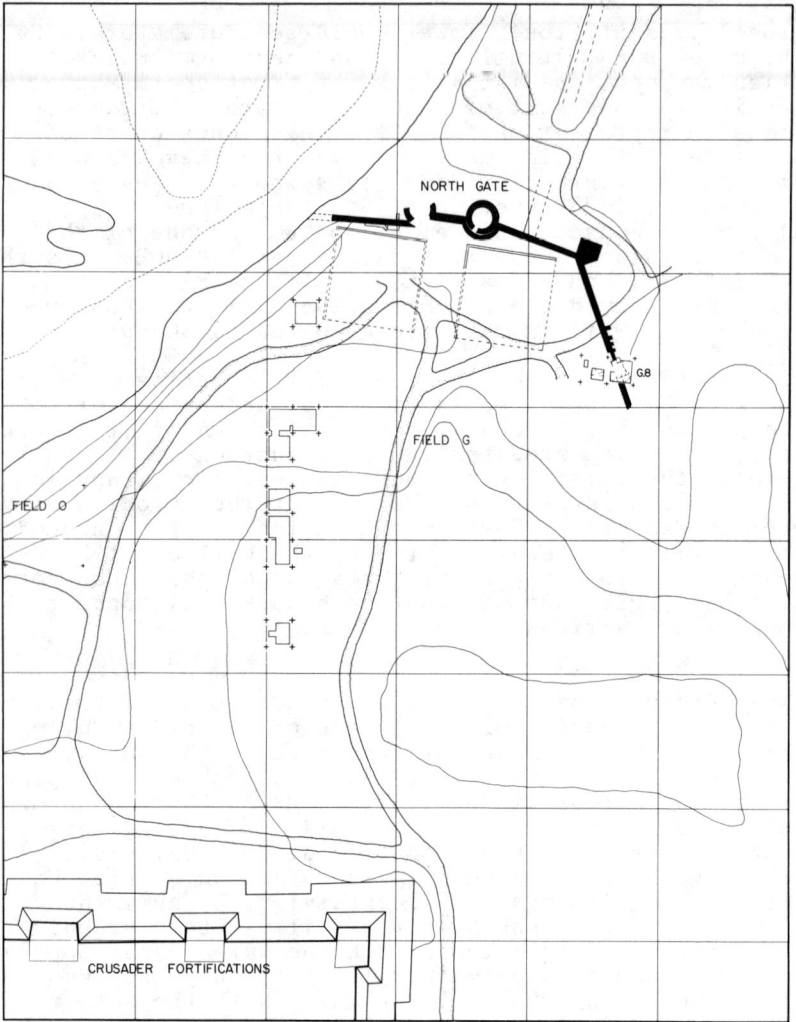

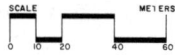

Fig. 1. Plan of Caesarea Maritima north of the Crusader city
(M. L. Govaars).

14

CAESAREA MARITIMA
AREA G/8
FINAL TOP PLAN   8.I.80
I:20   GRW

SCALE   METERS
0   I   2

Fig. 2. Plan of Area G 8 at the conclusion of excavation (G. Wing and M. L. Govaars).

Fig. 3. Elevation of the inner fortification wall in Area G 8 (G. Wing and M. L. Govaars).

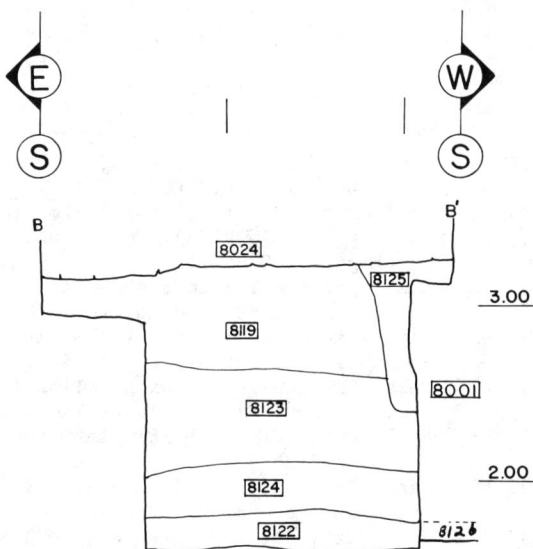

CAESAREA MARITIMA
AREA G/8
SOUTH BAULK   1:20
MLG/LFL   7.31.80

Fig. 4. Subsidiary south section against the inner fortification
wall, G 8001 (M. L. Govaars from an original by Blakely).

17

FIGURE 5

	Locus	Registry No.	Form	Description of Ware
1	G8123	G.8.501.2	Jar	Ext light reddish brown (5YR6/4). Int reddish brown (5YR4/2). Core reddish yellow to pale brown (5YR6/6-10YR6/3).
2	G8124	G.8.501.1	Bowl	Ext red slip (2.5YR5/8-10R4/6). Int red slip (2.5YR5/8). Core very pale brown (10YR8/4).
3	G8124	G.8.501.25	Body	Ext and Int very pale brown (10YR7/4) Core reddish yellow (5YR5/8). Ext incised markings.
4	G8123	G.8.500.1	Cup	Ext reddish brown to weak red slip (2.5YR4/4-2.5YR4/2). Int red slip (10R4/6). Core red yellow (5YR7/6).
5	G8123	G.8.500.11	Bowl	Ext reddish yellow (5YR6/6). Int pink (7.5YR7/4). Core red yellow (7.5YR7/6).
6	G8123	G.8.500.9	Bowl	Ext red slip (10R5/6). Int lacking. Core reddish yellow (5YR7/6).
7	G8123	G.8.500.10	Bowl	Ext and Int light red (2.5YR6/6). Core gray (10YR5/1).
8	G8123	G.8.500.5	Bowl	Ext red slip (10R5/6). Int reddish yellow (5YR7/6). Core light brownish gray (10YR6/2).
9	G8123	G.8.500.7	Bowl	Ext and Int reddish yellow (5YR7/6). Core light reddish brown (6YR6/4).
10	G8123	G.8.500.15	Cook Pot	Ext gray (5YR5/1).Int weak read (2.5YR 4/2).Core red-gray (5YR5/6-5YR5/1).
11	G8123	G.8.500.19	Cook Pot	Ext and Int reddish yellow (5YR7/6). Core reddish yellow (5YR6/6).
12	G8123	G.8.500.17	Cook Pot	Ext red (2.5YR5/6). Int weak red (2.5YR5/2). Core dark gray (2.5YRN/4).
13	G8123	G.8.500.13	Cook Pot	Ext and Int red (2.5YR5/8). Core reddish brown (2.5YR4/4).
14	G8123	G.8.500.3	Jug	Ext,Int, and Core pale yellow (5Y8/4).
15	G8123	G.8.500.12	Lid	Ext, Int reddish yellow (5YR6/6).Core pale brown (10YR6/3). Rim smoked.
16	G8123	G.8.500.18	Jar	Ext very pale brown (10YR8/4). Int and Core light red (2.5YR6/8).
17	G8123	G.8.500.4	Base	Ext very dark gray slip (2.5YRN/3). Int reddish yellow (5YR7/6). Core reddish yellow (5YR6/6).
18	G8123	G.8.500.16	Base	Ext reddish gray (5YR5/2).Int reddish brown (5YR5/3).Core weak red (10R5/4).
19	G8123	G.8.500.2	Baking Tray	Ext reddish brown (5YR5/4). Int pink gray (715YR6/2).Core very dark gray ((5YR3/1).Ext pockmarked, burnished.
20	G8123	G.8.500.42	Base	Ext pale yellow slip (2.5Y8/4). Int very pale brown (10YR7/4). Core reddish yellow (5YR6/6).

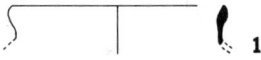

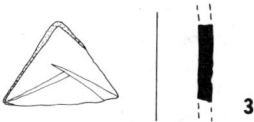

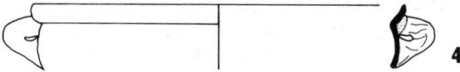

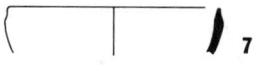

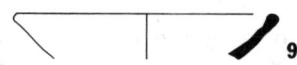

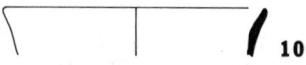

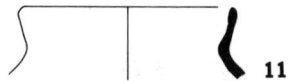

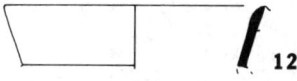

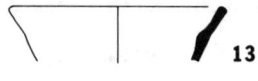

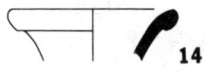

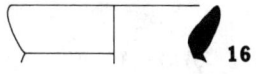

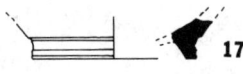

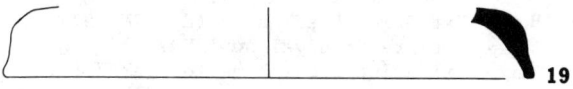

Fig. 5. Pottery from G 8124 and G 8123.

FIGURE 6

	Locus	Registry No.	Form	Description of Ware
1	G8119	G.8.488.19	Bowl	Ext dark reddish gray, red slip (5YR 4/2 & 2.5YR4/3).Int red slip (10R4/8). Core reddish yellow (5YR7/6).
2	G8119	G.8.489.8	Bowl	Ext reddish brown slip (5YR4/4). Int red slip (10R4/8).Core pink (7.5YR7/4).
3	G8119	G.8.489.10	Bowl	Ext dark red brown slip (2.5YR3/4). Int red brown slip (2.5YR4/4). Core reddish yellow (7.5YR8/6).
4	G8119	G.8.498.1	Bowl	Ext very dark gray slip (5YR3/1). Int dark reddish brown & red slip (2.5YR 3/4 & 2.5YR4/8).Core reddish yellow (7.5YR8/6).
5	G8119	G.8.488.10	Bowl	Ext reddish brown slip (5YR4/3). Int red slip (10R4/8). Core very pale brown (10YR7/4).
6	G8119	G.8.490.6	Bowl	Ext & Int very dark gray slip (5YR3/1). Core very pale brown (10YR8/4).
7	G8119	G.8.489.13	Bowl	Ext reddish brown slip (5YR4/3). Int red slip (10R4/6). Core reddish yellow (5YR7/6).
8	G8119	G.8.490.15	Cup	Ext & Int red slip (10R4/8). Core very pale brown (10YR7/4).
9	G8119	G.8.475.6	Plate	Ext dusky red slip (2.5YR3/2). Int very dusky red slip (2.5YR5/2). Core very pale brown (10YR8/4).
10	G8119	G.8.488.21	Bowl	Ext & Int red slip (10R4/8). Core reddish yellow (5YR7/6).
11	G8119	G.8.488.11	Plate	Ext & Int black slip (2.5YRN2.5/). Core pink (7.5YR7/4).
12	G8119	G.8.489.14	Bowl	Ext slip flaked off.Int black slip (2.5YRN2.5/).Core light brownish gray (2.5Y6/2).
13	G8119	G.8.488.36	Bowl	Ext black slip (2.5YRN2.5/).Int very dusky red (2.5YR2.5/2). Core very pale brown (10YR7/4).
14	G8119	G.8.498.58	Bowl	Ext black slip (2.5YRN2.5/). Int red slip (10R4/6). Core reddish yellow (7.4YR7/6).
15	G8119	G.8.488.6	Bowl	Ext red slip (10R5/8). Int slip flaked off. Core pink (7.5YR7/4).
16	G8119	G.8.499.10	Bowl	Ext & Int red slip (10R4/8). Core reddish yellow (5YR7/6).
17	G8119	G.8.490.1	Bowl	Ext & Int black slip (2.5YRN2.5/). Core reddish yellow (5YR7/6).
18	G8119	G.8.475.5	Jug	Ext & Int reddish yellow (5YR7/6). Core reddish yellow (5YR6/6).
19	G8119	G.8.489.9	Jug	Ext & Int reddish yellow (5YR7/6). Core very pale brown (10YR7/4).
20	G8119	G.8.475.4	Jar	Ext very pale brown (10YR7/4).Int pink

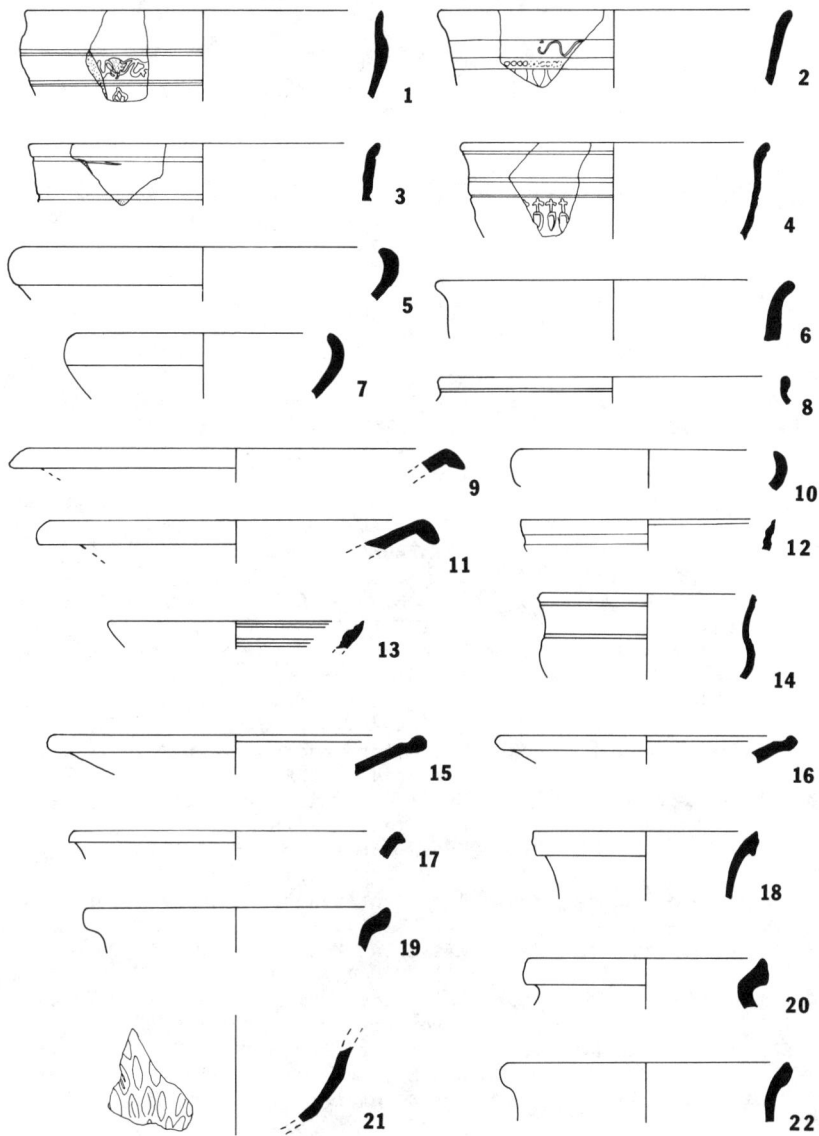

G 8119

Fig. 6. Pottery from G 8119.

FIG. 6 (cont)

				(7.5YR7/4).Core red yellow (5YR7/6).
21	G8119	G.8.489.20	Body	Ext red to dark red gray slip(10R4/6-10R3/1).Int dusky red slip (10R3/2). Core reddish yellow (7.5YR8/6).
22	G8119	G.8.490.11	Jug	Ext white (2.5Y8/2).Int very pale brown (10YR8/3).Core very pale brown (10YR7/3).

FIGURE 7

1	G8119	G.8.488.16	Jar	Ext & Int white (2.5Y8/2). Core red (2.5YR5/8).
2	G8119	G.8.490.4	Jar	Ext & Int pink (7.5YR7/4). Core light yellowish brown (10YR6/4).
3	G8119	G.8.475.8	Jar	Ext,Int, & Core light gray (10YR7/2).
4	G8119	G.8.475.7	Jar	Ext pale yellow slip (2.5Y8/4). Int pink (7.5YR7/4).Core reddish yellow (5YR7/6).
5	G8119	G.8.475.3	Jar	Ext pale yellow (2.5Y8/4). Int pink (7.5YR7/4).Core light brown (7.5YR6/4).
6	G8119	G.8.488.15	Jar	Ext pale yellow (2.5Y8/4). Int very pale brown (10YR8/4). Core reddish yellow (5YR7/6).
7	G8119	G.8.490.7	Casserole	Ext red brown (5YR5/4).Int red brown (5YR5/3).Core red (2.5YR5/6).
8	G8119	G.8.498.12	"	Ext weak red (2.5YR5/2).Int red brown (2.5YR5/4).Core dark brown (7.5YR4/2).
9	G8119	G.8.490.2	Cook Pot	Ext & Int reddish brown (5YR5/4). Core red (2.5YR4/6).
10	G8119	G.8.489.5	"	Ext red (10R4/6).Int red (10R4/8). Core red (10R5/8).
11	G8119	G.8.488.12	"	Ext & Int light red (2.5YR6/6).Core gray (2.5YRN5/).
12	G8119	G.8.488.30	Body	Ext & Int red slip (10R5/6).Core pink (7.5YR7/4).
13	G8119	G.8.488.22	Base	Ext & Int red slip (10R4/6).Core pink (7.5YR7/4).
14	G8119	G.8.490.19	Base	Ext & Int dusky red slip (10R3/3). Core very pale brown (10YR8/4).
15	G8119	G.8.489.11	Base	Ext & Int very dusky red slip (2.5YR 2.5/2). Core pink (7.5YR7/4).
16	G8119	G.8.488.23	Base	Ext & Int red slip (10R5/8). Core pink (7.5YR7/4).
17	G8119	G.8.488.1	Lamp	Ext, Int & Core dark gray (10YR4/1). Smoke blackened.
18	G8119	G.8.488.2	Lamp	Ext, Int & Core dark gray (10YR4/1).
19	G8119	G.8.475.1	Jug	Ext red slip (10R5/8). Int & Core pink (7.5YR7/4).

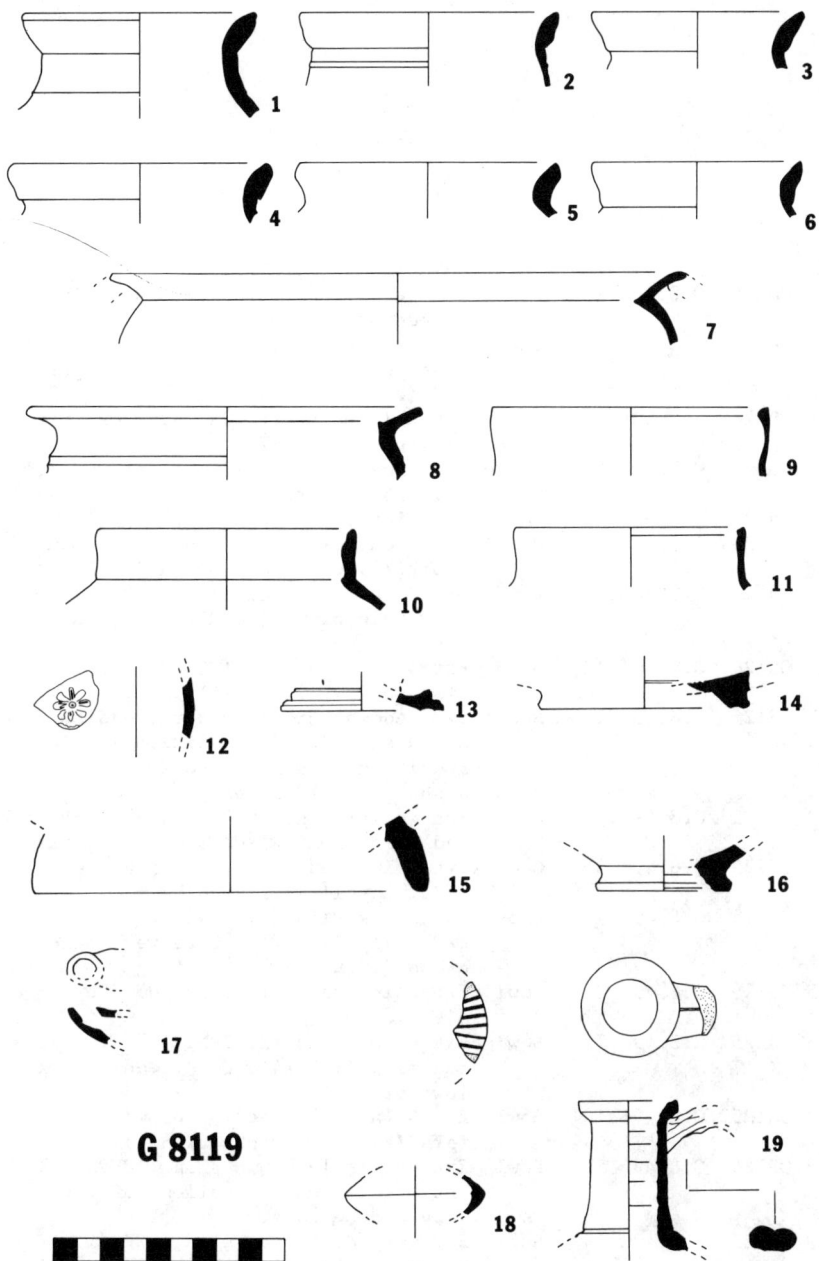

Fig. 7. Pottery from G 8119.

FIGURE 8

	Locus	Registry No.	Form	Description of the Ware
1	G8126	G.8.504.3	Plate	Ext & Int very dark gray slip (5YR 3/1). Core white (10YR8/2).
2	G8126	G.8.504.4	Bowl	Ext very dusky red slip (10R2.5/2). Int red slip (2.5YR5/6). Core very pale brown (10YR7/3).
3	G8126	G.8.505.1	Bowl	Ext red slip (2.5YR5/6). Int slip flaked off. Core pink (7.5YR7/4).
4	G8126	G.8.504.2	Jar	Ext reddish yellow (5YR7/6). Int reddish yellow (7.5YR7/6). Core light red (2.5YR6/6).
5	G8126	G.8.504.5	Jug	Ext & Int pink (7.5YR7/4). Core very pale brown (10YR7/3).
6	G8126	G.8.504.6	Casserole	Ext weak red (2.5YR5/2).Int red brown (2.5YR5/4).Core dark brown (7.5YR4/4).
7	G8126	G.8.504.7	Lamp	Ext, Int & Core pink (7.5YR7/4).
8	G8126	G.8.504.10	Handle	Ext red yellow (5YR7/6).Int brown (10YR6/3).Core pale brown (10YR7/3).
9	G8126	G.8.504.22	Bondy	Ext & Int weak red slip (5YR5/2).Core very pale brown (10YR7/4).Ext incised lines.
10	G8126	G.8.504.13	Body	Ext & Int red slip (10R4/6). Core reddish yellow (7.5YR7/6).
11	G8125	G.8.497.1	Bowl	Ext reddish brown to dark reddish brown slip (2.5YR5/4-5YR2.5/2). Int reddish gray slip (5YR4/2). Core reddish yellow (7.5YR6/6).
12	G8125	G.8.497.6	Cup	Ext weak red slip (2.5YR5/2). Int weak red slip (10R4/4).Core pink (7.5YR7/4).
13	G8125	G.8.496.9	Cup	Ext & Int red slip (2.5YR5/6). Core reddish yellow (5YR7/6).
14	G8125	G.8.496.17	Plate	Ext black slip (2.5YRN2.5/). Int dark gray slip (5YR5/1). Core very pale brown (10YR7/4).
15	G8125	G.8.497.3	Bowl	Ext & Int red slip (10R5/6). Core reddish yellow (5YR7/6).
16	G8125	G.8.496.7	Bowl	Ext black slip (2.5YRN2.5/). Int weak red slip (10R4/4). Core reddish yellow (5YR7/6).
17	G8125	G.8.496.10	Bowl	Ext & Int dark reddish brown slip (5YR3/2). Core pink (5YR8/4).
18	G8125	G.8.496.12	Bowl	Ext very pale brown slip (10YR8/3). Int & Core reddish yellow (5YR7/6). Very coarse ware.
19	G8125	G.8.496.14	Bowl	Ext very dark gray slip (5YR3/1). Int red slip (10R4/6). Core reddish yellow (7.5YR7/6).
20	G8125	G.8.496.15	Bowl	Ext black slip (2.5YRN2.5/). Int dark reddish brown slip (6YR3/2). Core light reddish brown (5YR6/4).

24

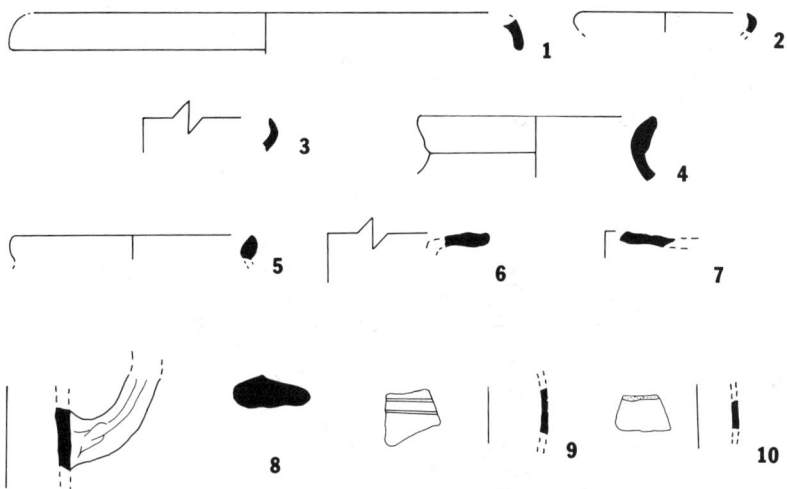

G 8126

G 8125

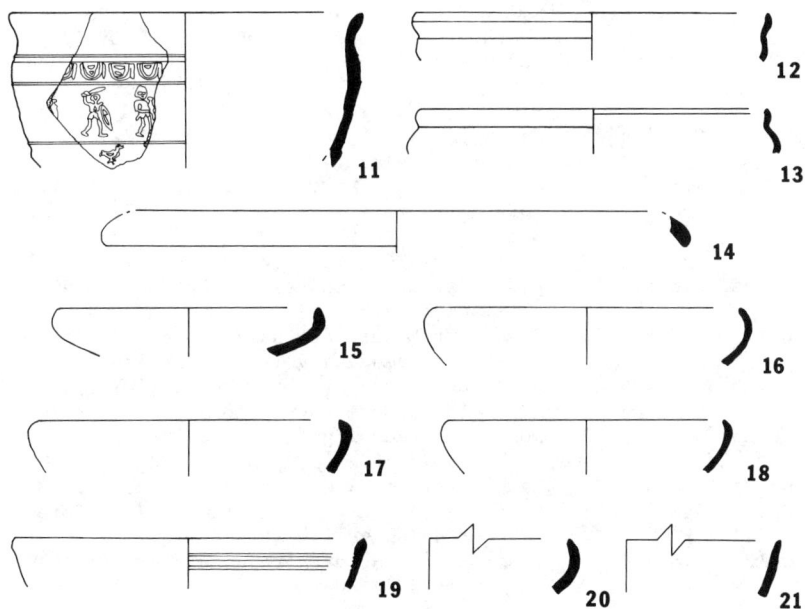

Fig. 8. Pottery from G 8126 and G 8125.

FIG. 8 (cont)
21 G8125 G.8.496.18   Bowl   Ext black slip (2.5YRN2.5/). Int very
                               dusky red (2.5YR2.5/2). Core reddish
                               yellow (5YR5/6).

FIGURE 9
1 G8125 G.8.497.5   Bowl   Ext black slip (5YR2.5/1). Int weak
                               red slip (2.5YR4/2). Core reddish
                               yellow (7.5YR8/6).
2 G8125 G.8.496.13   Jug   Ext light red (2.5YR6/6). Int light
                               reddish brown (5YR6/4). Core yellow-
                               ishred (5YR4/6).
3 G8125 G.8.497.4   Bowl   Ext & Int red slip (2.5YR5/6). Core
                               reddish yellow (7.5YR7/6).
4 G8125 G.8.496.5   Cook   Ext & Int red (10R4/6). Core dark
                        Pot   red (2.5YR3/6).
5 G8125 G.8.496.2   Casse- Ext red (2.5YR4/6).Int red yellow
                        role   (5YR6/6). Core dark gray (2.5YRN3/).
6 G8125 G.8.496.8   Jug   Ext, Int & Core white (2.5Y8/2).
7 G8125 G.8.496.3   Jar   Ext very pale brown slip (10YR8/4).
                               Int & Core reddish yellow (5YR7/6).
8 G8125 G.8.496.1   Jar   Ext white slip (2.5Y8/2).Int pale
                               brown (10YR7/4).Core pink (7.5YR7/4).
9 G8125 G.8.496.6   Am-   Ext very pale brown slip (10YR8/3).
                        phora Int & Core reddish yellow (5YR7/6).
10 G8125 G.8.496.7   Jar   Ext pale yellow slip (2.5Y8/4). Int
                               very pale brown (10YR7/3). Core red-
                               dish yellow (7.5YR7/6).
11 G8125 G.8.496.21   Jar   Ext & Int white slip (2.5Y8/2).
                               Core pink (7.5YR7/4).
12 G8125 G.8.496.20   Casse- Ext & Int very dark gray (10YR3/1).
                        role   Core very dark gray (7.5YRN3/).
13 G8125 G.8.496.25   Base   Ext slip flaked. Int weak red slip
                               (10R4/4). Core red yellow (7.5YR7/6).
14 G8125 G.8.496.39   Body   Ext & Int red slip (10R5/8). Core
                               pink (7.5YR7/4).
15 G8125 G.8.496.24   Base   Ext & Int very pale brown (10YR7/4).
                               Core reddish yellow (7.5YR7/6).
16 G8125 G.8.496.23   Base   Ext very pale brown slip (10YR8/3).
                               Int & Core very pale brown (10YR7/4).
17 G8125 G.8.496.43   Body   Ext red slip (10R5/6). Int red slip
                               (10R4/6). Core pink (7.5YR7/4).
18 G8125 G.8.497.2   Lamp   Ext, Int & Core gray (7.5YRN6/).
19 G8125 G.8.497.13   Base   Ext & Int red slip (2.5YR5/8). Core
                               reddish yellow (5YR7/6).
20 G8125 G.8.496.28   Base   Ext & Int dark reddish brown slip
                               (5YR3/3). Core pink (7.5YR7/4). Ext
                               scratched lines.
21 G8125 G.8.496.32   Base   Ext pale brown (10YR8/3). Int pale
                               brown (10YR8/4). Core pink (7.5YR7/4).
22 G8125 G.8.496.27   Base   Ext & Int red slip (10R4/6). Core

26

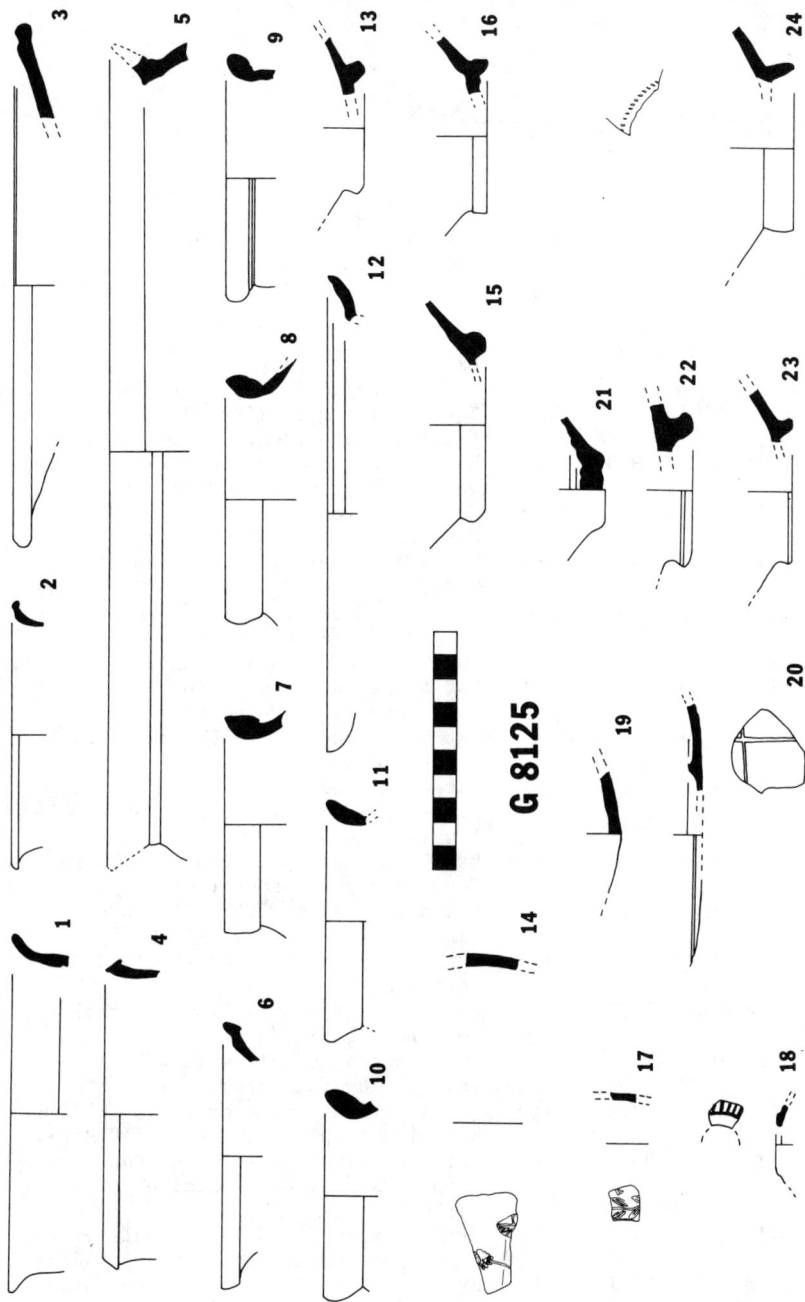

Fig. 9. Pottery from G 8125.

27

FIG. 9 (cont)

pink (7.5YR7/4).

23 G8125 G.0.496.26 Base Ext & Int red slip (10R4/6). Core reddish yellow (5YR7/6).

24 G8125 G.8.496.11 Base Ext dark gray slip (2.5YRN3/). Int slip flaked. Core pale red (2.5YR6/2).

FIGURE 10

1 G8118 G.8.485.11 Cup Ext dusky red slip (10R3/3).Int red slip (10R4/6).Core pink (7.5YR7/4).

2 G8118 G.8.485.3 Jug Ext reddish gray (5YR5/2).Int brown (7.5YR5/2).Core dark brown (7.5YR3/2).

3 G8118 G.8.469.9 Bowl Ext & Int red slip (10R4/6). Core very pale brown (10YR8/3).

4 G8118 G.8.472.3 Bowl Ext & Int red slip (10R5/8). Core reddish yellow (7.5YR7/6).

5 G8118 G.8.474.1 Bowl Ext & Int dark reddish brown slip (5YR3/2).Core light brown (7.5YR6/4).

6 G8118 G.8.471.4 Bowl Ext very dark gray slip (5YR3/2). Int very dark gray to red slip (5YR3/1-10R4/8). Core reddish yellow (5YR6/6).

7 G8118 G.8.472.2 Plate Ext & Int red brown slip (2.5YR4/4). Core very pale brown (10YR7/4).

8 G8118 G.8.485.16 Bowl Ext & Int red slip (10R5/6). Core light red (2.5YR6/6).

9 G8118 G.8.473.4 Bowl Ext dusky red slip (2.5YR3/2). Int red slip (10R4/6). Core reddish yellow (7.5YR7/6).

10 G8118 G.8.471.1 Jar Ext & Int very pale brown (10YR8/4). Core very pale brown (10YR7/4).

11 G8118 G.8.472.7 Jar Ext & Int white (2.5Y8/2). Core light yellowish brown (10YR6/4).

12 G8118 G.8.483.2 Jar Ext & Int very pale brown (10YR8/3). Core pink (7.5YR7/4).

13 G8118 G.8.485.6 Jar Ext & Int reddish yellow (5YR6/6). Core red (2.5YR5/6).

14 G8118 G.8.485.5 Jar Ext & Int pale yellow (2.5Y8/4). Core pale yellow (2.5Y7/4).

15 G8118 G.8.483.4 Jug Ext & Int very pale brown (10YR7/3). Core light yellowish brown (10YR6/4).

16 G8118 G.8.485.13 Base Ext red slip (10R4/6). Int dusky red slip (10R3/2). Core reddish yellow (5YR6/6).

17 G8118 G.8.485.14 Base Ext red slip (10R5/8).Int pale brown (10YR7/3). Core pale brown (10YR6/3).

18 G8118 G.8.473.12 Body Ext red slip (10R4/8). Int red slip (10R5/6). Core pink (7.5YR7/4).

19 G8118 G.8.483.19 Lamp Ext dark red gray slip (10R3/1). Int pink (7.5YR7/4). Core pink (7.5YR8/4).

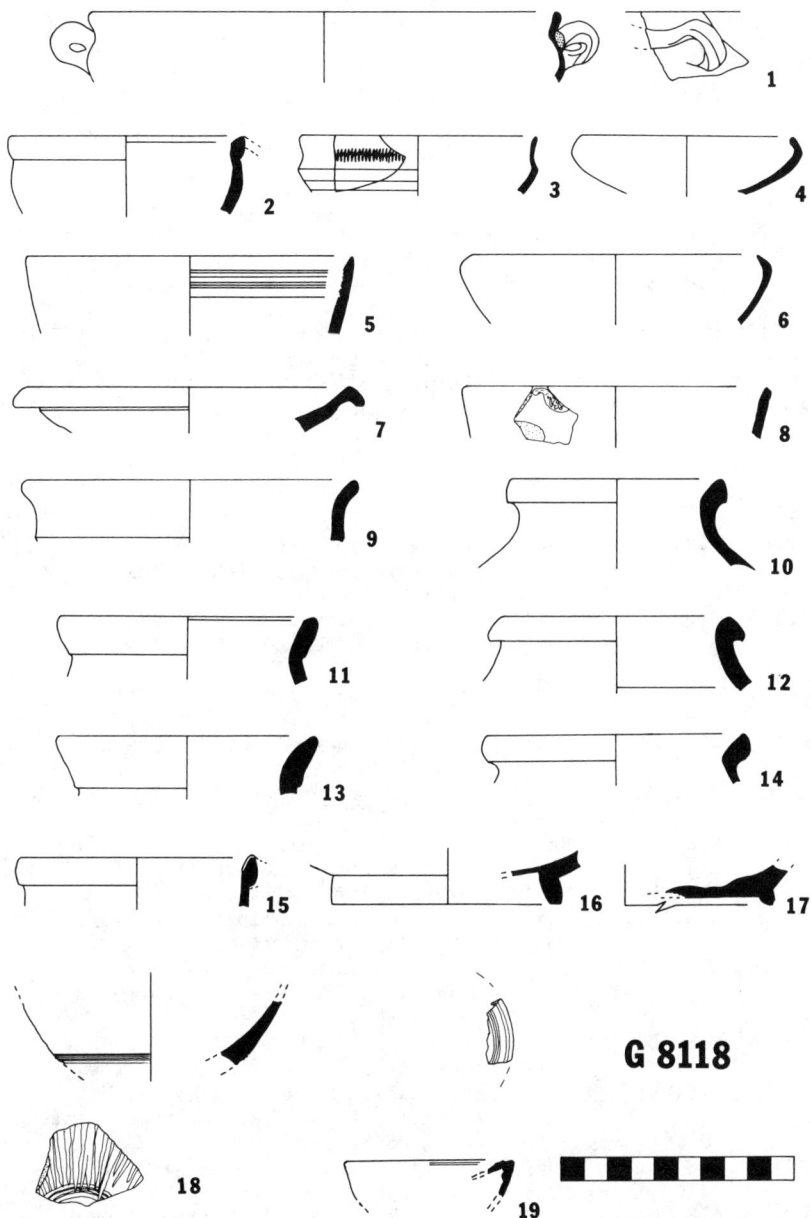

G 8118

Fig. 10. Pottery from G 8118.

29

FIGURE 11

	Locus	Registry No.	Form	Description of the Ware
1	G8118	G.8.470.1	Cook Pot	Ext, Int & Core light red (2.5YR6/8). Smoke blackened base and body.
2	G8118	G.8.473.6	Krater	Ext & Int reddish yellow (5YR7/6). Core light red (2.5YR6/8).
3	G8118	G.8.471.2	Casse-role	Ext dark reddish gray (10R4/1). Int weak red (10R4/2). Core red (10R4/6).
4	G8118	G.8.469.8	Flask	Ext very pale brown to pink (10YR8/4-5YR8/4).Int & Core red yellow (5YR7/6).
5	G8118	G.8.469.3	Cook Pot	Ext light reddish brown (5YR6/4). Int redish yellow (5YR7/6). Core brown (10YR5/3).
6	G8118	G.8.483.5	Handle	Ext & Int very pale brown (10YR8/4). Core reddish yellow (5YR7/6).

FIGURE 12

	Locus	Registry No.	Form	Description of the Ware
1	G8000	G.8.503.3	Cup	Ext red slip (10R4/6). Int red slip (10R5/8). Core reddish yellow (5YR7/6).
2	G8121	G.8.491.10	Bowl	Ext & Int very dark gray slip (5YR3/1). Core reddish yellow (7.5YR8/6).
3	G8121	G.8.494.1	Bowl	Ext & Int pink (7.5YR7/4). Core brown (10YR5/3).
4	G8000	G.8.502.12	Bowl	Ext, Int & Core light yellowish brown (10YR6/4).
5	G8000	G.8.502.5	Plate	Ext & Int red slip (10R5/6). Core pink (5YR7/4).
6	G8121	G.8.494.5	Bowl	Ext very dark gray slip (2.5RN3/). Int dark reddish brown slip (2.5YR3/4). Core pink (7.5YR7/4).
7	G8121	G.8.491.3	Plate	Ext & Int black slip (2.5YRN2.5/). Core pink (7.5YR7/4).
8	G8000	G.8.503.8	Bowl	Ext dark brown slip (7.5YR4/2). Int black slip (7.5YRN2.5/). Core reddish yellow (7.5YR7/6).
9	G8000	G.8.502.34	Casse-role	Ext weak red (2.5YR4/2). Int very dark gray (5YR3/1). Core red (10R5/8).
10	G8121	G.8.491.1	"	Ext reddish brown (2.5YR5/4). Int reddish yellow (5YR6/6). Core light red (2.5YR6/6).
11	G8121	G.8.491.16	Jug	Ext yellowish red (5YR5/6). Int red (2.5YR5/6). Core red (2.5YR4/6).
12	G8000	G.8.502.19	Casse-role	Ext dark gray (2.5YRN4/). Int weak red (2.5YR4/2). Core weak red (2.5YR5/2).
13	G8121	G.8.495.2	Jug	Ext, Int & Core reddish yellow

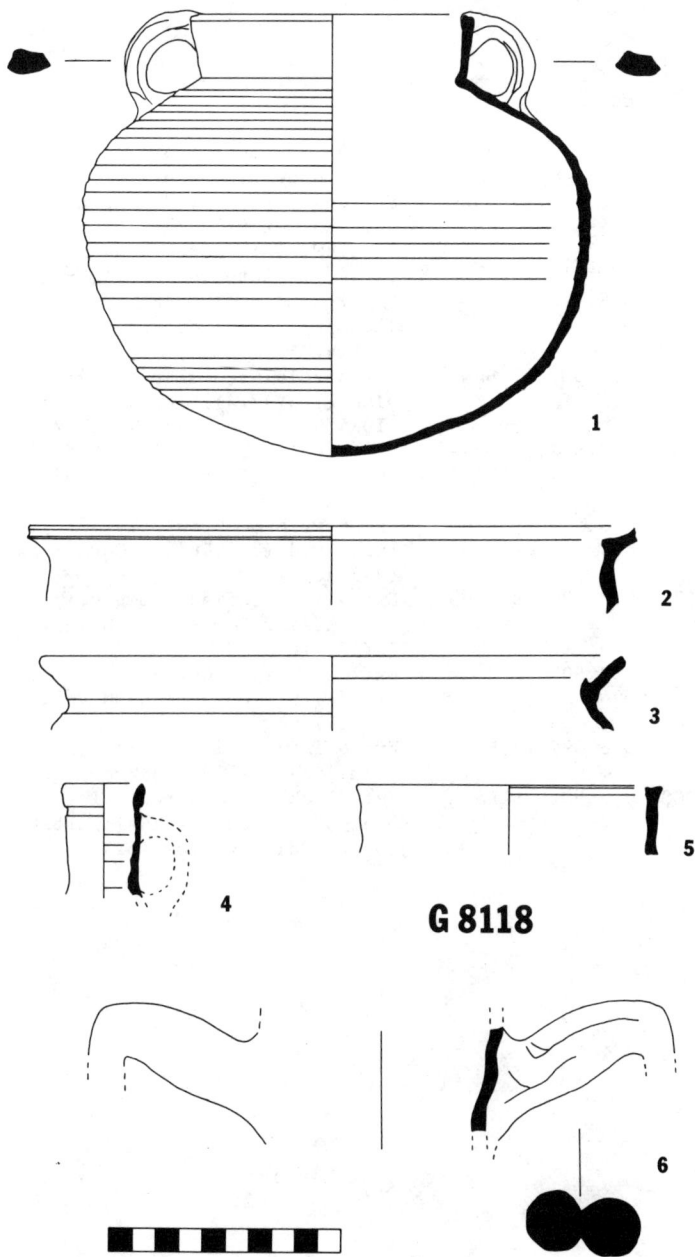

G 8118

Fig. 11. Pottery from G 8118.

FIG. 12 (cont)

				(5YR7/6).
14	G8121	G.8.493.3	Juglet	Ext & Int pink (7.5YR7/4). Core light brown (7.5YR6/4).
15	G8121	G.8.495.1	Base	Ext dusky to very dark gray slip (2.5YR3/2-2.5YRN3/). Int black slip (2.5YRN2.5/). Core reddish yellow (5YR7/6). Int two seal impressions.
16	G8121	G.8.492.9	Base	Ext red slip (10R5/8). Int red slip (10R4/6). Core reddish yellow (7.5YR7/6).
17	G8000	G.8.503.12	Base	Ext partial red slip (10R4/6). Ext pink (7.5YR7/4). Int weak red slip (10R4/3). Core pink (7.5YR7/4).
18	G8000	G.8.502.39	Base	Ext reddish brown slip (2.5YR4/4). Int pink (7.5YR8/4). Core pink (7.5YR7/4).
19	G8121	G.8.491.9	Base	Ext very pale brown (10YR8/3). Int light red (2.5YR6/6). Core light red (2.5YR6/8).
20	G8121	G.8.491.28	Base	Ext & Int reddish brown slip (2.5YR5/4). Core reddish yellow (5YR7/6).
21	G8000	G.8.502.37	Body	Ext red slip (10R4/8). Int red slip (2.5YR4/8). Core reddish yellow (7.5YR7/6).
22	G8121	G.8.492.10	Base	Ext & Int reddish yellow (5YR7/6). Core light yellowish brown (10YR6/4).
23	G8000	G.8.502.38	Base	Ext black to dark red slip (2.5YRN2.5/-2.5YR3/6). Int black slip (5YR2.5/1). Core reddish yellow (5YR7/6).

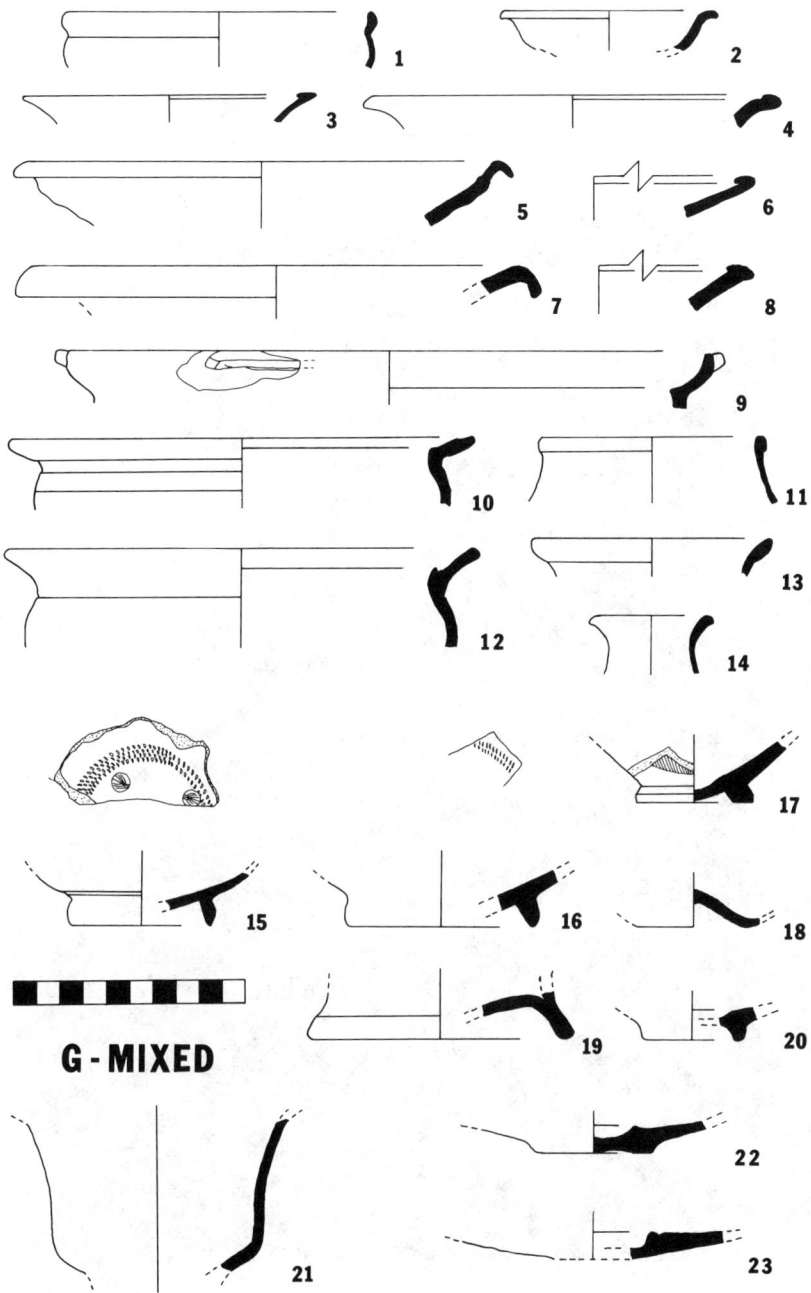

G - MIXED

Fig. 12. Pottery, mixed.

33

Plate 1. East face of the inner fortification wall and foundation courses in Area G 8. Photo by Ewald and Johnson; courtesy Drew Institute for Archaeological Research.

Selected Locus Summary

Each locus listed below is either described in the preceeding text
or found in the figures. Other loci have been excluded. Each entry takes the form of the following example. Since a detailed a-
nalysis of the pottery is presented in the body of the study, a
basket-by-basket field analysis is not included. For those loci,
the proper figure reference is given. For those for which the pottery was not examined, field analysis is presented. It should be
noted that this examination of the pottery has shown a tendency
for the field analysis to place the date of the pottery too late.

Locus	Stratum	Locus Above	Top Level	EW Extent	NS Extent
		Locus Below	Bottom Level	Loci combined with this	
				locus	

Contiguous elements (only loci described in this study are
included)
Description of the locus
Pottery baskets listed by year and basket number
Artifacts listed by year, registry number, and description

Abbreviations (local dates for Roman and Byzantine from Toombs,
232):

AR	Artifacts		LR	Late Roman (200-330 CE)
B	Byzantine (330-640 CE)		MR	Middle Roman (100-200 CE)
EB	Early Byzantine (330-450)		PB	Pottery Basket
ER	Early Roman (10 BCE-100 CE)		R	Roman (10 BCE-330 CE)
H	Hellenistic (332-10 BCE)		ud	undetermined
LH	Late Hellenistic (198-10 BCE)			

G8000 ER exposed   7.16 m EW Extent 2.3 m NS Extent 9.0 m
            G8126   1.66 m
        contiguous to North balk, subsidiary South balk, G8024, 8100,
        8118, 8120, 8124, 8125
        dry-laid, limestone wall with a seven course superstructure
        and 4 course foundation. Stones c. 1.2 x 0.6 x 0.35 m.

G8024 MR G8016, 8017, 8044 5.06 m EW Extent 2.91 m NS Extent 2.43
            G8119, 8125   3.14 m
        contiguous to East balk, subsidiary East balk, subsidiary
        South balk, G8001, 8100, 8120, 8127
        six-course limestone wall bonded with humra. Stones c. 0.51
        x 0.72 x 0.27 m. Abutts Wall G8001.

G8100 MR   G8101   4.26-4.20 m EW Ext 3.96 m NS Ext 8.56
            G8118, 8120, 8127 4.01-3.88 m Combined with locus G8074
        contiguous to North balk, East balk, subsidiary East balk,
        G8001, 8024
        packed sand and clay (10YR5/4) below Surface G8101
        PB 1980 #325 R, Mr, B?; #335 R, ER, LR?; #466 H, ER, LR; #467
            B, EB; #468 R, ER, MR, LR; #479 R, ER, MR, LR; #480 R, ER,
            MR. LR, B; #481 R, ER, MR, LR; #482 R, ER, MR, LR.

AR 1980 #7.20.4 iron nail, #7.23.2 iron fragment, #7.23.3
glass, $7.23.4 iron fragment, Coin-10 ud, Coin-11 procur-
torial 1st cen CE, Coin-12 ud, Coin-17 1st Jewish War
69 CE.

G8118 ER $\underline{\quad G8100 \quad}$ 4.4 m $\quad$ EW Extent 9.96 m MS Extent 8.56 m
$\overline{G8119, 8125}$ 4.26-4.2 m
contiguous to N. balk, E. balk, subsidiary E. balk, G8001,
8120
loose sand (10YR55/6). Cut by G8120
PB 1980 #469, 470 - 474, 483, 485. See figs. 10 and 11
AR 1980 #7.21.1 glass, #7.22.7 faience, #7.23.5 lead ring,
#7.23.7 copper fragments, $7.24.1 glass, Coin-13 Ptolemaic
3rd-1st cen BCE, Coin-14 Antiochus III, 222-187 BCE

G8119 LH $\underline{G8024, 8118, 8120}$ 3.42 m EW Extent 3.96 NS Extent 8.56 m
$\overline{\qquad G8123 \qquad}$ 2.60 m
Contiguous to N. balk, subsidiary E. balk, subsidiary N.balk
G8120, 8125
loose sand (10YR7/4, 10YR7/3) with random charcoal flecks.
Cut by G8120, 8125
PB 1980 #475, 488-490, 498 (possible contamination), 499
(possible contamination). See figs. 6 and 7
AR 1980 #7.27.1 faience, #7.28.4 copper frag, #7.28.5 faience, #7.28.6 iron frag, #7.28.7 iron frag, Coin-18 Tyre 1st
cen BCE-1st cen CE, Coin-19 ud, Coin-20 Alexander III, 128-
123 BCE, Coin-21 Seluecid 3rd-1st cen BCE, Coin-22 same,
Coin-23 Antiochus III 222-187 BCE

G8120 MR $\underline{G8100, 8127}$ 3.54 m EW Extent 2.92 m NS Extent 0.21 m
$\overline{G8119, 8125}$ 3.14 m
contiguous to subsidiary E balk, G8001, 8024, 8118, 8119, 8125
sand filled trench (10YR7/4) cut through G8118, 8119 and
8125 for Wall G8024
PB 1980 #486 R, ud; #487 R, MR

G8121 mix $\underline{G8119}$ 2.85 m EW Extent 2.00 m NS Extent 1.25 m
$\overline{G8122}$ 1.60 m
mixed loci G8119, 8122, 8123, 8124, 8125
PB 1980 #491 - 5. See fig. 12
AR 1980 #7.27.3 chert chip, Coin-24 Seleucid 3rd-1st cen BCE,
Coin-25 Antiochus IV 175-164 BCE, Coin-26 Antiochus III?

G8122 -- $\underline{G8124, 8126}$ 1.62 m EW Extent 2.28 m NS Extent 8.56 m
$\qquad$ -- $\qquad$ -- $\qquad$ Combined with locus G8081
contiguous to N balk, subsidiary E balk, subsidiary S balk,
G8126
virgin sand (5YR6/6)

G8123 LH $\underline{G8119 \quad}$ 2.60 m $\quad$ EW Extent 2.28 m NS Extent 8.56 m
$\overline{G8124}$ 2.21-1.79 m
contiguous to N balk, subsidiary E balk, subsidiary S. balk,
G8125
loose sand (10YR 7/4) with random charcoal flecks. Cut by
G8125

PB¨1980 #500. See fig. 5
AR 1980 #7.27.2 ud, Coin-28 imitation Seleucid 3rd-1st cen

G8124 LH G8123, 8125 2.21-1.79 m EW Extent 2.28 NS Extent 8.56 m
             G8122   1.62 m
      contiguous to N balk, subsidiary E balk, subsidiary S balk,
         G8001, 8125
      loose sand (10YR8/6). Cut by G8125
      PB 1980 #501. See fig. 5
      AR 1980 #7.29.3 chert chip, #7.29.4 iron fragments

G8125 ER G8118, 8120 3.14 m EW Extent 0.48 m NS Extent 8.26 m
             G8124   1.97 m
      contiguous to N balk, subsidiary S balk, G8001, 8119, 8120
         8123, 8124
      sand-filled trench (10YR7/3) cut through G8119, 8123, and
         8124 for Wall G8001. Cut by G8120
      PB 1980 #496, 497. See figs. 8 and 9
      AR 1980 #7.28.1 metal hook, #7.28.2 metal hook,#7.28.3 glass
         bead, Coin-27 ud

G8126 ER G8001 1.66 m EW Extent 0.50 m NS Extent 8.26 m
         G8122 1.55 m Combined with locus G8082
      continguous to N balk, subsidiary S balk, G8122
      compacted sand (10YR6/3) under Wall G8001
      PB #360, 504, 505. See fig. 8

G8127 MR G8100 4.00 m EW Extent 0.15 m NS Extent 0.52 m
         G8120 3.90 m
      contiguous to subsidiary E balk, G8024
      layer of humra (10R6/3) encountered in balk trim

BIBLIOGRAPHY

F.-M. Abel, La Liste Géographique du Papyrus 71 de Zénon. Revue
1923   Biblique 32:409-15.
Pessah Bar-Adon, Another Settlement of the Judean Desert Sect at
1977   'En el-Ghuweir on the Shores of the Dead Sea. BASOR 227:
          1-26.
Jeffrey A. Blakely, William D. Glanzman, and L.J. Tiede, Observa-
coming   tions on Late Hellenistic and Roman Pottery from Caesarea.
J. W. Crowfoot, Grace M. Crowfoot and Kathleen M. Kenyon, The Ob-
1957   jects of Samaria. Samaria-Sebaste III; London: PEF.
David F. Grose, The Syro-Palestinian Glass Industry in the Later
1979   Hellenistic Period. Muse 13:54-67.
John W. Hayes, Ancient Lamps in the Royal Ontario Museum I: Greek
1980   and Roman Clay Lamps. Toronto: Royal Ontario Museum.
James A. Hodges, The Building Program of Herod the Great. Chicago:
1970   University of Chicago. Unpublished Ph.D. dissertation.
Flavius Josephus, Antiquities of the Jews, nd.
1959   The Jewish War; Middlesex: Penguin.
E.-M. Laperrousaz, Remarques sur les pierres à bossage préhérodi-
1974   ennes de Palestine. Syria 51:104-28.

Nancy Lapp, ed., The Third Campaign at Tell el-Ful: The Excavation
1981   of 1964. AASOR 45; Cambridge: ASOR.
Paul W. Lapp, Palestinian Ceramic Chronology, 200 B.C. - A.D. 70.
          New Haven: ASOR.
Lee I. Levine, A propos de la fondation de la Tour de Straton. Re-
1973   vue Biblique 80:75-81.
1974   The Hasmonean Conquest of Strato's Tower. IEJ 24:62-9.
1975   Roman Caesarea: An Archaeological-Topographical Study.
          Qedem II. Jerusalem: Hebrew University.
Eric M. Meyers, James F. Strange, and Carol L. Meyers, Excavations
1981   at Ancient Meiron, Upper Galilee, Israel 1971-2, 1974-5,
          1977. Meiron Excavation Project III. Cambridge: ASOR.
Avraham Negev, Studies of Caesarea: Discovery of Hellenistic Cae-
1966a   sarea. Mada 10:341-4 (Hebrew).
1966b   Roman Caesarea. Mada 11:136-44 (Hebrew).
Ehud Netzer and Eric M. Meyers, Preliminary Report of the Joint
1977   Jericho Project. BASOR 228:15-28.
Avner Raban, The Ancient Harbors of Caesarea. Qadmoniot XIV Nos.
1981   3-4:80-8 (Hebrew).
Avner Raban and Robert L. Hohlfelder, The Ancient Harbors of Cae-
1981   sarea Maritima. Archaeology XXXIV, No. 2:56-60.
Avner Raban and Elisha Linder, News from Israel: Caesarea. Inter-
1978   national Journal of Nautical Archaeology and Underwater
          Exploration VII:240-3.
John A. Riley, The Pottery from the First Session of Excavation in
1975   the Caesarea Hippodrome. BASOR 218:25-63.
Joseph Ringel, Cesaree de Palestine: etude historique et archeolo-
1975   gique. Paris: Editions Ophrys.
Duane Roller, Hellenistic Pottery from Caesarea Maritima: A Prelim-
1980   inary Study. BASOR 238:35-42.
          The Wilfrid Laurier University Survey of Northeastern Cae-
1982   sarea Maritima. Levant 14:90-103.
forth-   The Northern Plain of Sharon in the Hellenistic Period.
coming   BASOR 248.
Susan I.Rotroff, The Athenian Agora: Hellenistic Pottery, Athenian
1982   and Imported Moldmade Bowls. American School of Classical
          Studies at Athens 22. Princeton: ASCS at Athens.
James A. Sauer, Hesbon Pottery 1971: A Preliminary Report on the
1973   Pottery from the 1971 Excavations at Tell Hesban. Andrews
          University Monographs VII. Berrien Springs, MI: AU Press.
Anonymous, Scavi di Caesarea Maritima. Rome: Bretschneider, 1966.
James F. Strange, Late Hellenistic and Herodian Ossuary Tombs   at
1975   French Hill, Jerusalem. BASOR 219:39-67.
Lawrence E. Toombs, The Stratigraphy of Caesarea Maritima. Pages
1978   223-32 in Archaeology in the Levant: Essays in Honor of
          Kathleen Kenyon ed. P.R.S. Moorey and P.J. Parr. Warmin-
          ster: Aris & Phillips.
Moses S. Zuckermandel, ed., Tosefta. Jerusalem. 1970.

SOME ASPECTS OF ARCHAEOLOGY -- TACTICS AND STRATEGY

Roger S. Boraas

The excavator is brought to ever broader and more technically demanding questions as one prepares to excavate a site. The pressures are produced by the technical applications of scientific disciplines, increasingly sharpened zones of archaeological ignorance and higher costs of all aspects of the work from travel to equipment and labor. I propose to examine some dimensions of such decisions in the context of three recent excavations -- one a modest sounding,[1] another a full scale five-season grid excavation on a virgin site,[2] and the third a project still developing both in strategy and tactics.[3] Professor Toombs has given a long and fruitful career to wrestling with these issues, and the writer happily acknowledges his debt of interest in the subject to the stimulus provided by this astute and thoughtful teacher.

Funding limits have almost always affected such decisions in some way. The excavators of Megiddo modified their strategy from the original goal of reducing the entire site to selecting portions thought to be most fruitful for further work. Some limitations have been faced in one degree or another by almost every expedition mounted. However, if one looks at the enterprise from a long time perspective, such limits may have had some positive strategic value. The unparalleled rapid pace of improved data recovery which has marked the craft of archaeology particularly since World War II focuses the awareness that even the most modern methods will soon be replaced by even better procedures for retrieval and modes for study and classification than we now possess. It can therefore be recognized by far-sighted practitioners that the complete excavation of any major phenomenon prevents anything more being learned from it by future generations working with superior retrieval and interpretive techniques.

This is usually no problem for the excavator of a modest preliminary sounding. The function of the sounding is to provide an admittedly and deliberately limited test of the range of stratigraphic evidence available on a given site. To avoid major architecture (and the delay and complications from dismantling massive construction) one tries to place such soundings in locations which promise to give maximum stratigraphic indications with minimal disturbance of major features. The tactical choices in such cases are usually decided from ground surface observations, and choices can be narrowed astutely by careful use of topographic clues.

For example, the location of the sounding at Rujm el-Malfuf (North) was put outside the two major visible structures, but it was set at an angle attempting to intercept the foundation trenches for both the ca. 20.00 meter diameter stone tower and the adjacent quadrilateral structure east of the tower. The placement was designed to do minimal damage to both structures and to get the stratigraphic record from ground surface to bedrock. Placement of the preliminary sounding at Tell Hesban was determined by the combination of available land, obvious extensive architectural features in the acropolis and similarly extensive wall fragments showing through ground surface along the north, west and south sides of the acropolis. This led to plotting the sounding on the southwest shelf where both a small nearly level platform and the absence of protruding wall lines suggested a fruitful location. At Khirbet Iskander the first season's work placed two preliminary 4.00 meter by 4.00 meter squares on the site. One was at the highest portion of the site, the northwest corner. It attempted to sample the stratigraphy in what might have been expected to be public construction, if any were located on the site. The second square was placed adjacent to some ground surface evidence of a major tumbled wall line cutting the site east to west. At test in this sector was whether this debris reflected Nelson Glueck's earlier observed defense perimeter at that approximate location.[4]

In all these cases the tactics of sounding placements were based on avoiding major architecture in ground-surface clue patterns and on attempting to get rapid maximum stratigraphic penetration in the shortest feasible time. The tactical judgments fit the overall strategic consideration of avoiding the complete destruction of any major feature while accomplishing the immediate aim of full stratigraphic index retrieval.

As the plans for an excavation expand, the financial, scientific, tactical and strategic questions begin to trip over each other. The overall issue is usually some form of the question: how can one get the most information most quickly and most cheaply? Here

40

even the nature of the material which can be published
and the effect this has on fund-raising might become an
issue. There is merit in the long-standing cliche of
going for broad lateral exposures which are easily
photographed, good for publicity and make for spectacular presentations at professional society meetings.
This strategy is especially helpful for reaching broad
popular audiences as one interprets the work.[5] It
makes for good slide lectures both in and out of the
classroom.

The usual strategic alternative is to settle for
less breadth and go for more depth. Here the results
are never as visually spectacular and they make less
impressive publication photos with less easily discerned
analyses of architectural features. The meticulous
separation of soil-layers in relatively restricted space
sacrifices the publishable visual perception of architectural extents for the sake of more modest stratigraphic correlations. But it is sometimes a less expensive way to get more information within an equivalent
time/labor effort.

It becomes a more critical issue which of these to
choose when the stratigraphic depth of a site is unclear
or simply unknowable from any other sources of information. To illustrate, the preliminary sounding at Rujm
el-Malfuf hit bedrock at about 1.00 meter below ground
surface in the square external to the two visisble
structures. This, given the time, funding and staff
available, allowed the extension of the work to include
a second square placed at the presumed juncture of the
two buildings so as to test their interior architectural
relations. In contrast to the outer space where no architecture was involved other than the two main units
evident in the original placement decision, the second
square uncovered interior architecture comprising two
stories and a basement, bedrock being reached in the
latter component, although in extremely limited breadth.

At Tell Hesban international political developments
had forced excavation of the preliminary sounding to
become part of the first regular full season's work
rather than the normal preference that it precede such
full-scale inquiry.[6] It took three seasons' work to
reach bedrock in that case, and while the merit of the
sounding as the most rapid penetration of the stratigraphic history of the site was retained throughout the
process, its "lead" was sometimes tenuous. Also, there

were gaps in the occupation sequence uncovered there, especially for the earliest period represented on the site to date. It did work as a location for good sounding information in spite of its cutting across part of a major Byzantine kiln and a large Hellenistic stone wall foundation, set in a very deep and broad trench dug into the fill layers of an abandoned reservoir.

At Khirbet Iskander, despite diminished size of the squares involved, the effort to reach maximum depth within the first season led to restricting the zone excavated within both squares. Major architectural features forced work into less than a third of one square, but late deep trenching in the other was unimpeded by architectural barriers. In contrast to Hesban, however, the homogeneity of the pottery evidence made discerning the stratigraphic phases a task of much more refined stratigraphic work. Uncertainty of the depth at which bedrock or virgin soil might be encountered persisted even after the 1982 season when concentrated efforts to extend depth penetration in the lower sounding were further limited by the erosion damage between seasons. The geological contours around the site suggested a possible depth for bedrock of up to 20.00 meters. That indicated that several additional normal seasons' work might be needed to complete the sounding even in restricted breadth exploration.

However, as important as the effects of these considerations may be on overall strategy, no dimension afflicts the tactical decisions of a Director more broadly than the demands of available scientific analyses. It usually appears in the matrix of research design as affected by both social and natural sciences. The Rujm el-Malfuf project never had to face the problem fully, because it was intended and completed as a preliminary sounding on a property threatened by expanding modern urban development on the west side of Amman.[7]

The developing pressures generated by the new applications were illustrated through the years of the Tell Hesban excavation. Within the traditional goals of excavating a site to provide information on its public buildings, its private housing, its defenses, water supply systems, burial practices, and any specialized industrial or other economic support systems, there was agreement from the beginning that all bone materials would be saved for analysis, that geological studies and

42

lithic identifications would be done, and that the
usual horizons of ceramic, epigraphic, numismatic,
architectural and artifactual data would be dealt with
fully and responsibly. This meant that field tactics
would involve restricting the expedition to a stratigraphic "slicing" of the site along an east-west and a
north-south axis anchoring the main grid. Work was to
be focused in the southwest quadrant of the site but
was to cover the ground from the acropolis center (where
major pillar bases appeared to be in situ) down the west
and south slopes.[8] The original goal of a three-season
expedition, given uncertainty about the depth of debris
on the site, resulted in placing a series of squares on
the west edge (to sample defenses and possibly cut half
of a gateway), a group of squares in the acropolis center (to get the major public architecture there), a
string of squares running down the south slope (inter-
cepting both the fortifications of the acropolis and
the approach constructions from that side), and the preliminary sounding on the southwest slope. All squares
were set in positions so as to allow eventual direct
connections along the main axes if the depths of debris
would allow such extensions as would be needed. Given
the architecture evident at the end of three seasons,[9]
the sponsors decided to go for two full additional
seasons in order to complete the picture yet only partly exposed. That goal was reached over the five seasons,
when squares were excavated linking all Areas to a continuous section line running from the west edge of the
site up to the acropolis center, then down the south
slope and reaching slightly westward to connect with
the original sounding square.

At the same time, however, scientific interests
were expanded to include geological mapping, meteoro-
logical observations, ethnographic studies, procedures
of froth flotation and pollen sampling, ornithological
observations, site-catchment survey, and other related
studies.[10] The demands of these additional dimensions
affected the size and composition of the staff, field
procedures in both excavation and recording, auxiliary
facilities needed for laboratory work in the field, and
cost of shipping and processing, to say nothing of publication. It was further recognized that the real
value of some of these studies would only become available to future generations' work. For example, the
tactics of taking soil, pollen and froth flotation samples to the same degree and extent from a site in the
Transjordan hills was at the time unmatched in any east

43

bank effort. It was done to establish a baseline of data as a reference for comparative studies as other expeditions might provide comparable data, as well as to learn what could be grasped from such data for the site's preliminary reports in such zones as weather patterns, geological history, ceramic raw material resources, natural environmental changes observable, and the historic shifts in population as reflected not only in burials but in the patterns of discarded or treated food supplies and other related studies. The value of the environmental data retrieved -- from seeds to molluscs -- would reside primarily in establishing a clear catalog of items and changes in the items for the periods under survey (Iron I to Mamlūk). It would thus be a reference scale for other explorations in the region as future expeditions added similar data to the reservoir. For this reason it was decided to sample every locus from ground surface to bedrock in three sectors of the site as the excavation completed its work. Such data profiles from the acropolis, the west slope and the south slope would provide a basis not only for internal comparisons and supplement where gaps had occurred in one square, but would allow future comparative studies of the environmental data in the region for all periods reviewed. In the writer's opinion this provided one of the major payoffs of the decision to go for stratigraphic depth at the price of more spectacular breadth as the overall strategy for work on the site. Only the future studies and the relative helpfulness of the Hesban data base can confirm or refute this judgment, but as a practicing excavator I find the decision a happy one.

As additional testimony concerning this pressure, it is clear from proposals being submitted to the National Endowment for the Humanities in the field of Archaeology that the expectation of increased scientific applications continues to grow in the consciousness of expedition directors. This involves not only adapting recording systems to computer capabilities but experimenting with increasingly sophisticated machinery for data retrieval, which can range from the satellite photographic techniques to laser surveying to the most advanced trace-element analyses requiring specialized and highly trained processors. The struggles to accommodate such technical advances raises questions beyond the limits imposed by dust, short water supply and no electricity in the field. Should one restrict excavation now by a diminished emphasis on architectural

44

remains and focus more on the detailed analyses of each locus' soil by any and all scientific procedures ready in the wings, if not in the field itself? Is the relative value of what can be learned in the dust-free labs of major research facilities more vital than getting the full expanse of that gateway? Ideally, funding should accommodate both, but in the real world these choices impinge ever more intensely.

The issue of how to use the money becomes the pressure to reassess what is hoped to be learned. That is, research design and its relative cost components become paramount. In the case of Rujm el-Malfuf, the main question the excavation sought to answer was the date range of the site's occupation, and, if possible, the founding dates of the architectural units evident from ground surfaces. It comprised about as narrow a research focus as one might imagine.

In contrast, for Hesban there were specific historical questions about Israelite migration in the Late Bronze Age. The design included establishing the chronology of the site's occupation, exploring some of the more obvious architectural features evident from ground surface clues, and expanding the base of scientific knowledge, both in environmental data and in cultural anthropology data which might be available. Tactical decisions concerning the locations of the squares where flotation and other sampling would be drawn from every excavated locus nourished the scientific inquiry. Site-catchment survey, efforts to locate and explore burials for all periods of occupation, and analysis of butchering techniques met more directly the cultural anthropology goals.

At Khirbet Iskander the expedition's main goal was to test the accuracy of a particular historical hypothesis, namely that EB IV was a nomadic or pastoralist occupation period.[11] Already the 1982 season has shown by the architectural patterns uncovered in three sectors of the site that it was instead a very sophisticated society of stone masons and building designers, pertaining both to domestic dwellings, defense wall repair and modification (if not construction), and gateway design. The further work planned at the site at this writing is aimed to elaborate or correct the accuracy of these judgments and to extend the historical inquiry into the details of the transition from EB III culture to the EB IV life in this Transjordan hill country site.[12]

45

Scientific data retrieval in the 1982 season was limited in part by water shortage and severely restricted electrical service at the site camp.[13] What future logistic adaptation will allow as expansion of scientific data recovery is under constant scrutiny and revision by the Director of the expedition. Funding in this instance is a major part of the formula that will determine what will be possible as the work is drawn to its planned three-season completion.

When the question of the level and complexity of natural science studies to be included has been settled, there are still competing forces affecting the strategic and tactical decisions of how to excavate the site. These simpler lines of competing aims involve the present goals versus the future lines of information to be sought. Several considerations play at once even within this narrower field of decisions. What are the priorities of information to be gotten? How do they affect the scope and nature of materials one ought to reserve for future excavators with their better methods? Is this humility a false or a legitimate characteristic of the field excavator? Should one "go for broke" on all possible fronts simply because one happens to be the explorer currently interested and on the scene? Does any form of reserve for future generations' inquiries comprise a hesitation damaging to the results one can rightly expect to achieve in the present operations? Whether such questions even arise may be resolved in part by external factors.

Soundings or salvage work provide semi-automatic answers for different reasons. Soundings are modest by definition, and by that definition may rightly reserve the bulk of the site for future exploration. Genuine salvage work, that is, exploring material about to be destroyed by forces of human development or by nature, can exploit ruthlessly with present methods all aspects of the site threatened because the future will mean total loss of learning potential from the site anyway. It is the simplest form of work to do from the point of view of the questions under review.

However, the dilemma is sharpened with large sites, obviously complex in layout and data. With the exception of the Byzantine Church and its sub-structures on the Hesban acropolis, one can say that one had left much, much more for future work by better methods than one had destroyed even in a major expedition's five

seasons of intense labor. Given the protective consequences of the decision to preserve the Islamic bath on
the Hesban acropolis, even portions of the Byzantine
Church and the Roman sub-structures remain for others
to explore. The entrance features of the Church and
unknown aspects of the Roman sub-structures remain un-
disturbed for future delineation and cross-checking.
One might hope that a hundred years or so would be
allowed to elapse in order that the small portions remaining might not be sacrificed to procedural gains of
minor proportions. There certainly remain intact substantial portions of the architecture inside the acropolis and in the approximately three-fourths of the site
not disturbed around the acropolis on the northwest,
east and southeast. One can rest assured that future
work will have plenty of data to run through its more
sophisticated procedures in the next century.

The tactical and strategic decisions yet to be
made for further work at Khirbet Iskander sharpen the
focus of the questions in several respects. Does a
research design focused on a particular historical
question or the nature of an historical transition
justify clearing both halves of a presumed gateway on
the southeast corner of the main site slope? Or should
one proceed stratigraphically to open greater depth
beneath the uppermost architectural reaches for the sake
of the transition and the scientific environmental data
which might be reached there before extending the lateral breadth for the sake of more complete plans and
better plan photographs? How much exposure is really
needed to demonstrate the nature of citizen housing on
the site? The situation is less acute regarding the
defense sequence on the north edge of the site. The
substantial portions of walls exposed at the northwest
corner suggested that there are more than adequate sectors of the defense perimeter in well preserved condition along both the north and west edges of the site to
satisfy any future inquiry's needs.

The issue of what other features of the site should
be explored within a three-season projection, two seasons remaining at this writing, is less easily settled.
From work already done, it is clear that no bedrock or
virgin soil is likely to be reached in less than three
seasons. The question of what can be gained by large-
scale lateral exposure opposes the values of what will
be missed by failure to penetrate to the bottom of occupation in the ten squares already under excavation.

Given the pattern of extremely complex architectural
data obviously involved in all but one square presently
under investigation, the data suggests that extensive
lateral exposure will maximize loss, minimize gain and
risk incomplete investigation of that already exposed.
The value of intensifying and expanding the variety of
natural scientific data retrieved for analysis by logistic solutions in a fairly primitive setting might
be viewed as more important than additional architectural layouts, given the current three-season limit on
exploration plans.   Such are the tactical decisions facing the Director, and the answers given will affect
staff recruitment, logistical arrangements, transport
and storage budgets, equipment procurement, shipping
costs, post-season workup expenses and publication
costs.

From one point of view, these decisions are nothing
but the ordinary heat an excavation Director has to
face.   From the experience of this writer, however,
these decisions are becoming increasingly difficult because of both the pace of scientific developments to be
considered for application in the field and the rapid
rise in costs of all processing involved in even the
most standard forms of data analysis.   One is tempted
at such times to "think small" for the sake of efficien-
cy.   That applies to research design so that modest
goals might be achievable.   It applies to the scope of
results expected from the enterprise so that future
generations will have ample data with which to cross-
check and correct our fumbling 20th century efforts
from the advantageous perspectives of the 21st or even
the 25th centuries.

FOOTNOTES

1.   The site of Rujm el-Malfuf, Jordan was excavated in the summer
of 1969 under the joint sponsorship of Upsala College and The American Schools of Oriental Research. The preliminary report is Roger
S. Boraas, "A Preliminary Sounding at Rujm el-Malfuf, 1969," Annual
of the Department of Antiquities of Jordan XVI (1971), 31-45.
2.   The excavations at Tell Hesban, Jordan were initiated by Siegfried Horn of Andrews University and joined by a consortium of institutions in subsequent seasons. Work was started in 1968, then in
1971, '73, '74, and '76.   Preliminary reports were issued by Andrews
University Press in 1969, '73, '75, '76 and '78 respectively. Full
additional reports available are in Boraas and Lawrence T. Geraty,
Heshbon 1976; Berrien Springs, MI: Andrews University Press, 1978,
especially pp. 1-2.
3.   Excavation at Khirbet Iskander, directed by Suzanne Richard of

of Drew University was begun in 1981 and the first full season of work was completed in 1982. The preliminary report is forthcoming in the Bulletin of the ASOR.

4.   Nelson Glueck, Explorations in Eastern Palestine, Part 3, Annual of the ASOR 18-19 (1939); New Haven: ASOR, Fig. 47.

5.   Typical of this procedure is the current work of the University of Rome at Tell Mardikh, Syria. The Director, Paolo Matthiae, presented a report on the work which reflected this point of view both in slides used and in comments responding to questions at a Symposium, "Ebla: Its Excavation and Implications," at the University of Pennsylvania Museum, 26 Mar 83.

6.   The initial season had been planned and prepared for 1967. The war between Israel and her neighbors necessitated rescheduling the first season for the summer of 1968. One result was less lead-time for the sounding as a preview of the stratigraphy to be anticipated in other portions of the excavation.

7.   The property lines of one private home already had impinged on the southeast corner of the site when work began in 1969. The field still under cultivation just south of the main stone tower has now been used for the construction of a private home. Rescue of the site itself by the Department of Antiquities has allowed its subsequent development as a public park.

8.   The fact that the southwest quadrant lay within land owned by the Department of Antiquities spurred the decision to locate the main excavation work there, rather than to enter negotiations for land use permissions with numerous local owners of other portions, especially on the east side of the tell. It was also the case that the general contours and surface evidences showed the southwest quadrant to be as likely a fruitful zone of inquiry as any other portion would have been.

9.   The primary puzzles remaining for diagnosis were a major reservoir installation on the south slope (Area B), a large defensive installation on the west slope (Area C) and unclear boundaries of the Byzantine church on the acropolis (Area A). See Boraas and Geraty, Heshbon 1974; Andrews University Press, 1976, p. 6.

10.   The degree of growth of scientific studies is best seen when comparing the first and last season preliminary reports. For the 1968 season, only Robert M. Little's "An Anthropological Preliminary Note on the First Season at Tell Hesban," appeared in the first volume, pp. 232-9, Heshbon 1968 ed. Boraas and Horn; Andrews University Press, 1969. By contrast and improvement, there were six special articles included in the report of the fifth season, pp. 201-303, Heshbon 1976 ed. Boraas and Geraty; Andrews University Press, 1978. The latter was judged among the most favorable efforts at integrating such studies by William G. Dever, "The Impact of the 'New Archaeology' on Syro-Palestinian Archaeology," BASOR 242 (Spr 81), 18, 24, n. 20.

11.   See S. Richard, "Toward a Consensus of Opinion on the End of the Early Bronze Age in Palestine-Transjordan," BASOR 237 (Wint 80) 5-6.

12.   The lack of any clear stratigraphic or ceramic evidence of EB

III layers in the work of either the 1981 or 1982 seasons has moved this level of the inquiry to focus for the projected 1984 and 1986 seasons.

13. Restrictions on water use led to adaptations in the froth flotation procedures employed during the 1982 season. To allow maximum conservation of water, froth flotation was concentrated in a few work days during the season, rather than daily as the soil samples came in. Electrical service to the base camp was provided by a community generator operated for the local agricultural settlement. Hours normally were limited to operations from 10 a.m. to noon, and from c. 6 to 10 or 11 p.m. daily.

VILLAGE SUBSISTENCE AT AI AND RADDANA IN IRON AGE I

Joseph A. Callaway

The period of transition from Late Bronze to Iron Age I has been of special interest to Larry Toombs for more than twenty years. One would think that a consensus of agreement would be reached on its related problems over twenty years, but that is not the case. If anything, there is more disagreement today on the time and manner of Israel's entry into Canaan and the nature of the settlement than there was in 1960. Toombs could spend another career on the same problems. But alas, the torch must be passed to another generation. Fortunately, he has worked with and influenced many students and there should be several who will carry on his work. Because of this wide contribution to both archaeology and the next generation of archaeologists, as well as a close personal comradeship over the years, it is with special pleasure that I join in the celebration of his sixty-fifth birthday. May it be simply a milestone in a continuing career!

New approaches to the study of Israel's settlement in Canaan have been opened up with the application of interdisciplinary methods in archaeological research. Before 1970, little attention was given to such matters as settlement patterns and subsistence strategies of villages and towns in the highlands of central Canaan. There seemed to be an impatience to get on with establishing connections between the Bible and history, and most scholarly discussion focused upon the manner of those connections. An example is the symposium on early Israelite history held in Jerusalem in 1975 to celebrate the seventy-fifth anniversary of the American Schools of Oriental Research. The papers that dealt with problems of early Israelite history did little more than reiterate long-standing positions of different schools of thought on the manner of the conquest and settlement (See Cross 1979). No significant new perspectives on the problems were presented.

It seems obvious that we must go back to the primary sources of archaeological research and find new ways to study the early history of Israel. This was impressed upon me during the excavations at Ai, when the most common question asked was "Have you found any Late Bronze pottery?" If I had said "Yes," there would have been no more questions about the Iron Age I

settlement. Nobody asked who the settlers may have
been, where they came from, how they made a living, or
what happened to them at the end of Iron Age I. Over
the final years of work, after 1969, these unasked
questions began to assume major importance with me,
because I saw that answers to them could give new perspectives on the problems of early Israelite history.
In this paper, therefore, I should like to deal with
the subsistence strategy of the Iron Age I settlers at
Ai and the nearby site of Raddana, and begin answering
questions about the central highland villagers that
should have been the focus of attention long ago.

The Introduction of Hill Country Dry Farming

In the early 1970s, Lawrence E. Stager directed a
survey of ancient agricultural terraces in the highlands of Israel from Shechem to Hebron, an area of
about 4,200 km^2 (Stager 1981:1). The survey found a
dramatic increase in the number of permanent settlements during the transition from Late Bronze to Iron
Age I, actually an increase from 23 in the former to
114 in the latter. Stager's estimate was that the population increased from about 14,000 to more than 38,000
in a very short period of time. This, of course, was
too much to attribute to natural growth; the increase
in population must be ascribed to movement from elsewhere. But where, he asked, was "elsewhere"?

Traditionally, this influx has been associated
with the entry of Israel into Canaan, either by conquest
as reflected in Josh. 1-11, or by infiltration and more
peaceable settlement as reflected in the accounts in
Judges. The sites of Ai and Raddana were a part of the
almost 100 new settlements established at the beginning
of Iron Age I, and thus have some evidence bearing upon
the radical expansion of occupation during the period.
Like most of the new villages, they were established
either on the abandoned ruins of earlier sites, as at
Ai, or on unoccupied hilltops that had never before
supported settlements, as at Raddana. In either case,
the subsistence strategy was unlike that of the previous
inhabitants of the area. Indeed, the new villagers introduced a revolutionary new way of wrestling a living
from the arid hills of central Canaan; they employed
techniques that may be characterized as dry farming.
Because the dry farming techniques were so new, yet
apparently fully developed when the settlers arrived,

it seems that a closer look at these practices may be instructive concerning the larger questions of population movements and the manner of entry into the land, and thus Stager's question about the origins of the settlers is put aside for the moment.

There were two basic innovations in hill country dry farming that came to central Canaan about 1200 B.C. First, the newcomers conserved water for household use by digging cisterns on the rocky hilltops where their houses were located. This enabled the location of small villages some distance from natural water sources in the valleys. And second, the hillsides around the villages were terraced on contours to conserve both soil and water for food production. Because the hillsides were steep, terraces at Raddana, for instance, were very narrow and inefficient for grain production, but the objective of the settlers seems to have been survival so that inefficiency was tolerated.

The Settlements at Ai and Raddana

Both Ai and Raddana are examples of the villages supported by dry farming, and are representative of settlements established upon the abandoned ruins of ancient cities, or of new settlements built "de novo" on hilltops. A great city flourished at Ai during the Early Bronze Age, from about 3200 B.C., but destruction by an unknown adversary overtook the heavily fortified urban center about 2400 B.C. The inhabitants were either captured, or they fled the city, and it lay abandoned and in ruins until the Iron Age I villagers came about 1200 B.C.

The subsistence base of the Early Bronze city was agriculture, animal husbandry, and trade. It dominated the plateau region north of Jerusalem and west of Jericho from the secure enclosure of massive walls around some 27.5 acres of houses, an industrial area, and a temple palace compound on the acropolis. Since the only natural water source during the third millenium B.C. was a spring in the Wadi el-Jaya about 500 meters outside the walled city, an artificial reservoir was constructed inside the walls at the southeast corner. This reservoir, constructed much like a modern pond with a dam on the low side, had an estimated capacity of about 1,800 m³, or enough to support a population of 1,500 to 2,000 in normal times.

53

When the site was destroyed about 2,400 B.C., a
considerable depth of silt had accumulated in the reservoir, and over the years of abandonment from that time
until about 1,200 B.C., the reservoir filled with eroded
earth and lost its identity. The newcomers apparently
did not recognize the reservoir when they arrived. The
houses and other structures on the east slope of the
tell seem to have fallen down and eroded earth covered
them also. Thus the settlers were faced with 27.5
acres of stony and earth-covered ruins, probably over-
grown with vegetation and shrubs, enclosed by the broken
down ruins of the Early Bronze walls.

On the acropolis were the standing walls of the
ancient temple-palace compound. The newcomers seem to
have moved into the temple building, built a crude
divider wall across its middle, and established a residence in either end. On the contour around the east
side of the temple site, houses were constructed on
terraces that were built up to support them. At Site
B, which was excavated from 1964 until 1972, a long
divider wall running straight down the east slope separated the closely built compounds of houses. The limits
of the small settlement were at our contour 845, which
defined the acropolis area.

The village at Raddana, on the other hand, was
established on a hilltop across a deep valley from present-day Ramallah which had never before supported a
settlement. Packed huwwar floors were laid out on exposed bedrock, and the only evidence of previous visitors was fragments of handmade pottery in the cracks of
bedrock that dated to at least 3,200 B.C. The houses
at Raddana were constructed in the same style as those
at Ai: they were simple rectangles with a row of hewn
stone pillars or stacked piers on one side of center to
support roof beams. Some houses had a room across the
rear of the basic rectangular structure, and at Raddana,
there were up to three houses clustered around a common
courtyard. These seem to have been family compounds,
and there were only five or six compounds in the entire
settlement at Raddana. At both Ai and Raddana there
were no fortification walls around the villages.

Cistern Construction at Ai and Raddana

As noted above, the new Iron Age I settlements
could be located on hilltops some distance from natural

water sources because the newcomers dug cisterns to capture rainwater for use in the dry season. Bell-shaped cisterns were excavated underneath the huwwar and bedrock floors of houses, and on the uphill sides along the house walls in a consistent size and pattern that indicates an established tradition of cistern building brought in by the villagers. Like the houses, the cisterns were plain and functional, yet they reveal a sophistication in construction techniques that could come only from some experience in the use of cisterns.

At Ai, for instance, one house compound was supplied with three cisterns. All were cut into a thick layer of Senonian chalk that was exposed on the surface of the ground, and all were bell-shaped, tapering inward from bottom to top and culminating at a small round opening about fifteen inches in diameter. The openings were small to minimize the introduction of contaminants, and to enable a secure closure with a flat round capstone.

Two of the three cisterns had openings along the uphill side of the house, and a channel cut in rock brought rainwater into the reservoirs. However, the channel led to only one of the two. About eighteen inches from this cistern, a pit had been cut in the path of the channel and, filled with small stones, it served as a trap to filter out large contaminants. Water from the first cistern flowed to the second and third ones through holes cut in the lower walls less than two feet from the bottom. Thus the bottom of the first cistern served as a settling basin which filled with water before the second and third cisterns were filled through the spillway holes in the sides. The third cistern was directly underneath the floor of the greatroom above, and a round capstone, still in place since the village was abandoned about 1050 B.C., gave access to the water supply from the room.

An adjacent house at Ai had a twin-cistern arrangement in the greatroom itself. Rainwater was channeled into a large reservoir at the end of the room, and access to it was provided by a round capstone opening. Beside the large cistern was a smaller one which was filled by way of a small round aperture cut near the top of the large installation. When the large cistern filled, overflow water spilled into the smaller reservoir, filling it with cleaner water since the larger one served as a settling basin.

The introduction of cistern technology at the beginning of Iron Age I made feasible the building of
small villages on hilltops throughout central Canaan.
Where sites have been extensively excavated, the number
of cisterns has been amazing. Wampler, for instance,
characterized Tell en-Nasbeh as "...truly a place of
cisterns," because fifty-three of them were discovered
in various places (Wampler 1937:127). Albright believed
that the revolutionary development of waterproof lime
plaster at the beginning of the period enabled dependence on rock cut cisterns, and he attributed the settlement of Iron Age I villages to this development
(Albright 1971:113). My investigations at Ai and Raddana, however, indicate that lime plaster was not used
to waterproof cisterns used only in Iron Age I, and
that plaster was found only in those reservoirs which
were re-used at a later time. Apparently the Senonian
chalk in which the cisterns were dug had a self-sealing
quality that minimized loss through seepage. The revolutionary development was the introduction of cistern
technology, not the introduction of lime plaster for
use in cisterns.

Agricultural Terracing

The hillsides in the Ramallah region are staircases
of narrow terraces today, as Stager observed in his
survey report. In fact, Z. Ron has calculated that
56.4% of the Israeli part of the Judean hills consists
of terraced hillsides (Ron 1966:33). Valleys at the
base of the hills are very narrow and would support
only about half the population that is presently being
supported. It has been apparent for some time that
many of the terraces are quite ancient, but specific
evidence to document the exact age has not been available until recently.

A part of the strategy in excavating at Ai was to
discover the limits of the Iron Age I village, as noted
earlier. The limits were found at contour 845, just
below the acropolis on the site plan. An unexpected
dividend in defining the extent of the village was the
discovery of the first agricultural terrace constructed
on contour 840 by Iron Age farmers over the ruins of
Early Bronze Age houses. To our surprise we found that
the newcomers, having built their tiny village on the
ancient acropolis area, had put the remaining nine-
tenths of the city ruins into cultivation. Apparently

it was easier to terrace and farm the Early Bronze ruins than it was to cultivate the barren, rocky slopes outside the Early Bronze walls. The built-up destruction debris and earth fill must also have appeared more fertile than the hillsides.

At Site G on contour 840 of the site plan, flattened ruins of Early Bronze houses were found on bedrock, following the natural slope eastward without any kind of terraced foundations. A street in the middle of Site G actually was stepped between house walls with rooms founded on bedrock. After the city was destroyed and abandoned about 2400 B.C., eroded soil and fallen rocks accumulated against the downhill walls of houses, and natural contours following the broken edges of layers of bedrock became evident. These contours on the site from 840 down to 795 at Site J continued outside the city walls where the breakings of bedrock determined the topography.

The Iron Age I newcomers built a simple wall of fieldstones along contour 840 and allowed it to act as a retainer for the debris backed up to the edge of contour 845. This wall was constructed in the same manner as barrier dams across narrow valley floors which impede the flow of water and trap eroding soil. If Stager's observations that the newcomers were pushed into the highland by more aggressive settlers in the lowland areas, the art of terrace construction would have developed from barrier construction in lowland valleys.

There is evidence at Site G that the terrace wall was rebuilt one time, after soil and stones built up to the top of the original wall. Thus there were two major phases of construction during the Iron Age I occupation at Ai, from about 1200 B.C. to 1050 B.C. The contour lines on the site plan are drawn from present-day terraces over the ancient Early Bronze ruins. We found at Site G that subsequent repairs and rebuildings of the terrace system there simply extended and strengthened the original Iron Age I terrace. Phases identified in the vertical profile were Iron Age I, Roman-Byzantine, Islamic, and modern. At Site C on the plan, present-day farmers still plow through dark gray ashy soil beneath whose surface lie Early Bronze house remains.

The Inhospitable Hill Country Sites

I doubt that we appreciate just how inhospitable the sites of Ai and Raddana were when the Iron Age I settlers arrived. Never before had the hillsides supported agriculture nor the arid hilltops villages. It was certainly not a place "flowing with milk and honey," as later tradition would suggest. In fact, the central hills seem to have offered a last chance for survival for a peaceful, agricultural population that chose to move on rather than fight. There is a short passage hidden away in Josh. 17:14-18 that seems to reflect the sociological dynamics that led to settlements such as those at Ai and Raddana being established. The tribe of Joseph is reported to have said, "The hill country is not enough for us; yet all the Canaanites who dwell in the plains have chariots of iron, both those in Beth-shean and its villages and those in the Valley of Jezreel" (Josh. 17:16).

Prevented from expanding into the fertile valleys by superior forces, and desperate for room to live because of population pressures, the tribe of Joseph was told, "...the hill country shall be yours, for though it is a forest, you shall clear it and possess it to its farthest borders..." (Josh. 17:18). Whether this passage refers to the settling of the Ai-Raddana region is not really significant, because the population pressures that led to expansion in the hills near Jezreel must have been the same as those at Ai and Raddana.

Besides the task of digging cisterns for a water supply, and constructing agricultural terraces on narrowly contoured hillsides, the newcomers had a "forest" to clear to make way for the settlements. Our perception of what confronted them is usually that of heavily wooded land like that which confronted pioneers in our country two centuries ago. However, this is not an accurate perception of the "forests" in ancient Judea and Samaria.

The word ya'ar, translated "forest," means "wild, untilled land carrying permanent vegetation." It included the cedar forests of Lebanon (1K. 7:2, etc.), open woodlands (1 Sam. 14:25-26), or thickets and scattered shrubs (Isa. 21:13). The precise meaning in any given usage must be determined by the geographical and archaeological contest. In the case of Ai and Raddana, is there evidence of either open woodlands, or thickets

and scattered shrubs? The question can be answered
best in the light of archaeological findings at the
sites.

At Ai, the houses of the Early Bronze city (about
3200-2400 B.C.) were built with foundations and floors
mainly on bedrock. Uneven places were filled with red
clay and huwwar. The temple-palace complex on the
acropolis had floors laid on bedrock, and streets along
the south city wall as well as those between houses at
Site G, for instance, were constructed on bedrock.
This suggests that topsoil on the hilltop site was not
much, if any, thicker 5000 years ago than it is on
neighboring hilltops today, which are arid and barren.
It is highly unlikely that a stand of trees, such as
one finds in open woodlands, existed on the site at Ai.

The Iron Age I settlers came 1200 years after the
city was destroyed and abandoned about 2400 B.C. What
did they find? Were the hillsides wooded in 1200 B.C.?
Or was the city ruin inside the Early Bronze walls
wooded? Apparently there were no significant stands of
trees anywhere in the area. The two house units built
inside the walls of the Early Bronze temple cella had
floors laid only a few inches above the plaster floors
of the ruined structure. In the area excavated by
Marquet-Krause, Iron Age I house floors lay on bedrock,
and some were extremely uneven and uncomfortable-look-
ing because of the rough natural surface. On the east
slopes east of contour 845, which were put into cultivation, there may have been thickets and bushes, perhaps an occasional tree, but we found no evidence of
tree stumps or roots. The city ruin at Ai in 1200 B.C.
was a ya'ar in that it was wild and untilled, but it
was not a forest of trees.

The hilltop site at Raddana likewise seems to have
been covered only by bushes, possibly thickets, but no
trees. Early Bronze pottery dating to the beginning of
the period about 3200 B.C. was found in crevices of
bedrock on top of the hill, suggesting that the surface
of bedrock was exposed at the time. The first pillar-
type houses of the Iron Age I settlers were built about
1200 B.C. on the same exposed bedrock, and the main
house in the small village actually had a bench along
the wall of the greatroom shaped from a ledge of bedrock. When the houses were abandoned about 1050 B.C.,
they gradually crumbled before the ravages of sun, wind,
rain, and occasional visitors. However, the buildings

do not seem to have been covered with a thick growth of vegetation, because Byzantine pottery left by a shepherd 1500 years after the Iron Age I settlers abandoned the site was found in one of the original rooms which by then was only a roofless shelter against the wind.

The sites of Ai and Raddana were, therefore, open sites covered with bushes, perhaps some thickets, and an occasional tree when the Iron Age I newcomers arrived, but they were not forested in the sense that we understand the term. This type of vegetation could be removed with the crude mattocks and blades that were found, so that clearing a place to live and raise a minimum supply of foodstuff was within their capabilities. We must keep in mind, however, that mere existence was marginal, because these people were true pioneers who learned to eke out a living where nobody had tried to do so before.

The Size of the Villages

Since no evidence of farming the hillsides and valleys around the ancient city ruin at Ai was found, we may assume that the terraced 25 acres or so inside the Early Bronze walls would support a very small population. Of course the village was not completely dependent upon farming this 25 acres, because we found bones of sheep and goats in every house, and a cistern was discovered a kilometer eastward in the Wadi el-Jaya with Iron Age I pottery in it, suggesting a watering place for the flocks. Nevertheless the grain and vegetables raised in the enclosure of the ruin would have been the major source of food to supplement milk, meat, and cheese supplied by the flocks.

A more exact way of estimating the population is to work from cistern capacity for each household and check the resulting calculations of people supported against the floor area of the houses. Both Ai and Raddana had meager springs located quite a distance away from the hilltop villages which would have provided a survival source of water, but not a regular supply. The spring in the Wadi el-Jaya north of Ai was studied in 1970, and its flow was calculated to be about 12½ gal. per hour. This is not insignificant, but it would serve mainly as a backup source. The basic water source for everyday use was that captured in cisterns.

60

Two houses at Ai supplied by three cisterns each were carefully studied by James B. Davis, a graduate student at Southern Seminary, and capacities of 21.6 m^3 and 17.7 m^3 were calculated for the two systems. This would convert to 21,600 liters for one household, and 17,700 liters for the other. One unpublished study of water consumption in arid regions of the Middle East concluded that people adapted to the environment could get along quite well on 2 m^3, or 2,000 liters per year. If we assume replenishment of the cisterns regularly during the rainy season, the maximum period of dependence on the cisterns would be about 250 days. Assuming a requirement of 2,000 liters per person for 250 days, there would be about 8 liters, or two gallons per person per day. This, of course, assumes also optimum conditions, which rarely prevail. Nevertheless, we may conjecture that the norm would be near these calculations. On this basis, as many as ten persons could live in the larger household, and about eight in the smaller.

Another way of estimating population is that of relating floor area to the requirements of shelter per person. A study made recently by G. Edwin Harmon, also a graduate student at Southern Seminary, found that 10 m^2 per person was an accepted formula used in determining population of primitive villages. Using this formula at Ai, the twenty Iron Age I house complexes would accommodate about 100 persons, or an average of five per household. This is considerably lower than the eight to ten persons indicated by a calculation of water usage, and is probably too conservative because it does not take into account the use of outside space for household tasks.

At Raddana, houses were clustered around common courtyards, and every house had a fireplace for cooking outside the roofed area. It seems evident that much of the food preparation and cooking were carried on outside the greatroom area, and that unroofed courtyards must be included in the floor area calculations. When these areas are added to that of the actual houses, the average of five persons per household is increased to seven or eight, which agrees in general with the calculations of water needs and supplies. The village at Ai would have had no more than 150 persons, therefore, and possibly as few as 125. Raddana would have accommodated in its five or six houses no more than 50 persons.

These numbers pose problems at Ai in particular
with regard to subsistence. The 25 acres inside the
city ruin would not provide food for even 125 persons.
It seems evident, therefore, that some farming was done
on the adjacent hillsides and valleys, although evidence
cannot be produced. The area immediately east of the
tell where contour lines 795 and 790 continue would provide good soil for farming, although the terraces become more narrow. Also the valley south of the tell
has wide areas between contours that could and probably
were farmed. There is one other major item of subsistence, however, that enabled the settlers to live in
their marginal environment, an item that has been mentioned but not discussed. That is the practice of animal husbandry.

Sheep and Goats

One can only estimate the part that sheep and
goats played in the subsistence at Ai and Raddana, but
the estimate can be based upon some factual evidence.
First, we have seen that cultivation of grain and other
foodstuffs was on a small scale. The 25 acres inside
the ancient city ruin at Ai and adjacent areas would
barely provide bread for a village of 125 to 150 persons. At Raddana, the staircase terraces were too narrow for efficient grain production, but they were apparently cultivated to provide a bare survival type of
subsistence. Taken in its totality, the sources of
subsistence from farming would be inadequate in themselves, without the significant contribution of animal
husbandry.

A surprising discovery at Ai was a series of animal enclosures built adjacent to the houses in which
people lived. In fact, only the house wall separated
the quarters of people and animals, with the animal
enclosures being on the east side between contours 850
and 845. There was a practical reason for this layout.
With prevailing winds from the west, odors from the
sheepfold would blow away from the house and toward the
Jordan Valley. Nevertheless, the odors of sheep and
goats must have penetrated the entire area in spite of
westerly winds.

This method of quartering animals in close proximity to one's living quarters was apparently continued
from the Iron Age period, because we discovered a stable

with the skeleton of a cow adjacent to a Byzantine house at Khirbet Haiyan, dating 500-700 A.D. Actually, in the modern village of Deir Dibwan where our excavation staff was quartered, some of the older houses have animals quartered on the ground level and the occupants of the house live on the floor above. Access is gained by a long flight of steps from the ground level. Odors do not seem to be a problem, and one would assume they were not a problem at Ai and Raddana.

In the compound of buildings at Ai, more space is given to animal enclosures than to the roofed area of houses. Entrance to one of the rectangular animals enclosures was by way of a perfectly arched doorway 80 cm high, with a rough hewn keystone at the top. Considerable care, therefore, was given to the care of animals in providing shelter and safety from predators, and having ready access to milk for yogurt and cheese. It is probably not out of line to estimate that one-half of a family's subsistence came from these animals.

Conclusions and Implications

The Iron Age I villagers at Ai and Raddana are examples of settlers throughout the hill country of central Canaan who moved into the arid inhospitable area that had never before supported a way of life which they introduced. Bringing with them a technology of cistern construction and agricultural terracing, the newcomers pioneered a marginal subsistence based upon agriculture and animal husbandry, and made it succeed until the beginning of the monarchy. Events connected with the establishment of the monarchy caused the villages at Ai and Raddana to be abandoned, never to be occupied again. What happened to the inhabitants we do not know.

These are the people usually identified as Israelites who either took the highlands of central Canaan by conquest at the end of the Late Bronze Age, or infiltrated and settled the land as opportunity afforded during Iron Age I. Leaving aside the identity of the villagers, it seems obvious from a study of Ai and Raddana that the occupants would be a military threat to no one. In fact, they seem to have fled to the marginal environment of the arid hill country to escape the threat of conflict. It would be very difficult to envision any combination of these highland villagers as an army led by the biblical Joshua.

Also, the theory of peaceful infiltration and settlement has some problems. It is true that settlements seem to have been established where there was no resistance, thus they could be characterized as peaceful. However, there seems also to have been a general movement into the hill country that was not strung out over a long period of time. The paramount question is the one raised by Stager in his observation that the people moved into the highlands from elsewhere: where was "elsewhere"?

Present evidence seems to point to a movement from the lowland areas in west Palestine into the hill country, and from the plains areas north of Samaria southward.   Houses with the pier-technique of roof support are found in the coastal plain area as far north as Abu Hawam (near modern Haifa), and they appear at the transition from Late Bronze to Iron Age I.   In fact, they may precede in time the construction of similar buildings in the highlands by newcomers in Iron Age I such as those at Ai and Raddana.   Metal chisels, mattocks, and axes are found in the context of pier-type houses in the lowlands, exactly like those recovered at Ai and Raddana, and tuyeres as well as crucibles for melting metal ingots are common in all the major sites.   The architecture and general culture of highland villages have their counterpart in the lowlands and coastal plain as far north as Abu Hawam, and eastward in the Esdraelon plain to Afula.

If the population movement of highland villagers was from the west and north, then we must reevaluate the archaeological and historical evidence for an entry by Israelites from the east and south.   This calls for some new perspectives for studying the Deuteronomic history in Joshua and Judges.

BIBLIOGRAPHY

W. F. Albright, The Archaeology of Palestine, 2nd ed.; Gloucester, Mass.: Peter Smith, 1969, reprinted 1971.
F. M. Cross, Symposia; Boston: ASOR, 1979.
Z. Ron, "Agricultural Terraces in the Judean Mountains," IEJ 16 (1966).
L.E. Stager, "Highland Village Life in Palestine Three Thousand Years Ago," The Oriental Institute Notes and News, No. 69 (1981).
J. C. Wampler, Tell en-Nasbeh I; New Haven: ASOR, 1937.

35°10' 170 35°15' 180 35°20' 190 35°30' 200 35°35' 210,000

160,000

TO NABLUS

JORDAN RIVER

32°00'

BIR ZEIT

TAIYIBA

150

(ET-TELL)
AI (+855 M)

RAMMUN (RIMMON)

31°55'

KH. RADDANA

BEITIN (BETHEL)

KH. KHUDRIYA

TO AMMAN

DEIR DIBWAN
KH. HAIYAN

RAMALLAH (+869 M)

BIREH

BURQA

MUKHMAS (MICHMASH)

TELL ES-SULTAN

140

EL-JIB (GIBEON)

JERICHO (-258 M)

31°50'

ANATA

TO AMMAN

TO TEL AVIV - JAFFA

JORDAN RIVER

JERUSALEM

130

31°45'

BEIT JALA

BETHLEHEM

BEIT SAHUR

120

DEAD SEA (-392 M)

31°40'

SCALE KILOMETERS

0 2 4 6 8 10

110

TO BEER-SHEBA

HEBRON

TO YATTA

31°30'

160,000

35°10' 170 35°15' 180 35°20' 190 35°30' 200 35°35' 210,000

WWE

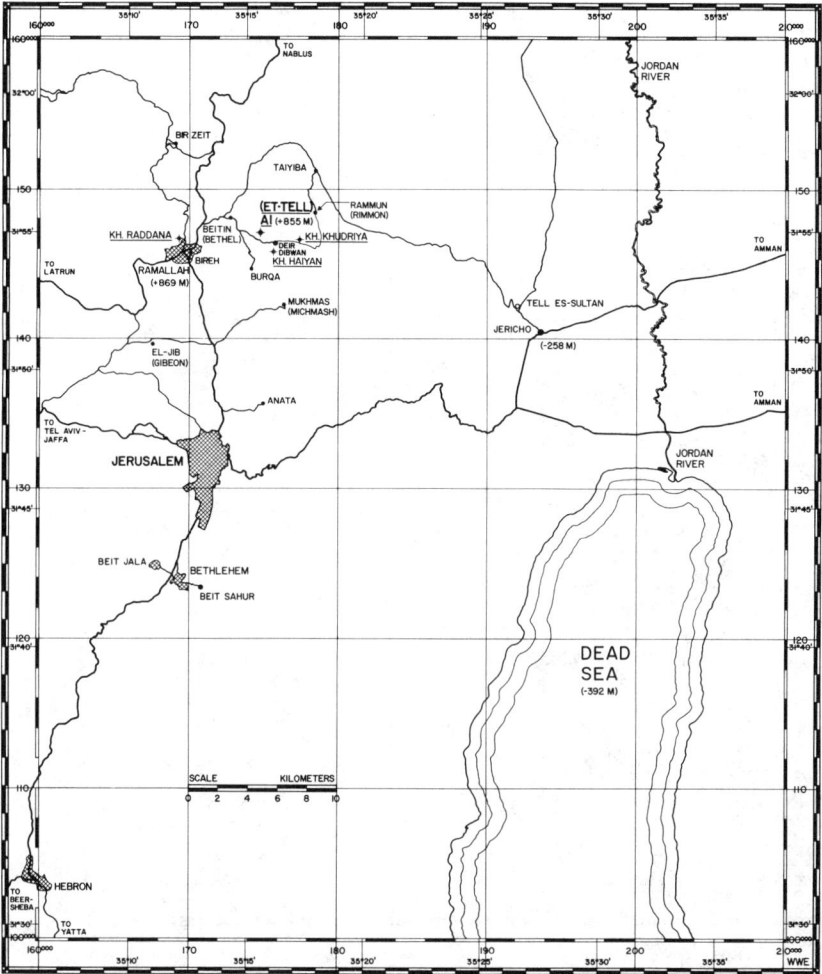

Fig. 1.   Regional map locating Ai and Raddana near Ramallah,
north of Jerusalem.

65

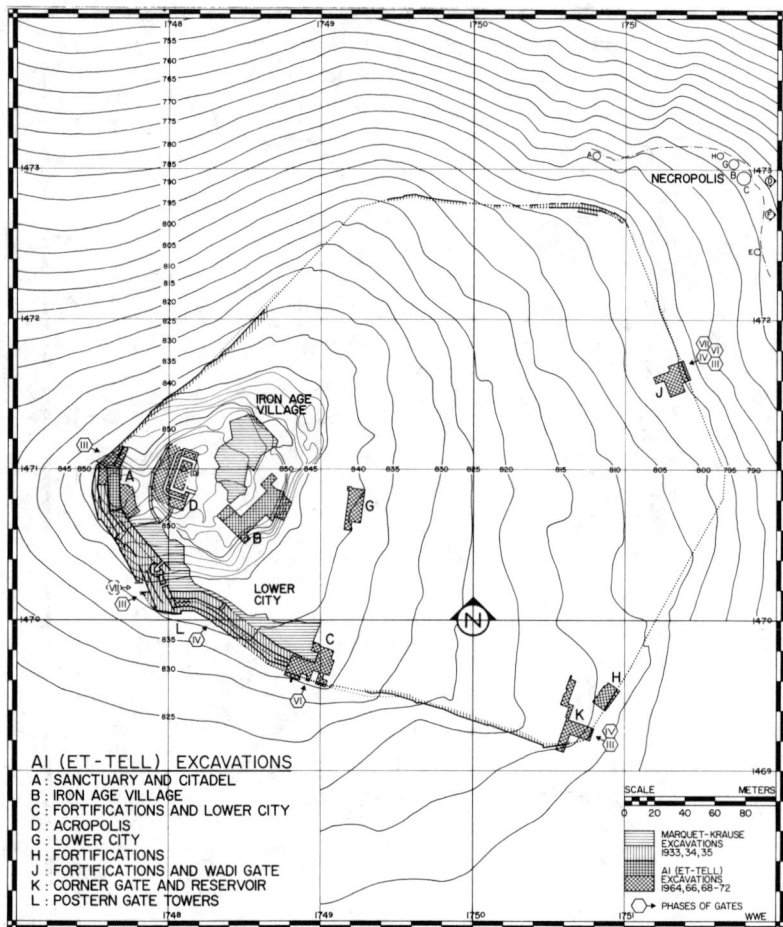

AI (ET-TELL) EXCAVATIONS
A : SANCTUARY AND CITADEL
B : IRON AGE VILLAGE
C : FORTIFICATIONS AND LOWER CITY
D : ACROPOLIS
G : LOWER CITY
H : FORTIFICATIONS
J : FORTIFICATIONS AND WADI GATE
K : CORNER GATE AND RESERVOIR
L : POSTERN GATE TOWERS

SCALE   METERS
0   20   40   60   80

MARQUET-KRAUSE
EXCAVATIONS
1933, 34, 35
AI (ET-TELL)
EXCAVATIONS
1964, 66, 68-72
PHASES OF GATES

Fig. 2.   Site map of Ai (et-Tell) locating the Iron Age I
         village above contour 845. Terraces from 845 to
         795 were farmed by the villagers.

66

The Boundary Between Ephraim and Manasseh

Edward F. Campbell

It was at Lawrence E. Toombs' urging, back in 1964, that the Joint Archaeological Expedition to Tell Balatah/Shechem added to its agenda a regional survey of occupation. Site explorations went on intensively from 1964 to 1968; there have been sporadic additions to the survey's coverage since. Meanwhile, German and Israeli colleagues have contributed new data, corroboration and correction.[1] This brief article presents the results of the survey as they pertain to one specific topographic problem. Since the interpretation here emerges from collaboration with my McCormick colleague, Robert G. Boling, as he prepared his Joshua commentary in the Anchor Bible series, we hope Dr. Toombs will receive it as a joint salute.[2]

In Joshua 16:5-9 and 17:1-10 we are given boundary information about the tribal holdings of Ephraim and Manasseh, which in all likelihood stems from the time of the tribal confederacy -- the Iron I period archaeologically.[3] The two passages bristle with difficulties, some of which will probably never be resolved. Nevertheless, if we combine information from the Shechem regional survey with suggestions from Karl Elliger and the results of an analysis of the geographical terminology used in Joshua 15-19 by H. vanDyke Parunak,[4] we can advance a step or two beyond what students of the problem have already established.

The two passages allow us to pick out a boundary running from the Jordan near Jericho northwestward through Naaran/Naarath[5] and Ataroth to Janoah and Taanath-Shiloh -- at which point we are east of a place designated "the Michmethath." Michmethath lies, we are told, 'al-p^{e}ne, "to the face of," Shechem. From it, the boundary turns south to Tappuah, and then goes down the brook Qanah to the Sea.

Michmethath is the pivot of the central segment of this line, marking apparently the northernmost point. Where in the Shechem region does it lie? To get at that, we need to decide what 'al-p^{e}ne signifies. Because directions in the OT are usually indicated by "right"= south and "left"= north, one might expect "to the face of" would mean east. In the boundary lists, however, we have at Joshua 15:8 and 18:14 instances where 'al-p^{e}ne is used for places which are explicitly not east of the given reference point. And when one looks at all the texts employing this expression in geographical contexts, it is clear that "opposite" or "over against" is the more precise meaning -- with the implication that one point is in sight of the other. Equally important is the fact that the majority of such places are salient features, in a good many instances mountains (e.g., Josh. 15:8, 18:14 & 16; Num. 21:20; Deut. 32:49; Judg. 16:3; 1 Sam. 26:1; 2 Sam. 2:24; 1 Kings 11:17). Michmethath ought to be, then, a visible and probably lofty location opposite Shechem. For the rest of the boundary indicators in our two passages to make sense, it should lie out in the vista one sees from Shechem's east gate.

Two places proposed for Michmethath do not meet these tests. Khirbet Makhneh el-Foqa = Khirbet en-Nebi (General Map site 35) has a full range of Iron age pottery -- that is, examples from the Shechem corpora for Strata XI through VII -- and W. F. Albright once proposed a relationship between its modern name Makhneh and the ancient name Michmethath,[6] but it lies out of sight of Shechem around the corner of Mt. Gerizim, and it is not a particularly salient spot. To place Michmethath here would require taking 'al-p^{e}ne to mean only something colorless like "in the vicinity of."[7]

Khirbet Kefr Beita (site 18) has been proposed for Michmethath, most recently by L. Wächter.[8] It does indeed lie east, but again out of Shechem's view, in the low contours of the mountain ridge which constitutes the south edge of the Shechem vale's east-extending arm. Wächter found two sherds he dates to Iron II here, while our survey found none from that period nor from Iron I on two separate and wide-ranging visits to the site; it may have been occupied in the time of the Israelite monarchy, but the case for locating Michmethath here is really very weak.

What in fact does lie opposite Shechem are two mountain complexes, Jebel el-Kebir along the north of the east arm and the mountain ridge which corners at the bend of the vale. On a peak just at this bend is Khirbet Ibn Naṣir (site 19). On Jebel el-Kebir, two locations might qualify: Salim/Khirbet esh-Sheikh Naṣrallah (one occupation spread on two adjacent knolls, sites 11 and 12)[9] and Khirbet Shuweiha (site 14).[10] Both display Iron age pottery, although neither the

German explorers nor we found Iron I pottery at the former. This period was well-represented at the latter. But neither of these stands out as salient; one has to know where to look in order to spot them from Shechem's east gate.

By all odds the best location for Michmethath opposite Shechem is Khirbet Ibn Naṣir. But is this a town or even a settlement of the Iron age? A fine small orchard now sits on its crown, the trees growing among random wall segments within a circling wall which encloses an area with a diameter of about 50 meters. The soil inside may reach to 50 or possibly 100 centimeters in depth, but some of that soil has doubtless been brought in recently for the orchard. An Elliger photograph from 1930 shows no trees, and a description by Dalman dating to 1911 speaks of an incomplete ringwall. There is very little pottery to be found on the surface. Animals have dug holes in the orchard floor, in the sides of which we found no indication of stratigraphy or sherds. The edges of a square exploratory trench excavated sometime in 1967 or 1968 to bedrock just outside the ring-wall on the west are likewise sterile, and the soil lacks the grayish-brown tinge referred to as jedr, marking human occupation. Alt found Iron age sherds here in 1930, according to his report to Elliger.[11] In three visits to the site we have found about five distinctive Iron I jar handles, and the Israeli explorers have found the same. This raises an interesting question about surface pottery collections. These jar handles all belong to portable water vessels characteristic of Shechem Stratum XI (12th century); so far there has been no report of typical domestic pottery, such as cooking pots, lamps, or huge store jars -- vessels that stay put in a settlement. Herdsmen might easily carry -- and break -- water jars on a site such as this one. In short, we lack evidence of settlement here.

This is where Professor Elliger's suggestion becomes pertinent. He observes that Michmethath does not have to be a settlement, but could well be a topographic salient. Michmethath must designate the spur now capped by Khirbet Ibn Naṣir.[12]

From Michmethath eastward, the boundary's next point is Taanath-Shiloh. Surveys by a number of explorers have made it clear that either of two sites now called Tana can qualify, upper Tana or Tana el-Foqa

(site 16) and lower, Tana et-Tahta (site 17); Tana re-
calls the ancient name.13 Eusebius clearly places
Taanath, for him "Thena," at site 17, and our findings
support him. We are told in Joshua 16:6 that the boundary turns eastward from Michmethath to Taanath-Shiloh,
and then it bulges out around (Hebrew: 'br)14 to reach
a point east of Janoah. Courses for such a boundary
can be drawn so as to loop out around either Tana, then
to return slightly westward to a point east of Janoah --
which is to be located at modern Yanun, or better at
the small ruin called Khirbet Yanun, two kilometers
north of the modern town. (Note the arrow and question
mark on the Regional Map).15

Going the other way from Michmethath, we have next
to do with Tappuah, which consensus places at Tell
Sheikh Abu Zarad.16 While this site lies outside the
Shechem regional survey's planned coverage, we visited
the site several times. Our findings coincide with
those of German and Israeli colleagues: the tell shows
some Early Bronze pottery, and then evidence of continuous occupation from 1800 B.C.E. to Crusader times. It
is of sufficient size to qualify as a Canaanite city
(Josh. 12:17). To its north is a fertile narrow valley
which leads northeastward toward the Shechem vale,
coming out at modern Huwwara just west of site 33 on
the General Map. To the west of Sheikh Abu Zarad is a
bay in the mountain contours which is fertile; this bay
is drained by a water course which becomes one of the
two main sources of the Wadi Qanah = biblical Qanah.

The course of the boundary from Tappuah westward,
we are told, separated Tappuah from its lands (Josh
17:8). This would be the bay to the west and/or the
valley to the north, with the boundary then dropping to
the Qanah farther west. The interesting note about
separating a town from its lands suggests that a key
concern in drawing boundaries was the distribution of
fertile land.

That very issue becomes pertinent to the course of
the border between Michmethath and Tappuah. It raises
a related question as well: Where most sensibly did
ancient boundaries run? On water courses like the
Qanah? Or might they run on the divides between watersheds? Both make sense with reference to human concerns. They represent ways of coping with possible
conflict over water rights and good land. Water courses
separate the flanks and bottom lands of their valleys

70

-- though one can imagine that the bed of the stream
during the dry season could become a bone of contention,
and there would be a question about who controls the
water when the stream is flowing. Divides between
watersheds might be less of a problem. In the absence
of forestation, such divides are likely to have had
virtually no soil accumulation, and almost by definition not to have held water.[17]

With this in mind, it seems likely that the boundary from Michmethath to Tappuah would not run down the
center of the fertile Shechem vale, but would follow
the heights-of-land on one side or the other of the
south arm of the plain, turning westward at the south
end to run to Tappuah. If we have placed Michmethath
correctly, the question is whether the boundary jumped
the plain to run down its west side, splitting it so as
to give the south arm to Ephraim and the east arm to
Manasseh; or, instead, stayed on the east side, crossing
on the saddle at the south which divides the Shechem and
Lubban plains.

The second option seems the more likely. It is
difficult to imagine where the line would most logically
have crossed the plain, so as to reach some point on the
Gerizim massif -- which, by the way, we would expect to
be designated by name. One can readily imagine contin-
ual dispute over where the division of agricultural
rights lay. It makes better topographical sense to
leave the entire plain in Manasseh. But if we do that,
there can be no doubt that Manasseh gets the better of
the arrangement -- probably in the Taanath-Shiloh
region, certainly in the vale itself and at Tappuah.

Perhaps we shall never have enough information
about population size and spread, about agricultural
potential, or about the relative strength of the
Manasseh and Ephraim "brother" tribes, to move much
farther in visualizing the human environment here in
the central hill country. But important beginnings
have been made, and there looks to be an interesting
ongoing agenda of research for geographers, agronomists
and archaeologists to tackle together.[18]

On the basis of the regional survey and a closer
understanding of the textual evidence, then, this picture emerges: the boundary approached Shechem after a
bulge to incorporate Taanath-Shiloh on the range of
mountains at the south edge of the east arm of the vale;

it cornered at Michmethath, and hop-scotched south on
the mountain spurs east of the south arm. Settlements
on the edge of the plain would go with the plain itself
to Manasseh; only settlements well up in the mountains
would have been Ephraim's. At the far south end of the
plain, the boundary crossed on the water divide approximately where the modern road to Yasuf and Tell Sheikh
Abu Zarad leaves the Jerusalem-Nablus road, ran along
the north edge of Tappuah to the south edge of the bay
west of the city, and then dropped to the course of the
Qanah to the Sea. Thorough occupational survey over
the past 25 years undergirds the identification of
Tappuah; it votes against Khirbet Kefr Beita or Khirbert
Makhneh el-Foqa as the site of Michmethath, and for a
different understanding of what "the Michmethath"really
was, placing it at Khirbet Ibn Naṣir. It prefers Tana
et-Taḥta over Tana el-Foqa, but commends either, as the
location of Taanath-Shiloh. All things considered, it
suggests a boundary which favors Manasseh regularly.
And it brings into focus an agenda for cooperative
research.

FOOTNOTES

1. Descriptions of 41 sites are given in R.J. Bull and E.F. Campbell, BASOR 190 (Ap 68), 19-41. For Israeli contributions, see M.
Kochavi, ed., Judaea, Samaria and the Golan: Archaeological Survey
1967-68 (1972), hereafter IS. German research will be cited infra.
2. R.G. Boling and G.E. Wright, Joshua, Anchor Bible; Garden City:
Doubleday, 1982, notes and commentary on relevant passages.
3. On the date, see A. Alt, Kleine Schriften I:193-202. Among many
studies of the texts see esp. K. Elliger, ZDPV 53 (1930), 265-309;
M. Noth, Josua, 2nd ed., HAT, 1953, 96-107; J. Simons, The Geographical and Topographical Texts of the Old Testament, 1959, 158-69;El-
liger article in next note; and Boling-Wright, Joshua.
4. Elliger in A. Kuschke and E. Kutsch, eds., Archäologie und Altes
Testament, 1970, 91-100; H. vanDyke Parunak, "Geographical Terminology in Joshua 15-19," unpublished paper presented to the graduate
seminar, Dept of Near Eastern Languages and Literatures, Harvard
University, Nov 76; used by permission. On taking the verbs in the
boundary lists as technical terms, cf. O. Bächli, ZDPV 89 (1973),1-
14, esp. 5-8. Parunak seems to me to have more penetrating insight
into the meanings of the verbs than has Bächli.
5. Boling-Wright, Joshua, 402.
6. Albright, AASOR 4 (1924), 152-3.
7. In the floor of the plain, east of Khirbet Makhneh el-Foqa, is
Makhneh et-Taḥta, "Lower Makhneh." Now a military site - and its
name means just that - it has not been available for exploration by
archaeologists. Wright reports a visit to it in 1957, which showed
Roman occupation; nothing earlier was noted. Shechem, 1965, 12-3.

8. Wächter, ZDPV 84 (1968), 55-62.

9. Alt, Palästinajahrbuch 25 (1929), 52-4; H.J. Stoebe, ZDPV 82 (1966), 11-2; Wächter, ZDPV 84:63-72.

10. A. Kuschke, ZDPV 74 (1958), 15.

11. Cited by Elliger, ZDPV 53 (1930), 290.

12. Michmethath carries the definite article in both our texts, the only two occurrences of the name. It is not unusual for Hebrew place-names to do this, but Elliger rightly sees it as further reason to consider Michmethath a geographical feature. Cp. Abraham's cave Machpelah, always with definite article, and the hill Ḥakilah in 1 Sam 26:1, among others. Elliger also likes Abel's suggestion in RB 45 (1936), 105, to read Hebrew m'šr, "from Asher," in Josh 17:7 as m'śd, "from the flank of," a tantalizing way out of the difficulty that this verse seems to jump from a reference to the tribal territory of Asher at the northwest edge of Manasseh to Michmethath on Manasseh's south border. Boling-Wright accept this change.

13. In BASOR 190:31, I reported that we had found only Byzantine at el-Foqa, Roman and Byzantine at et-Taḥta, and added we had visited them on a very hot day in a hurry. A subsequent visit in 1973 gave a very different picture. Tana el-Foqa showed possible LB, certain Iron II 8th century B.C.E. and at least one piece of Hellenistic pottery. Tana et-Taḥta yielded clear representation of Shechem XIII (LB), and sherds of Iron I through all phases of Iron II known at Shechem. Our observations are now in accord with what German colleagues found. See G. Wallis, ZDPV 77 (1961), 38-45; Wächter, ZDPV 84:55-7; Elliger, in Kuschke & Kutsch, 95-7; IS 167, No. 27.

14. Parunak's rendering. Josh. 16:6 contains the word 'ōtô after the verb, apparently the Hebrew accusative case marker with masc. sing. suffix. If the antecedent is a place name, we would expect the fem. suffix, and thus we would have a plain grammatical error. Many assume instead a textual error and delete 'ōtô, but the same construction occurs in Josh. 19:14; two instances of a mistake in similar texts seems highly improbable. The appearance of 'ōtô in 19:14 also tells against the suggestion of G. Wallis, ZDPV 77:43-4 to read the relic of a proper name such as Taanath-Otho in 16:6. Perhaps we have two instances of an odd reflexive idiom: "(The border) bulged/turned itself..," that is, "made a bulge/turn."

15. Wallis, ZDPV 77:43-5, reports Iron I and II pottery at both sites; see also K. Jaroš and B. Deckert, Studien zur Sichem-Area (1977), 25 and n. 70 on 57. Khirbet Yanun seems to fit slightly better the distance Eusebius gives from Neapolis (Nablus) to Janoah, though the course taken by the Roman road is uncertain.

16. Another of the difficulties in Josh. 17:7-10 is ".. to the inhabitants of (Hebrew: yôsebê) En- (= the spring of) Tappuah." Abel, RB 45:103-22 proposed to follow the Septuagint and read instead ".. to Yashib, the spring of Tappuah." He connected Yashib to modern Yasuf, the village at the copious spring barely a kilometer northeast of Tell Sheikh Abu Zarad. However, E.Jenni, ZDPV 74:35-40, found only Roman and Byzantine sherds at Yasuf. Apparently Tappuah and Yasuf constitute paired sites, Yasuf replacing Tappuah in the last two centuries B.C.E. As a town at the spring, named prob-

ably Yashub or Yashib, came into prominence, it found its way into the intertestamental and later works Abel has collected, including presumably the Septuagint. What the original Hebrew of Josh. 17:7 was eludes us. Elsewhere in Josh. 15-19, there is mention of towns by reference to "the inhabitants of N.," but not in true boundary lists (15:15, 63; 17:11); perhaps our verse was contaminated by these. In any case, Tell Sheikh Abu Zarad is the key location.
17. Parunak proposes that the verb yṣ', "to go out," and its related noun twṣ'wt, "outgoings," are used designedly in boundary descriptions where the boundary follows a watercourse (16:8 about the lower end of the Qanah, 16:7 about the run from Jericho to the Jordan). Other verbs may then designate something correlative, such as following watershed dividers. Thus Hebrew hlk suggests jumping from height to height. So Boling: "skips" in 16:8 for the stretch from Tappuah westward, "steps" for the stretch from Michmethath southward (17:7).
18. G.E. Wright, Eretz-Israel 8 (1967), 57-68, esp. 61-4, in defining the Solomonic districts in 1 Kings 4:7-19, makes effective use of the observations of geographers about agricultural and thus economic potential, notably those of D.H.K. Amiran, IEJ 3 (1953), 65-78, 192-209, 250-60. In spite of the rebuttal of Y. Aharoni, Tel Aviv 3 (1976), 5-15, esp. 12, these ventures on the part of Wright should be followed up. An important ingredient of future research should be studies of agricultural terracing, such as that of L.E. Stager in his article, "Agriculture," Interpreter's Dictionary of the Bible, Suppl. Vol. (1975), 11-3. [Cf. also Callaway's article in this volume.]

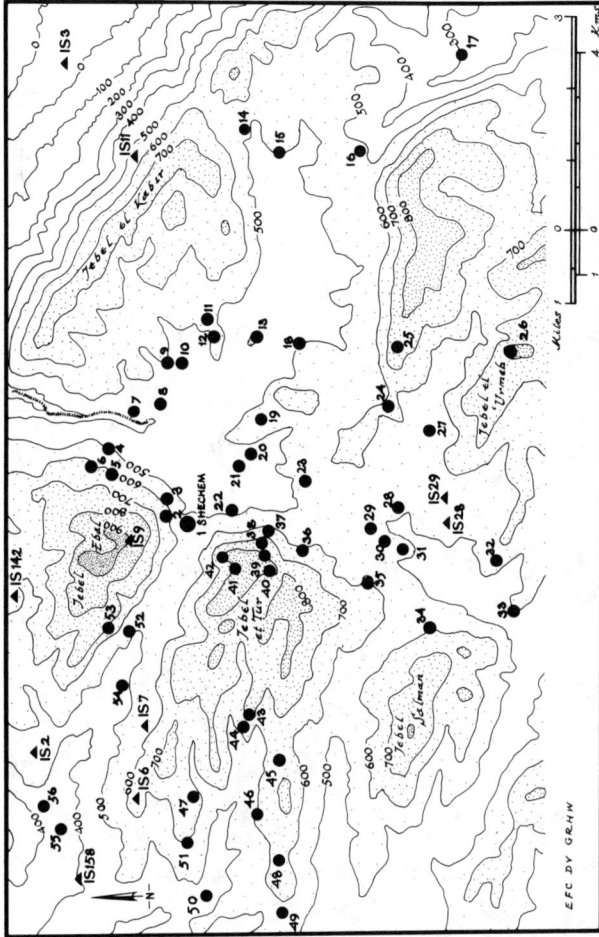

Fig. 1. General Map of the Shechem Plain, showing sites of ancient occupation. Sites 11, 12, 14, 16, 17, 18, 19 and 35 are discussed in the text. Prepared by G.R.H. Wright.

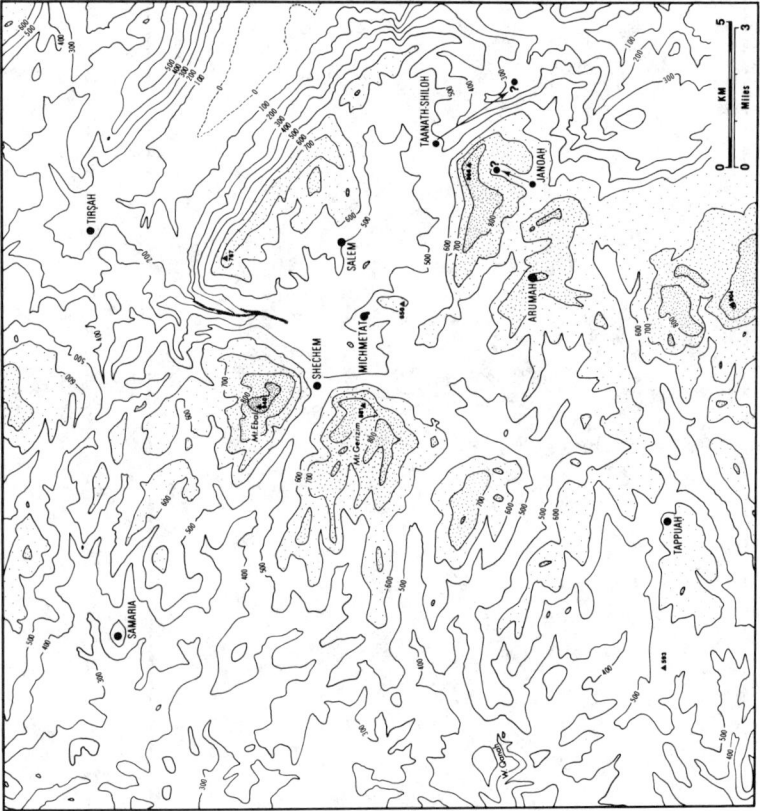

Fig. 2. Regional Map of the Central Portion of the Ephraim-Manasseh Boundary.

TELL EL-HESI: AN IMPORTANT SITE

IN THE DEVELOPMENT OF ARCHAEOLOGICAL METHOD

Valerie M. Fargo

Introduction

When Sir Flinders Petrie began his brief excavation at Tell el-Hesi in 1890 on behalf of the Palestine Exploration Fund, he initiated a series of excavations which would make major contributions to the history of archaeological work in Palestine. Although his expedition was in the field for only six weeks, Petrie used the materials found at Hesi to establish the significance of ceramic chronology for stratigraphic analysis. His work was continued from 1891 to 1893 by an American, Frederick Jones Bliss. In the course of four lengthy seasons, Bliss removed the entire northeast quadrant of the tell, so that a gaping hole is still readily visible today. After a hiatus of 80 years, a new team of American archaeologists returned to the site in 1970. The Joint Archaeological Expedition, affiliated with the American Schools of Oriental Research, is still active at Hesi and carried out its eighth season of field work in 1983. This expedition brought with it the improvements in field techniques developed since the 1890's in an effort to verify and expand the conclusions of Petrie and Bliss. An important member of the Joint Expedition's staff is Lawrence E. Toombs, the "Hakam of Hesi." In the capacity of chief stratigrapher, he has contributed greatly to the advancement of knowledge and the improvement of methods, and has aided the Joint Expedition in moving in new directions.

The Palestine Exploration Fund Expedition

After arriving in the Hesi region in 1890, Petrie briefly investigated a number of sites in the area, and concluded that Hesi was clearly the most promising because of its size and the range of pottery sherds visible on the surface. Excavation was hindered by the fact that the summit of the mound was under cultivation. As a result, Petrie was limited to probing along the slopes and in the 25-acre Lower City which surrounds the tell on three sides. Despite this restriction, he was able to identify a number of major structures and

77

to present a summary of the history of occupation at
the site.

Petrie carried out about 40 probes in the Lower
City, where he discovered archaeological remains up to
a maximum of 3.5 meters deep. These materials were
uniformly early, and Petrie dated them to the Amorites
whom he believed to have been the first to inhabit the
site around 1700 B.C.[1]

The focus of his work, however, was the east slope
of the tell, adjacent to the Wadi Hesi. The action of
the water there had cut away some of the mound and had
produced a fairly steep slope. The probes along the
east face revealed several walls and buildings. He
illustrated these features with both a composite plan
and a schematic section (Figs. 1 and 2). The section
is especially significant because Petrie correlated the
structures and their elevations with the associated
artifacts and pottery, and in this way he formulated
his history of the site.

The waters of the Wadi Hesi had washed away the
eastern portion of almost all the structures Petrie
found. Along the north side of the tell, however, he
was able to identify three wide mudbrick walls. The
lowest of these measured about nine meters in width and
had been rebuilt several times (A in Fig. 1; I in Fig.
2). He traced this wall all along the north side of
the mound. His interpretation was that it was the city
wall of the earliest Amorite settlement at the site,
dating to 1670 B.C.[2] Above the Amorite wall was
another mudbrick wall, also traced along the north face
of the tell (B in Fig. 1; H in Fig. 2). Petrie dated
this wall to the 10th century, probably to the period
of Rehoboam. Several small walls immediately above
Rehoboam's wall were attributed to the 9th and 8th
centuries.[3] To the period of Manasseh belonged the
large wall which Petrie traced all around the north,
west, and south of the site (C in Fig. 1; A and G in
Fig. 2). In Petrie's view, Hesi was to be identified
with Lachish, and it had been one of the fortified
sites besieged by Nebuchadnezzar.[4]

Along the southern portion of the Wadi face were
several major constructions. A roughly square building
featuring stone slabs with pilasters in low relief was
named the Pilaster Building. Petrie considered this
building to be contemporary with the Rehoboam wall on

78

the north. Above the Pilaster Building was a "long range of chambers" whose eastern portion had been washed away. Petrie located a 25-meter expanse of this mudbrick wall with its associated cross walls forming chambers. He claimed that these chambers had become filled with rubbish and that the structure was completely covered over by the time the crushed stone glacis was built by Hezekiah. Immediately above the glacis was the south portion of the Manasseh wall.[5]

Petrie was a keen observer, and he provided measurements and numerous descriptive details for each feature. He also attempted to interpret the history of the site and to link up the archaeological evidence with known historical events. He accepted the earlier identification of Hesi with Lachish, as argued by Conder and Kitchener,[6] and this assumption colored his interpretation.

He also attempted to assign specific dates to the major features at the site. The earliest level, which is attributed to the Amorites, was dated to 1670 B.C. We now know that the Amorite levels belong to the Early Bronze Age and so date to the mid-third millennium B.C. Petrie's late dating of the early levels led to a compression of the occupational history of the site, although he was much more accurate on the later periods.[7] He called the Late Bronze and Iron Age levels Phoenician, and dated them from 1350-850 B.C. The end of occupation he placed at 450 B.C. Since he was not able to work on the summit of the mound he apparently did not see very much of the Persian and Hellenistic pottery, nor did he find any structural remains from these periods. The latest structures he identified were the long range of chambers and the Manasseh wall, which date to the Iron II period.

Probably the most important single contribution Petrie made was in the realm of pottery chronology. He looked upon Hesi as an excellent place to determine the pottery sequence for Palestine, because of the extended period of its occupation.

When analyzing the Hesi pottery, he observed:

> Once settle the pottery of a country, and the key is in our hands for all future explorations. A single glance at a mound of ruins,...will show as much to anyone who

79

knows the styles of the pottery, as weeks of work by a beginner.[8]

Petrie published several plates of line drawings and sections of sherds, with each identified by a brief description, a suggested dating, and the level from which it came. This method of presenting pottery was entirely new, and this publication marked the first use of pottery as a chronological indicator based on its stratigraphic location.

He divided the pottery into three groups corresponding to the major occupational periods: Amorite, Phoenician, and Jewish. As noted above, the Amorite is actually Early Bronze, the Phoenician Late Bronze and Iron Age. The Jewish pottery in Petrie's mind represented a mixture of characteristics neither strictly Amorite nor Phoenician, and it was typical of the later divided monarchy. In fact, this pottery does contain some later elements, including Persian and Hellenistic. Also identified by Petrie as belonging to the Jewish period were a range of Attic imports, now dated to the Persian period.

When Bliss came to the site in 1891, he was able to arrange the excavation of the summit of the mound. He chose to excavate the northeast quadrant, which enabled him to make use of the information gathered by Petrie. At the end of four seasons, Bliss had removed the entire quadrant, nearly one-third of the tell. His method of excavation was to begin by marking off 10-foot squares and putting a worker in each.[9] As walls were discovered and traced, their lines tended to obscure the distinctions between the original areas.

Immediately below the surface the workers encountered "rude Arab graves" and earth disturbed by plowing. These burials were the remains of a medieval Arabic cemetery. Beneath this cemetery were many layers of architectural features which Bliss classified into eight "cities" (Fig. 3). His extensive excavation improved the understanding of the structural fragments Petrie found in the east face of the tell, but since Bliss followed the chronology established by Petrie, his dating of the earlier levels was much too low. Bliss depended heavily on Petrie's interpretive framework, and so he did not make major contributions in that area. Also he devoted little attention to pottery and referred the reader to Petrie's volume. Bliss

focused on the architecture and the artifacts, and provided detailed descriptions and plans of the major
structures in each City.

City I contained the earliest remains, chiefly
traces of mudbrick buildings that were too fragmentary
for Bliss to draw their plans.[10] In this level the
lowest of Petrie's walls was found. This wall was
actually the corner of a large tower with a central
chamber (Fig. 4). West of the tower the wall continued
to the extent of excavation. This structure was dated
by Bliss to the Amorite occupation.[11]

Cities II and III were marked by Phoenician pottery, and Bliss dated them to the 15th century. In
City III he discovered a kiln containing large quantities of slag. Analysis of the slag indicated that it
was not from iron smelting, and so Bliss was at a loss
to identify it.[12] In City III a cuneiform tablet of
the Amarna type came to light. It was found in an area
of bricky debris adjacent to a large building which
filled nearly half of the excavation area. Cities II
and III are to be dated to Late Bronze, and so Bliss's
dating was fairly accurate.

City III was covered by the thick ash layer previously noted by Petrie (E in Fig. 2). Ranging from
one meter to 2.5 meters deep, this deposit actually
consisted of many thin lenses of ash. Petri attributed
the ash to "alkali burners,"[13] while Bliss attempted to
relate it to the kiln of City II.[14] This interpretation is not supported by the stratigraphy, since City
III intervened between the kiln and the ash layer. The
thick ash is still visible in the vertical face of
Bliss's trench. It appears to be the result of industrial activity.

Above the ash was City IV, which contained a
large, thick-walled building about 18 x 18 meters in
size. Bliss also assigned Petrie's Pilaster Building
to this phase.[15] This is unlikely, since the pottery
of City IV is Late Bronze, while the Pilaster Building
contained pilasters in the Proto-Aeolic style of the
9th century. City IV was dated to 1400-1300 B.C. by
Bliss, a dating which has held up.

Parallel rows of stone pillar bases characterized
the chief structures of City V. Bliss was unable to
develop an explanation for this construction,[16]

although it was probably a storehouse of typical Iron II type. It is likely that the Pilaster Building which Petrie dated to 1000-900 B.C., belongs in this phase. With City V the Jewish pottery appeared, and the pottery of this phase is characteristic of Iron II.

Beginning with City VI, Bliss's plans are fragmentary and probably represent composites. These strata contained many pits, which are now known to have typified the site during the Persian period. Between Cities VI and VII was almost 10 feet of earth without structural remains. Bliss did not explain this feature, but it was probably the fill between some of the walls composing Petrie's long range of chambers. In City VII there were residential remains which had been destroyed by fire. Above this destruction was a mixture of architectural fragments, along with Persian and Hellenistic pottery and Attic imports. Bliss dated Cities VI through VIII from 800-400 B.C.,[17] and today we can say that these strata represented the 9th-3rd centuries B.C.

As a result of Bliss's large-scale excavation, an overview of the occupational history of Hesi was achieved. Clearly there had been a major occupation in the Early Bronze Age, when both the tell itself and the surrounding Lower City had been occupied. In later periods the settlement was confined to the Acropolis. Bliss found very little evidence from the Middle Bronze period, but there was a significant occupation during the Late Bronze Age, and then the site was probably in continuous use through the Hellenistic period.

Although the reports published by Petrie and Bliss were not full-fledged archaeological reports by modern standards, they were pioneering efforts that turned Palestinian archaeology in a new direction. For the first time in Palestine a stratigraphic approach to the structures and the artifacts was followed. The data, particularly the architecture and the ceramics, were carefully recorded and presented in a sequential manner. This allowed the formulation of a preliminary interpretation of the site's occupational history and provided information for later excavators. The illustration of pottery in section initiated a method which has become standard procedure. As stratigraphic methods have developed, the use of section drawings for architectural features has become mandatory. And of course, the correlation of pottery with the stratigraphy in which it occurs is the backbone of the relative dating of archaeological sites.

The Joint Archaeological Expedition[18]

In 1970 a new team of excavators returned to Hesi. There had been many changes in field methods since the days of Petrie and Bliss, and the Joint Expedition staff hoped to apply the most advanced stratigraphic procedures to the site in order to expand on the results of the earlier excavators. Another goal was to integrate scientific disciplines for the purpose of providing a broader data base and interpretive results.

The Joint Expedition's methodology developed out of a long tradition of ASOR projects, particularly Shechem and Gezer. Hesi also absorbed some influences from the new archaeology movement in the United States. The result was an approach which combined aspects of both biblical archaeology and the new archaeology in an interdisciplinary method. The focal points of this approach were an interest in cultural change, the importance of man's relation to the environment, the necessity of providing explanation rather than mere description, and the view that the Expedition was a scientific enterprise.[19] In general, the Joint Expedition adopted a problem-solving point of view and applied carefully controlled stratigraphic excavation along with input from the scientific staff in answering questions about the site's occupational history.

This method proved very successful and has enabled the Joint Expedition to contribute new interpretations about Hesi and its surrounding region. Particularly important is the better understanding of the ancient environment. For example, we now know that Hesi's climate during EB was wetter and milder than today and that the area supported rich vegetation including forests. Plants grown during EB would have some difficulty surviving in today's drier conditions.

The Joint Expedition began its work on the summit of the mound. The southern edge of Bliss's cut and the east face of the tell where Petrie had worked were used as controls, and the first squares (Field I) were laid out adjacent to these locations (Fig. 5). Work was also carried out along the south slope of the acropolis (Field III) and at several points in the Lower City

(Fields II, IV - IX). While the Joint Expedition has
produced many significant results,[20] for the purposes
of this paper we will limit ourselves to stratigraphic
issues and in particular the connections between the
work of Petrie and Bliss and that of the Joint Expedition.

An initial surface survey confirmed the occupation
of the site from the Chalcolithic through Hellenistic
periods, although evidence for MB was meager. As excavation began, the Arabic cemetery noted by Bliss was
encountered in most of the fields. The Expedition
chose to record all details of the burials, using the
computer to quantify and analyze the data, and the result was a thorough-going report of medieval Islamic
burial practices.[21]

Modern military trenching (Stratum I), the Arabic
cemetery (Stratum II), and occasional Arabic use of the
summit (Stratum III) had badly damaged the underlying
remains of the Hellenistic period. This helped to explain Bliss's difficulty in isolating the architecture
of his Cities VI through VIII. The Hellenistic remains
of Stratum IV consisted of three sub-phases of mudbrick
and stone structures and a number of pits. Pits were
also particularly characteristic of the four sub-phases
of Stratum V, belonging to the Persian period. These
large pits, often more than a meter wide and at least
that deep, were used mainly for grain storage. The
Persian period occupants also undertook extensive
building activities from the 6th to 4th centuries.

Up to this point the Joint Expedition was not able
to establish a definitive correlation with Petrie or
Bliss. Petrie did not excavate the summit and did not
identify any Persian, Hellenistic, or later structures
in the east face. Bliss, on the other hand, excavated
these periods but was unable to disentangle them because of the complex nature of the stratigraphy and the
limited knowledge of pottery in his time.

With the Iron Age remains, however, specific correlations could be made. The latest Iron II phase was
a sixth century house in the south end of Field I
(Stratum VI). Beneath this were four additional phases
of Iron II ranging from the 9th to 6th centuries. The
later subphases of Stratum VII were domestic structures,
and the final phase had been destroyed by fire, probably
by the Babylonians. This resulted in a very dark ash

layer covering the calcined bricks of this phase.

The earlier Iron II construction of the 9th to 8th centuries consisted of the Stratum VIIc courtyard building[22] and the Stratum VIId construction phase immediately beneath it. Portions of this construction can be identified with Petrie's long range of chambers and his Manasseh wall.[23] The Stratum VIId structures (Fig. 6) formed a level platform for the VIIc courtyard building and also raised the level of the Acropolis by 5 to 7 meters. On the south slope the consolidating material was surrounded by a double wall system, the upper wall being the Manasseh wall.

The first element to be built was the lower wall in Field III (#2 in Fig. 6). A series of terraces up the south slope (#1 in Fig. 6) served as working platforms, and each was filled in as the builders moved up the slope (#3 in Fig. 6). At the same time the chamber and fill system on the summit was under construction (#4 in Fig. 6). This chamber/fill system of alternating mudbrick walls with consolidating fill between them is the long range of chambers observed by Petrie in the east face of the mound. While the chamber/fill system was being built the lower portion of the upper (Manasseh) wall was begun. The area between the upper wall and the chamber/fill system was filled with consolidating material, producing a sloping surface, and this slope was secured by means of a pebble and lime-plaster glacis (#5 in Fig. 6).[24] Once the glacis was in place, construction of the upper wall could continue. This wall's inner face was not vertical, but extended northward and overlapped the glacis. As a further support for the upper wall, additional fill layers were placed to the south of its outer face (#5 in Fig. 6). The final step (#6 in Fig. 6) was to fill in the area above the upper wall to achieve a horizontal surface for the VIIc building.

The Joint Expedition was anxious to find a definitive link between Petrie's long range of chambers and the chamber/fill system on the Acropolis. To achieve this it was necessary to examine the steep east face of the tell. Scraping here revealed fragments of Petrie's chambers, and the resulting measurements enabled the placement of the chambers on the Expedition's grid (Fig. 7). The evidence indicates that three sides of the construction consisted of a series of double walls connected by cross walls, while the north side was composed of only a single wall. The enclosed area was entirely filled with consolidating material.

In the Iron II period Hesi was a relatively small site. The massive construction effort described above was probably undertaken for military purposes. Hesi dominates the surrounding plain and provides an excellent view of all the roads in the area. Its location just a few miles southwest of Lachish suggests that the site may have served as an outpost to give early warning of enemy invasion.

The Joint Expedition has also begun an extensive excavation of the Lower City, occupied only during the Early Bronze period. From numerous soundings Petrie and Bliss had determined that the Lower City had been occupied only briefly during the so-called Amorite period. The Joint Expedition's exploration of the EB has focused on the southern dune system, where there were traces of a large wall. Fields V, VI, and IX (Fig. 5) have exposed portions of this mudbrick wall and an associated crushed limestone glacis (Fig. 8).

In Field VI excavation has uncovered a rectangular tower 9.6 meters wide, preserved to a length of over 20 meters. The western end of the tower has eroded away. Within the tower were two chambers connected by a narrow corridor. A second corridor continued to the east of the easternmost chamber. On the floor of this corridor was an irregular layer of large, flat stones, perhaps the remains of a stairwell to the top of the tower. The floors of the chambers were covered with flat-lying pottery, basalt grinding stones, and a black ash layer.

It was not necessary to look far to find comparative material. In his City I Bliss had found a tower about nine meters wide, with two chambers connected by a corridor (Fig. 4). This tower had been identified as a wall by Petrie, and was the lowest wall in the northern part of this section. Although this tower's dimensions are somewhat smaller than those of the Field VI tower, the plan is virtually identical. The Amorite pottery found near the wall by Petrie and Bliss belonged to EB, and all of the pottery smashed on the floor of the Field VI tower dates to EB III. Thus it is likely that both towers were contemporary.

Conclusion

This brief summary of the excavations at Hesi has outlined the major finds of both expeditions and has indicated the initial correlations the Joint Expedition has made with the work of Petrie and Bliss. Without their pioneering work Palestinian archaeology would not have developed in quite the way it has. The Joint Expedition's methods are the result of an evolution from Petrie's early emphasis on stratigraphic recording and the chronological significance of pottery. At the same time, the Joint Expedition has attempted to move in a new direction through the development of an interdisciplinary, problem-solving approach.

FOOTNOTES

1. W.M.F. Petrie, Tell el Hesy (Lachish); London: Palestine Exploration Fund (PEF), 1891, p. 31 and Pl. I.
2. Ibid., p. 21.
3. Ibid., pp. 22, 26-8.
4. Ibid., p. 29.
5. Ibid., pp. 29, 33-4.
6. C.R. Conder and H.H. Kitchener, Survey of Western Palestine, III: Judaea; London: PEF, 1883, pp. 261, 290-91.
7. J.M. Matthers, "Excavations by the Palestine Exploration Fund at Tell el-Hesi, 1890-1892," in Tell el-Hesi: The Site and the Expedition ed. K.G. O'Connell, S.J. and B.T. Dahlberg. Excavation Reports of the ASOR: Tell el-Hesi 4; Winston Salem: Wake Forest University, in press.
8. Petrie, op. cit., p. 40.
9. F.J. Bliss, A Mound of Many Cities; London: PEF, 1894, p. 8.
10. Ibid., pp. 31-2.
11. Ibid., pp. 27-34.
12. Ibid., pp. 46-51, Fig. 94.
13. Petrie, op. cit., p. 16.
14. Bliss, op. cit., pp. 64-5.
15. Ibid., pp. 71-4.
16. Ibid., pp. 90-96.
17. Ibid., pp. 138-9.
18. The Joint Expedition has carried out eight seasons of field work in 1970, '71, '73, '75, '77, '79, '81, and '83. The Expedition affiliates with the American Schools of Oriental Research (ASOR) and is supported by a consortium of institutions of higher education and other participating institutions. The following have supported the Expedition in one or more seasons: Hartford Seminary, Oberlin, Seabury-Western, Holy Cross, Smith, Trinity Lutheran Seminary, Wilfrid Laurier, Virginia Theological, Wake Forest University, Oklahoma State, Wartburg Theological, Central State University. John Carroll University, Phillips University, University of

Oklahoma, Golden Gate Baptist Theological, Consortium for Higher Education-Religious Studies (CHERS), General Theological, Ashland Theological, Research Team for Religion and Culture in the Aegean in New Testament Times (Harvard Divinity) Christian Theological. Major grants have been received from: Canada Council, NEH, Smithsonian. Other participating institutions: Weston School of Theology, Harvard Semitic Museum, EARTHWATCH and the Center for Field Research.

19. D.G Rose, "The Methodology of the New Archeology and Its Influence on the Joint Expedition to Tell el-Hesi," in O'Connell and Dahlberg, op. cit.

20. For summaries of the work, see the preliminary reports: Toombs, "Tell el-Hesi, 1970-71," PEQ 106 (1974), 19-31; Rose and Toombs, "Tell el-Hesi, 1973 and 1975," PEQ 108 (1976), 41-54; O'Connell, Rose and Toombs, "Tell el-Hesi, 1977," PEQ 110 (1978), 75-90; O'Connell and Rose, "Tell el-Hesi, 1979," PEQ 112 (1980), 73-91; Toombs, "Tell el-Hesi, 1981," PEQ 115 (1983), 25-46.

21. L.E. Toombs, Tell el-Hesi: Modern Military Trenching and Muslim Cemetery in Field I (Strata I-II) ed. K.G. O'Connell, S.J. Excavation Reports of the ASOR: Tell el-Hesi 2; Waterloo, Ontario: Wilfrid Laurier University Press, in press.

22. O'Connell, Rose and Toombs, op. cit., pp. 79-82.

23. Cf. Figs. 1 and 2.

24. The "glacis" was meant solely to serve as a support within the construction and was not above the surface level. It certainly did not serve a defensive function as is usually suggested by the use of the term glacis.

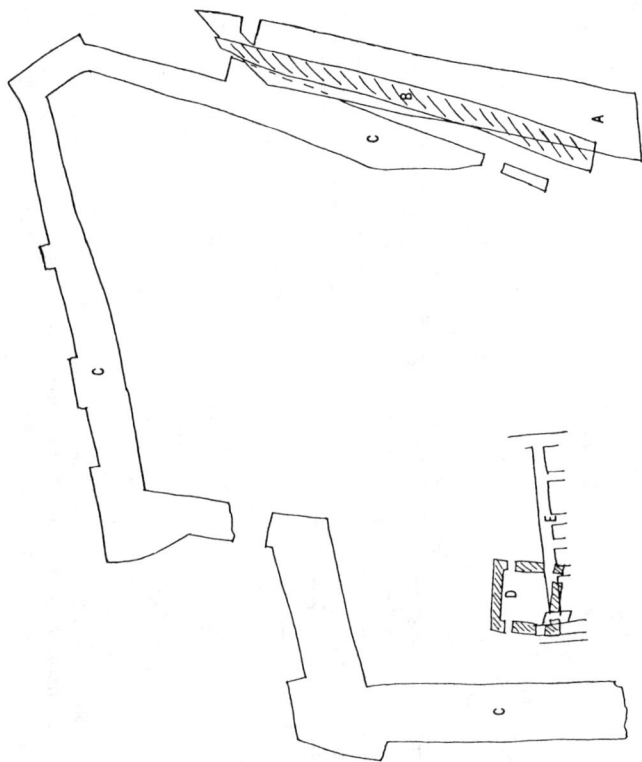

1:600

Fig. 1.   Composite plan of walls discovered by Petrie: A. Amorite wall;   B. Rehoboam wall;   C. Manasseh wall;   D. Pilaster Building;   E. Long Range of Chambers.   After Petrie, Tell el Hesy,
Pl. II.

89

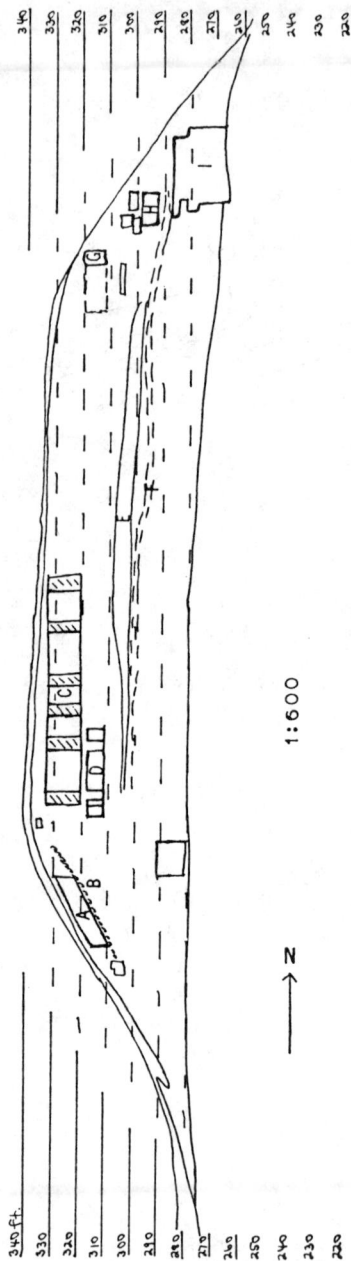

Fig. 2. Petrie's schematic section of the east face of Hesi. A. Manasseh wall; B, Glacis; C. Long Range of Chambers; D. Pilaster Building; E. Thick Ash; F. Pebble Layer; G. Manasseh wall; H. Rehoboam wall; I. Amorite wall. After Petrie, Tell el Hesy, Pl. III.

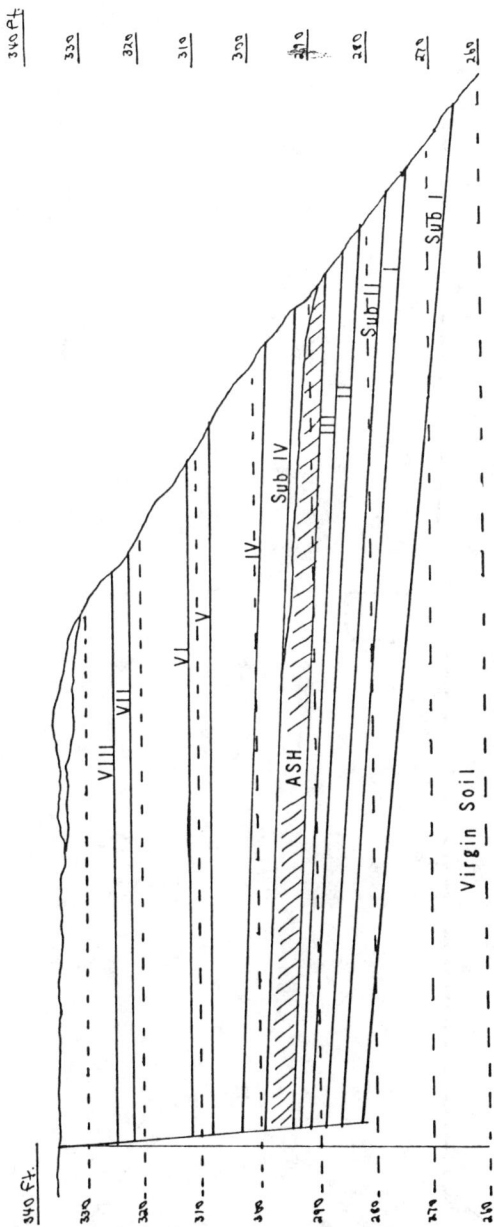

Fig. 3. Schematic section showing the eight Cities identified by Bliss. After Bliss, A Mound of Many Cities, Pl. II.

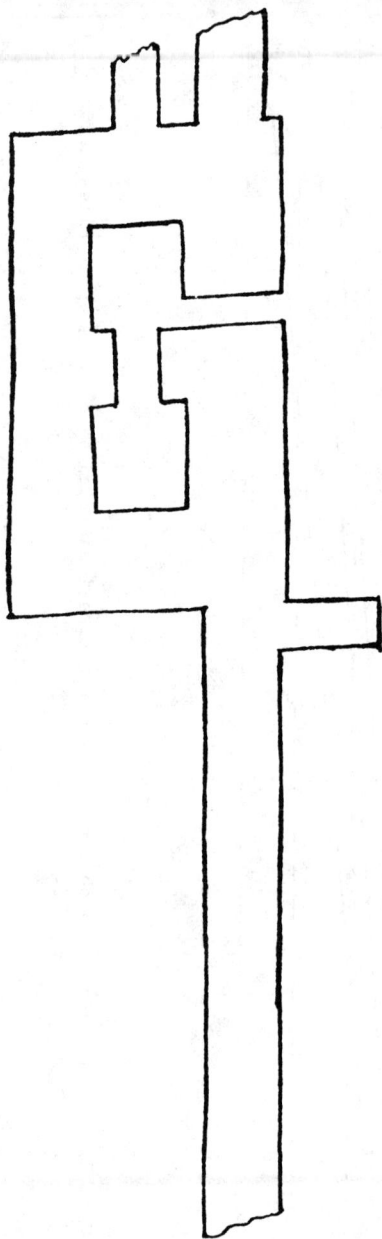

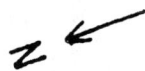

Fig. 4. Amorite tower found by Bliss, to be identified with Petrie's Amorite wall. After Bliss, A Mound of Many Cities, p. 26.

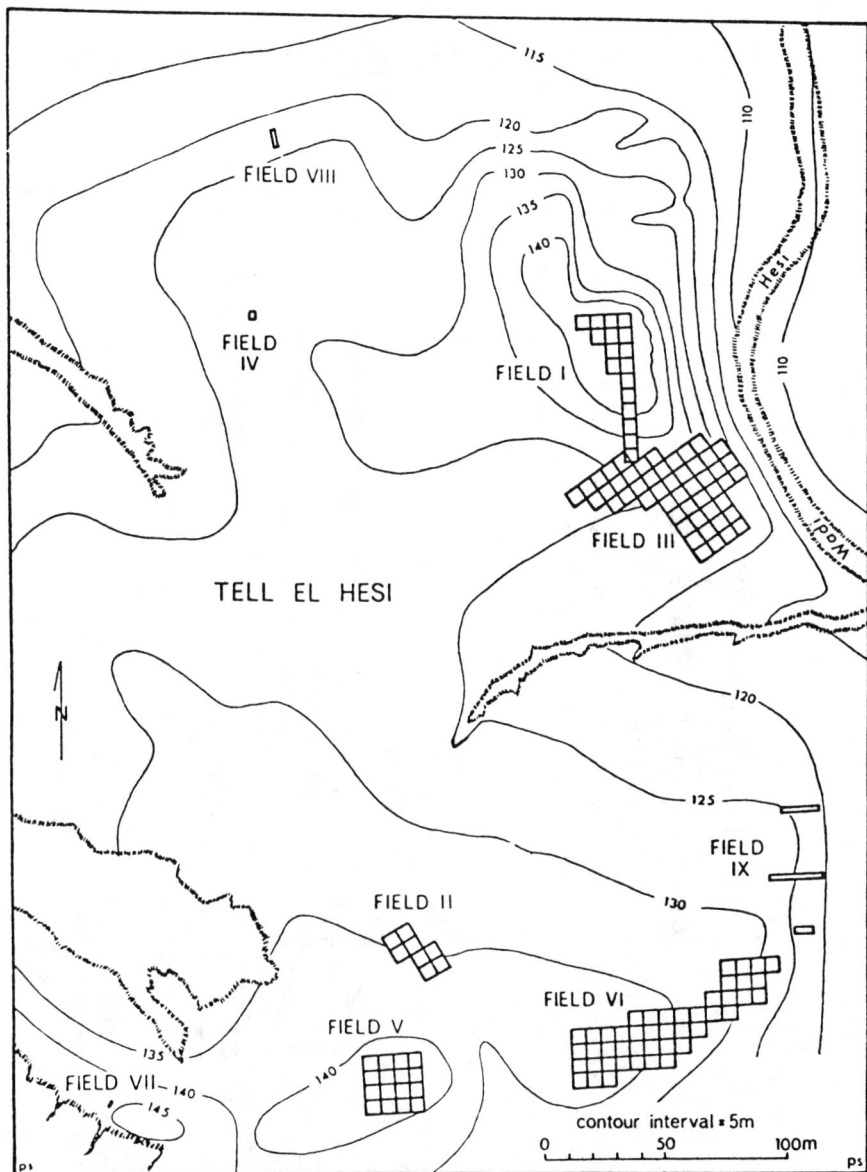

Fig. 5. General plan of Tell el-Hesi showing the location of the
Joint Expedition's excavation areas. Drawing by P. Schaus.

93

TELL EL-HESI 1981

STRATUM VIId – SCHEMATIC SECTION

Field I 1-91 and III 107

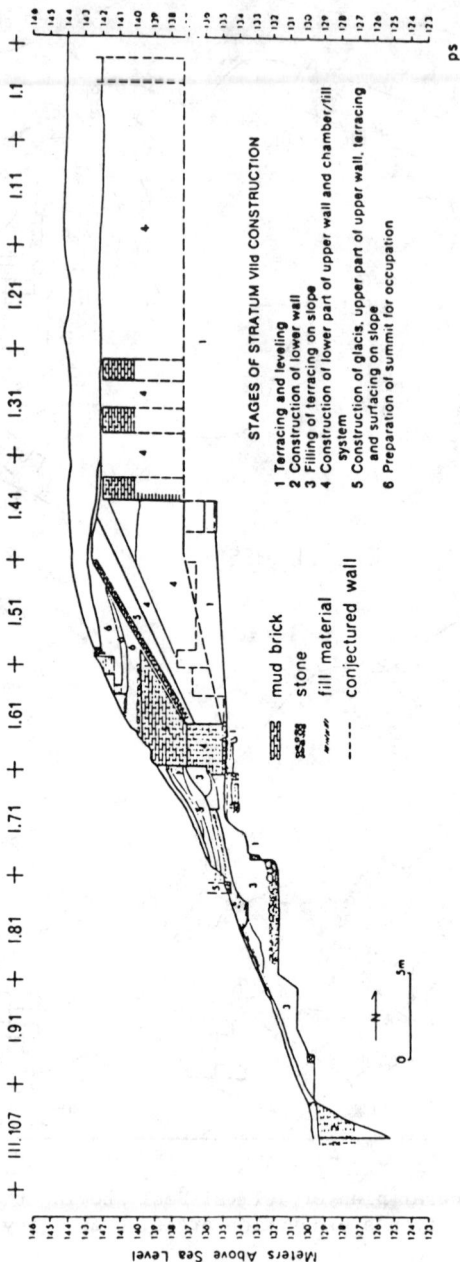

STAGES OF STRATUM VIId CONSTRUCTION

1 Terracing and leveling
2 Construction of lower wall
3 Filling of terracing on slope
4 Construction of lower part of upper wall and chamber/fill system
5 Construction of glacis, upper part of upper wall, terracing and surfacing on slope
6 Preparation of summit for occupation

mud brick
stone
fill material
--- conjectured wall

N

0   5m

Meters Above Sea Level

III.107 + I.91 + I.81 + I.71 + I.61 + I.51 + I.41 + I.31 + I.21 + I.11 + I.1

Fig. 6. Schematic section of the Stratum VIId construction. Drawing by P. Schaus after an original by L. Toombs.

94

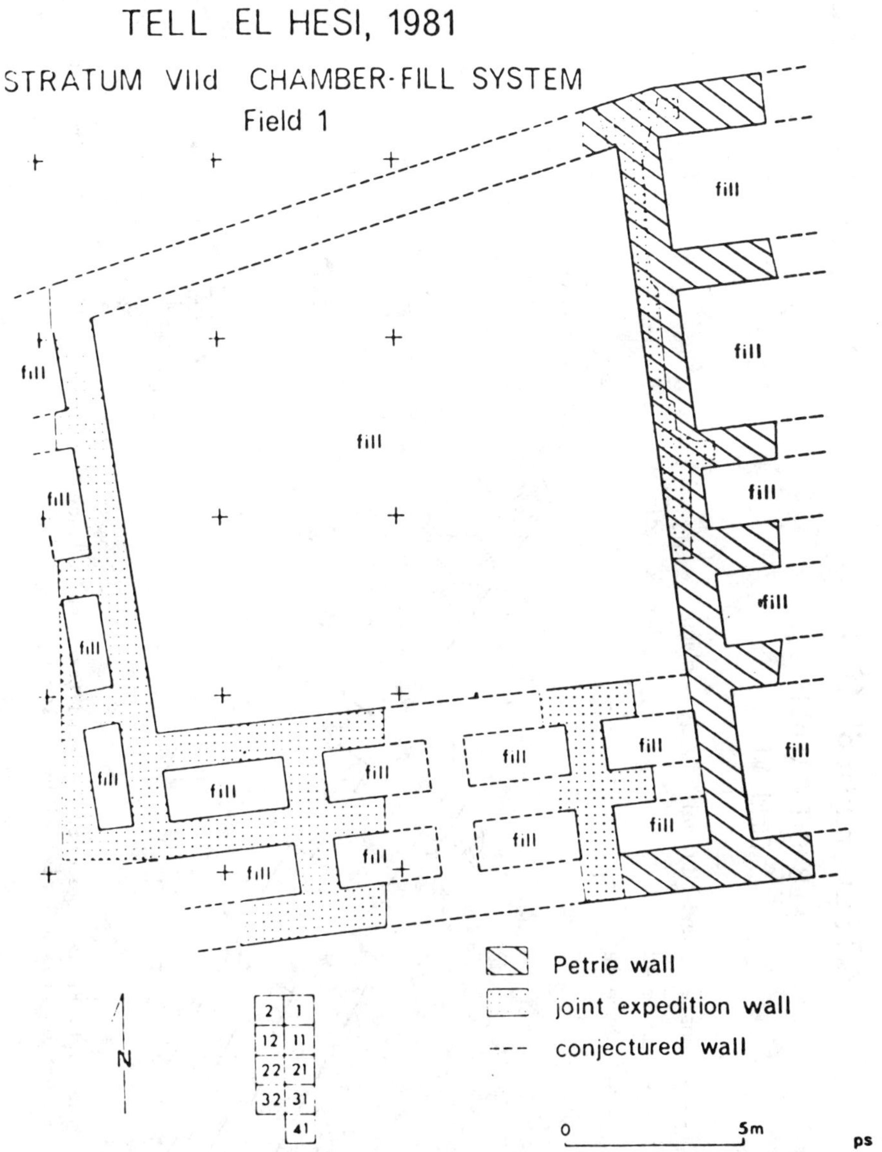

Fig. 7. Plan of the chamber and fill system on the Acropolis.
Drawing by P. Schaus after an original by J. Blakely.

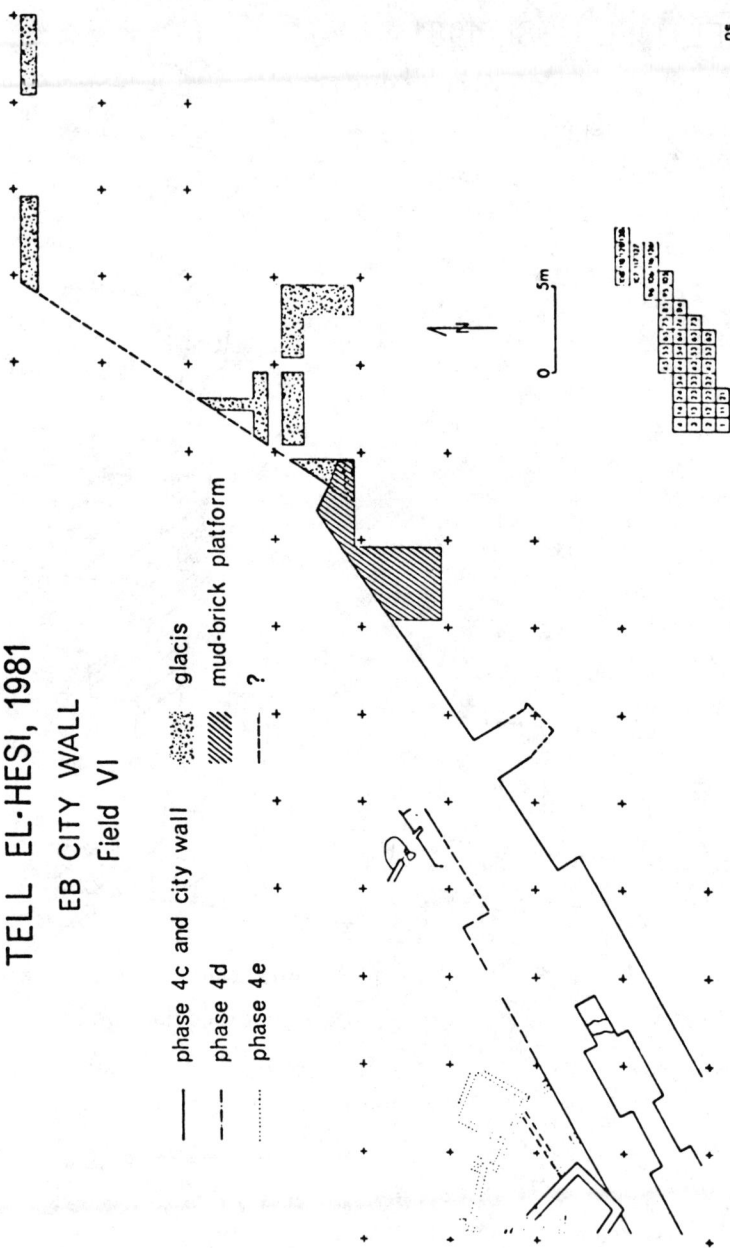

TELL EL·HESI, 1981

EB CITY WALL
Field VI

— phase 4c and city wall
-·- phase 4d
···· phase 4e

glacis
mud-brick platform
? ---

Fig. 8. The Early Bronze Age city wall and tower and adjacent structures in Field VI. Drawing by P. Schaus from an original by L. Toombs.

96

THE ARCHAEOLOGICAL FIELD GRID:
A DISCUSSION OF ITS ATTRIBUTES AND USE

Lawrence T. Geraty and Colin L. House

This contribution to field technique honors
Lawrence E. Toombs, known to so many in Palestinian
archaeology as "Mr. Field Technique" himself. We
hope it carries to a logical conclusion principles
adumbrated in his "Principles of Field Technique",
Appendix 1 in G. E. Wright's Shechem: The Biography
of a Biblical City (New York: McGraw-Hill, 1965) and
his Tell el-Hesi Field Manual (Cambridge, Mass.: ASOR,
1980), successor to his earlier Pella manual.

Among the many changes that archaeology has undergone since the early days of artifact gathering[1] is the
steady search for an adequate, accurate, yet comprehensive field grid system. Analysis of a broad cross-
section of excavation reports[2] reveals an apparent
direct relationship between the rise of the stratigraphic method of excavation and increasing awareness
of the necessity for accurate recording of an artifact's
context so that reliable recovery and reconstruction
data may be obtained. As a result, the archaeologist's
aims and excavation strategy can often be deduced from
the overt features of the field grid.[3]

Excavation Methodology and the Grid

Historically, the field grid system initially displayed essentially navigational concerns for archaeological constraints related primarily to the search
for architectural features. It was pointless to excavate within the confines of a five meter square if the
sole aim was to clear away the overlying "debris" from
the extant remains of some ancient temple/palace complex. Artifacts encountered were "interesting"; of
paramount importance were the spectacular, impressive,
valuable, crowd-gathering museum attractions. The grid
systems served as map co-ordinates.[4] Careful following
of the directions rewarded the "traveler" (armchair or
otherwise) with the position or sight of a usually magnificent piece of ancient architecture.

The modus operandi of earlier searchers for

architectural features often included   the long narrow excavation trench, both with and without an overlying grid.[5] Among the matters that concern us now,
but obviously hardly concerned the "explorers,"[6] are
the lack of findspot assemblages, accurate stratigraphic analysis, adequate context, and horizontal
exposure--all problems native to this method.[7] However,
short of that "abomination of desolation"--the bull-
dozer, it is acknowledged that the long narrow trench
probably offers the quickest results in the hunt for
hidden architecture.

An alternative to the narrow trench was the excavation of total portions of the tell, usually reserved
today for small excavation areas such as a burial or
group of tombs[8] where the alternating quadrant system
is often used. But that notwithstanding, for all
practical or statistical purposes, financial or ethical
constraints, as a serious excavation technique for
large tells, such a method should be laid to rest. The
gaping hole left by Petrie's efforts in the NE quadrant
of Tell el-Hesi[9] illustrates the difficulty of cross-
checking what is no longer there. Everything related
to that area depends entirely on the records left to
us; whether or not the records are accurate is hardly
the point. The relevant fact is that those records are
all that we have. Controls are no longer possible and
if cross-checks of findspots, a la Shuruppak, need to
be made, the confirmation or discrediting of the interpretation of the recorded data is impossible.

As meticulous recovery and precise reconstruction
of the artifact's context became more accurately con-
trollable by stratigraphic excavation, there arose the
necessity of an equally accurate regulatory field
device to which all loci could ultimately be referred.
We believe that our proposed field grid system is but
another evolutionary step in the search for archaeological utopia.

The Proposed Grid

Twenty-five Near Eastern[10] excavations were ana-
lyzed according to the criteria below. The inadequacy
of any particular grid system (regardless of whether it
contained or divided the tell), was usually directly
associated with the lack of balance between the attributes of navigation and regulation. Accurate, initial

recovery and viable, subsequent reconstruction were thus virtually impossible for many scientific disciplines.[11]

It is apparent that our proposed field grid is basically a montage of the positive features of the following fundamental attributes (which have been culled from the analysis of the proposed grid's historical antecedents), adapting and focusing them upon the needs of the modern archaeologist. We believe that the "ideal" field grid should be able to answer these questions in the affirmative.

Is the Field Grid Nomenclature:

    1. **Unique?**

        Y[es]   Non-repeatable numbers

        N[o]   Confusable numbering

    The numbers and letters should not repeat; the nomenclature for each "square" must be unique,[12] otherwise independent status cannot be assumed for each of the "squares" in the "field sectors."

    2. **Sequential?**

        Y   Mathematical/Spatial sequence

        N   Random/Chronological choice

    It will be sequential if it follows strict but simple mathematical and spatial laws.[13]

    3. **Logical?**

        Y   Position deduceable from nomenclature

        N   No spatial deduction easily made

    The reader should be able logically to deduce the relative position of each "square" from the combinations of the numbers and letters themselves.[14]

    4. **Simple?**

        Y   Easily recordable/reconstructable

        N   Pattern complex—potentially confusing

    Simplicity will be evident in the shortest possible number of digits and letters without the sacrificing of either accuracy or independence.[15]

Is the Field Grid:

    5. **Extensive?**

        Y   Covers tell and immediate surrounds

        N   Partial cover

    6. **Extendable?**

        Y   Easily include survey without negating 4.

                        N   Extensive modifications required
          As well as coverage of the whole tell, the field
grid system must be capable of considerable extension to
accomodate the needs of the field survey crew.[16] Their
finds should be related to the tell in a manner that
retains overall proportion and perspective.

Does the Field Grid Aid:

    7. **Stratigraphic**
       Control?   Y   Squares small/horizontal, large/
                                 vertical
                           N   Too large for precise horizontal
                                 control
          In retaining the above characteristics, sitewide
horizontal stratigraphic control[17] will be evident
through the choice of appropriate "square" sizes. We
recommend a "square" of five meter sides with one meter
balks.

Is the Field Grid's:

    8. **Orientation**
       Uniform?   Y   Alignment of all fields uniform
                           N   Not uniform or worse, haphazard
          Tight vertical stratigraphic control by means of
large cross-sectional reconstructions and balk analysis,
will be greatly assisted by the uniform orientation of
the "fields" of excavation.[18]

Does the Field Grid:

    9. **Create Large**
       Sectors?   Y   Field grid sectors can include archi-
                                 tecture
                           N   Not large enough
          Adequate combinations of "squares" will ensure
that the "field grid sectors" will be large enough to
contain the search for and the eventual exposure of
architectural features.[19] We recommend "field grid
sectors" of one hundred "squares."

    10. **Regulate the**
        Excavation?   Y   Excavation follows field grid lines
                           N   Excavated areas not regulated
          The "squares" laid out by the surveyor must
regulate the excavation.[20] It seems pointless to have a
grid at all if it is ignored during the excavation.

Does the Field Grid Assist:

    11. **Navigation?**
                           Y   Definite aid
                           N   Cumbersome
                          100

12. **Reconstruction?**

　　　　　　Y　　Cross-sections easily reconstructable
　　　　　　N　　Difficulty exists; possibly
　　　　　　　　　criteria 8
　　　　If the nomenclature of the "square" is unique,
sequential, and logically simple, it will be of positive
assistance in intrasite navigation as well as eventual
reconstruction.[21]

Is the Field Grid's:

13. **Direction of**
Notation　　　Y　　Uniform direction across tell
Uniform?　　　N　　Non-uniform

　　　　　　Although placing the field grid's datum and base
on the tell leaves our logical sequence of nomenclature
fundamentally unchanged (the datum is always collapsed
into the base),[22] dissection of the tell should be
avoided because it alters the uniform direction of
notation.[23]

Is the Field Grid's Architectural:

14. **Nomenclature**
Discrete?　　　Y　　No indisriminate use of similar terms
　　　　　　　　N　　Easily capable of confusion
　　　　Rather than using similar terminology
indiscriminately, archtitectural features should be
described with grid nomenclature, again aiding both
navigation and reconstruction.[24]

Does the Nomenclature of the Field Grid:

15. **Aid Computer**
Entry of　　　Y　　Nomenclature keys easily
Data?　　　　N　　Difficulty exists
　　　　　　Archaeology has now broadened from mere
chronological inquiry and typological classification to
include inferential, distributive, and quantitative
analysis for the attempted reconstruction of cultural
life-ways.[25] Computer entry of the nomenclature must be
readily possible[26] to aid the various programs that will
be utilized to identify correlations and/or search and
record enormous quantities of data both in the field and
at the archaeologist's base.

Does the Field Grid Assist:

16. **Statistical**
Tests?　　　　Y　　Adequate regulation enables viable
　　　　　　　　　　testing
　　　　　　　　N　　Statistical sampling not possible
　　　　In order that accurate statistical data can be

provided—to be used eventually in the creation and/or
support of inferential statements—acceptable gathering
criteria must be followed. The grid must regulate the
tell into manageable, testable units.[27]

Analysis on the basis of the criteria, (a N[o], -
[unable to determine], or Y[es] was "objectively" assigned), resulted in Table 1.

As demonstrated in Fig. 1, our proposed grid admir-
ably fulfills these demanding criteria. By arranging the
upper case alphabetic letters along the base and the arabic numerals along the datum, the progressive, systematic, mathematical, and symmetrical collapse of the datum
into the base provides the archaeologist with a unique,
sequential, logical, simple, and extensive grid system
that with but one use of the lower case alphabetic letters reaches to thirty seven and a half kilometers in
the base of the survey grid. (See footnote 14 for a full
description of methodology and Fig. 2 for illustration
of the survey grid).

Conclusion

It seems apparent that the major factors involved
in the development of our tightly controlled, extensive,
accurate and yet simple grid system have been paralleled not only by the rise of the stratigraphic method but
by the expansion in emphasis that has taken place in
archaeological inquiry. No longer are the questions related solely to where and how big were the temples, palaces, and theaters; no longer is inquiry obsessed with
chronology, museum treasure-hunts and the like; a broad-
ening of scope has occurred that has often been evidenced
by an expansion in the attitudes, goals and skills of
the archaeologists themselves. Rather than exist solely
in the sterile, dusty debates of academia, it seems
right and proper that modern inquiry should relate the
people of the artifact and/or inscriptional record, the
people who created the context we so eagerly, expensive-
ly, and carefully seek, to their functional, operational,
or intellectual counterparts today.[54]

It now seems fitting that the "whos," "whys," and
"hows" as well as the "whens" and "wheres" should receive scholarly attention; for in assuming that distributions of material remains are not simply the random
scatterings of some cosmic mole, we should be delighted
that these very remains, recovered in their original contexts, appear to reveal reactions and relationships not
altogether dissimilar to our own, thus giving our lives
a sense of continuity with our past and hopefully a de-

CRITERIA

EXCAVATION	1	2	3	4	5	6	7	8	9	10	11	12	13	14	15	16	N	-	Y
Shuruppak DOG[28]	N	N	N	N	N	N	N	N	N	N	N	N	N	N	N	N	16	0	0
Byblos[29]	N	N	N	N	N	N	Y	N	N	Y	N	N	N	N	N	N	13	0	3
Tell el-Hesi[30]	N	N	N	Y	N	N	Y	N	N	Y	N	N	N	N	N	N	13	0	3
Bab Edh Dhra[31]	N	N	N	Y	N	N	Y	N	N	N	Y	N	N	-	Y	N	11	1	4
Beth-Zur[32]	N	N	N	Y	Y	N	Y	N	N	N	N	N	N	-	Y	N	11	1	4
Dura-Europus[33]	Y	N	Y	N	N	N	N	Y	Y	N	N	N	Y	N	Y	N	10	0	6
Warka[34]	Y	Y	Y	Y	-	N	Y	N	N	Y	N	N	Y	N	N	N	8	1	7
Babylon[35]	Y	Y	Y	Y	N	N	Y	Y	N	N	N	N	Y	N	Y	N	8	0	8
Nimrud[36]	Y	Y	Y	Y	Y	N	N	N	N	Y	N	N	Y	N	Y	N	8	0	8
Tell Agrab[37]	Y	Y	Y	Y	Y	N	Y	N	N	N	N	N	Y	N	Y	N	8	0	8
Jericho[38]	Y	Y	Y	Y	-	N	N	Y	N	Y	N	N	Y	N	Y	N	7	1	8
Tell Mevorakh[39]	Y	Y	Y	Y	Y	N	Y	N	N	N	N	N	Y	N	Y	Y	7	0	9
Heshbon '71[40]	Y	Y	Y	Y	N	N	N	Y	Y	Y	N	N	Y	N	Y	N	7	0	9
Heshbon '76[41]	Y	Y	Y	Y	N	N	Y	Y	N	Y	N	N	Y	N	Y	N	7	0	9
Aphek-Antipatris[42]	Y	Y	Y	Y	Y	N	Y	Y	N	Y	N	N	Y	N	Y	N	6	0	10
Atchana[43]	Y	Y	N	Y	N	N	Y	Y	Y	Y	Y	Y	N	-	Y	N	5	1	10
Carthage[44]	Y	Y	Y	Y	Y	Y	Y	N	N	Y	N	N	Y	N	Y	N	6	0	10
Selenkahiye[45]	Y	Y	Y	Y	Y	-	Y	Y	Y	Y	N	N	N	N	Y	N	5	1	10
Tell Beit Mirsim[46]	Y	Y	Y	N	N	N	Y	N	Y	Y	Y	Y	Y	N	Y	Y	5	0	11
Tell Mardikh[47]	Y	Y	Y	Y	Y	N	Y	Y	Y	Y	Y	N	N	-	Y	N	4	1	11
Khirbet Shema[48]	Y	Y	Y	Y	Y	Y	Y	Y	N	Y	Y	N	Y	-	N	N	4	1	11
Cartesian Co-ord[49]	Y	Y	Y	Y	N	N	Y	Y	Y	Y	Y	Y	Y	N	Y	N	4	0	12
Hazor[50]	Y	Y	Y	Y	Y	N	Y	Y	Y	Y	N	N	Y	N	Y	Y	4	0	12
Tell Mureybet[51]	Y	Y	Y	Y	Y	Y	Y	Y	Y	Y	Y	N	N	-	Y	N	3	1	12
Tell el Abd[52]	Y	Y	Y	Y	Y	Y	Y	Y	Y	Y	Y	Y	Y	-	N	N	2	1	13
Shuruppak UP[53]	Y	Y	Y	Y	Y	Y	Y	Y	Y	Y	Y	Y	Y	Y	Y	Y	0	0	16
Proposed Grid	Y	Y	Y	Y	Y	Y	Y	Y	Y	Y	Y	Y	Y	Y	Y	Y	0	0	16

TABLE 1

sire for unity here and continuity hereafter.

Precisely these reasons demand the usage of a grid system similar to that which we have proposed. We think Larry Toombs would agree that to wish for or be happy with anything less is to possess a distinct aptitude for the digging of mere potatoes.

FOOTNOTES

1. Knudson 1978:477; Joukowsky 1980:2; Binford 1972:135-161, have been excellent discussions regarding the necessity, history, and process of change. Cf. Wheeler 1954:82-83 for an early list of criteria for what he calls an "area excavation."
2. No claims are made as to the "exhaustiveness" or "representativeness" of the discussion. Indeed, reports were random selections from the sources available in the Andrews University library, accepted if they contained a diagram of the grid system used at the dig, or rejected because they did not.
3. Despite note 2, it is interesting to observe that analysis of the available excavation reports according to the criteria developed below, appeared to pattern the excavations into a broad expression of time. Generally, the earlier digs are at the top of our analysis and the more recent excavations towards the bottom. It appears that the later the grid system used, the more likely it is that it will express aptitude for the accomodation of our criteria.
4. The majority of the early "expeditions" could hardly be described otherwise for it seems that geographical, regional, or even travel information was considered more important than the recording of precise findspot data. Cf. Waterfield 1963, an exceptional, colorful volume where the majority of the time Layard spent in the Near East is clearly presented as travelling and exploring.
5. The Shuruppak Deutsche Orient-Gesellschaft (DOG) expedition (Martin 1975:pl. 37, fig. 1) apparently did not employ one while the excavators of Agrab (Delougaz and Lloyd 1942:map) clearly did.
6. People who carved their names on priceless ancient artifacts (Knudson 1978:456) or crawled about under cover of darkness (Knudson 1978:457; Kubie 1964) could hardly be called archaeolgists.
7. These very shortcomings forced the University of Pennsylvania (UP) to return to Fara-Shuruppak to clarify many points not adequately represented by the earlier DOG expedition which employed the long narrow trench (Martin 1975:pl. 37, fig. 1). While DOG had recorded the findspots of the tablets in relation to the trench, because their goals were architecturally oriented, very little material was recorded illustrating assemblages. Subsequently when tablet findspots and assemblages became important, UP was able to duplicate comparable findspots to DOG by using strict, gridded excavation techniques. This enabled them to solve many enigmas that had annoyed scholars for "no one had hitherto known whether the tablets were the records of one huge palace or temple, or whether they had come from

many small and scattered offices." The reconstruction of the comparable findspots "supports the theory that the economy of an Early Dynastic city state depended on many separate household units." It now appears that "none of the Suruppak archives can be proven to come from a palace or temple." Therefore, "for our knowledge of the economics of Shuruppak, it is tragic that the only temple found, was the only building of any size not to have yielded tablets." Given the fact that temple tablets appear to have been the rule and not the exception, allied with its limited fulfillment of modern archaeological criteria, it would appear - at least from this example - that the long narrow archtectural-feature-hunting trench should be buried. (Quotes from Martin 1975:173-182).

8. Joukowsky 1980:145-6; Dever and Lance 1978:14.

9. Rose and Toombs 1978:111.

10. Angel Site, Indiana (Dancey 1981:68), is an excellent example of how the need for tight stratigraphic control, uniform orientation and regulation of the excavation, unique nomenclature, and expandable grids, has been recognized elsewhere. However, with this attempt, terminology has become somewhat clumsy ("square" numbers like K13B5R3, with locus and object numbers still to come), and the opposing field orientations cannot possibly aid in reconstruction.

11. It is impossible or worse, foolhardy, to make inferential, quantitative, or distributive claims about a site - and history is replete with the dismal records of those who have persisted - unless either complete excavation or a sound statistical sampling technique has been used. For example, "Having found no Mycenaean pottery, he [Garstang] legitimately came to the conclusion that the occupation of the enclosure [of Hazor] came to an end PRIOR to the appearance of the Mycenaean pottery in the area, that is, roughly before 1400 BC. One can readily imagine our excitement, therefore, when we uncovered an abundance of Mycenaean pottery on the floor of the two topmost strata!" (Yadin 1975:29). Yadin is being kind for Garstang had not the slightest right to make such sweeping dogmatic assertions on the basis of such scantily verified silence. Based on the amount he had dug, his confidence level would have had to be very low. Reconstructions and inferences drawn from collected data must have viable, empirically testable bases for collection as well as interpretation. To adequately infer anything about the complete site new, accurate, and acceptable methodology must be employed or endeavors in these regards could be considered null and void. It is one thing to be able to say that during a particular period or within the confines of a particular stratum, certain objects, artifacts or important features were discovered. It is entirely another to quantify the results in such a manner as to ensure that the inferential or distributive hypotheses drawn will be both accurate and supported.

12. It is not that each "square" employs unique terminology, for no such terminology exists, but rather that the simplest combinations created are unique. As presented in their illustration (Sellers et al. 1968:plan 1), the terminology used in the overall plan of the 1931 and 1957 excavations at Beth-Zur is somewhat less than unique for each "square." Confusion is distinctly possible in that the da-

tum's alphabetic letters are identical north and south of dividing
row "A," yet the base's arabic numerals are divided according to
their being odd or even.
13. Many excavations appear to have numbered the "square" according
to its chronological excavation. Heshbon (Boraas and Horn 1973:16)
and Tell el-Hesi (Rose and Toombs 1978:111) illustrate the total
lack of spatial sequence that results and the absolute futility of
trying to get the approximate position of a "square" from its name.
14. In our proposed grid, by collapsing the datum into the base, a-
malgamation of the digits produces spatially sequential, mathematically viable combinations. For example, the darkened "square's" unique number (cf. fig.1) can be ascertained by looking to the DATUM
(left) and locating 2, then moving to the BASE (right) and finding
B, the simple combination of which naturally coicides with the description of that "field grid sector" - 2B. Identical procedures within this "field grid sector" 2B provide us with the "square" number
of 67. Therefore, the completely unique description of that "square"
is 2B67. The same rules apply for deducing the relative position of
the "square" from the digits alone. The numeral/s left of the upper
case alphabetic letter (2-B67) will be found on the DATUM and the
letter (2-B-67) will always be found on the BASE. Moving to the two
numerals right of the letter/s, the numeral to the left (2B-6-7)
will again be found on the DATUM and the numeral to the extreme
right (2B6-7) will again always be found on the BASE. Therefore within each "survey grid sector" of 625 "field grid sectors," not only
does/do the letter/s always apply to the "field grid sector," they
also always divide the "field grid sector" (left) from the "square"
(right). It then follows that, without exception, all numerals left
of the letter/s apply to the "field grid sector," and all numerals
to the right of the letter/s apply to the "square."
15. Because most tells will be totally contained within the coverage
of "survey grid sector" 1a (fig. 2), in reference to the "square"
this could be assumed. While dealing with the "survey grid sector"
1a, a single letter will suffice and until double numerals/letters
are schematically demanded, combination produces but four digits.
Even the printer found the combinations used in the excavation at
Warka (Perkins 1957:122) a little combersome - he inadvertently repeated one of them. Even though we consider their 20m "squares" too
big to control the accuracy of the horizontal stratigraphic record,
further dissection would require the addition of at least one more
numeral or letter, rendering unthinkable the already unworkable.
(The terminology used at Warka was 1 upper case alphabetic letter
with 5 lower case sub-units and 1 roman with 5 arabic numerical sub-
units. To divide the 20m "squares" yet again would introduce combinations such as O.e.XVII.2.14; up to 10 digits.)
16. Intrinsic to the "ideal" field grid system is the ability to
substantially extend. Tel Masos (Avi-Yonah and Stern 1977:816) illustrates the usefulness of this where the remains of the Iron I city were found 200m away from the main tell in a single-component
site, and the remains of the Middle Bronze enclosure were discovered
about 800m away in the opposite direction. Many of the analysed grid

106

systems would be incapable of including these important periods of occupation history within their original framework.

17. The dual aspects of horizontal and vertical stratigraphy are an excellent mutual check, for over-exposure in one area will immediately lead to under-exposure in the other. Excavating a series of related "squares" while maintaining tight control of the horizontal strata, followed by the removal of the balks enabling large cross-sections of the vertical stratigraphy to be recorded, is excellent methodology. In such cases, however, theories are only as good as those who put them into practice.

18. The sequential mixtures displayed at Heshbon (Boraas and Horn 1973:16) and Tell el-Hesi (Rose and Toombs 1978:111), with apparent lack of order in the field placement, orientation, numerical se-- quence, and nomenclature, make the reader's and especially the re-constructor's job ever so difficult. Trying to get a continuous cross-section of the tell through certain squares of Areas B and D (Heshbon) and Fields I and III (Hesi), is futile due to differing orientations. Hazor (Yadin 1960:map section) shows that even when separate grids are used for each "field," if attention is given to their orientation and alignment within a master grid, they can be readily subsumed at any time.

19. Combining 100 six meter "squares" provides a "field grid sector" area of 3600sqm over/within which a field supervisor could work (cf Field 2C, fig. 1). If located in "field grid sector" 4H, a temple could easily be described for navigation purposes as Temple4H. If extremely large complexes are found, then several excavation fields could be combined and given another conceptual name with little re-semblance to the grid nomenclature. Because excavation "fields" are but conceptual arrangements of "squares," combining several and e-ventually even crossing into another "field grid sector" to expose a highly complex urban structure, palace/temple or administrative center, will be quite easily accomodated through the continued use of conceptual nomenclature. Excavation "fields" could be named after people, fruit, colors and so on. Then again, just as the square supervisor can oversee more than one square, so field supervisors can control several fields with overlapping archtecture.

20. The long narrow trench excavation technique used at Tell Agrab (Delougaz and Lloyd 1942:map section) together with the excavations at Jericho (Kenyon 1957:42) and Heshbon (Boraas and Horn 1973:16), all failed to derive any benefit from their published field grid a-part from its probable function as a navigational aid.

21. Regardless of whether the nomenclature is unique, sequential, logical or simple, because the excavation sites at Carthage (Stager 1978:fig. 22) lack uniform orientation and regulation as a direct result of the lack of a master grid, they (like Heshbon and Hesi; cf n. 18) are also unable to be combined to get a continuous strati-graphic record.

22. Cf. n. 14.

23. Although Tell Beit Mirsim (Albright 1943:pl. 1) tried to hold a tight control over stratigraphic reconstruction through the use of simple, accurate notation, in our opinion it is difficult to see

how this could be done on a "square" as large as 400sqm. However, squares of 100sqm would have introduced unacceptable confusion by necessitating doubling or repeating of nomenclature before entire coverage was achieved. Barely tolerable for TBM (the ability to extend in any direction is strictly limited), the 400m base is totally inadequate for large mounds such as Hazor and Tell Mardikh. Further, the separate directions of notation within each quadrant are potentially confusing to workers and supervisors who may be moved from one quadrant to another; it is imperative they remember that "up" may now mean "down" and vice versa. Anybody working with the published materials must also take careful note of these differing orientations.

24. Jericho (Kenyon 1957:42) and Mardikh (Matthiae 1980:43,126-7) both show a somewhat arbitrary method of naming excavation areas and revealed architecture. At Jericho, excavations HII, HIII, HIV, HV and HVI all lie in grid square H6; EI, EII, EIII and EIV are in E7; but F1 is in G4, M1 is in F5, and AI and AII are in E5. At Mardikh, the nomenclature of the grid is indiscriminately used to refer to the architectural features as is well illustrated by residential sector B being located in master grid area DIV (Matthiae 1980:126) and temple N is in FVII (Matthiae 1980:127). Clearly no one is able to logically deduce from the nomenclature where residential sector B or temple N should be expected to be found on the master grid.

25. Cf. Knudson 1978 where virtually the whole volume is an apologetic for the processualist archaeological approach.

26. Khirbet Shema (Meyers 1976:4) is a genuine attempt to create unique numbers, adequate coverage through reasonable size of "field grid sector," and strict horizontal stratigraphic control by manageable "square" size. However, having chosen the quadrant schema and the arabic numerals for nomenclature, they were forced to use an altogether different numbering system to separate the "field grid sector" numbers from those of the "square." Had they not done so, the potential for error would sooner or later have been realized; NE4.26 can become NE42.6 by the simple change of decimal. Creating 4NE26 by putting the arabic numeral first is invalid for the quadrant is of primary significance. (cf. n. 23 for discussion of notational direction.) This grid is limited to an east-west expansion of 180m. It is small, but very accurate in terms of regulation and reconstruction - adequate for the site itself but distinctly limited where ecological, topographical or environmental studies are envisaged. Because roman numerals were chosen to separate the "field grid sector" numbers fromthose of the "square," the popularity of the grid is likely to suffer due to the general lack of expertise in that numbering system. Warka (n.15) shows digits are easily confused.

27. Regulation of the tell into sufficient quantities of units of uniform size aids in the application of valid statistical sampling techniques, the results from the proper use of which are essential for creating or validating inferential statements.

28. Martin 1975:pl.37, fig. 1.

29. Dunand 1954:viii.
30. Rose and Toombs 1978:111.
31. Rast and Schaub 1978:fig. 1.
32. Sellers et al 1968:plan 1.
33. Rostovtzeff 1944:map section.
34. Perkins 1957:122.
35. Koldewey 1914:fig. 3.
36. Ibid, fig. 114.
37. Delougaz and Lloyd 1942:map section.
38. Kenyon 1957:42.
39. Stern 1978:fig. 22.
40. Boraas and Horn 1973:16.
41. Boraas and Geraty 1978:16.
42. Kochavi 1975:22-3.
43. Woolley 1955:map section.
44. Stager 1978:fig. 1.
45. van Loon 1979:fig. 1.
46. Albright 1943:pl. 1.
47. Matthiae 1980:43,126-7.
48. Meyers 1976:4.
49. Herr 1982:fig. 16.
50. Yadin 1960:map section.
51. Cauvin 1979:20.
52. Bounni 1979:54.
53. Martin 1975:pl. 37, fig. 2.
54. "[The archaeologist] handles the actual things which helped men
to pass their lives: the pots from which they ate and drank, the
weapons with which they hunted or killed one another, their houses,
their hearthstones and their graves. Such material keeps him much
closer [than the historian] to the essentials of history. He must
be concerned with the lives and achievements of countless ordinary,
anonymous people." Hawkes 1949:cited in Heizer 1959:preface.

BIBLIOGRAPHY

W.F. Albright, The Excavation of Tell Beit Mirsim; New Haven:
AASOR 21 & 22 (1943).
M. Avi-Yonah & E. Stern, Encyclopedia of Archaeological Excavations
in the Holy Land; Englewood Cliffs: Prentice-Hall, 1977.
L.R. Binford, An Archaeological Perspective; NY: Seminar, 1972.
R.S. Boraas & L.T. Geraty, "Heshbon 1976: The Fifth Campaign at Tell
Hesban," Andrews University Seminary Studies (AUSS) 16 (1978), 1-17.
Boraas & S.H. Horn, "Heshbon 1971: The Second Campaign at Tell Hes-
ban," AUSS 11 (1973), 1-16.
A. Bounni, "Preliminary Report on the Archaeological Excavation at
Tell al-Abd and Anab al-Safinah (Euphrates) 1971-2," AASOR 44
(1979), 49-61.
J. Cauvin, "Les Fouilles de Mureybet (1971-4)," AASOR 44:19-48.
W.S. Dancey, Archaeological Field Methods: An Introduction; Minnea-
polis: Burgess, 1981.
P. Delougaz & S. Lloyd, Pre-Sargonid Temples in the Diyala Region;

Chicago: University of Chicago, 1942.

W.G. Dever & H.D. Lance, A Manual of Field Excavation; Cincinnati: Hebrew Union College, 1978.

M. Dunand, Fouilles de Byblos 1933-8; Paris: Libraire d'Amerique et d'Orient Adrien Maissoneuve Vol. 2, 1954.

C. & J. Hawkes, Prehistoric Britain; Baltimore: Penguin, 1949.

R.F. Heizer, The Archaeologist at Work; NY: Harper, 1959.

L. Herr, Proposed Jalul Field Manual, 1982.

M. Joukowsky, A Complete Manual of Field Archaeology; Englewood Cliffs: Prentice-Hall, 1980.

K.M. Kenyon, Digging Up Jericho; NY: Praeger, 1957.

S.J. Knudson, Culture in Retrospect; Chicago: Rand McNally, 1978.

M. Kochavi, Aphek-Antipatris, 1972-3; Tel-Aviv: TAU Institute of Archaeology, 1976.

R. Koldway, The Excavations at Babylon; London: Macmillan, 1914.

N.B. Kubie, Road to Nineveh: The Adventure and Excavations of Sir Austin Henry Layard; NY: Doubleday, 1964.

H. Martin, Le Temple et le Culte: The Tablets of Shuruppak; Leiden: Nederlands Historich-Archeologisch Institut te Istambul, 1975.

P. Matthiae, Ebla: An Empire Rediscovered; NY: Doubleday, 1980.

E.M. Meyers et al., Ancient Synagogue Excavations at Khirbet Shema, Upper Galilee, Israel, 1970-2; Durham, NC: AASOR 42 (1976).

A.L. Perkins, The Comparative Archaeology of Early Mesopotamia; Chicago: University of Chicago, 1957.

W.E. Rast & R.T. Schaub, "A Preliminary Report of the Excavations at Bab edh Dhra, 1975," AASOR 43 (1978), 1-32.

D.G. Rose & L.E. Toombs, "Four Seasons of Excavation at Tell el-Hesi: A Preliminary Report," AASOR 43 (1978), 109-149.

M.I Rostovtzeff, The Excavations at Dura-Europas; New Haven: Yale, 1944.

O.R. Sellers et al., The 1957 Excavations at Beth-zur; Cambridge: AASOR 38 (1968).

L.E. Stager, "Excavations at Carthage 1975, The Punic Project: First Interim Report," AASOR 43 (1978), 151-190.

E. Stern, Excavations at Tel Mevorakh, 1973-6; Jerusalem: Hebrew University Institute of Archaeology, 1978.

M. van Loon, "1974 and 1975 Preliminary Results of the Excavations at Selenkahiye near Meskene, Syria," AASOR 44 (1979), 97-112.

G. Waterfield, Layard of Nineveh; London: John Murray, 1963.

M. Wheeler, Archaeology from the Earth; Baltimore: Penguin, 1954.

C.L. Woolley, Alalakh; Oxford: Oxford University, 1955.

Y. Yadin, Hazor II; Jerusalem: Hebrew University, Magnes, 1960.
_____, Hazor; NY: Random House, 1975.

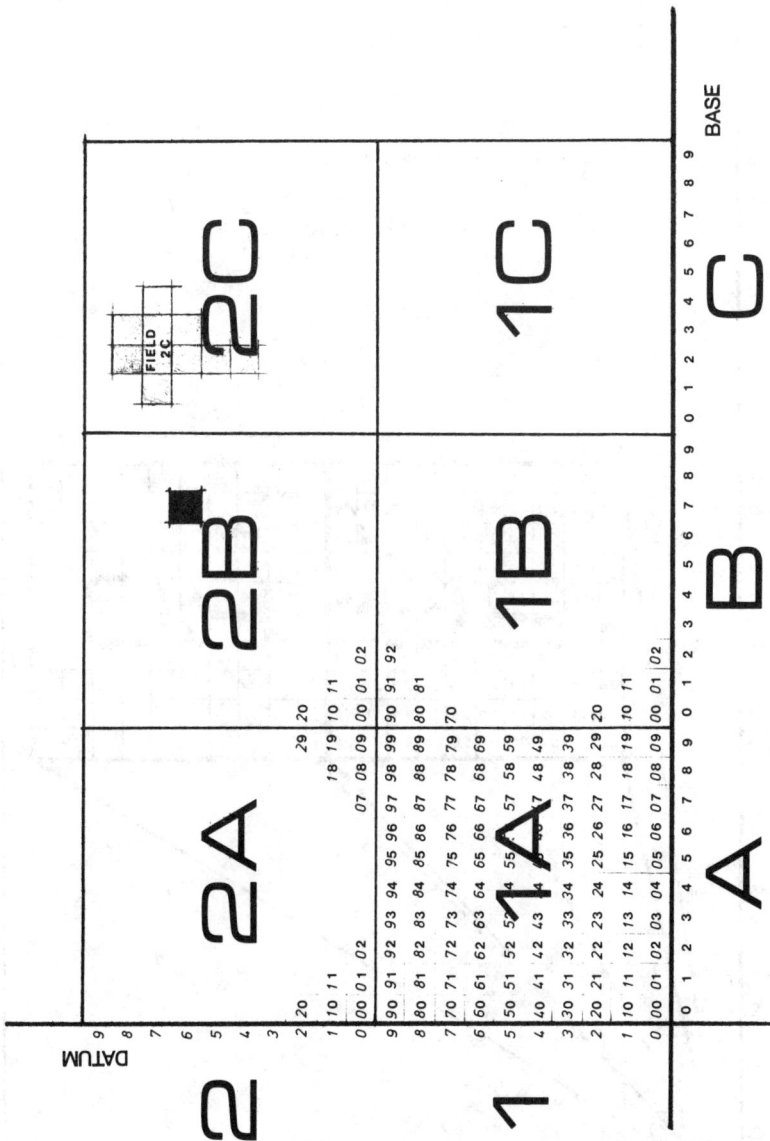

Fig. 1: " Field " grid sectors and " Squares."

111

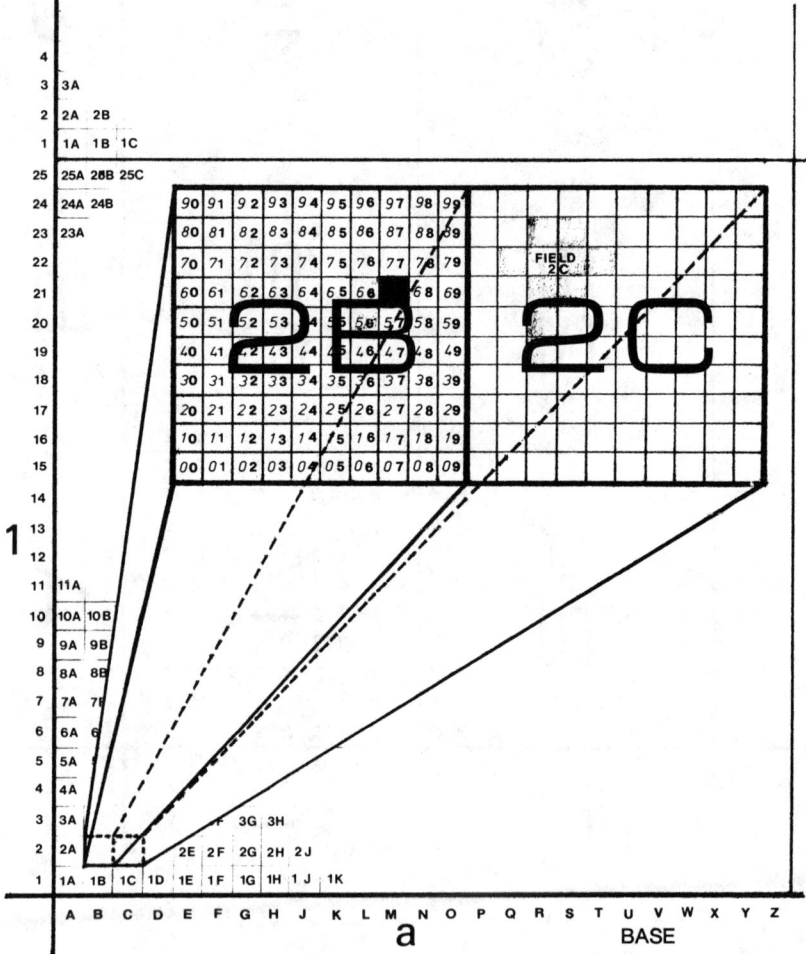

Fig. 2:

Illustration of the relationship between the

"Survey" and "Field" grid sectors.

Note "Field" 2C and "Square" 2B67.

THE WADI EL HASĀ ARCHAEOLOGICAL SURVEY

Burton MacDonald

Glueck's Edomite Fortress System

Shortly after the beginning of his explorations in
Eastern Palestine in the 1930's, Glueck began to form a
theory of a system of fortresses which bounded the territory of Edom in Southern Jordan. In his Explorations
in Eastern Palestine, II he spelled out quite clearly
the northern, southern, eastern, and western border
fortress posts of Edom (1935:105-106; 112, notes 320,
321, and 323). In his "The Boundaries of Edom" Glueck
envisioned the northern boundary of Edom as a line of
fortresses extending "from er-Ruweihah near the east
end of the border of Edom to Rujum and Kh. Kerakeh
near its west end, with Rujm Jâ'ez and Kh. Bâkher in
between" (1936:143). In the same article he treats of
the eastern boundary of Edom as a "line of fortresses
which runs a few kilometers west of the north-south
line on which Dā'jānîyeh is located. They include Kh.
Tawîl Ifjeij, Rujm Rās el-Ḥâlā, Rujm Ḥâlā el-Qarâneh,
and probably Kh. el-Jeḥeirah.[1] These fortresses are
all situated on the highest hills in the arid, unculti-
vated area between the Desert and the Sown...." (143-
144). As regards the southern boundary of Edom he
comments: "The southern boundary extends along the top
of the Neqb overlooking the Ḥismeh Valley, and is
guarded by Kh. Neqb esh-Shtâr and Kh. esh-Shedeiyid...."
(144). This is the same listing as in his 1935 writing.
For the western boundary he merely lists some Early Iron
Age I-II sites in the 'Arabah and he adds Mene'îyyeh
and Umm el-'Amad in the foothills to the east of Feinân
to the list of his 1935 writing (1936:144-145).

After further work in Southern Jordan he expanded
upon this list of border fortresses. In Explorations
in Eastern Palestine, III he lists the eastern frontier
of the Edomite Kingdom as being marked by a line of
fortresses which "commencing with er-Ruweihah, overlooking the Wadi el Ḥesā (the River Zered) at the n.e. corner of Edom, the eastern Edomite border is further
marked, going from north to south, by Rujm Jâ'ez, Rujum
Abū el-Aẓâm, Kh. Bâkher, Rujm Mughâmes, Rujm el-Ḥamrā,
Rujm Rās el-Ḥâlā, Rujm Ḥâlā el-Qarâneh, Rujm el-Baḥash,
Rujm el-Jeḥeirah, Kh. Tawîl Ifjeij, Kh. el Meqdes (?)
Kh. el-Far'ah (?), Kh. el-Moreighah, and Kh. esh-
Shedeiyid (?) and Kh. Neqb esh-Shtâr at the s.e. corner"

(1939:24). In this enumeration he adds the sites of er-
Ruweiḥah and Kh. Neqb esh-Shtâr as the n.e. and s.e.
fortresses for the eastern boundary respectively. These
sites were formerly listed as northern and southern
border fortresses respectively but their addition to the
eastern border list is no surprise. However, besides
adding er-Ruweiḥah as a site previously listed in the
northern boundary fortress list he adds two more sites,
namely Kh. Bâkher and Rujm Jâ'ez to the eastern fortress
line. These sites were formerly listed as belonging to
the northern boundary fortress system. Moreover, he
adds Kh. esh-Shedeiyid with a question mark to the eastern line of fortresses. This site was previously listed
along with the s.e. corner site of Kh. Neqb esh-Shtâr
as a southern border fortress. Thus he now has three
sites, namely Kh. Bâkher, Rujm Jâ'ez, and er-Ruweiḥah,
serving as both northern and eastern border fortresses
and two, namely Kh. Neqb esh-Shtâr and Kh. esh-
Shedeiyid (?), serving as both eastern and southern
border sites.[2]

Commenting further about the eastern boundary of
Edom in this 1939 publication he states: "If we com-
mence with Rujm el-Ḥamrā, from which Ḥâlā el-Qarâneh is
visible, we find that east and north of eth-Thuwâneh
there was an irregular line of border fortresses running
down to the Wadi el-Ḥesā. In this line are included
Rujm el-Ḥamrā, Rujm Mughâmes, Kh. el-Bâkher, Rujm Abū
el-Aẓâm, Rujm Jâ'ez, and er-Ruweiḥah. This line does
not include all the possible EI sites along this line,
because there are several along this line, and a few to
the east of it, which we were still unable to get to"
(53). In a footnote he states further that "some of
these sites, such as Kh. el-Bâkher, Rujm Abū el-Aẓâm,
and Rujm Jâ'ez may also properly be included in the
northern border posts of Edom" (53, note 166).

Thus if one looks carefully at Glueck's listing of
northern and eastern border fortresses of Edom in the
publications up to 1940 it is evident that he sees such
sites as Rujm Jâ'ez, Rujm Bakher, er-Ruweiḥah, and Rujm
Abū el-Aẓâm as forming part of both the northern and
eastern frontier of Early Iron I-II Edom.

In his concluding remarks to Explorations in
Eastern Palestine, II he dates the Edomite civilization
to which the border fortresses belong when he writes:
"There was a highly developed Edomite civilization,
which flourished especially between the thirteenth and

the eighth centuries B.C. From the eighth century on
there was a rapid disintegration of the power of Edom"
(1935:138). He maintained this dating in his "Conclusions" to Explorations in Eastern Palestine, III (1939:
269).

In his 1940 edition of The Other Side of the
Jordan he again treats of the border fortresses of Edom
and lists Kh. Neqb Shtâr and Kh. Shedeiyid as southern
boundary fortresses (130). He lists Kh. Ṭawîl Ifjeij,
Rujm Jeḥeirah, Rujm Ḥâlâ el-Qarâneh (131-133) as three
eastern border fortresses and about the other frontiers
he states that "the northern and western boundaries of
the kingdom of Edom were no less strongly protected
than the eastern and southern, although there were not
actually as many fortresses and police-posts" (134).
He dates these fortresses to the beginning of the 13th
century B.C. when a new agricultural civilization appeared in Edom (1940:125) or to between the 13th and
8th centuries B.C. (1940:128, 145-147). This system
according to Glueck was set up by the 13th century B.C.
since he relates it to the Exodus of the Israelites
through Transjordan (1940:146).

In an article published in The Biblical Archaeologist in 1947 Glueck reiterated what he had written
in the thirties and early forties about the border
defenses of Edom and their dating (1947:77-84) and
again in 1967 this position was repeated (1967:433-436).

In his revised edition of The Other Side of the
Jordan Glueck is less certain about the dating of these
fortresses as he states: "The archaeological survey of
Edom and Moab and of the other Iron Age Kingdoms of
Jordan revealed the presence of strong fortresses along
their frontiers. It remains to be demonstrated through
excavations how early in the Iron Age they came into
existence" (1970:161). In this work he dates the
Edomite, Moabite, Ammonite, and Gileadite pottery to
the twelfth-sixth centuries B.C. (1970:179). He goes
on, however, to state: "Of a particularly formidable
looking character are many of the Iron Age sites in
Ammon and South Gilead, whose history, like that of the
contemporary sites in Edom and Moab, extends from the
thirteenth to the sixth century B.C." (1970:181). He
reiterates the date for the beginning of this new agricultural civilization belonging to the Edomites,
Moabites, Ammonites, and Amorites as being "sometime
before the end of the Late Bronze Age, well before the

beginning of the thirteenth century B.C." (1970:157).

Thus the above survey shows the importance that Glueck held for a system of Edomite border fortresses. Moreover, it points out that he dates the sites making up this line of defense to the Early Iron Age and certainly not much later than the twelfth century B.C.

Responses to Glueck's Position

The above described position of Glueck of a developed Edomite state with a well established system of border fortresses at the beginning of the Iron Age I was widely accepted for many years.[3] However, especially because of Bennett's work at Umm el-Biyara (Bennett 1964, 1966a, 1966b, 1966c, 1967), Tawilan (Bennett 1967/68; 1969, 1970, 1971a), and Buseira (Bennett 1973, 1974, 1975, 1977; Puesh 1977) this early dating for the beginning of Edomite civilization was seriously questioned since these sites, according to the excavator, are no earlier than the ninth or eighth centuries B.C.

Bartlett, coming at the matter from another angle, also questioned the early dating of Edomite civilization put forth by Glueck. He states that "whatever the strength of the early settlers of Edom, it is most unlikely that there was any national unity in Edom before the mid-ninth century B.C...." (1972:26). He sees the population of Edom as being mainly semi-nomadic in the thirteenth century B.C., with some more permanent settlements beginning to come into existence (1973:232). He calls for the precise dating of the border fortresses in Edom by careful archaeological study (1973:231).

At about the same time that Bartlett was raising objections to the dating of the civilization and border defense system of Glueck, Franken and Power wrote a review of Glueck's Explorations in Eastern Palestine in which they stated: "It is now, however, becoming increasingly clear that the other part of Glueck's work, that is to say the pottery study, and the conclusions drawn from that study are in many ways both defective and misleading" (1971:199). Most recently Miller points out the disaffection with Glueck's ceramic chronology insofar as it relates to the work of the Central and Southern Moabite Archaeological Survey (1982:172).

The Wadi el Ḥasā Survey

The Wadi el Ḥasā Archaeological Survey (WHS) carried out three seasons of work along the south bank of the Wadi el Ḥasā in Southern Jordan between 1979 and 1982 (MacDonald, Banning, and Pavlish 1980; MacDonald, Rollefson, and Roller 1982; MacDonald, Rollefson, Banning, Byrd, and D'Annibale 1983). This survey covered only the northern portion of the territory of Edom and was, therefore, not nearly as extensive as Glueck's work in the southern part of Jordan. In the process of this survey many of the sites that Glueck surveyed in the 1930's were again visited, sherded, and photographed. These sites along with other sites in the area that Glueck had not visited turned up Iron Age pottery especially in the western segment of the survey area (MacDonald 1982:39, 41, Fig. 4, 42). There does appear to be permanent, albeit small, settlements along the south bank of the Wadi el Ḥasā by the 12th century B.C. (MacDonald, et al. 1982:126-127; MacDonald, et al. 1983). Among those sites surveyed by the WHS were five of Glueck's so-called Edomite fortresses, namely Rujm Karakā (MacDonald, et al. 1980:176; MacDonald 1982:41) Khirbat Karakā (MacDonald 1982:41), Rujm Jā'is (MacDonald, et al. 1982:126), Rujm Bākher and Er Ruweiḥi (MacDonald, et al. 1983).[4] In June 1983 the writer along with E. B. Banning visited one more of what we believed to be a Glueck Edomite fortress, named Rujm Umm el-'Aḍhām=Rujm Abū el-'Aẓām,[5] because of its proximity to the survey area and because of its believed importance for the interpretation of the sites surveyed along the south bank of the Wadi el Ḥasā (Fig. 1; Table 1). These six sites belong to Glueck's northern and/or eastern Edomite border system. Each of these sites will be studied individually. The ones along the Wadi el Ḥasā will be treated in a west to east order while Rujm Umm el-'Aḍhām, located to the south of the survey area, will be treated last.

Khirbat Karakā is situated on a hill overlooking the Wadi 'Afrā. It commands an excellent view to the west, the Wadi 'Afrā and its settlements, and the plateau to the northeast. Animal pens and caves at the site indicate that it is used at least seasonally by shepherds. There is at least one cistern on the site. The foundations of walls can be seen on the summit and slopes of the site. Iron IC-IIA (1000-721 B.C.) sherds were collected at the site (Table 1). Glueck states that "although no sherds were found, it seems likely

that Kh. Kerakeh may also have been an Edomite
site...." (1935:109).

Rujm Karakā is located one km to the southeast of
Kh. Karakā. It is probably a watchtower and what
strikes one about this relatively small site, built of
chert blocks, is its visibility from almost any point
on the plateau south of the Wadi el Ḥasā. It provides
an excellent vantage point from which to view the surrounding terrain and even the Dead Sea can be seen on
a clear day to the northwest. The site is now in a
ruined state but still stands ca. three meters high.
We were able to measure one level of the structure and
it measured ca. 8.50 m². It gives the impression of
having been built in a step-like fashion. It is now a
burial place and many human bones can be seen among
the stones that constitute its makeup. A large cistern,
cut into bedrock, and stone aqueducts which at one time
channelled rain runoff into it, is located immediately
north of the site. The identifiable pottery collected
at the site dates to several different periods one of
which is Iron IC-IIA and another of which is Iron II.
Glueck found some Edomite sherds at the site (1935:108)
(Table 1). From the WHS pottery collected at the sites
of Rujm and Khirbat Karakā it would seem that they are
contemporaneous.

Rujm Jā'is, situated on a terrace west of the Wadi
Jā'is, provides an excellent view of the Wadi as well
as the oasis of El-'Ainā to the north. It is situated
above a spring in the Wadi. There are many foundation
walls still visible and there appears to be a tower
measuring ca. 9.00 m² at the eastern extremity of the
site. The only sherds found at the site by the WHS
were dated to the Iron IIA-B period. Glueck found a
new Edomite EI I-II sherds at the site (1935:102)
(Table 1).

Further to the east, on the eastern edge of the
plateau between the Wadi el-'Ālī and the Wadi Aḥmar
(Fig. 1) is the large and prominent watchtower of Rujm
Bākher. The WHS had visited the site in 1982 and estimated its size as being ca. 24.00 m² and still standing
ca. 3.00 m high. The writer was unable to return to it
in 1983 because of its inaccessibility. Glueck gives
this description of the site: "It is a strongly built,
almost square structure..., oriented practically north
and south and measuring 25.5 by 24.8 metres. There
seem to have been rooms built against the sides of the
wall on the inside of the building. In the center of

118

the building are visible the foundations walls of a
superimposed tower (?), measuring 9.4 by 8.8 metres...
Around the Khirbeh are the foundation walls of a number
of small houses. The present walls of the Khirbeh seem
to have been reconstructed in the mediaeval Arabic
period with large stones taken from an earlier structure. The rows are irregular, with small stones between
them" (Glueck 1935:106-107). These small houses that
Glueck speaks about around the site give the impression
of having been recently used as animal pens and windbreaks. However, they could very well cover over more
ancient structures. The predominant identifiable pottery collected at the site was Ottoman. The WHS found
no identifiable pottery earlier than the Late Roman-
Byzantine period at the site. However, Glueck claims
to have found several EI I-II sherds (1935:107) (Table
1).

Approximately 12 km to the southeast along the
Wadi el Ḥasā from Rujm Bākher is the very large fortress
of Er Ruweiḥi. The site is irregular in shape and follows for the most part the contours of the terrain. It
consists of an upper citadel (?) and a lower segment.
There are sharp descents from the site to nearby wadis
especially on the eastern and northern sides. The site
is located at the junctures of the Wadi el Ḥasā to the
northeast, the Wadi Abū eḍ Dibā' to the west, and the
Wadi er Ruweiḥi to the north. The upper segment of the
site measures ca. 30.00 m wide and is separated by a
wall from the lower segment. A gateway measuring ca.
4.00 m was noted in this wall. The upper segment has
also a slightly smaller gate on its northern wall with
possible exterior towers. The lower segment measures
ca. 60.00 m (north-south) by ca. 82.00 m (east-west) at
its greatest extent. There is another gateway measuring
ca. 6.15 m in the south wall of the lower segment with
two flanking exterior towers measuring ca. 6.00 m
(north-south) by 5.30 m (east-west). A series of
rooms (?) and a passageway are located on the eastern
side of the site. A number of towers (?) are located
around the site, especially on the east side facing the
Wadi el Ḥasā. The wall thickness for the main enclosure
wall of the site is from 1.30-2.00 m at what is now the
top of the wall. The WHS found no sherds earlier than
the Nabataean period at the site (Table 1). However,
Glueck claims to have found a number of coarse sherds
which he identifies as Edomite Early Iron (1937:24).

Finally, Rujm Umm el-'Aḍhām, probably one of

119

Glueck's northern and eastern Edomite Fortress sites,
located to the south of the WHS survey territory, must
be considered. This site is located on one of the highest hills in the entire area and, therefore, can be
seen from most parts of the region. It was passed repeatedly by the WHS team in both the 1981 and 1982
seasons as we made our way from the Tafila-Jurf ed-
Darāwish road near 'Abūr to work along the south side
of the Wadi el Ḥasā between the Wadi Jā'is and the Wadi
Aḥmar (Fig. 1). The site, located on Jebel el-'Idhām,
overlooks the entire region to the north from Rujm
Karakā on the west to Er Ruweiḥi on the east. It,
therefore, commands an excellent view of the Roman
Road, Via Nova Traiana (MacDonald, et al. 1982:128-12),
along the plateau south of the Wadi el Ḥasā. To the
south and southeast it commands a view of the entire
territory with 'Abūr clearly visible. It is located
ca. one-half km east of the Via Nova between mile 55
and mile 54 from Petra. It is constructed of chert
blocks and now appears as a very large pile of stones.
Two government markers are clearly visible at the highest point of the site. It is impossible to determine
the original plan of the structure without the expendi-
ture of a great deal of work necessary to move the
large stones. The stone pile still stands at least
4.00 m high and has an estimated diameter of ca. 20 m
at ground level and ca. 5.00 m at the highest point.
Foundations of structures were noted on the east side
of the site. These may be ancient but they could have
served most recently as animal pens and/or windbreaks.
Only a few indicator sherds were collected at the site
and the identifiable ones were dated to the
Nabataean-Roman period. Glueck says that the pottery
at the site was Roman to Byzantine but, nevertheless,
he lists this site in both the northern and eastern
border fortress list of Edom (1939:51).

A comparison of the six, above-described sites
which Glueck lists as either northern and/or eastern
Edomite border fortresses and the pottery collected by
the WHS at the same sites leads to the following conclusions:

1. Glueck found Edomite pottery at four of these six
    sites while the WHS collected Iron Age pottery, no
    earlier than Iron IC (ca. 1000 B.C.), at only three
    of these six sites.
2. Glueck states that he did find Edomite Early Iron
    pottery at Er Ruweiḥi where the WHS found nothing

earlier than the Nabataean period.

3. Glueck calls Khirbat Karakā and Rujm Abū el-'Aẑâm (=WHS Rujm Umm el-'Adhām) Edomite border fortresses even though he does not claim to find pottery from this period at either site. WHS found Iron IC-IIA at the first of these two sites.

4. Three of these six sites, namely Rujm Karakā, Rujm Bākher, and Rujm Umm el-'Adhām are definitely watchtowers. Er Ruweiḥi is undoubtedly both a watchtower and a fort. Rujm Jā'is, because of its location in a barren area and because of its construction, appears to be a fortress. There is the possibility that Khirbat Karakā may be either a watchtower and/or a fortress.

A further comment is in order: Glueck extends Early Iron Age Edomite occupation along the south bank of the Wadi el Hasā as far east as Er Ruweihi. The WHS, however, found little evidence of Iron Age occupation east of the Wadi el-'Ālī (MacDonald, et al. 1983) (Fig. 1).

In concluding this section of the paper it is safe to say that only excavations will determine more precisely the nature of these six sites and the time period to which they belong.

Prospects for Further Work on the Edomite Border System along the South Side of the Wadi el Hasā:

From the above discussion I would conclude that sites such as Kh. Karakā, Rujm Karakā, and Rujm Jā'is are good possibilities for Iron II fortresses and/or watchtowers along the south bank of the Wadi el Ḥasā. My present position is that such sites as Rujm Bakher, Er Ruweiḥi, and Rujm Umm el-'Adhām are probably not to be associated with an Iron Age, fortress system but belong to a later period. However, there are other possibilities for an Iron Age II fortress system along the south bank of the Wadi which require further investigation along with the above, discussed sites. These sites, namely El Maqhaz, Rabāb, Kh. 'Ain Saubalā, Rujm Muhawish, Ed-Dair, and WHS Site 647, will also be discussed in a west to east direction.

El-Maqhaz, WHS Site 187, is located on a spur overlooking the southern end of the Dead Sea in the western extremity of the survey area (MacDonald, et al.

1980:177). It consists of a modern animal pen which is surrounded by a heavy stone scatter and what appears to be a stone platform just to the west of the pen. The site commands an excellent view of the plain along the southeastern end of the Dead Sea. The predominant pottery collected at the site was Iron II (Table 2).

Another site, not unlike El-Maqhaz, although larger, WHS Site 172, Rabāb, is located to the north of the previously discussed site and is also situated on a spur oriented roughly east-west. It too provides an excellent view of the area leading down to the southeast end of the Dead Sea. What are probably structural foundations are visible at the lowest levels as well as on the slopes of the site. The highest elevations of the site have what may be one or two earthen platforms. The ceramic material found at the site represents many periods, one of which is Iron II (Table 2).

Kh. 'Ain Saubalā, WHS Site 61, is another candidate for an Iron II fortress system. The site is predominantly Early Bronze I as far as ceramic material is concerned (MacDonald, et al. 1980:172). However, there is one segment of the site which appears to be an Iron II tower. It is located at the northeastern extremity of the site on the western side of the Wadi 'Afrā. This tower/platform measures ca. 31 x 14 m and the only pottery found in association with it is possibly Late Bronze but more likely Iron II (Table 2).

Rujm Muhawish, WHS Site 248, is probably a large fortress structure dating from the Iron II period. It is located on the highest hill in the area on the plateau west of the Wadi el Lā'ban.[6] It consists of a polygonal building with towers at the corners and long narrow structures, 4-5 m wide, running between the towers (MacDonald, et al. 1982:126-127). Here again the dominant ceramic material collected at the site is dated to the Iron II period. The site commands an excellent view in all directions and is clearly visible from such sites as Kh. and Rujm Karakā.

Ed-Dair, WHS Site 367, is a major site on the west side of the Wadi el Lā'ban just to the southwest of 'Ain el Lā'ban. It is located on a spur, with a tower to the north and a major building, constructed of well-laid roughly-hewn blocks, immediately to the south. This building is ca. 25 x 10 m and appears to be divided into three rooms. To the west there is what may be another similar building (MacDonald, et al. 1982:126). The predominant pottery at the site is within the Iron I-II horizon (Table 2).

Such a fortress system as outlined above and consisting of three of the sites in Table 1 and the six sites of Table 2 is merely a hypothetical Iron Age, most likely Iron Age II, fortress system. It does require verification by means of further investigation such as excavation. Such a system has the advantage, however, of protecting the south bank of the Wadi el Hasā and the major north-south wadis entering this Wadi (Fig. 1).

FOOTNOTES
1. This latter site is an addition to the 1935 list.
2. He says the sites he lists "with the question mark behind them are Edomite EI I-II sites, but are not proper border fortresses, being located really in cultivable areas and being somewhat too far west perhaps to be listed in that category" (1939:24).
3. Most recently for this see the summation of Weippert, "Remarks on the History of Settlement in Southern Jordan during the Early Iron Age," in Studies in the History and Archaeology of Jordan I ed. Adnan Hadidi; Amman: Department of Antiquities, 1982, 153 n.5.
4. Glueck's spelling has been used until now but hereafter the WHS spelling is used, based on current maps. In some cases, local spelling is used. Er Ruweiḥi is incorrectly placed on the map Qal'at el Ḥasā, Map Sheet 225/025, Scale 1:25,000.
5. Rujm Umm el-'Adhām is likely the same as Glueck's Rujm Abū el-'Azâm which he describes thus: "About 6 km. in a straight line east from Kh. edh-Dherîḥ is Rujm Abū el-'Azâm (51), overlooking the upper part of the Seil el-Qaṭṭâr from the west. Rujm Abū el-'Azâm is built on top of a hill strewn with flint blocks, which is situated in a broken and bleak area. From the top of the site the Wâdī el-Ḥesā is visible, with the modern road zigzagging down its n. side. This rujm represents a large, almost completely destroyed fortress buried within the mass of its own fallen, roughly hewn flint blocks. It is oriented n.w. by s.e., measures 18 m. square at the bottom, and supports an inner tower or platform which is about 10 m. square. The ruins are still about 4.5 m. high. On the top of the rujm is a modern grave. To which historical period the construction of the site belongs is impossible to say. The few scraps of worn sherds which were found seem to be Roman-Byzantine. The fort may have served as a Roman fortress guarding the approaches from the Wâdī el-Ḥesā to the north, and from the infertile areas to the east, to the fertilearea between 'Aineh and eth-Thuwâneh which is crossed by the Roman highway." (1939:51).
    Glueck's location of Rujm Abū el-'Azâm as given above, i.e., 6 km in a straight line east from Kh. edh-Dhariḥ, ought to place it

within WHS territory. However, there is no site of this description in the area where Glueck says it is. In another place, he writes: "A considerable number of Nabataean-Roman-Byzantine sites were examined in the broken plateau land north and south of the Jurf ed-Derāwîsh - eṭ-Ṭafîleh road, including such sites as Khan Qillus, Kh. ef-Freij, Rujm el-Mughâmes, Rujm Abū el-'Aẓâm, Qefeiqef, and Rujm el-Hamrā" (1937:15). This description of the location of Rujm Abū el-'Aẓâm fits the location of Rujm Umm el-'Adhām well. Moreover, the description of the site itself fits well with the description of Rujm Umm el-'Adhām. I am of the opinion that Glueck's Abū el-'Aẓâm and Umm el-'Adhām are the same site. We call it Umm el-'Adhām, the name given to us by two different groups of Bedouin.
6. Rujm Muhawish is incorrectly placed on the map Buṭeina, Map Sheet 210/025, Scale 1:25,000.

REFERENCES
J. R. Bartlett, "The Moabites and Edomites," in Peoples of Old
1973   Testament Times ed. D.J. Wiseman; Oxford: Clarendon, 229-258.

_____, "The Rise and Fall of the Kingdom of Edom," PEQ 104:26-37.
1972
C.M. Bennett, "Excavations at Buseirah, Southern Jordan, 1974: Pre-
1977   liminary Report," Levant 9:1-10.

_____, "Excavations at Buseirah, Southern Jordan, 1973: Prelimi-
1975   nary Report," Levant 7:1-19.

_____, "Excavations at Buseirah, Southern Jordan, 1972: Prelimi-
1974   nary Report," Levant 6:1-24.

_____, "Excavations at Buseirah, Southern Jordan, 1971: Prelimi-
1973   nary Report," Levant 5:1-11.

_____, "A Brief Note on Excavations at Tawilan, Jordan, 1968-
1971a   1970," Levant 3:v-vii.

_____, "An Archaeological Survey of Biblical Edom," Perspective:
1971b   A Journal of Pittsburgh Theological Seminary 12:35-44.

_____, "Chronique archéologique: Ṭawîlân (Jordanie)," RB 77:371-
1970   374.

_____, "Chronique archéologique: Ṭawîlân," RB 76:386-390.
1969

_____, "The Excavations at Tawilan, Nr. Petra," ADAJ 12/13:53-55.
1967/68

_____, "A Cosmetic Palette from Umm el-Biyara," Antiquity 41:197-
1967   201.

_____, "Des fouilles à Umm el-Biyara: Les Edomites à Pétra,"
1966a   Bible et Terre Sainte 84:6-16.

_____, "Exploring Umm el Biyara, The Edomite Fortress-Rock which
1966b   dominates Petra," ILN 30 (April), 29-31.

_____, "Fouilles d'Umm el-Biyara: Rapport préliminaire," RB 73:
1966c   372-403.

_____, "Chronique archéologique: Umm el-Biyara," RB 71:250-253.
1964
H. J. Franken and W.J.A. Power, "Glueck's Explorations in Eastern

1971   Palestine in the Light of Recent Research," VT XXI:119-23.
N. Glueck, The Other Side of the Jordan, rev.; Cambridge: ASOR.
1970
_____, "Transjordan," in Archaeology and Old Testament Study ed.
1967   D. Winton Thomas; Oxford: Clarendon, 429-453.
_____, "The Civilization of the Edomites," BA X:77-84.
1947
_____, The Other Side of the Jordan; New Haven: ASOR.
1940
_____, Explorations in Eastern Palestine, III. AASOR XVIII-XIX
1939   for 1937-1939; New Haven: ASOR.
_____, "An Aerial Reconnaissance in Southern Transjordan," BASOR
1937a   67:19-27.
_____, "Explorations in Eastern Palestine III," BASOR 65:8-29.
1937b
_____, "The Boundaries of Edom," HUCA XI:141-157.
1936.
_____, Explorations in Eastern Palestine, II. AASOR XV for 1934-
1935   1935.
A. Hadidi, ed., Studies in the History and Archaeology of Jordan I;
1982   Amman: Department of Antiquities.
B. MacDonald, G.O. Rollefson, E.B. Banning, B.F. Byrd, and C. D'An-
1983   nibale, "The Wadi el Ḥasā Survey 1982: A Preliminary Re-
        port," ADAJ XXVII (in press).
B. MacDonald, G.O. Rollefson, and D.W. Roller, "The Wadi el Ḥasā
1982   Survey 1981: A Preliminary Report," ADAJ XXVI:117-131,
        Pls. XXVIII-XXXIV.
B. MacDonald, "The Wadi el Ḥasā Survey 1979 and Previous Archaeo-
1982   logical Work in Southern Jordan," BASOR 245:35-52.
B. MacDonald, E.B. Banning, and L.A. Pavlish, "The Wadi el Ḥasā
1980   Survey 1979: A Preliminary Report," ADAJ XXIV:169-183.
J.M. Miller, "Recent Archaeological Developments Relevant to Anci-
1982   ent Moab," in Hadidi, op. cit., pp. 169-173.
E. Puech, "Documents epigraphiques de Buseirah," Levant 9:11-20.
1977
M. Weippert, "Remarks on the History of Settlement in Southern Jor-
1982   dan during the Early Iron Age," in Hadidi, op. cit., pp.
        153-162.

TABLE 1

Sites Common to WHS and Glueck's Edomite Fortress System:

WHS Site Name - # (Glueck's Site Name - #)	Coordinates*	Elevation	WHS Field Reading** (Glueck's Field Reading)
Kh. Karakā - 31 (Kh. Kerakeh - 234)	133350*	1117	LIslam(49);Iron IC-IIA(21);Byz(7);Mod(3);Ud(237). (No sherds saved)
Rujm Karakā - 24 (Rujm Kerakeh - 233)	138343	1148	Iron IC-IIA(71);Iron II(11);LIslam(10);LRom(8);Byz(6);Ud(283). (Some Edomite)
Rujm Jā'is - 311 (Rujm Jā'ez - 217)	205380	645	Iron IIA-B(17 indicators + 192 body sherds).(A few Edomite EI I-II sherds and several mediaeval Arabic)
Rujm Bakher - 716 (Kh. Bākher - 224)	298333	936	Ott(33);LRom-Byz(6);Ud(32). (Several EI I-II sherds, several Nabataean and mediaeval Arabic sherds)
Er Ruweihi - 764 (er-Ruweiḥah - 53)	378292	825-847	Nab(73);LRom-Byz(18);Nab/Rom(15);LByz(13);Nab-Rom(11);LRom(8);Byz(7);EByz(5);Nab,poss(4);Ayy-Mam ?(1);Ud(25). (Numerous Nabataean sherds; coarse sherds.... Edomite Early Iron)
Rujm Umm el-'Adhām (Rujm Abū el Aẓâm - 51)	234295	1173	Nab(2);Rom(2);Ud(3). (Roman-Byzantine)

126

* The abbreviated form of the coordinates is given.
** The most frequently occuring sherds are given priority in the readings.

TABLE 2

Prospects for Further Work on An Iron II Fortress System Along the South Bank of the Wadi el Ḥasā:

WHS Site Name – #	Coordinates*	Elevation	WHS Field Reading**
El-Maqḥaz – 187	069359	745	Iron II(32);Iron I(28);Ott(22);LIslam(19);Byz(8);Hell, poss(1);Ud sherds, pss EB(3);Ud sherds(149).
Rabāb – 172	066366	925	Byz(157);Nab(37);Nab,poss(13);Iron II(26);MB/LB/Iron Age(4);LB,poss(2);LRom(2);Ott/Mod(1);EB IV(1);Ud sherds(846).
Kh. 'Ain Saubalā – 61	112403	569	EB I(444);EB I,prob(12);LB(?) or Iron II(?)(22);Iron II(135);Nab(4);Byz(2);Ud sherds(239).
Rujm Muhawish – 248	147306	1198	Iron II(350);Nab/Rom(3);Iron I(6);Nab(1).
Ed-Dair – 367	166351	760	Iron I-II(295);EB and Iron Age body sherds(95);Nab(24); Iron IIA(5);EB I(5);Ott/Mod(3).
No Name – 647	227365	660	Byz(16);Iron II(12);LOtt(12);Cl(7);Ud sherds(18).

* The abbreviated form of the coordinates is given.
** Sherds are ordered according to predominence.

127

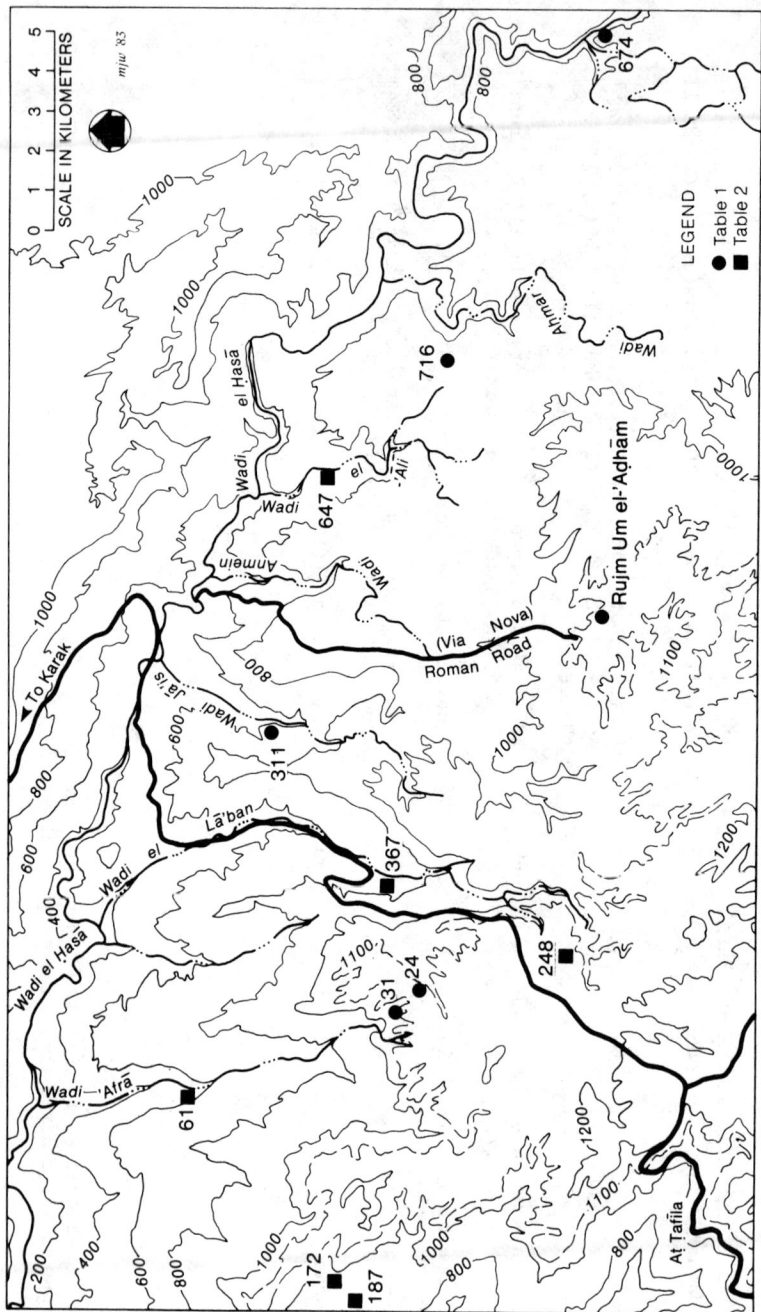

FIGURE 1

RECENT COMPUTER APPLICATIONS IN ANCIENT

NEAR EASTERN ARCHAEOLOGY

James F. Strange

Before 1970, the application of the computer to problems in Ancient Near Eastern (ANE) archaeology was hardly more than a dream. Yet, as we shall soon see, in the decade from 1970-1980 the use of computer-assisted analyses of various kinds, not to mention data base management, graphics, and other applications, have moved from the realm of _posse_ _est_ to that of _necesse_ _est_.

Although it might be of some interest to speculate about the reasons for turning to the machine for information storage, retrieval, and analysis, the purpose of this small essay is simply to describe some of the major applications to which the computer has been put in the field of ANE archaeology. Thus, in the nature of the case, much will be omitted from the discussion in terms of computer applications in European and classical archaeology that might intrigue and fascinate the reader. Rather our limited presentation here is intended to be instructive and, we hope, pragmatic. It is simply our plan to review some of the major uses of the computer in ANE archaeology in three areas: (1) data base establishment, (2) data base management, and (3) data analysis. This leaves out of the running some important possibilities, as many readers will know, but perhaps we can save these for another time and place.

I. Data Bases in ANE Archaeology

A leader in establishing a data base in ANE archaeology was the Expedition to Caesarea Maritima, under the direction of Robert J. Bull of Drew University. Bull was interested in using the computer for data recording as early as 1970 when he was Annual Director of the W. F. Albright Institute for Archaeological Research in Jerusalem. He was then planning the first season in the field at Caesarea and was exploring various alternatives in registration systems and recording systems. It was fairly obvious that a site of such enormous size as ancient Caesarea would likely be a veritable mine of the material culture of the Roman and Byzantine Periods: coins, sculpture, pottery, oil lamps, small finds of

every kind. If the computer was not relied upon simply
to record this massive amount of information, then the
sheer volume of the data threatened to overwhelm any
traditional registration system.

Bull found ready assistance from the hand of Dr.
Donald Fisher, then Professor and Chairman of Computer
and Information Science at Oklahoma State University in
Stillwater. Fisher devised the information system or
data base design, using the pottery encoding system
developed by Lawrence Toombs of Wilfrid Laurier University in Ontario. The Expedition to Caesarea Maritima
developed this immense data base over several seasons,
but it was never used by the archaeologists.[1]

Another early entry into this late-blooming discipline among ANE archaeologists was the Joint Expedition
to Khirbet Shema, directed by Eric M. Meyers of Duke
University. The present author became an Associate
Director of this expedition in 1971. In that year I
learned to program in Fortran IV and developed a mini-
data base from the artifact registration of the first
season's work in square B.1 at Caesarea, the square I
had directed. In the course of learning to program it
had become abundantly clear to me that computers would
soon be a sine qua non for data analysis for ANE archaeologists, though the seemingly insurmountable problem
was cost effectiveness. Computer time was expensive.

One of the duties of successive artifact Registrars
of the Joint Expedition to Khirbet Shema was therefore
to see to it that artifacts were recorded in an identical format. This system was in lieu of the expensive,
specially printed IBM keypunch forms used by Don Fisher
and his assistants at Caesarea. Thus after the field
season a series of keypunch operators at the Computer
Center at the University of South Florida read the
registration records directly from spiral notebooks--
though not without protest--and keyboarded the data
onto IBM punchcards. These cards were then read immediately into computer memory and printed out in lists.
These lists remained the primitive data base for the
staff of the Khirbet Shema' project until its end in
1972.[2]

The successor to the Joint Expedition to Khirbet
Shema' was the Meiron Excavation Project, also directed
by Eric M. Meyers and with largely the same staff. The
Registrars again made sure in successive excavation

seasons to use the same registration format in the familiar spiral notebooks. This did not represent in itself an advance. However, we also began to amass two other data bases; namely, pottery field readings and coin readings. Therefore at the time of analysis of the data, it became clear that we needed file merging. That is, in order to produce the Locus List, dear to the hearts of all archaeologists, it would be necessary to merge the coin list, pottery reading list, and locus descriptions. This was accomplished in a pilot run in 1977 as the senior staff completed the final report.

The next step up for the Merion Excavation Project, then, was the use of the terminal "in the field." This was certainly not a new idea, as it had been tried in the early 1970's by a variety of archaeologists.[3] Our idea was to make it economically feasible by taking a microcomputer into camp and building files there. In effect we would be moving the data base out of the university office and making it available to the archaeologists in the field.

During the 1980 excavations at Nabratein, Israel, the Meiron Excavation Project used the Radio Shack TS-80 with 32K Random Access Memory (RAM), two cassette recorders for mass storage, and a printer. Staff members Strange and Longstaff wrote the software for building and updating the artifact registration files and the pottery reading files (coins were included with artifacts).[4]

This experiment had its difficulties, but the immediate effect was to make clear to the staff of the Expedition that such immediate access to the data base is simply a necessity for intelligent field decisions. Recent advances in field methods have resulted in recovery of ever greater amounts of information. The archaeologist is therefore continually confronted with a mass of data too large to digest, and therefore may make poor field decisions. Even the simple making of lists helps the field archaeologist know where certain types of artifactual material are coming from, and therefore which areas to pursue, in terms of the objectives of the excavation.

A somewhat different application of a computer generated data base was that of Z'ev Yeivin of the Department of Antiquities of Israel. In this case Yeivin decided to encode all instances of the published

Iron Age pottery of ancient Israel and the lands adjoining Israel. His objective was to enable the researcher to search for parallels to pottery that he or she might be examining at the moment. Yeivin skirted the thorny problem of encoding profile drawings directly by the simple expedient of encoding the name of the vessel, as there is fair unanimity among archaeologists what to call each vessel. It was also necessary, of course, to encode the name of the publication, the site, locus identification, and many other categories, including a description of the pot itself.

Yeivin took advantage of the state of the art by having special forms printed for an optical reader. That is, a machine read the file cards, which were prepared by Dr. Yeivin and his assistants, directly into computer memory. This is an important innovation, as it meant there was only one clerk entering the data into the machine (ignoring for the moment the second clerk who verified the cards against the original publications). It is a rule in electronic data processing that the fewer clerks who handle the data, the fewer errors will creep into the data base.[5]

Yeivin accessed his data base via about 29 categories or combinations of categories. That is, he could query the data base to print out all instances of chalices associated with Gezer bowls, or all instances of cooking pots with specific types of rim, or any other way he chose. The only constraint on the system was the complexity of the search program and the organization of the data within the data base. This became an invaluable aid for the archaeologist preparing his or her pottery for publication.[6]

Yet another approach to a similar data base was provided by Tom McClelland, a doctoral candidate at the University of Pennsylvania. McClelland's objective was no less than the complete re-seriation of the published Iron Age pottery of ancient Palestine, relying on modern, sophisticated statistical techniques. To realize this aim he needed an accurate data base of all published Iron Age pottery from the area.[7]

McClelland's data base was equally no less than a completely uniform reclassification of the data. McClelland discovered five problems in assembling his data base: (1) There are internal discrepancies in vessel counts and classifications in the catalogues from any given site. (2) Not all interpreters of the Iron Age classify their pottery the same way. (3) Certain categories overlap, as, for example, the chalice or goblet.[8] (4) Stratum and locus descriptions use not only different numbers and letters for the same thing, but also presuppose different definitions of the smallest excavable unit. (5) The site publications and Duncan's Corpus may disagree about the number of vessels and types found at any given site.[9]

Thus McClelland's strategy was to develop a uniform system of classification of all published Iron Age vessels, to resolve the discrepancies in the vessel counts and classifications at a given site, and to preserve the "locus" and provenience designations in each site report translated into Arabic numerals. For example, Megiddo stratum VIIA is reported as stratum 7-1.[10] This allowed him to develop five regional occupational sequences that seemed to have meaning: (1) Hazor, (2) Megiddo/'Amal/Beth Shean, (3) Lachish/Tell Beit Mirsim, (4) Jemmeh/Zuwayid/Tell el-Farah (S), and (5) Deir 'Alla.[11]

If McClelland is right, his work should have the most impact in terms of his complete chronological reseriation of Iron Age pottery in ancient Palestine.[12] In any case his storage of ancient Iron Age ceramics in an accurate, easily revisable data base provided him with a research tool that would have been simply impossible before the advent of the computer. With the coming of huge amounts of permanent storage on microcomputers and with the development of sophisticated software for micros, we will likely see extensions of McClelland's research on much more compact machines than he used.

Another recent use of the computer for assembling a data base from a single site has been that of the Heshbon Excavation Project in Jordan under the direction of Larry Geraty of Andrews University. In this case the staff, particularly Oystein LaBianca and Larry Geraty, became convinced of the value of computerizing the existing locus descriptions, artifact registration, and other related information. They began after the fact, but managed to encode all the information they deemed relevant, verify the data, update the data base, and continue to enlarge it up to and including their last season in the field, namely, 1980.[13]

133

This was very much an "in-house" project, using
the Andrews University computer and the services of
James Brower, Director of the Computer Center. The
result included the production of an encoding manual
written by Larry Mitchell in 1978 and subsequently updated.[14] The complete system allowed the encoding,
storage, and retrieval of information keyed to the excavated unit, including data on soil descriptions, architecture, stratigraphy, artifacts, pottery, coins,
biodata, and photographs and other records.[15] That is,
the result was probably the most complete computerized
data base of field information ever assembled in
Ancient Near Eastern archaeology.

Still another recent application of the computer
for on-site encoding and retrieval of data was that
developed by Debra Katz for use at Tell Mikhal, Israel,
since 1978.[16] In the words of V. A. Walsh, the design
of the system "...allows continuous updating of the
data-base structure and definitions, immediate responses to the excavators, and modification of excavation
procedures as indicated by computer analysis."[17] No
description of this data-base or of the preliminary
results of its implementation have yet appeared in
print. Nevertheless, if fully implemented, this application may mark a significant step in such computer
usage.

Finally, it seems proper to mention here the computer assisted cataloging system developed for artifacts from Tell Akhmim, Egypt by Sheila McNally and
Vicki Walsh.[18] In this case the data base is designed
to allow efficient processing of large numbers of artifacts, and also to support cross-cultural comparisons.
In other words the data base allowed for sorting and
classification of large numbers of artifacts rapidly
and accurately. On the other hand the same system also
enabled the archaeologists to make intra-cultural and
cross-cultural inferences from artifact characteristics.

McNally and Walsh devised a pottery and artifact
classification and encoding system that was clear and
simple, yet used objective, global definitions of artifacts so that artifacts from different cultures could
be compared. To this end the cataloguing system was
divided into several stages so that the first stage was
simple and global. The second stage of cataloging was
more specific and included the simplification and reduction of variables. The result of the cataloging system

was a set of encoding sheets from which the data could
be entered by keyboarding directly into the computer.

McNally turned to a commercially available data
base management system, the System 2000, for it seemed
to fit her needs.[19] This package was also already
readily available at the host institution, the University of Minnesota. System 2000 is a software package
of several machine-language programs to ease encoding,
editing, and management of the data base.[20] For example the system contains a feature called REPORT
WRITER that enables the user to call up data in whatever format the user desires. System 2000 can sort
through the data bank on virtually any number of variables and print out the results according to the
user's needs. This is a normal feature of a good data
base management package.

Another example of the use of the System 2000 for
a data base application in ANE archaeology is also from
the University of Minnesota. In this case a team of
scholars entered all available cuneiform documents from
the second millenium Old Babylonian town of Kutalla
into the computer. This required transliteration of
102 documents into a Roman alphabet, identification of
eighty-eight components of the economic transactions
thus recorded (buyer, seller, item, date, etc.), and
eventually a search of the data base for a series of
variables relative to the aims of the project. In this
case the researchers were asking for the economic history of Kutalla.[21]

For the sake of introducing some comparative data,
certain documents from ancient Ur and Dilbat were also
entered into the data base. The entire file was then
searched with a concordance command (TALLY). Other
special reports were generated with the REPORT WRITER
command, which could and did retrieve entire documents.
Finally the entire data base was searched to produce a
tabulation of all sales of land, reducing the price of
each piece of property to common figures.

The study provided some important insights into
the economic history of an Old Babylonian site, but
more importantly it illustrates the utility of such
computerized studies. In this case the computer made
possible what traditional scholarly approaches would
regard as untenable. This is the value of such a computerized data base.

It goes without saying that most archaeologists, unlike those in the previous examples, have approached a computerized data base with limited plans in mind. For example the staff of the Joint Expedition to Khirbet Shema originally had very limited goals in mind when we turned to the computer. After we had labored with encoding the artifact registration into the computer, we asked for no more than a comprehensive artifact list. However very shortly we looked at that list and instantly realized that the computer could just as easily print out all the artifacts by material. This would help us answer questions like, "Where are all these iron nails coming from?" The next step is rather obvious, namely, have the computer search by material, but also by field, square, and locus and print out the report in the same sequence. What seems so obvious now was manna from computer heaven in the early 70's. The final step, or data base management, has become a reality only ten years later.

II. Data Base Management

It may be valuable here to realize that early users of the data bases mentioned generally thought of the electronic file of archaeological information in much the same way they may have thought of their 3x5 cards in the past. In other words, the information so stored was regarded essentially as a static, unchanging well of information from which one dipped from time to time in order to trace an artifact or look at some information relative to an isolated problem. Notice, however, that even with 3x5 cards any researcher finds that he or she must do at least three things: (1) Correct the information. (2) Write in new information. (3) Delete irrelevant information. These are important in effective data base or data bank management.

Users of an artifact file system may also find it necessary to present the same information in different ways. For example, art historians will probably find it necessary to discuss whatever art motifs are found on the artifacts in question, while the historians of technology may treat the same motifs solely in terms of the ancient methods of manufacturers. In other words, the choice of organization of the data may change from presentation to presentation, even though the file itself may not change. We may identify any machine-supported capacity to change either the content or

136

organization of a file as a kind of data base management.[22]

Upon reflection, then, the reader may realize that those data bases treated in section 1 of this essay were probably examples of data base management as much as they were simply of data base establishment. The staff of the Caesarea Maritima expedition would probably find it necessary to update their computer files to the extent that they used them. It was certainly the case that the data base established by the Joint Expedition to Khirbet Shema and by its successor, the Meiron Excavation Project, had to be managed, and is still being managed as changes are necessary. This element of relative permanence is the mark of a true data bank, which may be defined as a large file of information that will be accessed or used by (ordinarily) a group of researchers.

An example of a system designed expressly for data bank management is that prepared for the explorations at Sepphoris in lower Galilee for 1983. The data bank management system is a set of programs written in BASIC for the Radio Shack TRS-80 model III. The programs are designed for "friendly" use, meaning that they do not require a computer expert to enter or revise the data. The system allows a designated user to sit before the screen and type in (keyboard in) information about four areas: (1) artifact registration, (2) pottery readings, (3) coin readings, and (4) locus descriptions. The system also allows the user to update or correct faulty information, fill in blanks, and add new information as it becomes available either during excavation or later during interpretation. The system also allows printing out or presentation of the stored information in a variety of formats, either on the screen or on the printer or both.

The final goal of this data bank will be the complete locus list, which means merging the four files listed above. The locus list, after all, is traditionally what the archaeologist involved in the ANE works from, especially at the level of interpretation. Thus the researcher can retrieve from this data bank any one of the four files mentioned, or any record from any one or more of the files, or any datum or pattern of data that he or she may discern. This amounts to imposition of control of the whole array of data that the archaeologist has unearthed, which is the ultimate aim.[23]

This, of course, is the entire reason for using the computer, for the machine becomes an effective tool in managing or controlling the huge amounts of information that advanced excavation methods force upon us.

Data Bank management, then, is as necessary in classical and ANE archaeology as it is in European and American archaeology. It just so happens that our colleagues in Europe and North America have responded to the need first. Therefore it may be a surprise for some to hear that the first conference in data banks in archaeology was held at the University of Arkansas in 1971, about the time that practioners in the ANE were sizing up the situation and first trying out machine storage of their data.[24] The second such conference took place in 1972 in France.[25] By 1981 Sylvia Gaines could report that European archaeologists had access to no less than thirty-three archaeological data banks in seventeen countries.[26] The American situation is somewhat more restricted, for Data Bank Applications in Archaeology reports on seven archaeological data banks, of which only four are from the United States, though that is hardly an exhaustive list.[27]

In this short essay we have reported on seven data bases (or data banks). These include the Caesarea Maritima project, which is housed at Oklahoma State University. The data bank associated with the Joint Expedition to Khirbet Shema and the Meiron Excavation Project is housed at the University of South Florida. Some of the later material from the Meiron Excavation Project is both at the latter institution and at Colby College in Waterville, Maine. Yeivin's data is at the Hebrew University in Jerusalem. McClelland's data base is at the University of Pennsylvania, where it was developed. The Heshbon Project's data bank is at Andrews University, while the Tel Mikhal, Israel, data is at the University of Minnesota. This last university also houses the data bank from the Akhmim, Egypt, excavations, and the file of Kutalla's Old Babylonian records.

III. Data Analysis

By far one of the most powerful uses of the computer is in data analysis, which need not always be the use of powerful and sophisticated statistical programs. Yet one of the first uses of the computer for data analysis for ANE archaeology is just such a detailed

analysis. In this case the data was recovered from
Ksar Akil in Lebanon and amounted to about 15,000
Paleolithic stone cores, blanks, and tools that needed
description and interpretation. Use of the computer
as an interpretive aid was more or less inevitable,
given the sheer volume of data.[28]

The site of Ksar Akil, near Beirut, is a Paleolithic rock shelter with C14 dates between 40,000 and
30,000 BP. The mass of lithic materials that was recovered offered a large enough data sample that it appeared feasible to infer in some detail the development
of a set of lithic industries at a single site over
several thousands of years. To this end Azoury used an
existing system of description and developed a specialized set of analyses.[29]

Azoury classified the 15,000 stone artifacts hier-
archically according to the system of F. Bordes. Level
One of this system classifies all lithic artifacts as
either (1) cores, (2) tools, (3) blanks, or (4) waste
flakes. In Level Two the Bordian system separates
cores into seven types, tools into three types, and
blanks into two types. Azoury did not consider waste
flakes. Each of the classifications in Level Two were
further refined into Level Three's sub-types.[30] Thus
all stone artifacts were classified in a system that
used three levels.

In practice this meant that one described each
piece individually by making two or three strokes on a
worksheet, checking off only a few of the 128 attributes
listed. In this way the fourteen stone tool assemblages
from the fourteen strata at Ksar Akil were inserted into a data matrix of 14 rows and 128 columns. This could
be printed out as a suitably labeled matrix. The data
were also treated by "constellation analysis."[31]

Without describing the theory and application of
constellation analysis in detail, suffice it to say
here that it is a statistical method that looks for
structures within the data beyond the three dimensions
to which the human mind is accustomed.[32] In this case
Azoury identified eight general groups or "constellations" of artifacts that he thought helped to isolate
major trends in lithic industries at Ksar Akil over the
ten millenia of the site. He next calculated the mathematical "difference" between each constellation and
all others. When all such calculations were completed,

he had a picture of lithic industry development at the
site, though he had to combine both typological and
technological data on the artifacts to do so. He also
found that a reduced type-list of butts, blanks, and
cores correlated +89% with the results of an exhaustive
type list. This is an important methodological discovery, for it implies that less descriptive detail,
when developed properly, allows the researcher to discover the structure within the data about as well as an
exhaustive list, saving much time and money.[33]

It is often the case that scholars trained in ANE
archaeology do not necessarily have the statistical
sophistication to undertake such an analysis such as
that of Azoury. This was certainly the case of the
Joint Expedition to Khirbet Shema, whose staff was
trained in textual methods as scholars and in field archaeology as practicing ANE historians. Therefore,
under the tutelage of George J. Levenbach, the staff
sought to use the computer to detect structures within
the data that did not require study equivalent to a new
academic degree.[34]

During the 1970's one of the most promising methods
in automatic classification of archaeological data was
cluster analysis.[35] Various archaeologists had experi-
mented with a number of types of such analyses, though
very few were active in ANE archaeology. I stepped into this vacuum with some trepidation, but still guided
by George Levenbach. The result was an attempt to
classify the Squares (the smallest excavated plot) from
the excavations at Khirbet Shema by comparing their
artifact distributions by material. It was certainly
possible to classify the Squares in this manner, though
it was not clear what the resulting dendrogram actually
meant.[36]

Meanwhile Levenbach applied himself to various
statistical problems in ANE archaeology, including an
analysis of the pottery from ancient Mycenaea. In this
case Levenbach and Mertz asked themselves how much information about dates is lost when one reduces the number of variables used to describe ancient pottery.
This may be particularly important when examining the
data from a series of sites in order to deduce the distribution of pottery types chronologically.[37]

Levenbach and Mertz used the Mycenaean pottery
studies of Furumark, which are well known among ANE

archaeologists.[38] They used Furumark's counts of pottery forms, which are described by Type, Site, Context, Decorative Motif, and Date. They then used a computer program to construct a series of two-way contingency tables, which means that they compared all 336 types to all 80 decorative motifs, then all types to all sites, then all types to all contexts, etc. As one can readily see, this is not a process that lends itself to hand work.

A major problem for statistical methods in comparing such tables is the zeros entered at any point. For specific mathematical reasons, zeros are very troublesome in some comparative statistics. However, in the case of information theory, it is very easy to handle such information. The authors of this study ordered the sites from richest to poorest in each table, using the zeros as important information for such ordering. The computer then calculated the interdependence of rows and columns. In its next run, the computer calculated the interdependence of rows and columns with the "pottery poor" sites eliminated.

The result was similar to what Azoury had deduced in his study, but in a different analysis and for a different reason. Levenbach and Mertz concluded that, if the eight "poorest" site groups are discarded from a distribution analysis, only five percent of the pottery evidence would be missing, but twelve percent of the chronological information is lost. In other words, although there is still a relatively large amount of information remaining, the effect on the analysis is two and one half times greater than one might predict. Therefore, in terms of information theory, it would be prudent to include the "pottery poor" sites, if chronological inferences are desired.

Of course it is also possible to use far less sophisticated computerized procedures for exploratory purposes. For example recently the Meiron Excavation Project published its preliminary report on the 1980 season of excavation at Nabratein, Israel.[39] In the coin report, authored by Joyce Raynor, the staff provided some computer-generated calculations of the Pearson Coefficient of Correlation.[40] The reader can discover the meaning of this calculation in any elementary statistical text. Our point was to arrive at a quantitative estimate of the difference between the distribution of the coins at Nabratein and their

distribution at the three other ancient villages we
had excavated. Our impression from the number of coins
found was that Nabratein stood out from the other three,
but the calculation of the coefficient helped sharpen
and confirm that intuition. It was also possible to
convert the Pearson Coefficient into a mathematical
distance simply by subtracting the coefficient from
1.0000 and multiplying it by 100, rather like deriving
a percentage. This calculation was also easily accomplished on the computer. The calculations demonstrated
rather handily that our perceptions could be supported
mathematically, though we knew no statistician would
regard our calculations as rigorous.

There remains much more to be said. Recently
archaeologists have discovered the color graphics capabilities of computers in manipulating data and have
produced some stunning results.[41] Other archaeologists
have stayed with the relatively simpler scatter dia-
grams available in the Statistical Package for the
Social Sciences (SPSS),[42] or have discovered how to
sketch on the screen, sometimes in three dimensions.[43]
Some, following the lead of Tom McClelland, are trying
their hand at seriation, though the last great unex-
plored area, according to Jerry Sabloff, is modelling.[44]
Whatever may be the case, at least archaeologists involved in ANE archaeology will continue to build and
manage data bases, engage in data analysis of increasingly sophisticated order, and discover the graphics
and modelling capabilities of these ever more reliable
machines.

FOOTNOTES
1. Donald D. Fisher, "An Information System for the Joint Caesarea Maritima (Israel) Excavations," pp. 191-204 in Computers in the
Humanities ed. J. L. Mitchell; Minneapolis: University of Minnesota, 1974. For the encoding system used at Caesarea, cf. Lawrence E. Toombs and Norman E. Wagner, Pottery Coding Handbook; Waterloo, Ontario: Waterloo Lutheran University, 1971, and, Fisher
and Kyle M. Yates, Jr., Artifact and Pottery Coding Manual; Stillwater: Oklahoma State University, 1972. Cf. also L. E. Toombs,
"Appendix: Coding Pottery in the Field," pp. 25-8 in Coding and
Clustering Pottery by Computer by Wagner; Waterloo Lutheran University, 1971.
2. The published results of this first data base at Khirbet Shema
are to be found in Eric M. Meyers, A. Thomas Kraabel, and James F.
Strange, Ancient Synagogue Excavations at Khirbet Shema', Upper
Galilee, Israel, 1970-1972, AASOR XLII; Durham: Duke University
Press, 1976, pp. 269-280.

3. For early attempts at using the computer terminal in the field see P. Buckland, "An Experiment in the Use of a Computer for On-Site Recording of Finds," Science and Archaeology 9 (1973), 22-4; Sylvia W. Gaines, "Computer Use at an Archaeological Field Location," American Antiquity 39/3 (1974), 454-62; J. D. Wilcock, "An Experiment in the Use of a Computer for On-Site Recording of Finds: The Use of Remote Terminals for Archaeological Site Records," Science and Archaeology 9:22-5. An even earlier attempt (1969) is recorded by Robert G. Chenhall, Computers in Anthropology and Archeology, IBM Data Processing Application; White Plains: IBM Technical Publications No. GE 20-0384-0, 1971, p. 24.
4. James F. Strange, "Using the Microcomputer in the Field: The Case of the Meiron Excavation Project," Newsletter of the ASOR No. 4 (1981), 8-11.
5. Yeivin's work remains unpublished as of this writing.
6. Thus Yeivin was able to accomplish on the computer in a few minutes what would take a team of graduate students days or weeks to accomplish. This approximates Chenhall's second reason for using the computer in archaeology: "..analyses can be performed on the computer that, from a practical standpoint, cannot be accomplished any other way." Chenhall, "Computerized Data Bank Management," pp. 1-8 in Gaines, Data Bank Applications in Archaeology; Tucson: University of Arizona Press, 1981, esp. p. 8.
7. Thomas L. McClelland, Quantitative Studies in the Iron Age Pottery of Palestine; Philadelphia: University of Pennsylvania Ph.D. dissertation, unpublished, 1975.
8. Ruth Amiran, Ancient Pottery of the Holy Land; Jerusalem: Masada Press, 1969, p. 213.
9. McClelland, op. cit., Appendix V.
10. Op. cit., p. 815.
11. Op. cit., pp. 194-279.
12. McClelland made one of the most striking results of his study available as an article: "Chronology of the 'Philistine' Burials at Tell el-Far'ah (South)," Journal of Field Archaeology 6 (1979), 57-73.
13. Lawrence T. Geraty, "Computer Assisted Management of Heshbon Data: Coding Stratigraphic and Typological Data," a paper presented at the Annual Meeting of the ASOR, Nov 80, Dallas, TX.
14. Larry Mitchell, User's Manual: Heshbon Data Entry Forms; Angwin, CA: Pacific Union College, 1978.
15. Op. cit., pp. 14-37.
16. Peter C. Patton and Renne A. Haloien, eds., Computing in the Humanities; Lexington, MA: Heath, 1981, p. 160.
17. Vicky A. Walsh, "Part II: Computing in Archaeology and History," pp. 159-161 in Patton and Haloien (n.16).
18. Sheila McNally and Vicky Walsh, "The Data Bank for Akhmin, Egypt," Journal of Field Archaeology, in press; Patton and Haloien, op. cit., p. 160. See also D. Katz, J. Merkel, P.C. Patton and R.D. Ward, "System 2000 Applications in Ancient Studies," a paper presented at a System 2000 Users' Conference Ap 78, Austin, TX. McNally and Walsh cite the following systems as those that influ-

enced them, particularly in ceramic classifications: Ann Bennett, "Basic Ceramic Analysis," Eastern New Mexico University Contributions in Anthroplogy 6 (1974), 1-183. T. Loy and G.R.Powell, Archaeological Data Recording Guide; British Columbia Museum Heritage Records 3; BC Provincial Museum, 1977. C.L.Redman, R. Anzalone and P. Rubertone, "Qasr es-Seghir: Three Seasons of Excavation," Bulletin d'Archaeologie Marocaine 11 (1978), and, "Qasr es-Seghir: Ceramic Diagnostic Key Sheet" (mimeographed). Martha Joukowsky, A Complete Manual of Field Archaeology; Englewood Cliffs: Prentice-Hall, 1980. Irving Rouse, "The Classification of Artifacts," American Antiquity 25 (1960), 324-9. Charles Redman, "Multistage Fieldwork and Analytic Techniques," American Antiquity 38 (1973), 61-79. William G. Dever and H. Darrell Lance, A Manual of Field Excavation: Handbook for Field Archaeologists; Cincinnati: Hebrew Union College, 1977, esp. pp. 108-38.

19. McNally and Walsh, op. cit., p. 26 of MS.
20. MRI, System 2000 Reference Manual, rev.; Austin: MRI Systems Corp., 1974 (P.O. Box 9968, Austin, TX 78766).
21. Richard D. Ward and Renee A. Holoien, "A Computer Data Base for Babylonian Economic Documents," pp. 163-179 in Patton and Holoien, op. cit.
22. For a recent discussion of the idea of data base management in archaeology, see Chenhall, in Gaines, op. cit.
23. Chenhall, op. cit., p. 2.
24. Gaines, ed., Conferences, Newsletter of Computer Archaeology 6/4 (1971), 1-2.
25. J.C. Gardin, Les Banques de Donnees Archeologiques; Paris: Centre National de la Recherche Scientifique, 1974.
26. Gaines, "Computerized Data Banks in Archaeology: The European Situation," Computers and the Humanities 15 (1981), 223-6. This review is based mainly on F. Verhaeghe, ed., Archaeology, Natural Science and Technology: The European Situation, 3 vols.; Strasbourg: European Science Foundation, 1979.
27. Gaines, Data Banks.., op. cit. The American systems mentioned are ADAM (Archaeological Data Management) at Arizona State University, AMASDA (Automated Management of Archaeological Survey Data in Arkansas) at the University of Arkansas, AZSITE (apparently Arizona Sites) at the Arizona State University Museum, and ORACLE at Indiana University.
28. The final report of the site is in I. Azoury, A Technological and Typological Analysis of the Transitional and Early Upper Palaeolithic Levels of Ksar and Abu Halka; London: London University Ph.D. dissertation, unpublished, 1971. The computerized statistical data analysis is reported by Azoury and F.R. Hodson, "Comparing Palaeolithic Assemblages: Ksar Akil, a case study," World Archaeology 4/3 (1973), 292-306. A useful, brief discussion of the computerized data analysis as a whole is found in J.E. Doran and Hodson, Mathematics and Computers in Archaeology; Cambridge: Harvard University Press, 1975, pp. 257-74.
29. The descriptive system is that of F. Bordes, Typologie du Paleolithique Ancien et Moyen; Bordeaux: Delmas, 1961.

30. For the sub-types see D. de Sonneville-Bordes and J. Perrot, "Lexique typologique du Paleolithique superieur," Bulletin de la Societe Prehistoire Francaise 51 (1954), 327-35; 52 (1955), 76-9; 53 (1956), 408-12, 547-59.
31. M.H. Newcomer and Hodson, "Constellation Analysis of Burins from Ksar Akil," pp. 87-104 in D.E. Strong, ed., Archaeological Theory and Practice; London and NY: Seminar Press, 1973.
32. For more on constellation analysis, see Doran and Hodson, op. cit., pp. 205-9.
33. But no attention was paid here to the question of the proportion of information lost. See below n. 37.
34. His guidance is visible in Meyers, Kraabel and Strange, op. cit., pp. 99-102, 243-7.
35. For an earlier, jargon-filled but understandable treatment (called "agglomerative hierarchical procedures") see Doran and Hodson, op. cit., pp. 175-85.
36. The dendogram appeared in Meyers, Kraabel and Strange, op. cit. p. 101. A dendogram is a tree-like diagram showing classification into groups.
37. Richard P. Mertz and George J. Levenbach, "An Information Theory Application to Mycenaean Pottery," pp. 29-33 in S. Laflin, ed., Computer Applications in Archaeology 1978: Proceedings of the Annual Conference at the Computer Centre, University of Birmingham; Birmingham, England: University of Birmingham, 1978.
38. Arne Furumark, The Chronology of Mycenaean Pottery; Stockholm: Victor Pettersons, 1941.
39. Eric M. Meyers, James F. Strange amd Carol L. Meyers, "Preliminary Report on the 1980 Excavations at en-Nabratein, Israel," BASOR 244 (1981), 1-26.
40. Ibid., p. 16. Pearson's Moment assumes the linear relationship of the data, but on occasion it is useful to violate the assumptions of a statistical procedure knowingly in order to gain a mathematical perspective on an archaoelogical intuition.
41. The least known and perhaps most sophisticated application of color graphics to archaeological data is in Norman I. Badler and Virginia R. Badler, "Interaction With a Color Computer Graphics Systems for Archaeological Sites," Computer Graphics 1/11 (Oct 78), 12018. In this article, the illustrative material is all from Troy. The authors cite their own system: Badler and Badler, SITE: A Color Computer Graphics Systems for the Display of Archaeological Sites and Artifacts; Philadelphia: Dept. of Computer and Information Science, Technical Report 77-76 (Aug 77). See also Badler and Badler, "A New Analysis of Thermi," AIA, 79th Annual Conference Abstracts; Atlanta: Dec 77. One of the most recent discussions of archaeological computer graphics is in J.B. Arnold III, "Archaeological Applications of Computer Graphics," pp. 179-216 in M.B. Schiffer, ed., Advances in Archaeological Method and Theory, vol. 5: NY and London: Academic Press, 1982.
42. This is a highly developed package of statistical routines designed, as its name implies, for use with social sciences data: N. H. Nie, C.H. Hall, J.C. Jenkins, K. Steinbrenner, and D.H. Bent,

Statistical Package for the Social Sciences, 2nd ed.; NY: McGraw-Hill, 1975.
43. Interactive graphics systems, as they are called, are now simply legion. The American Institute of Architects schedules seminars on computers and computer graphics at its annual meeting. These seminars focus on issues such as computer graphics, systems drafting by computer, and computerized design. In addition, the capability of digitizing a two or three dimensional image for rotation, scaling, and merging with other images is now available on relatively inexpensive microcomputers. Someone should soon deduce how to use this capability in a cost effective and timely manner in archaeology.
44. J. A. Sabloff, ed., Simulations in Archaeology; Albuquerque: University of New Mexico Press, 1981. This is one of the most important books to appear in the field and needs to be better known.

MADABA - AN IRON AGE TOMB

Henry O. Thompson

The city of Madaba is widely noted for its
Byzantine mosaics and the remains of at least 14
churches.[1] One of the church mosaics is the famous
map of Palestine and Jordan, dating from c. 560 A.D.[2]
The mosaics, religious and secular, are so extensive
that very little remains from earlier periods. A Roman
reservoir to the east of the city marks that empire's
presence here. An occasional coin serves as a reminder
of the Nabataeans.

Ancient literature, including the Bible, suggests
a fuller history for Madaba. The site is 25 km. southeast of where the Jordan River empties into the Dead
Sea, and 37 km. southwest of Amman on the Old King's
Highway between Amman and Dhiban. Egyptian and other
sources suggest the Highway has been in use since 3000
B.C. Madaba may mean "full waters" in the ancient
semitic languages. One could speculate that the place
has been a way station on the highway for millennia.
The earliest specific reference to Madaba is the Bible.[3]

The book of Numbers 21:30 mentions Madaba in relation to Hesban. The date of this passage is heavily
disputed. The events may have taken place in the 13th
century B.C. The date when the verse was written down,
is quite uncertain.[4] According to this account, Madaba
was in territory ruled by an Amorite King named Sihon.
He had captured it from the Moabites. Traditionally
the territory north of the Wadi Mojib belonged to the
Ammonites. It is in their hands in the 10th century
B.C. (I Chronicles 19:7). It is back in Moabite hands
in the 9th, according to the Moabite Stone in which
King Mesha claims to have built (perhaps "rebuilt")
Madaba.[5] The town is included in Moabite territory by
the Hebrew prophet Isaiah (ch. 15:2) in the latter part
of the 8th century. The intervening centuries are unknown but in the mid-2nd century B.C. it was once again
in Ammonite hands.

The archaeological data for the Iron Age at Madaba
is also limited. Several tombs have been found on
nearby Mt. Nebo. Father Sylvester J. Saller published
two of these, discovered by Professor Julio Ripamonti.[6]
Several of the pottery forms are comparable to the material published here and will be noted in the

147

comparison section. Tomb 20 was a natural cave with a
natural arch (0.6 m. x 6.0 m.) entry. It consisted of
two chambers, 10.35 m. x 15.50 m. and 4.9 m. x 3.6 m.
Arabic, Roman and Iron Age pottery was found in three
layers. There was a great deal of pottery and a large
number of burials. Excavation halted when a large
chunk of rock broke loose and fell on Ripamonti's
assistant, Jordi Cardona, breaking several bones.

Tomb 84 was also a natural cave with an arched entrance 1.0 m. high and 2.2 m. long. Steps led down into the tomb. This tomb also had two chambers 3.6 m. x
5.0 m. and 5.4 m. x 5.0 m. Both chambers were 2.0 m.
high. The excavators found Roman and Iron Age pottery
here. Ripamonti estimated 250 skeletons in Tomb 84 and
three times that in Tomb 20 though he did not mention
whether these were all Iron Age or various dates. He
estimated 800 vessels in Tomb 20 and 400 in Tomb 84,
not counting the broken sherds.

In Madaba itself, the remains are limited to two
tombs. The earlier one in both use and discovery is a
natural cave tomb east of Madaba.[7] It may date as
early as 1250 B.C. and was in use for a century. Harding notes that the pottery is very poor in quality -
badly made, badly fired, clumsy in form. In addition
to the pots, however, there were a number of important
objects. These included bronze daggers, at least one
of which had an inlaid wood handle. There were also
bronze arrow-heads and pieces of bronze scale armor.
There were both bronze and iron bracelets, anklets,
earrings and finger rings, toggle pins and beads of
stone and glazed paste. An Egyptian presence or influence is evidenced by scarabs typical of the XIXth
and XX Dynasties (1310-1170 B.C.). There was also a
glazed Egyptian eye amulet.

The biblical record says nothing at all about such
an Egyptian presence though Egyptian literary materials
refer to East Jordan sites. Egyptian artifacts are
also known from the early part of the Late Bronze Age
from the East Jordan area. They may represent trade
contacts rather than military conquest. The artifacts
were found in the Jordan Valley and along the King's
Highway.[8]

The second tomb to be considered here is the major
focus of this study. It had no Egyptian materials at
all and dates several centuries later. It was probably

148

in use from the 10th-8th centuries B.C.[9] There were no
tool marks visible except around the entrance. The general shape also suggests a natural cave. By the time
of the writer's exploration of the cave, several years
had passed since its discovery. By this time, the owner had enlarged one end of the cave in preparation for
the construction of a cistern. Hence considerable debris had accumulated so the floor depth at the southern
end and the southern end itself could only be estimated.
A large shelf in the natural bedding planes of alternate
limestone and chert was noted on the northwest edge of
cave. When the tomb was discovered, the shelf was em-
pty.[10]

The initial discovery was in February, 1967. Mr.
Salim Ali Abu Shunnar found the tomb while digging in
his front yard, at the southeast edge of the Madaba Refugee Camp. The tomb was cleared by the Department of
Antiquities of Jordan the following month, with a work
force of 10 men. Virgin soil was reached throughout
most of the cave. Disarticulated bones were scattered
in the fill. The latter was disturbed by rock fall,
possibly the result of recent blasting in the area. No
stratigraphic distinctions were found. They may have
been there, but were too badly disturbed by the rock
fall to see. No articulated skeletons were found however and this suggests ancient disturbance as well, with
later burials made without regard to earlier burials.
The bones were deteriorated so the number of burials was
not determined. Five stone objects were found. The oth-
objects are pottery. The attached inventory shows that
many of the pieces were of similar type so only a selection are presented here in the drawings.[11]

ABBREVIATIONS

AAP	Amiran, Ancient Pottery of the Holy Land
AASOR	The Annual of the ASOR
ADAJ	The Annual of the Department of Antiquities of Jordan
ANEP	Pritchard, The Ancient Near East in Pictures
ANET	_____, Ancient Near Eastern Texts
ANEST	_____, Ancient Near East, Supplementary Texts
ASOR	American Schools of Oriental Research
BA	Biblical Archaeologist
BANE	Wright, The Bible in the Ancient Near East
BASOR	The Bulletin of the ASOR
EI	Eretz Israel
FCTP	Fitzgerald, Four Canaanite Temples of Beth-shan, Pottery
IB	Interpreter's Bible
IDB	Interpreter's Dictionary of the Bible

IEJ	Israel Exploration Journal
LA	Studii Biblici Franciscani Liber Annus
Lachish	Tufnell, Lachish III
M	This item is in the Madaba Museum
Meg I	Lamon and Shipton, Megiddo I
Meg II	Loud, Megiddo II
MQS	McClellan, Quantitative Studies
PEF	Palestine Exploration Fund
PEFA	PEF Annual
PEQ	PEF Quarterly Statement
PRS	Pritchard, Recovering Sarepta
QDAP	Quarterly of the Department of Antiquities of Palestine
RB	Revue Biblique
TBM	Albright, Tell Beit Mirsim
TN	Wampler, Tell en-Nasbeh
SS	Crowfoot et al., The Objects from Samaria

FOOTNOTES

1. Cf. Van Elderen for a review.
2. Gold, BA XXI:50-71
3. Harding, Antiquities..; Grohman, IDB-318-9.
4. John Marsh called Num. 21:21-32 JE in the JEPD system of Julius Wellhausen. J is c. 950 while E is c. 750, both Iron Age. The conflation is presumably later. March, IB 2:245.
5. ANET-820-1. Max Miller suggests line 30 may be "bt" Madaba, i.e., Mesha built a house, a sanctuary or temple at Madaba.
6. Saller, LA XVI:165-298.
7. Harding, op. cit., pp. 17, 22, Pl. 4. Harding, "An Early Iron Age Tomb of Madaba," and Isserlin, PEFA 6. Isserlin dated the contents of the tomb c. 1200-1160 while Harding put them at 1250-1150.
8. Ward, ADAJ XVIII:45-6.
9. In an independent study, Piccirillo suggested an earlier date.
10. Mr. Samir Ghishan was Inspector of Antiquities when the tomb was found. His extensive assistance and the official cooperation of the Department of Antiquities is gratefully acknowledged.
11. The inventory list was prepared with Mr. Rafiq W. Dijani, now deceased. We were assisted by Mr. Mohammed Murshed Khadijah and other members of the Department. The drawings were made by Mr. Ismail, then of the Department. These efforts, the support of the Department and its permission to publish this material is deeply appreciated. A preliminary publication was submitted to The Archaeology of Jordan and other Studies, a Festschrift for Dr. Siegfried H. Horn. Permission of the editor, Dr. Lawrence Geraty, to reprint portions of that study are here gratefully acknowledged. The final study presented here includes the complete inventory list and completed comparative notes.

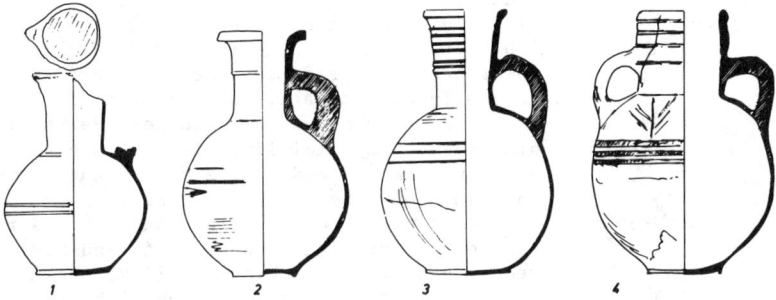

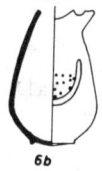

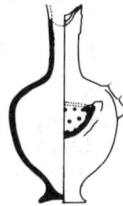

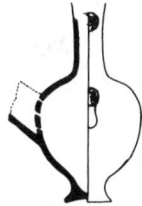

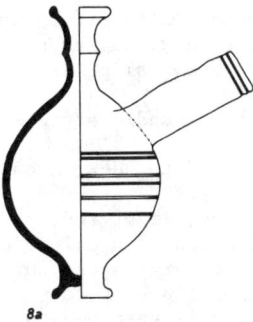

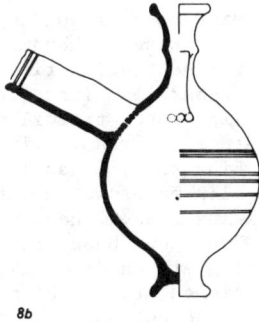

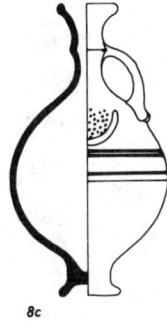

Figure I. Decorated and Sputed Jugs

151

FIGURE I. DECORATED AND SPOUTED JUGS

Fig. No.	Reg. No.	Description
1.	M59	Medium, broken handle and rim, pinched mouth, wide disc base, decorated with horizontal lines in dark red on light red.
2.	M148	1 handle attached to collar under rim, triangulated everted rim, concave disc base, dark gray slip on red ware, horizontal decoration
3.	M92	1 handle attached to collar under everted rim, disc base, parallel lines in red on creamy slip on neck and body horizontally and forming rings one the side. Repaired.
4.	M93	2 handles attached to collar under rolled rim, disc base, parallel lines on enck and body, trees on body - dark brown on light brown.
5.	399	Upper part of trefoil mouth jug, 1 handle attached to rim, brown decoration on light red - parallel lines, (?)trees on shoulder?
6.	359	Small beer jug, spout broken, 1 handle missing, neck missing, ring base, red gritty ware.
7.	130	Beer jug with strainer and spout, 1 handle missing, rim missing, long neck, low trumpet base, light red slip, burnished.
8.	250	Beer jug with strainer and half cylinder spout, 1 handle attached to collar under rim, 3 knobs under handle attachment to body profile, rolled rim, low trumpet base, light red decoaration with parallel lines in black, red in white in between. Repaired.

FIGURE II. JUGS

1.	M87	Carinated, 2 loop handles on shoulder, rolled everted rim, ring base, creamy slip on gray ware.
2.	230	Ring base, 1 handle broken, white gritty ware
3.	347	Ring base, 1 handle attached to collar under rolled flaring rim, dark brown slip, traces of parallel lines on body.
4.	M60	Ring base, trefoil mouth, 1 handle attached to rim, creamy slip.
5.	241	Ring base, 1 handle attached to neck, creamy slip on brownish ware, gritty.
6.	360	Ring base, 1 handle missing, light red, gritty.
7.	27	Round cut base, trefoil mouth, 1 handle missing attached to rim, short large neck, burnished, traces of parallel lines on body.
8.	233	Round cut base, 1 loop handle attached to neck, coarse ware, light to dark brown.
9.	149	Round cut base, 2 loop handles on widest part

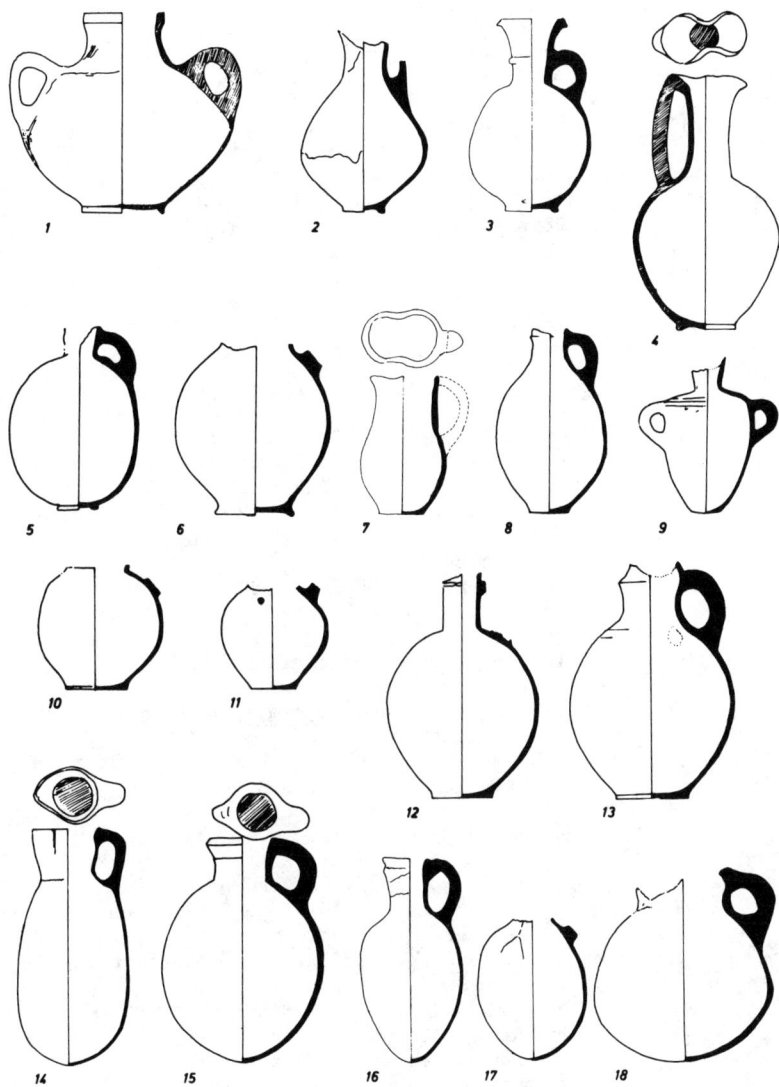

Figure II. Jugs

153

		of shoulder, rim missing, dark brown horizontal parallel lines on red poorly baked.
10.	371	Disc base, 1 handle missing, burnished, red.
11.	361	Round cut base, 1 handle missing, burnished, red, wheel made, re-used - 2 holes near neck.
12.	358	Disc base, 1 handle missing, red.
13.	282	Disc base, 1 handle attached to slight collar under rim, light red to dark brown, poorly baked.
14.	M157	Pointed base, 1 handle attached to rim, wide slightly pinched mouth, creamy slip.
15.	236	Round base, 1 handle attached to rim, pinched mouth, collar under rim, light red ware.
16.	132	Pointed base, 1 handle attached to rim, rim restored, light red.
17.	366	Round base, 1 handle missing, burnished, red, gritty ware, re-used - 2 holes in shoulder.
18.	365	Round base cook pot, 1 handle attached to rim and collar under rim, red, hard baked.

FIGURE III. JUGLETS, MISCELLANEOUS

1.	132	Cypro-Phoenician, 2 handles attached to collar under rim, round base, parallel lines in black on dark red slip. Repaired.
2.	90	Cypro-Phoenician, handle attached to collar under rim, round cut base, highly burnished, light brown.
3.	129	Imitation Cypro-Phoenician, 1 handle attached to collar under flaring rim, light red slip. Repaired.
4.	M170	1 handle attached to rim, slightly pinched mouth, round base, brownish color, dark slip.
5.	107	1 handle attached to rim, pinched mouth, round base, light red ware.
6.	39	1 handle attached to neck, rounded rim, blunt pointed base, light brown color.
7.	26	1 handle restored attached to neck, round but slightly pointed base, gray ware.
8.	124	1 handle attached to collar under flaring rim, round but slightly pointed base, light red.
9.	106	1 handle attached to slight collar under rolled rim, creamy slip on red.
10.	16	1 handle attached to slight collar under rim, light brown slip on brown ware.
11.	318	1 handle attached to collar under rolled rim, brownish slip on red ware.
12.	374	1 loop handle attached to narrow neck, round base. Repaired.
13.	22	1 handle attached to collar under rolled rim, round base, poorly baked.

154

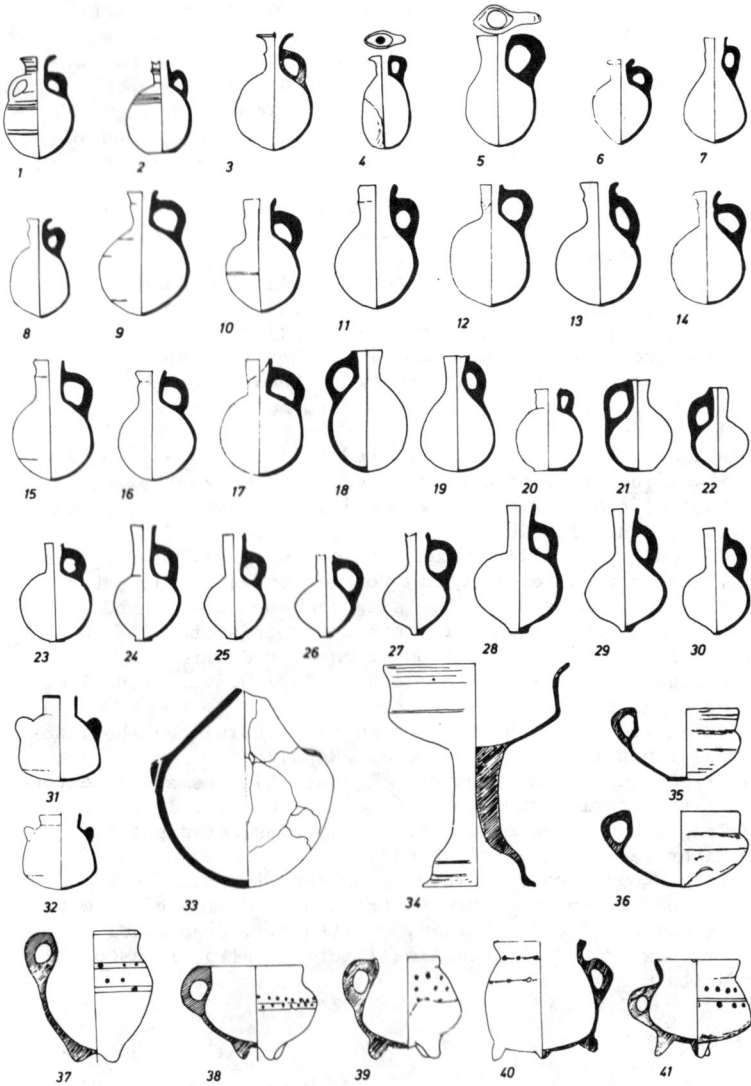

Figure III. Juglets, Miscellaneous

155

14. 122 1 handle attached to collar under rolled rim, chocolate slip on light red ware, round base.
15. 115 1 handle attached to collar under rim, light red, round base.
16. 4 1 handle attached to collar under everted rim, light brown ware, round base.
17. 50 1 handle attached to neck, brown slip on dark gray ware, traces of burnish, round base. Repaired.
18. 126 Black juglet, slightly flaring rim, round base.
19. 85 Black juglet, slightly flaring rim (broken), round base.
20. 323 Imitation Cypro-Phoenician, 1 handle, collared rim, red ware, disc base.
21. 32 Black juglet, 1 handle attached to neck, round cut base.
22. 9 Black juglet, 1 handle attached to narrow neck, vertically burnished, disc base.
23. 129 Black juglet, long narrow neck, small disc base.
24. 119 Black juglet, long narrow neck, small disc base.
25. 33 Black juglet, long narrow neck, small disc base.
26. 97 Dark brown, broken rim, small disc or knob base
27. 113 Long narrow neck, light red ware, knob base.
28. 30 Black juglet, 1 handle attached to neck, knob or small disc base.
29. 58 Black juglet, 1 handle attached to neck, knob base.
30. 59 Black juglet, 1 handle attached to neck, knob base.
31. M114 Conical type pyxis, 2 lug handles, straight rim, black ware, round flat base.
32. 111 Conical type pyxis, 2 lug handles, slightly flaring rim, light brown ware, slightly rounder base, poorly baked.
33. 171 Flask, 2 lug handles, red slip on brown ware, hand made. Originally drawn at 1:1 - other drawings at 1:2.
34. M147 Chalice, flaring rim, trumpet base, red ware.
35. M55 Carinated cup, 1 handle, light red slip, very fine limestone grits, round cut base.
36. M125 Carinated cup, 1 handle, brown slip, burnished, horizontal lines in red, round base. Repaired.
37. M104 Tripod cup incense burner, choclate slip, small limestone grits, poorly baked, perforated on the profile.
38. M227 Tripod cup incense burner, small holes, straight rim, light red slip, poorly baked.
39. M228 Tripod cup incense burner, straight rim, black ware.
40. M106 Tripod cup incense burner, triangulated rim, black ware.
41. M107 Tripod cup incense burner, everted rim, 2 parallel grooves around the profile, light red slip, limestone grits.

Figure IV.   Large Bowls

157

FIGURE IV. LARGE BOWLS

Fig. No.	Reg. No.	Description
1.	251	Large Bowl or cook pot, broad triangulated whole mouth rim, disc base, light red, wheel made.
2.	364	Carinated crater, 2 loop handles attached to triangular rim, light red grittey ware, poorly baked. Restored.
3.	M53	3 loop feet, triangulated rim, disc base, parallel lines in dark red on light red slip, burnished, small limestone grits.
4.	M163	3 loop feet, flattened inverted rim, gray gritty ware.
5.	305	Carinated crater or cook pot, 6 loop handles attached under triangular flat flaring rim, semi-disc base, dark brown, poorly baked. Repaired.
6.	356	Carinated crater, 7 handles attached to collar under a rolled rim and to widest part on the profile, creamy slip on light brown gritty ware, medium baked, disc base.
7.	M164	Deep bowl or cook pot, 8 handles attached to rim, disc and ring base, light red ware, gritty and coarse ware.

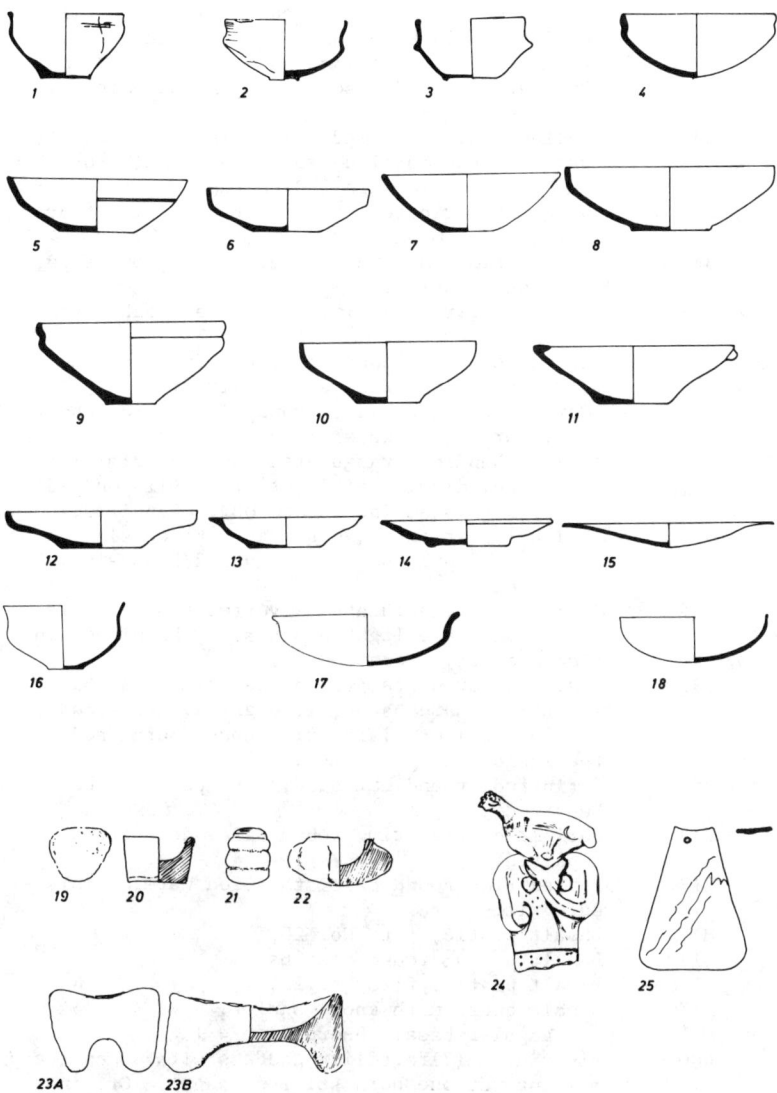

Figure V. Bowls and Objects

FIGURE V.   BOWLS AND OBJECTS

Fig. No.	Reg. No.	Description
1.	M182	Carinated, disc base, gray slip, gritty ware.
2.	M123	Carinated, concave disc base, light red slip.
3.	M131	Carinated, 14 knob handles, round cut base, light gray-black coarse ware. Repaired.
4.	311	Carinated, round base, dark gray ware and slip. Repaired.
5.	337	Rolled rim, wheel made, 2 incised grooves half way down the outside, round cut base, gray slip on coarse brown ware. Repaired.
6.	219	Slightly carinated, round cut base, light brown ware, wheel made.
7.	351	Rolled rim, round cut base, light brown slip, burnished inside.
8.	7	Carinated, rolled rim, disc base, light red, limestone grits.
9.	312	Carinated, disc base, red, highly burnished 2/3 outside and inside. Repaired.
10.	352	Carinated, disc base, brown slip inside and out, burnished, wheel made. Repaired.
11.	354	1 knob handle, trangulated inverted rim with flat top, disc base, light brown slip on red ware, burnished inside and out. Repaired.
12.	350	Slightly carinated, disc base, brown slip on red ware, burnished inside and 2/3 outside. Repaired.
13.	315	Carinated, triangulated inverted rim with flat top, disc base, light brown slip, burnished inside and out. Repaired.
14.	398	Flat bowl or plate, triangular rim, ring base, light red, hard baked, lime grits, wheel made.
15.	309	Shallow bowl or plate, ring base, burnished on the inside.
16.	357	Carinated, round cut base, red, poorly baked. Repaired.
17.	213	Carinated, flat rim, round base, dark brown. Repaired.
18.	217	Raised rim, round base, thin red ware, burnished, gritty ware.
19.	M175	Basalt pestle, fits No. 20.
20.	M179	Basalt quern, round flat base.
21.	M178	Basalt pestle, fits No. 22.
22.	M176	Basalt quern with knob handles.
23.	M177	Rectangular basalt quern with 4 legs.
24.	400	Figurine: (?)fertility goddess with sheep (head missing but one horn still present). Original drawing at 1:1 while others this page, 1:2.
25.	224	Triangular slate loom weight.

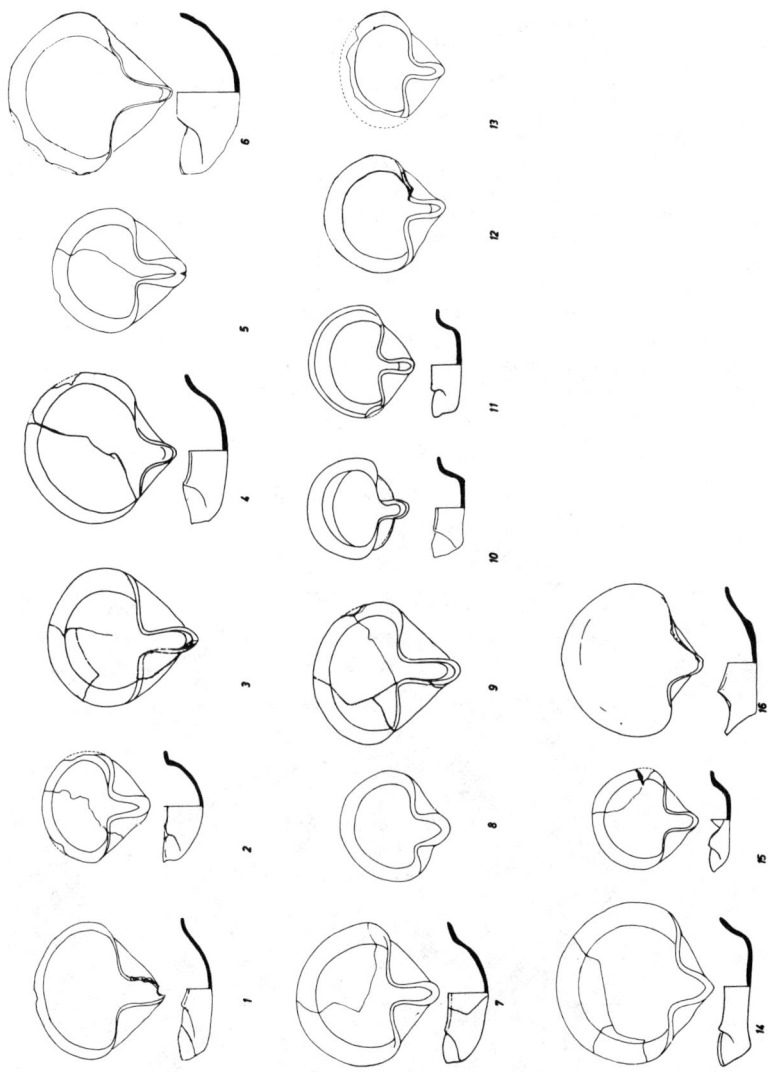

Figure VI. Lamps

161

FIGURE VI.   LAMPS

Fig. No.	Reg. No.	Description
1.	441	Shallow base, slightly flaring rim, brown, coarse ware.
2.	375	Deep base, round flaring rim, light red.
3.	244	Deep round base, dark red. Repaired.
4.	389	Deep round base, red, flaring rim.
5.	380	Deep round base, dark red, flaring rim.
6.	249	Thick deep round base, up raised rim, red, coarse gritty ware.
7.	192	Round base, flanged rim, light yellow, gritty ware.
8.	193	Round base, flanged rim, red.
9.	235	Round base, flanged rim, red.
10.	116	Round cut base, flanged rim, light yellow.
11.	206	Round cut base, flanged rim, light yellow.
12.	376	Round cut base, flanged rim, light yellow.
13.	393	Round cut base, flanged rim, light yellow.
14.	234	Flat base, flanged rim, red.
15.	382	Flat base, flanged rim, red.
16.	205	Disc base, flanged rim, red.

THE POTTERY: COMPARATIVE MATERIAL

Figure I:1-4

Mt. Nebo: Saller, Tomb 20, pp. 234-236, Fig. 21:8-14, 15, and Fig.
23:6,7,11-22.
Amman: Harding, QDAP XII:72, No. 36.
Lebanon: Chapman, Fig. 4:51, 52. c. 900 B.C.
Chatal Hüyük: Swift, p. 223, Fig. 43. Iron II (pp. 198, 201, 205).
Megiddo: Meg. I, Pls. 6:146-7, 7:162, 171, 174, 8:177 (Lev. V,
handles attached to ridge on neck and straight line decoration).
Meg. II, Pls. 75:7,8, 10, 11, etc. (decoration), 81:16,24, 88:
14,15 (handles attached at a ridge on the neck), 89:1,2 (re-
sembles our No. 4 but with a shorter neck). These examples are
from Strata VI-VA. Wright dated VI-V c. 1075-918 B.C. BANE-97.
Tell Abu Hawam: Hamilton, QDAP IV:Pl. XIII:82 has a shorter neck
but otherwise compares to our No. 1. Str. III, c. 1100-925?
Maisler, BASOR 124 (Dec 51), 21-5, suggested 980-815 B.C. BANE-
97 suggested 980-918.
Samaria: SS Figs. 2:4, 5:1, 22:5.
Nasbeh: TN-82, Pl. 35:620-22, c. 1000-600 B.C. Pl. 36:629, c. 1000
- our Nos. 2-3.
Lachish: Pl. 74:18,22,23 (Tomb 1002, c. 810-710 B.C.).
Cf. further, Hazor, TBM B3. Fara (S) and AAP-Pls. 84-91.

Fig. I:5. Cf. Fig. II:4.

Fig. I:6-8

Mt. Nebo: Saller, Tomb 20, pp. 238-9, Fig. 23:23,24.
Buseirah: Bennett, Levant VII:10, Fig. 6:2. The form also has 3
knobs below the handle, though in inverted triangle formation
rather than a straight line. The spout is broken but may have
been a half-cylinder. Rim and base are missing.
Sahab: Harding, QDAP XIII:Pl. 35:61, 9th-8th cen. B.C. The trough
like spout is shorter.
Amman: Harding, QDAP XI:Pl. 18, a zoomorphic vessel, a bull, with
a long half-cylinder spout.
Irbid: Dajani, ADAJ XI:89,97, Pls. 32:5, 33:3.
Lebanon: Hachman, Abb. 24:3, 25:4. Chapman, Fig. 2:4.
Beth-shan: James, Figs. 120:6, 56:7. Lev. VI. BANE-97 dated VI
to 12-1100 B.C.
Meg. I,Pl. 8:175. Str. V. Spouts on different forms of Iron II.
Meg. II,Pl. 75:20-22. Str. VIA. Long spout on earlier form.
SS Fig. 5:2. Lev. III. Spouts on different forms of Iron II.
Fara (S): KAHL-Fig. 66:4,6.
Lachish,Pl. 89:364 (undecorated, Tomb 521, c. 1000 B.C.). A close
parallel with a flatter base.
AAP-Pls. 84-91.

Figure II:1

Dolmens: Dajani, ADAJ XII & XIII:Pl. XXXI, Fig. 2:65. Our example
has a narrower neck.

<u>Fig</u>. II:4

Sahab: Harding, QDAP XIII:Pl. 35:48. Closer parallel than Amman,
  Samaria, Halif, Megiddo or Hazor.
Amman: Harding, QDAP XI:72, No. 36. Harding, ADAJ I:Fig. 1:26-8,
  31. Tomb C, 8th cen. B.C. Tufnell, PEFA VI:Fig. 22:109-10.
  Adoni Nur Tomb. Dajani, ADAJ XI:Pl. VI:60,44. Jabel Jofeh, 7th
  cen. B.C.
Meqabelein: Harding, QDAP XIV:Pl. XVI:20. 7th cen.
Lebanon: Chapman, Fig. 11:21.
Chatal Hüyük: Swift, p. 223, Fig. 41. 'Amuq Lev. O, Iron II.
Hazor: Yadin, Hazor III-IV:Pl. 177:15. Levels IX-X, 10th cen. Cf.
  Yadin, Hazor (1972), p. 200.
'Atlit: Johns, QDAP VI:Fig. 6:1, p. 142.
SS Fig. 10:16, Lev. VI.
Lachish, Pl. 86:241. Tomb 224, c. 860-820 B.C.
Halif: Biran, IEJ 20:Fig. 6:8-9. 10th-9th cen.
AAP-Pl. 92:108. This is a plate of Phoenician pottery, a term she
suggests is not wholly adequate (p. 272). Landes refers to the Am-
monite trefoil-mouth jugs: "Although possibly local products,
(they) show close affinity to a form which was fairly common at
sites on the Mediterranean, and which generally has been assigned
to an imported class in the Cypriote corpus of Red Slip I (III)
ware." However, Ms Tufnell suggested a Phoenician origin. Landes,
BA XXIV:87. Commenting on the Adoni Nur tomb, Tufnell said, "The
trefoil-mouth jugs nos. 109-10 could be local products on consideration of ware and quantity, and so far none have been found at Nim-
rud or at Nineveh. On looking west, however, to the coastal sites
of the eastern Mediterranean, they prove to be fairly common, and
they are an imported class in the Cypriote repertory -- Red Slip I
(III) ware. Mrs. Henschel-Simon noted the comparisons, which are
but few (QDAP XI, p. 79). If, as it appears, these jugs are foreign to Palestine (C. N. Johns, QDAP VI, Fig. 6, and pp. 129, 131,
141) and to Cyprus (E. Gjerstad, GSCE IV, pt. 2, p. 191 (Pl.
CXXVI:4)), they should perhaps, as Mr. Johns suggests, owe their
origin to Phoenicia, from whence they were diffused and locally
imitated." PEFA VI:68.
    One might speculate on their possible origin in the Ammonite
area, with examples now present from Sahab, Madaba, and Amman. Ammonites were engaged in extensive commercial activities and it is
not impossible that they originated pottery types which diffused
westward. The jug in question would be suitable for bulk quantities of perfume or smaller quantities of oils. So too, Johns noted that these oenochoai, especially the pear-shaped form, were
"trade receptacles for a product not necessarily Phoenician in origin. Phoenician traders seem to have reserved it for funeral use
and to have imported it or copied it wherever they went." He refers to Carthage, Sicily and Sardinia. He dated the 'Atlit tombs
in the 7th century, a period of Phoenician ascendency. However,
Tomb iva with the trefoil-mouth jug, may have been 6th century by
comparison of Cypriote material (pp. 121, 129-137). McClellan,

MQS-327, suggests Transjordan as the main manufacturing center, based on the high frequency of this jug in tombs. Chronologically he put it in his Period 4. Period 1 is Iron I and 2-5 are Iron II.

Fig. II:7

Beth-shan: FCTP Pl. XLVI:26.
TBM I Pl. 57:6,7 are squatter forms of the 9th cen. B.C.

Fig. II:9

Sahab: Dajani, ADAJ XV:Pl. IV:93.
Hazor: Yadin, Hazor II:Pls. 138:9, 187:2. An LB form which may have been a prototype.
Beth-shan: FCTP Pl. XLV:3, XLVII:26. Lev. V, a squatter form.
Taanach: Rast, Fig. 36:3. Similar in body but a wider neck. Per. IIB, c. 960-918 B.C.
Meg. I Pl. 9:23-4 (Str. i, III), 19:113-4, 22:130-31 (V).
'Atlit: Johns, QDAP VI:144, Fig. 8:1. Amphora disc or ring base, burial vii.
Lachish Pl. 74:14 (Tomb 223, c. 900 B.C.), 22 (Grave 132, c. 750) and Pl. 91:418-9 (c. 900 B.C.).
AAP Pl. 83:1-14.

Fig. II:14

Mt. Nebo: Saller, LA XVI:234, Fig. 23:1-4 (Tomb 20), 283, Fig. 33: 11, Fig. 34:23.
Dhiban: Tushingham, AASOR XL:Fig. 17:1,3. More globular.
Amman: Harding, ADAJ I:39, Fig. 1:20. Tomb C, 8th cen.
Taanach: Lapp, BASOR 173:Fig. 20:6. Late 10th cen.
Abu Hawam: Hamilton, QDAP IV:20, Figs. 58-9. Less comprative than Taanach.
Nasbeh: TN Pl. 38:678, c. 1000 B.C.
Lachish Pl. 88:282ff. c. 1000-700 B.C.

Fig. II:18

Taanach: Rast, Fig. 50, c. 960-918 B.C.
Meg. I Pls. 5:118 (Str. III-II), 119 (V-III), 7:167-9 (V).
Meg. II Pl. 81:7 (VI).
Abu Hawam: Hamilton, QDAP IV:22, Fig. 80. Lev. III.
SS Fig. 30:8, from "z" deep pit. A rounder form.
TN Pl. 45:954-68, 46:769-78.
Lachish Pls. 74:12,13 (Tomb 1002, c. 810-710), 75:22-23 (Tomb 106, c. 670-580), 84:186 (Tomb 1002), 187, 190 (Tomb 106).
As a concluding observation on jugs, it is of interest to note the absence of the the "decanter" jug of Iron IIC at Madaba. Cf. AAP-259, Pl. 88:1-4; Sahab, QDAP XIII:Pl. XXXV:57; Lachish Pl. 87:273-281 (c. 600 B.C.); TN Pl. 39:733-44; etc.

Figure III:1-3

Madaba: Isserlin (PEFA VI:36) noted there were Mycenean but no Cypriote imports in the earlier tomb.
Mt. Nebo: Saller, LA XVI:231, Fig. 20:4-7,17,20; 21:1,12; 22:1-11

(Tomb 20); 277-280, Fig. 34:10-13 (Tomb 84).
Dhiban. The type is common here. Cf. Tushingham, AASOR XL: Figs. 16, 21, 24, and Pls. XXV, XXIX, XXXII.
Buseirah: Bennett, Levant VI:20, Fig. 15:6.
Sahab: Harding, QDAP XIII:101, Fig. 7:64.
Amman: Harding, ADAJ I:37, Fig. 1:36-8. Tomb C, 8th cen.
Irbid: Dajani, ADAJ XI:Pl. 34:24.
Lebanon: PRS-83, Fig. 54, c. 800 B.C.
Beth-shan: James, Figs. 8:3, 9:2, 13:8, 18:21.
Taanach: Rast, Fig. 93, Per. IIB, c. 960-918 B.C.
Meg. I Plas. 1:40 (III), 5:123 (V-III).
Abu Hawam: Hamilton, QDAP IV:Pl. XIII:86.
'Atlit: Johns, QDAP VI:139, Fig. 4:1-2. Disc bases, 1 handle, no decoration.
Tel Zeror: Ohata, Tel Zeror II:Pl. X:1-2.
Tel Mevorakh: Stern, Fig. 17:15-16, Str. VII, 10th cen.
Azor: Dothan, IEJ 11:174, Pl. 34:7-8. Flat base, horizontal lines. Tomb 79, c. 9th cen.
SS Fig. 23:6-8,15.
Shechem: Wright, Shechem, Fig. 85.
TN Pl. 43:873-4, 976.
Halif: Biran, Fig. 9:14-17.
Lachish: Pls. 74:6 (Grave 147, c. 850 B.C.), 88:336 (c. 800), 337, 339 and 16 others.
TBM I:85, Pls. 39(A):13-19, 51:9 (c. 9th cen.).
TBM III:150, Pl. 15:4. Str. A, pre-7th cen.
Eẓ Ẓahiriyye: Baramki, QDAP IV:109-10, Pls. LXI-LXIII.
Beer-sheba: Aharoni, Beer Sheba I:Pl. 62:110-111, Str. II, 8th cen.
AAP Pl. 97:19,23,27.
Albright comments that these juglets appear c. 950-900 B.C. and disappear by c. 500 B.C. (TBM I:85). The round base is less common than the flat or disc base.

Fig. III:4-5

Mt. Nebo: Saller, LA XVI:232, Fig. 20:15; 22:15 (Tomb 20); 282, Fig. 34:16 (Tomb 84).
El-Jib: A. K. Dajani, Pl. IX:29-30.
SS Fig. 1:8. Lev. I, c. 900 B.C.
TN Pls. 40:758-74, 41:775-78.
Lachish Pl. 88:300-302,308, c. 850 B.C.
AAP Pls. 84:13-5, 85:12-3, 87:9-11, 88:16-8.

Fig. III:6-30

Mt. Nebo: Saller, p. 232, Fig. 20:16,19; 22:12,13,16 (Tomb 20).
Dolmens: Dajani, ADAJ XII & XIII:63, Pls. 30:48,109, 31:Fig. 2:15.
Deir 'Alla: Franken and Kalsbeek, pp. 226-7, 245-7, Fig. 70:49-52, Phase J, c. 1050 B.C.
Sa'idiyeh: Pritchard, The Cemetery.., p. 29, Fig. 46A:34,35. Early Iron Age but this form "seems to have had a long life, continuing on into the Iron II period."
Irbid: Dajani, ADAJ XI:90,94, Pls. 32:7,8, 33:9, 34:22.

Beth-shan: FCTP Pl. XLVIII:14, Str. V.
Taanach: Lapp, BASOR 173:38, Fig. 20:9. Rast, Fig. 40, Per. IIB.
  Cf. especially our 22-30.
Meg. I Pl. 2:49-54 (IV-I), 5:124-137 (V-IV).
Meg. II Pls. 87:15-8, 88:10-11 (V).
Abu Hawam: Hamilton, QDAP IV:Pl. XIII:91. Str. III.
Tel Zeror: Ohata II:Pl. X:5.
SS Fig. 23:2-4. Str. III-VI. Zayadine, Fig. 7:1-11. The tomb is
  dated to Samaria III.
Shechem: Wright, Fig. 85, 7th cen.
TN Pl. 41:798-807,810, 42:811-19,843-53, 43:854-71.
Lachish Pl. 88:309ff, c. 850 B.C.
Halif: Biran, Fig. 8:1-13, c. 10th-9th cen.
TBM I:Pl. 68(A):1-32 and TBM III:Pl. 18:1-9, c. 9th-7th cen., illus-
  trate the general type.
Azor: Dothan, IEJ 11:174, Pl. 34:1-4, c. 9th cen.
Beer-sheba: Aharoni, Pl. 62:126-8, Str. II, 8th cen.

Fig. III:31-2

Madaba: Harding, PEFA VI:30, Fig. 15:70-73.
Sahab: Dajani, ADAJ XV:32, Pl. III:278.
Dolmens: Dajani, ADAJ XII & XIII:62, Pl. XXXI:3,11.
Lebanon: Hachmann, p. 65, Abb. 25:2,7. Chapman, Fig. 22:84.
Taanach: Lapp, p. 38, Fig. 20:5. Rast, Fig. 40:12-14, c. 960-918.
Meg. I Pl. 19:98 (V).
Meg. II Pls. 77:7-10, 84:9-12 (VII-VI). These are examples of py-
  xis though without exact parallel to Madaba.
Abu Hawam: Hamilton, QDAP III:Pl. 23:19-21.
SS-177, Fig. 26:1,2 (VI). Zayadine, Fig. 7:12.
TN Pl. 74:1698.
Lachish Pl. 91:414-6, c. 8-900 B.C.
AAP-184-6, 262, 277-8, 284-5, Pl. 57:3, Pl. 96. Parallels include
Afula, Ain Shems, TBM, Fara, Tell Jemmeh. The pyxis is often trac-
ed back to an LB Mycenean form. It was widely copied on both sides
of the Jordan River throughout the Iron Age.

Fig. III:33

Madaba: Isserlin, PEFA VI:45, Fig. 15:77-86, p. 46, Fig. 16:87-93.
SS-100-101, 173-4, Fig. 1:6, Fig. 24.
TN Pl. 76:1752B.
Lachish Pl. 92, c. 9th cen., illustrates the flask. The examples
  do not compare in detail with Madaba.
AAP Pl. 96. The pilgrim flask is a very common pottery type from
the LB to the present. Our single example varies from the usual
with its lug handles and thin ware. Nasbeh is the closest example.

Fig. III:34

Amman: Harding, ADAJ I:39, Fig. 1:48.
Deir 'Alla: Franken, Fig. 69:28, Phase J, c. 1050 B.C.
Beth-shan: James, Fig. 62:8,9. Str. V.
Meg. II Pl. 90:8 (V) is somewhat comparable in the bowl though the

base is not. Pl. 87:5-9 (VI) are examples of chalices.
SS Fig. 25. Str. VI. Crowfoot thought the form might be a censor
or brazier.
Bethel: Kelso, Pl. 78:8,10.
TN Pl. 69.
Lachish Pls. 73:15 (Tomb 223, c. 900), 83:162 (Tomb 224, c. 860).
Halif: Biran, Fig. 4:8.
AAP Pl. 68. Our Madaba tomb had only two examples.

Fig. III:35-6

Mt. Nebo: Saller, pp. 212-3, Fig. 15:10,12-14; 17:1-4 (Tomb 20);
   p. 271, Fig. 31:4-7, 9; 32:11-16 (Tomb 84).
Dhiban: Tushingham AASOR XL:Fig. 1:13.
Beseirah: Bennett, Levant VII:8f, Fig. 5:16-17. Levant VI:20,22,
   Fig. 14:6.
Ezion Geber: Glueck, EI IX:Pl. VII:1. BASOR 188:32, Fig. 3:1-4.
Amman: Dajani, ADAJ XI:Pl. IX:69. Jabel Jofeh.
AAP-295,298-300. Photographs 304,315. Pl. 101:12. Amiran called
this type "definitely Judean" but does not illustrate the Judean
examples. The general form appears at Sahab, Buseirah, and Ezion-
Geber, as well as Amman, Dhiban and Madaba. Perhaps the form is
East Jordanian.

Fig. III:37-41
Pritchard, "On the Use of the Tripod Cup," has an extensive biblio-
graphy.
Mt. Nebo: Saller, pp. 205-212, Fig. 15:1-9 (Nos. 3,6,7,9 have a
   flat base); Fig. 16; pp. 267-70,292-3, Fig. 31:1-3; 32:1-10
   (Tomb 84).
Dhiban: Tushingham, AASOR XL:Figs. 16:14-18, 23:7,11. Pls. XXV:
   13-15, XXX:6-8.
Buseirah: Bennett, Levant VII:12, Fig. 7:18, no handle. Levant VI:
   20, Fig. 15:1.
Ezion Geber: Glueck, BASOR 188:32, Fig. 3:5-12.
Amman: Dajani, ADAJ XI:42. Jofeh.
Irbid: Dajani, ADAJ XI:92-3, Pls. 34:20, 39:20. Extensive biblio-
   graphy.
Lebanon: Hachmann, pp. 58,65,106, Abb. 25:1,3. No handles. Chap-
   man, Fig. 22:218.
Hazor II Pl. 55:43f (Str. VIII), 63:34 (VII, handleless). BANE-
   99 puts these strata between 900-750 B.C.
Beth-shan: James, Figs. 1:5, 3:4, 25:16. Lev. V. Nos. 4 and 16 are
   Upper V, c. 918-800. BANE-99 says 1100-980 B.C.
Taanach: Lapp, BASOR 173:38, Fig. 20:11. Rast, Fig. 51:3, c. 960-
   918 B.C. No handle.
Meg. I Pls. 23:20-23 (V-II), 31:146-7 (V).
SS-94,97,111-2,134,139,177, Figs. 5:8 (III), 26:5 (VI, post 722).
   Zayadine, Fig. 4:3.
Far'ah (N): de Vaux, RB 62:Pl. 18:1, Fig. 19:1, c. 800 B.C.
Lachish Pls. 76:16, 90:38081 (handleless), Tombs 120, 1002, c.
   800-700 B.C.
Kadesh-Barnea: Cohen, IEJ 32:70-71, Pl. 8:C, 8th-7th cen.

AAP-199-201, Pls. 62:27f, 63:15, 64:29, 65:21.
Pritchard's report confirms Grace M. Crowfoot's suggestion in 1940
that these perforated cups are incense burners. At Tell es-Sa'idiyeh, he found one surrounded by ashes in a depression on an altar.
He goes on to compare this type with non-perforated tripod cups.
Pritchard refers to 100 examples of tripod cups. There are 39 non-
perforated (wide, shallow) examples from the tombs of Amman. While
he recognizes that these may not have chronological significance,
at Sa'idiyeh they appear in Lev. II, while the deep, usually perforated cups appear in Levels IV-II. On this basis, he suggested
a date of c. 750 B.C. for the shallow cups. He noted a wide range
of 950-750 for the deeper cups. He listed a geographic ranges a-
long the rift of the Jordan Valley from the Biqa' in Lebanon to
the Dead Sea with extension westward to Gezer and Lachish and eastward to Amman. We can now add Madaba, Dhiban and Buseirah on the
eastern side of the Dead Sea. The form may have a Mycenean ancestry but Amiran noted that it is less common in Palestine than in
Transjordan. This raises the consideration of an East Jordan origin of the type. Amiran dated the incense burners Iron II, 1000-
586 B.C. McClellan, MQS-325, found their greatest frequency in
his Period 3 (Periods 2-5 = Iron II).

Figure IV:1

Mt. Nebo: Saller, pp. 246-9, Fig. 25:2 (Tomb 20); pp. 284-8, Fig.
     35:6-7 (Tomb 84).
Beth-shan: James, Fig. 52:2,13, 57:7, 59:12.
AAP Pl. 73:9. Rim forms vary but the whole mouth form is common.

Fig. IV:3-4
Mt. Nebo: Saller, pp. 251-2, Fig. 25:16-19 (Tomb 20); p. 287, Fig.
     35:8-10; 36:1 (Tomb 84).
Dhiban: Tushingham, Figs. 22:11,13, 24:26, Pl. XXVII:1,3,4. Decor-
     ated.
Buseirah: Bennett, Levant VII:14, Fig. 8:2.
Taanach: Rast, Fig. 10:4.
Meg. I Pl. 17:84 (IV-III) has loop feet on a large jar.
Meg. II Pls. 79:5, 85:6, and on a shallow bowl, 74:10 (all VI).
Tel Qashish: Ben-Tor, IEJ 31:153, Fig. 10:5.
Abu Hawam: Hamilton, QDAP IV:Pl. XIII:81. Decorated.
TN Pl. 63:1441.
Giloh: Mazar IEJ 31:18-20, Fig. 6:10, c. 1200 B.C.
Lachish Pls. 72:4, 81:118, a shallow bowl, Tomb 52, c. 1000 B.C.
The loop feet appear in MB and continue into Iron II. McClellan,
MQS-325, assigns them to his Per. 3.

Fig. IV:5-7
Mt. Nebo: Saller, pp. 240-46, Fig. 24:1-11 (Tomb 20); pp. 284-7,
     Fig. 35:1-5 (Tomb 84).
Dhiban: Tushingham, Fig. 17:16.
Hazor II Pls. 56:14 (Str. VIII), 68:5 (VI).
Beth-shan: FCTP Pl. XLVI:13, Str. VI-V.
Taanach: Rast, Fig. 41, c. 960-918.

Meg. I Pls. 18:89 (IV-III), 21:125, 32:167 (V). Meg. II Pls. 74: 12, 79:1-3 (VIIA-VIA).
SS Fig. 20:2, 3Li. III.
TN Pl. 65:1480.
Lachish Pl. 82:122 (III?), 124 (II).
Ashdod: Dothan, Ashdod II-III:22f, Fig. 4:4, Str. 8, Iron II.
AAP Pls. 69:1,3,6, 71:2,3,5, 73:3, 74:3,5. She suggested the multiple handles declined in Iron II after their appearance in I. While the 2-handled variety are common, Isserlin (p. 34) noted the absence of the multiple-handled form in the other Madaba Iron Age tomb.

Fig. V:1, 2, 16

TN Pl. 53:1154.
Muqanna: Naveh, IEJ 8:99, Fig. 6:1, Iron II, c. 900-600 B.C.

Fig. V:3, 11

Sahab: Harding, QDAP XIII:97, Fig. 3:11.
Halif: Biran, Fig. 4:7.
Lachish Pl. 81:99 (Tomb 521, c. 1000), 100 (Tomb 116, c. 875), 102 (Tomb 1002, c. 810-710 B.C.).

Fig. V:4, 9

Azor: Dothan, IEJ 11:173, Pl. 33:5, Burial 63, c. 1050-1000.

Fig. V:6

TN Pl. 55:1237.

Fig. V:8, 10

Abu Hawam: Hamilton, QDAP IV:21, Fig. 70, Str. III.
Muqanna: Naveh, Fig. 6:2.

Fig. V:14

Mt. Nebo: Saller, pp. 220-224, Fig. 19:17-27 (Tomb 20); pp. 275-7, Fig. 34:1-8 (Tomb 84).
Muqanna: Naveh, Fig. 6:4.
TN Pl. 68:1550, 1559.

Fig. V:15

Meqabelein: Harding, QDAP XIV:Pl. XVII:3,4.
TN Pl. 68:1551,1557.

Fig. V:18

Hazor II Pl. 79:8, Str. VB-VIII.
Taanach: Rast, Fig. 48:18, c. 960-918.
Meg. I Pl. 24:53-4 (IV-II).
TN Pl. 53:1176.
Halif: Biran, Fig. 4:4, c. 10th-9th cen.
TBM I Pl. 67(A):16, c. 9th cen.
AAP Pl. 101:4,6. The small bowls are of a general Iron Age type. The knobs of Nos. 3 and 11 are a bit unusual.

<u>Fig.</u> V:19-23

Beth-shan: James, Fig. 43:3,4,7,10 (V, c. 918-800 B.C.).
Meg. II Pl. 263:17 (VIB) resembles our No. 22.
Hazor II Pl. 77 shows the general type, Str. VI-VIII. Cf. also
    78:1-3 (VI-VIII), 103:19 (IV), 104:11 (VA).
The parallels are general rather than exact. The Madaba examples
follow the general pattern. Their uniqueness may simply reflect
local manufacture. The tripod form is more common our the four
feet of No. 23.

<u>Fig.</u> V:24

This broken figurine is presented as a goddess. If the dots on the
abdomen represent the pubic triangle, this interpretation holds.
In the original, this is not clear nor are the breasts prominent
as is common in female figurines. There is at least a possibility
the figurine is male. This encourages the interpretation of a tribute bearer. A bas relief of a warrior carrying a calf is pictured in ANEST-345, 37, No. 790. It is from Karatepe and is dated
8th cen. The Madaba excavator offerred an attractive suggestion.
This figurine may be an Ammonite forerunner of Christianity's "Jesus the Good Shepherd" art form. It is worth noting that Pritchard's earlier work does not show the motif of an animal around the
neck.

<u>Fig.</u> V:25

The Madaba piece appears to be unique. Meg. II Pl. 218:134 (VA)
is a thin serpentine pendant which is basically rectangular but
has a triangular top. Thus the concept is not unknown.

<u>Figure</u> VI

Mt. Nebo: Saller, pp. 199-204, Fig. 14:8-21 (Tomb 20); pp. 265-6
    (Tomb 84).
Amman: Harding, ADAJ I:37, Fig. 1:18, Tomb C, c. 8th cen.
Dhiban: Tushingham, Figs. 14:1,7,15,16, 15:1-10,16, 20:1,2,7,8,10,
    12-14, 23:14-17,19-21. Both round and flat bases.
Sahab: Harding, QDAP XIII:101, Fig. 7:75.
Tyre: Bikai, BASOR 229:53, Fig. 4:2, flat base.
Hazor II Pl. 61:16-24 (Str. VIII), 65:10-14 (VII), 74:5-10 (VI),
    88:13-15 (VA), 97:13-14 (VA).
Taanach: Rast, Fig. 51:1-2, c. 960-918 B.C.
Meg. I Pl. 37:10-15,17 (V-I). Meg. II Pls. 72:6, 74:13, 79:7-9,
    86:15,16 (VII-VI).
Abu Hawam: Hamilton, QDAP IV:4, Fig. 5, a close parallel to our
    No. 14. It is Str. II, late 6th-early 4th cen., though the le-
    vel could of course contain earlier material.
'Atlit: Johns, QDAP VI:139, Fig. 4:5 and p. 142, Fig. 6:6, 7th-6th
    cen.
Jenin: Tzori, p. 137, Fig. 2 = our No. 4.
Samaria: Zayadine, Fig. 9:1-5 = Samaria III.
TN Pl. 70. The stump base is illustrated Pl. 71:1663ff.

Ramat Rahel: Aharoni, Fig. 25:8. The base is not as flat as our
  Nos. 10-16 but it is flatter than our Nos. 1-9.
Lachish Pl. 83:140-8,150, c. 10th-7th cen.
Halif: Biran, Fig. 10:1-4, c. 10th-9th cen. These parallel our
  forms as does No. 5, 9th-6th cen., in contrast to the stump
  base, Nos. 6-8, 9th-6th cen.
Landes has pointed out that Ammonite lamps share the tradition of
Palestinian development (p. 87). Comparable examples appear on
both sides of the Jordan. For a general overview, cf. Smith. It
is of interest that we do not have stump or raised base lamps here.
While these appear in Buseirah (Bennett, Levant VII:12, Fig. 7:17),
Amman (Tufnell, the Adoni Nur tomb, PEFA VI:73, Fig. 21:82-6) and
Sahab (Harding, QDAP XIII:98), Amiran (AAP-291, Pl. 100:18-20) suggested this type is limited to southern Palestine in Iron IIC, c.
800-586 B.C. While she is wrong about the locale, the dates are
suggestive in a negative sense. The lack of stump-base lamps and
tripod shallow cups combine to a focus on the mid-8th cen. for our
Madaba tomb. If these items are of chronological significance,
their absence points to a terminal date of c. 750-700 B.C. for the
use of the tomb. This may, however, reflect cultural lag and the
accident of preservation. A beginning date of early 10th or late
11th century would seem appropriate.

INVENTORY (in addition to the numbered drawings)

Decorated Jugs
M152   Carinated, 1 broken handle, missing rim, small disc base,
        burnished red ware, traces of decoration - horizontal lines.

Trumpet Base
222   Part of a jug - a low trumpet base

Round Base
M119   Jug with 2 handles attached to rim, collar under rim, wide
        short neck, red ware.
170   Globular jug, 1 handle attached to collar under rim, broken
        rim, creamy slip on light red ware.

Round Cut Base Jugs
M146   Medium, 1 handle attached to collar under rolled rim, red
        ware, limestone grits.
M158   Slightly carinated, 1 handle, wide straight neck, red slip.
M161   See M146.
218   Medium, 1 handle attached to rim (broken and repaired), a
        slightly pinched mouth, wide neck, dark brown.
237a   Sharply carinated, 2 loop handles on shoulder, large short
        neck, red ware, rim broken and repaired; resembles pyxis.
240   1 handle attached to neck, neck missing, light red, coarse.
362   Sharply carinated, 1 handle (missing), neck missing.

Disc Base Jugs
M41   2 handles attached to profile of body, flat everted rim,
        wide neck, collar on neck, light red slip.

M45   See M41.
M103   Carinated, 2 handles on body, rolled collared rim, wide
        short neck, creamy slip on grayish body.
M115   1 handle attached to rim, broad straight neck, light red
        slip.
M149   Medium, 1 handle attached to rim, wide mouth, short neck,
        large disc base, light creamy slip on light red ware, grits.
M150   1 handle attached to collar under the rim, rolled everted
        rim, gray slip, poorly baked.
M151   Medium, 1 handle attached to rim and collar, wide short
        neck, large concave disc base, light gray slip, limestone
        grits, broken and repaired.
M159   See M115.
237b   Medium, 1 handle attached to collar under the rim, knife
        cut rim, gray slip, poorly baked.
286   1 handle attached to neck, rounded rim, wide neck, collar
        on neck and under the handle, gray slip on dark brown ware,
        poorly baked, broken and repaired.

Ring Base Jugs
M89   1 handle attached to collar under rolled rim, creamy slip,
        black ware, poorly baked.
M95   Large, 1 handle attached to collar under rim, pinched mouth,
        wide neck, gray slip, limestone grits, poorly baked.
M100   See M87 (Fig. II:1) but smaller and knife cut rim.
M102   See M100 except for rolled collared rim.
M108   Medium, 1 handle attached to rim, pinched mouth, wide neck,
        light red slip.
153a   Medium, 1 handle attached to rim, trefoil mouth, broad
        short neck, light red on dark gray ware.
M154   1 handle attached to collar under a collared rim, small
        ring base, gray slip, broken and repaired.
235   Lower part only, 1 handle missing, creamy slip on red ware.
397   Large, 1 loop handle, neck missing, light red.

"Beer Jug" with Strainer and Spout
131   1 handle attached to rim, ring base, neck broken.
137   Medium, carinated, 1 handle attached to neck (broken), rim
        missing, light red ware, clumsily made.
M153   1 handle attached to rolled rim, concave disc base, decor-
        ated horizontal lines (body only) black with white between
        on light red slip.
343   Cylindrical (about 2/3) spout, 1 double strand handle, flar-
        ing rim, collar on neck, metallic ware, upper part only.

Cooking Pots
M47   Medium, 1 handle attached to rolled collared rim, round
        base, gray slip.
M56   Carinated, collar under wide rolled inverted rim, large con-
        cave disc base, red ware, gritty.
M85   See M47.
M86   See M47.
M88   See M47.

173

M90   See M47.
M94   Up-raised rolled rim, large disc base, grayish lip on light
        gray ware, gritty.
M99   See M47 except red ware.
M109   See M47 except rolled vertical rim.
M168   Large, whole mouth, globular form, light red, gritty ware,
        broken and repaired.
355   Carinated crater or cook pot, 4 loop handles attached to
        broad flat triangular rim, large disc base, decorated with
        incised horizontal parallel lines on neck under rim and on
        shoulder, light red, medium baked, broken and repaired.

Dippers, 1 handle attached to rim
35   Long wide neck, big loop handle, globular body, small round
        cut base, light red, hard baked.
109   Pinched mouth, pointed base, light red ware.
160   Pinched mouth, collar under rim, round base, red slip.
344   Slightly pinched mouth, round base, light red.
473   Large, pinched mouth, collar on neck, round base, light
        brown, poorly baked.

Decorated and Imported Juglets
no #   Cypro-Phoenician, 1 handle, rim and part of neck missing,
        sharp carination on neck, round cut base, metallic ware,
        dark brown color, decorated with 5 horizontal parallel lines
        - black - with concentric circles above horizontal lines.
23   Imitation Cypro-Phoenician, 1 handle, globular, neck broken,
        decorated with horizontal parallel lines dark red on light.
58   1 missing handle, missing rim and part of neck, long neck,
        sharply carinated, trumpet base, burnished red ware.
77   Cypro-Phoenician, 1 handle attached to collar under rim,
        neck broken, small disc base, light red horizontal lines.
103   1 handle attached to rim, trefoil mouth, trumpet base (brok-
        en), decorated with parallel horizontal dark red lines on
        light red, with a few vertical parallel lines same color.
113   Small carinated, handle attached to rim, short wide neck,
        straight rim, small disc base, decorated horizontal lines
        in dark red on red ware.
117   Small imitation Cypro-Phoenician, 1 handle attached to col-
        lar under the everted rim, round base, light red slip.
130   Small, 1 handle, pinched mouth, narrow neck, round base,
        decorated parallel lines light red slip, small lime grits.
236   Imitation Cypro-Phoenician, 1 handle attached to collar un-
        der knife cut rim, round base, decorated parallel lines.
254   Small Cypro-Phoenician, 1 handle (missing), neck missing,
        round cut base, traces decoration parallel lines.
364   Cypro-Phoenician, handles and neck missing.
373   Globular, 1 handle (missing), neck missing, traces of decor-
        ation - black horizontal parallel lines on red ware.

Pointed Base Juglets
280   Small, red, 1 handle (missing), neck missing.
368   Black, 1 handle (missing), poorly baked.

Disc Base Juglets
M118 1 handle, long neck, light red slip, limestone grits.
156   Medium, 2 handles attached to very slight collar under roll-
      ed rim, gray slip, poorly baked.

Round Cut Base Juglets
61   2 handles attached to neck (1 handle missing), rim missing,
      light brown color.
M116 Small black, 1 handle, long neck.
266   2 handles (missing), neck missing, light red, poorly baked.

Globular Body (Round Base) Juglets
15   1 handle attached to collar under rim, dark brown.
17   1 handle attached to collar under rim, rim broken, light
      red, grits.
19   Medium, 1 handle attached to collar under rim, rim missing.
      light red slip on dark red ware, gritty.
21   Medium, 1 handle (missing), neck missing, light red slip.
25a   Medium, 1 handle (missing), attached to collar under rim,
      dark red.
27   See 25a.
66   Red, 1 handle (missing), neck missing.
71   Small, 1 handle, neck missing, light brown.
M108 1 handle attached to collar under rim.
152   See M108 but black.
167   1 handle attached to rim, pinched mouth, dark red slip.
242   1 handle attached to rim, red.
272   Medium, 1 handle (missing), neck missing, light red.
370   Red, 1 handle (missing), neck broken, poorly baked.

Round Base Juglets, 1 handle attached to neck/collar
31   Flaring rim, light brown.
37   Medium, handle (missing), neck missing, red.
39   Broken rim, light brown.
45   Black, collar under rim, broken rim.
47   Red, neck missing.
48   Long narrow neck, light brown ware.
54   Black, rim missing.
58   Neck missing, elongated body, brown ware.
60   Black, collar under rim, poorly baked.
62   Handle missing, neck missing, red.
74   Black, broken rim and neck.
83   Black, handle missing, neck broken.
86a   Handle missing, rim missing, red.
M127 Medium, collar under rounded rim, light red slip, lime grit.
M180 Light red slip, limestone grits.
M232 Dark brown slip.
M234 Medium, black, small tall neck, poorly baked.
252   Medium, handle missing, neck missing, light brown, poorly
      baked.
261   Handle and neck missing, slightly elliptical body, red.
263b Black, handle and rim missing, badly damaged.
275   Black, handle and rim missing.

175

276	Handle and neck missing.
313	Light brown.
314	Medium, handle and neck missing, light red.
466	Red, broken rim, wide short neck, squat body.

Knob Base Juglets, 1 handle attached to neck

8	Black, handle and rim missing
16b	Black, tall narrow neck.
18	Light red, broken rim, poorly baked.
20	Medium, handle restored, long narrow neck, dark brown ware.
25b	Black, rim and neck missing.
28	Black, neck restored.
31b	Rim missing, light red.
39	Medium, handle missing.
41	Black, medium, handle missing, long neck.
42	Red, rim missing, poorly baked.
43	Broken condition
49	Neck missing, brown.
51	Red.
53	Black, handle missing, long neck, burnished.
57	Long narrow neck, broken rim, gray.
72	Neck missing, light brown.
73	Neck missing, light red.
78	Neck broken, poorly baked.
79	Neck missing, light red.
80	Black.
81	Neck broken, dark brown on light brown.
85b	Black, handle missing, long narrow neck.
86b	Handle restored, rim missing, light red.
96	Black, handle restored.
114	Black, medium neck.
125	Broken rim, dark red slip on brown ware.
163	Black, short neck.
M174	Black, tall neck.
M226	Black, medium tall neck.
M230	Black, tall narrow neck, gray slip.
M231	Black, tall narrow neck.
M233	Tall narrow neck, brown slip.
M235	Black.
M241	Black, tall neck.
259	See 16, but handle missing.
261	Handle and neck missing, light brown.
262	Black, handle and neck missing, poorly baked.
264	Handle and neck missing, red slip on light red ware.
270	Broken rim and neck, light red.
273	Black, short narrow neck, handle restored.
279	Black, handle and neck missing.
281	Handle and neck missing, light brown.
342	Black, rim missing.
369	Black, handle missing, neck broken.

Pyxis, Conical Type, 2 lug handles

263a   Broken neck and rim, round base, light brown, poorly baked.
274   Round base, light red, poorly baked.

Chalices
243   Large, flaring rim, red ware, base broken off.
261   See M147 (Fig. III:34).

Handled Carinated Cups
M111   Large, handle attached to straight rim, round cut base,
       creamy slip.

Tripod Cup Incesnse Burner
346   Perforated on profile, handle and upper portion missing,
       light red ware.

Large Bowls
M64   Carinated, 2 knob handles, very large ring base, dark red
       slip.
M96   Deep carinated bowl or crater, 2 handles attached to rolled
       rim, collar under rim, large disc base, light red ware.
M97   Deep carinated bowl/crater, 2 handles attached to straight
       rim, collar under rim, disc ring base, light red ware.
M98   Deep carinated bowl/crater, 2 handles attached to trangu-
       lated rim which is both everted and inverted, collar under
       rim, large disc base, light red ware, gritty ware.
M52   Deep carinated, 1 bar handle, high ring base, gray slip.
M54   Rolled rim, disc base, burnished red ware.
M166   4 handles attached under broad flattened inverted rim, ring
       base, light red, gritty ware.
M167   4 handles attached to collar under flattened rim, disc
       base, light red slip on coarse red ware.
M202   Carinated, large disc base, dark gray slip.
M204   Everted rim, ring base, light red ware and slip, gritty ware.

Medium Bowls
M39   Carinated, 2 bar handles, rolled rim, disc ring base, light
       red ware, coarse and poorly baked.
M57   Carinated, raised rim, small disc base, burnished gray ware.
M67   Rolled inverted rim, round cut base, gray slip, poorly baked.
M110   Carinated, inverted rim, small round cut base.
M171   Round cut base, light red slip, gritty ware.
M173a Carinated, flat round base, light red ware.
M173b Rolled rim, shallw, flat base, dark gray ware.
M184   Straight rim, round flat base, burnished dark red slip.
M188   Rolled inverted rim, round cut base, burnished gray slip.
M189   Carinated, rolled rim, ring base, dark gray brownish color.
M190   Carinated, everted rim, round cut base, gray slip, poorly
       baked.
M191   Inverted rim, ring base, gray slip.
M192   Rolled inverted rim, dark gray ware and slip, gritty ware.
M194   See M190.
M195   Slightly carinated, disc base, light red ware.
M196   Flat rolled rim, round flat base, gray slip, poorly baked.
M197   Carinated, round cut base, light brown slip, poorly baked.

M198   Triangular rim, disc base, burnished gray slip.
M199   Carinated, 1 knob handle, ring base, dark gray slip.
M201   Carinated, raised tilted rim, disc base, dark gray ware.
M207   Flat flaring rim, round cut base, knife or shell burnished
        on outside and inside rim.
320   Round cut base, red, poorly baked, large grits, restored.

Small Bowls
M193   Raised rim, flat round base, gray slip on dark gray.
229   Rim missing, globular, deep body, poorly baked.
M13   Carinated, everted rim, disc base, gray slip on light red
        ware, poorly baked.
M62   Carinated, raised rim, disc base, light red slip on grayish
        ware, poorly baked.

Plates
M63   Medium, slightly carinated, rolled outside tilted rim, flat
        base, light red ware.
M187   Large flat, broad inverted rim, shallow gray ware, repaired.
M200   Large flat, ring base, dark gray ware and slip.

Deep Round Base Lamps, Flaring Rim
396   Large, light red.
202   Large, smoked nozzle, red.
214   Light brown.

Thick Deep/Round Base Lamp
M214   Medium, slightly flanged rim, pale slip, course ware, small
        limestone grits.

Round Base Lamps, Flanged Rim
153b   Small, deep, thin ware, light yellow.
199   Gritty ware.
M212   Deep saucer, raised rim, dark creamy slip, thick coarse
        ware, poorly made and baked.
M219   Medium saucer, light brown slip, limestone grits.
M221   Saucer, light red, limestone grits.
349   Large, dark brown slip.
377   Medium, red.
378   Red.
379   Broken, light red.
381   Large, gray.
388   Medium, light yellow.

Round Cut Base Lamps, Flanged Rim
M142   Large, slight flange, light red, limestone grits.
M143   Large, slight flange, slightly pinched nozzle, light red.
M144   Medium, pale slip, flat thick ware, limestone grits.
M145   Medium, smoked nozzle, light red, gritty ware.
203   Small, red.
204   Small, light yellow.
208a   Broken, deeply pinched nozzle, large round cut base, thin
        ware, light red.
209a   See 204.

211   Small, slight flange, light red slip, gritty ware.
245   See 204.
384   See 204 but broken rim.
386   See 204 but broken rim.
387   See 204 but red.
390   See 204 but slightly larger.
392   See 204.
394   See 204 but dark brown.
395   See 204 but flatter base.

Round Flat Base Lamps, Flanged Rims, Gritty Ware
M141   Large, light red slip.
M208b Medium, creamy slip, poorly baked.
M222   Large, light red slip.

Flat Base Lamps, Flanged Rims
M209b Small, dark creamy slip, thick ware, poorly baked, grits.
246   Red.
M265   Small, creamy slip, smoked nozzle.
M266   Small, light red, smoked nozzle.
383   Dark brown.
385   Small rim, large nozzle (broken).

Disc Base Lamp
391   Small, flanged rim, red gritty ware.

BIBLIOGRAPHY

Yohanan Aharoni, et al., Beer-Sheba I. Excavations at Tel Beer-sheba. 1969-1971 Seasons; Tel Aviv: Tel Aviv University, 1973.
Yohanan Aharoni, Excavations at Ramat Rahel, Seasons 1959 and 1960; Roma: Centro De Studi Semitici, 1962.
William F. Albright, The Archaeology of Palestine; Harmondsworth, England: Penguin - Pelican, 1956.
_____, "The Excavation of Tell Beit Mersim," AASOR XII (1930).
_____, "The Excavation of Tell Beit Mersim. Vol III. The Iron Age," AASOR XXI-XXII (1941-43).
Ruth Amiran, Ancient Pottery of the Holy Land; New Brunswick, NJ: Rutgers University Press, 1970.
Ruth Amiran and Yohanan Aharoni, "A New Scheme for the Sub-division of the Iron Age in Palestine," IEJ VIII (1958), 171-184.
D. C. Baramki, "An Early Iron Age Tomb at Eẓ Ẓahiriyye," QDAP IV (1934-35), 109-110.
Crystal-Margaret Bennett, "Excavations at Buseirah, Southern Jordan, 1972: Preliminary Report," Levant VI (1974), 1-24.
_____, "Excavations at Buseirah, Southern Jordan, 1973: Third Preliminary Report," Levant VII (1975), 1-19.
_____, "Excavations at Buseirah, Southern Jordan, 1974: Fourth Preliminary Report," Levant IX (1977), 1-10.
Amnon Ben-Tor, Yuval Portugali and Miriam Avissar, "The First Two Seasons of Excavations at Tel Qashish, 1978-1979: Preliminary Report," IEJ 31, Nos. 3-4 (1981), 137-164.

Patricia M. Bikai, "The Late Phoenician Pottery Complex and Chronology," BASOR 229 (Feb 78), 47-56.

Avraham Biran and R. Gophna, "An Iron Age Burial Cave at Tel Halif," IEJ 20 (1970), 151-169.

Marie-Louise Buhl and Svend Holm-Nielsen, Shiloh: The Danish Excavations at Tall Sailun, Palestine - The Pre-Hellenistic Remains; Copenhagen: National Museum, 1969.

Susannah V. Chapman, "A Catalogue of Iron Age Pottery from the Cemeteries of Khirbet Silm, Joya, Qraye and Qasmieh of South Lebanon," Berytus XXI (1972), 55-194.

Rudolph Cohen, "Kadesh-Barnea, 1980," IEJ 32 (1982), 70-71.

J. W. Crowfoot, "An Expedition to Balu'ah," PEQ 66 (Ap34), 76-84.

J. W. Crowfoot, Grace M. Crowfoot, and Kathleen M. Kenyon, The Objects from Samaria (Samaria-Sebaste Report No. 3); London: PEF, 1957.

Awni K. Dajani, "An Iron Age Tomb at Al-Jib," ADAJ 2 (1953), 66-9.

Rafiq W. Dajani, "Excavations in Dolmens," ADAJ 12/13 (1967-8), 55-64.

_____, "Four Iron Age Tombs from Irbid," ADAJ 11 (1966), 88-101.

_____, "An Iron Age Tomb from Amman," ADAJ 11 (1966), 41-47.

_____, "Iron Age Tombs from Irbid," ADAJ 8/9 (1964), 99-101.

_____, "A Late Bronze-Iron Age Tomb Excavated at Sahab, 1968," ADAJ 15 (1970), 29-34.

William G. Dever, H. Darrell Lance and G. Ernest Wright, Gezer I: Preliminary Report of the 1964-66 Seasons; Jerusalem: Hebrew Union College Biblical and Archaeological School, 1970.

Moshe Dothan, "Ashdod II-III: The Second and Third Seasons of Excavations, 1963, 1965, Soundings in 1967," Atiqot IX-X (1971), 1-219.

_____, "Excavations at Azor, 1960," IEJ 11 (1961), 171-5.

Moshe Dothan and David Noel Freedman, "Ashdod I: The First Season of Excavations, 1962," Atiqot VIII (1967), 1-171.

Gerald M. Fitzgerald, The Four Canaanite Temples of Beth-shan. The Pottery; Philadelphia: University Press, 1930.

Hendricus J. Franken and J. Kalsbeek, Excavations at Tell Deir 'Alla I; Leiden: Brill, 1969.

Hendricus J. Franken, In Search of the Jericho Potters: Ceramics from the Iron Age and from the Neolithicum; Amsterdam: North-Holland Publishing Co., 1974.

E. P. Einer Gjerstad, The Swedish Cyprus Expedition I-IV; Stockholm: The Swedish Cyprus Expedition, 1934-1937.

Nelson Glueck, The Other Side of the Jordan, rev.; Cambridge, ASOR, 1970.

_____, "Some Edomite Pottery from Tell el-Khelieifeh," BASOR 188 (Dec 67), 8-38.

_____, "Some Ezion-Geber: Elath Iron II Pottery," EI IX (1969), 51-60.

Victor R. Gold, "The Mosaic Map of Madeba," BA XXI (1958), 50-71.

Elihu Grant, Ain Shems Excavations, Part I (1931), II (1932), III (1934); Haverford.

Elihu Grant and G. Ernest Wright, Ain Shemesh Excavations I-V (Pottery); Haverford, 1938.

Edward D. Grohman, "Madaba," IDB III:318-319.

Philip L. O. Guy, Megiddo Tombs; Chicago: University of Chicago Press, 1938.

Rolf Hachman and Arnulf Kuschke, "Bericht uber die Ergebnisse der Ausgrabungen in Kamid el-Loz (Libanon) in den Jahren 1963 und 19-64," Saarbrucker Beitrage zur Altertumskunde 3 (1966), 7-107.

R. W. Hamilton, "Excavations at Tell Abu Hawam," QDAP IV (1934-5), 1-67.

_____, "Tell Abu Hawam," QDAP III (1933), 74-80.

G. Lancaster Harding, The Antiquities of Jordan; NY: Crowell, 1959.

_____, "An Early Iron Age Tomb of Madaba," PEFA 6 (1953),27-34.

_____, "An Iron Age Tomb at Meqabelein," QDAP 14 (1950), 44-8.

_____, "An Iron Age Tomb at Sahab," QDAP 13 (1948), 92-102.

_____, "The Tomb of Adoni Nur in Amman," PEFA 6:48-65.

_____, "Two Iron Age Tombs from Amman," QDAP XI (1944), 67-74.

_____, "Two Iron Age Tombs in Amman," ADAJ I (1951), 37-40.

E. Henschel-Simon, "Note on the Pottery of the 'Amman Tombs," QDAP XI (1944), 75-80.

Moawiyah Ibrahim and Gerit van der Kooij, "Excavations at Tell Deir 'Alla," ADAJ XXIII (1979), 41-50.

B. S. J. Isserlin, "Notes and Comparisons," PEFA 6:34-47.

F. W. James, The Iron Age at Beth Shan; Philadelphia: University Museum, 1966.

Cedric N. Johns, "Excavations at Pilgrims' Castle, 'Atlit (1933)," QDAP VI (1936-7), 121-152.

James L. Kelso, "The Excavation of Bethel (1934/1960)," AASOR XXXIX (1968).

Kathleen M. Kenyon, Archaeology in the Holy Land, 4th ed.; NY: W. W. Norton, 1979.

_____, "The Date of the Destruction of Iron Age I Beersheba," PEQ 108 (1976), 63-4.

_____, Digging Up Jerusalem; London: Ernest Benn, 1974.

_____, Excavations at Jericho: Vol. I. The Tombs Excavated in 1952-1954; London: British School in Jerusalem, 1960.

_____, Excavations at Jericho: Vol. II. The Tombs Excavated in 1955-1958; London: British School in Jerusalem, 1965.

_____, Jerusalem: Excavating 3000 Years of History; NY: McGraw-Hill, 1967.

Robert S. Lamon and Geoffrey M. Shipton, Megiddo I; Chicago: University of Chicago Press, 1939.

George M. Landes, "The Material Civilizations of the Ammonites," BA XXIV (1961), 65-86.

Paul W. Lapp, "The 1963 Excavations at Ta'anach," BASOR 173 (Feb 64), 4-44.

Gordon Loud, Megiddo II (Plates); Chicago: University of Chicago Press, 1948.

Edward N. Lugenbeal and James A. Sauer, "Seventh-Sixth Century B. C. Pottery from Area B at Heshbon," AUSS X, No. 1 (Jan 72), 21-69.

Thomas L. McClellan, Quantitative Studies in the Iron Age Pottery Palestine, I-III; Philadelphia: University of Pennsylvania Ph.D.

Thesis, 1975.

Farah S. Ma'ayah, "Recent Archaeological Discoveries in Jordan," ADAJ IV-V (1960), 114-116.

Benjamin Maisler, "The Stratification of Tell Abu Huwam on the Bay of Acre," BASOR 124 (Dec 51), 21-25.

Amihai Mazar, "Excavations at Tell Qasile. Part One. The Philistine Sanctuary: Architecture and Cult Objects," Qedem 12 (1980).

_____, "Giloh: An Early Israelite Settlement Site near Jerusalem," IEJ 31, Nos. 1-2 (1981), 1-36.

_____, "Iron Age Fortresses in the Judean Hills," PEQ 114 (1982), 87-109.

Benjamin Mazar, Trude Dothan and I. Dunayevsky, "En-Gedi: The First and Second Seasons of Excavations, 1961-1962," Atiqot V (1966), 1-100.

Max Miller, "The Moabite Stone as a Memorial Stela," PEQ 106 (1974), 9-18.

Abraham Negev, Archaeology in the Land of the Bible; NY: Schocken Books, 1977.

J. Naveh, "Khirbet al-Muqanna' - Ekron," IEJ 8 (1958), 87-100.

Kiyosha Ohata, ed., Tel Zeror I; Tokyo: Society for Near Eastern Studies, 1966.

_____, Tel Zeror II; Tokyo: Society for NE Studies, 1967.

M. Piccirillo, "Una Tomba Del Ferro I A Madaba," LA XXV (1975), 199-215.

James B. Pritchard, The Ancient Near East, Supplementary Texts and Pictures; Princeton: Princeton University Press, 1969.

_____, Ancient Near Eastern Texts, 2nd ed.; Princeton: Princeton University Press, 1955.

_____, The Cemetery at Tell es-Sa'idiyeh, Jordan; Philadelphia: University Museum, 1980.

_____, Gibeon; Princeton: Princeton University Press, 1962.

_____, "On the Use of the Tripod Cup," Mission de Ras Shamra 17 (=Ugaritca VI, 1969), 427-434.

_____, Palestinian Figurines in Relation to Goddesses Known Through Literature (AOS 24); New Haven: American Oriental Society, 1943.

_____, Recovering Sarepta, A Phoenician City: Excavations at Sarafand, Lebanon, 1969-1974; Princeton: Princeton University Press, 1978.

_____, Sarepta. A Preliminary Report on the Iron Age Excavations of the University Museum of the University of Pennsylvania 1970-1973; Philadelphia: University Museum, 1975.

_____, Winery, Defenses, and Soundings at Gibeon; Philadelphia: University Museum, 1964.

Walter E. Rast, Taanach I. Studies in the Iron Age Pottery; Cambridge: ASOR, 1978.

Sylvester John Saller, "Iron Age Tombs at Nebo: Jordan," LA XVI (1966), 165-248.

_____, "The Works of Bishop John of Madaba in the Light of Recent Discoveries," LA XIX (1969), 145-167.

Ovid R. Sellers, et al., "The 1957 Excavation at Beth-zur," AASOR

XXXVIII (1968).
Lawrence A. Sinclair, "An Archaeological Study of Gibeah (Tell el-Ful)," AASOR XXXIV-XXXV (1960).
Robert H. Smith, "The Household Lamps of Palestine in Old Testament Times," BA XXVII, No. 1 (1964), 1-31.
Ephraim Stern, "Excavations at Tel Mevorakh (1973-1976)," Qedem 9 (1978).
Gustavus F. Swift, Jr., The Pottery of the 'Amuq Phases K to O, and its Historical Relationships; Chicago: photocopy, 1958.
Olga Tufnell, et al., Lachish III: The Iron Age; Oxford: University Press, 1953.
Olga Tufnell, "Notes and Comparison (Adoni Nur Tomb)," PEFA 6:66-75.
A. Douglas Tushingham, "Excavations at Dhiban in Moab, 1952-53," BASOR 133 (Feb 54), 6-26.
_____, "The Excavations at Dibon (Dhiban) in Moab," AASOR XL (1972).
Nehemia Tzori, "New Light on Engannim," PEQ 104 (1972), 134-8.
Gus W. Van Beek, "Cypriote Chronology and the Dating of Iron I Sites in Palestine," BASOR 124 (Dec 51), 26-29.
Bastiaan Van Elderen, "Excavations of Byzantine Churches and Mosaics in 1973," ADAJ XVIII (1973), 83-84.
Roland de Vaux, "Les Fouilles de Tell El-Far'ah, Pres Naplouse," RB 62 (1955), 541-589.
Joseph C. Wampler, Tell en-Nasbeh II. The Pottery; Berkeley and New Haven: Palestine Institute of the Pacific School of Religion and ASOR, 1947.
William A. Ward, "A Possible New Link Between Egypt and Jordan During the Reign of Amenhotep III," ADAJ XVIII (1973), 45-46.
Theodore A. Wertime and James D. Muhly, eds., The Coming of the Age of Iron; New Haven: Yale University Press, 1980.
Fred B. Winnett and William L. Reed, "The Excavations at Dhiban in Moab. Part I: The First Campaign 1950-51; Part II: The Second Campaign 1952," AASOR XXXVI-XXXVII (1957-1958).
G. Ernest Wright, "The Archaeology of Palestine," pp. 73-112 in The Bible and the Ancient Near East ed. Wright; Garden City: Doubleday, 1961.
_____, Shechem: The Biography of a Biblical City; NY: McGraw-Hill, 1965.
Yigael Yadin, Hazor; London: The British Academy, 1972.
Yigael Yadin, et al., Hazor I: An Account of the First Season of Excavations. 1955; Jerusalem: Hebrew University, 1958.
_____, Hazor II: An Account of the Second Season of Excavations. 1956; Jerusalem: Hebrew University, 1960.
_____, Hazor III-IV (Plates); Jerusalem: Magnes Press, 1961.
Shemuel Yeivin, et al., Ancient Pottery of Erez-Yisra'el; Jerusalem: Department of Antiquities, 1958.
Fawzi Zayadine, "Une Tombe du Fer II a Samarie-Sebaste," RB LXXV (1968), 562-585.

Section

B

BIBLICAL

STUDIES

SOJOURNERS IN THE LAND

George Wesley Buchanan

Introduction

Dwellers on the earth. A group of people to whom
reference is made in the Book of Revelation has been
called by the RSV "those who dwell on the earth" (Rev.
3:10; 6:10; 8:13; 11:10; 13:14; 14:6), "all who dwell
on earth" (13:8), "the earth and its inhabitants"
(13:12), or "the dwellers on earth" (17:2, 8). There
are problems with this translation, however, because
the people involved do not include all of the people
on the earth, even when the adjective "all" was used in
reference to them (13:8). In that instance "all" of
the dwellers were set in contrast to still others whose
names were written in the Book of Life (13:8). They
were also contrasted with those who would be kept from
the hour of testing (3:10), and the seer prayed that
God would punish them for the martyrdom of those who
had been killed for the word of God (6:9-10). These
dwellers rejoiced when the two witnesses were killed
by the "beast," because those anointed prophets had
earlier tortured these dwellers (11:7-10).

Hebrew hypotheses. Charles[1] correctly noted that these
could either be considered "those who dwell on the
earth" or "those who dwell on the land," meaning the
land of Palestine. He was further accurate in observing that it would be impossible for all the inhabitants
of the earth to learn of the death of the witnesses and
send each other presents within three and one half
days.[2] He concluded that these dwellers were Palestinian inhabitants and also Jews.[3] In other examples
(3:10; 6:10), Charles thought these dwellers were non-
Christians or heathen.[4] Charles held that the expressions katoikountes epi tēs gēs, katoikountes tēn gēn
are rendered yošebym 'al ha'ares or yošebe ha'ares.
This is a reasonable deduction, since the root yšb
means to sit, dwell, reside, or remain, but Charles'
conjecture is not the only one possible. That root was
translated by 80 different terms in the LXX,[5] most of
which were some form of oikein or kathizein. Eight of
these were rendered by paroikos, which translates
either gēr or tošab "stranger" or "sojourner." It
seems evident that the crucial Hebrew terms behind this
Greek is yašab and 'eres, because the dwellers seem not

187

to have occupied all of the earth, and because the same
group in one instance is rendered tous kathēmenous epi
tēs gēs --"those seated on the land or earth" (14:6).⁶
Since the root yašab can mean both "sit" and "dwell,"
some translator evidently mistranslated it to mean
"seated," even though "seated" makes no sense in that
context. Some LXX translator also confused yašab with
šub and rendered it by apostrephein (Prov. 20:3). With
eighty different words used to translate yašab in the
LXX, with kathēmenoi confused for katoikountes in the
Book of Revelation, with 'ereṣ meaning both "earth" and
"land," there are other possibilities for the underlying Hebrew than Charles' conjecture, and English translation possibilities other than the RSV's offering.
One of these will be considered here.

Sojourners in Palestine

The earth and the land. The term yošebē ha'areṣ was
used in the OT four times when it probably meant "the
inhabitants of the earth" (Is. 24:6; Jer. 25:30, 31;
Ps. 33:14). RSV additionally renders Zeph. 1:18 "inhabitants of the earth." The term yošebē tēbēl also
had this meaning (Is. 26:18; Lam. 4:12; Ps. 33:8). The
great majority of cases, however, identify the yošebē
ha'areṣ as those who lived on the land of Palestine
(Ex. 23:31; 34:12, 15; Josh. 2:9, 24; 6:12; 7:9; 9:14;
10:18; 13:21; 24:18; 25:29, 30; Jdgs. 1:32-33; Ezek.
7:7; Hos. 4:1; Joel 1:2, 14; 2:1; Zech. 11:6) and
should be rendered "inhabitants of the land" rather
than "inhabitants of the earth."

     From the same Hebrew root comes both the expres-
sion tošab, one who dwells or sits, and also yošab,
meaning one who dwells, but tošab has the special meaning of one who dwells temporarily. Inhabitant is a
general expression, whereas sojourner is a more distinctive term. Those who were strangers or sojourners in
the land were those who lived in the land of Palestine
but who either belonged someplace else or were believed
by the citizens of Palestine to belong somewhere else.
These dwellers seem more likely to qualify for identification with those in the Book of Revelation than do
earthly inhabitants in general. The next step of this
study will be to examine the sojourners in the land to
learn their characteristics.

OT usage. Sojourners held an important role in the

formation of Hebrew life and religion. Abraham lived in Canaan as a stranger (gēr = paroikos) and a sojourner (tosab = parepidēmos) (Gen. 23:4). This evidently means that he lived there but was not assimilated among the local residents. The author of Hebrews said Abraham lived as a stranger in the land of the promise, the land he was afterwards to inherit (Heb. 11:9). He did not become a Canaanite citizen. Israelite law prohibited a priest's sojourner or hired servant from eating holy food restricted for priests (Lev. 22:10). The "sojourner" in the priest's home was apparently the priest's guest whom the priest might have been tempted to serve the kind of food he himself ate. Israelites were reminded that even when they owned land in Palestine, which they had received as an inheritance, they were still strangers and sojourners with the Lord (Lev. 25:23). They were obligated to redeem the land. The land belonged to the Lord, so covenanters were only tenants, so far as the Lord was concerned. Jews could be evicted (I Chron. 29:15; Ps. 39:12). The fellow Israelite who had to work off his debt lived with his creditor as a stranger and a sojourner (Lev. 25:35, 40). Someone who lived in the same community but was not a member of the Israelite family was called a stranger and a sojourner, even though he was wealthy, settled, and probably owned the property where he lived (Lev. 25:47). From the point of view of the Israelite invaders, all Canaanites, Hittites, and other local residents might have been classed as temporary residents to be expelled and replaced as soon as possible, even though the land they owned had been in the family for centuries. Cities of refuge were provided for strangers and sojourners who were fleeing from avengers (Num. 35:15). Rabbis distinguished between the stranger, who was a tenant, and the sojourner, who was a proprietor (GenR. 58:6), but that distinction was not always valid. The two terms were often applied jointly to the same person who could not have been both a tenant and a proprietor at the same time. These sojourners were all short term residents or non-citizens in a certain geographical area. Abraham was a sojourner in the midst of the Canaanites. Some were guests in a priest's house. Other sojourners were with God on the promised land which they were obligated to redeem. The debtor was a sojourner in the home of his creditor. In one way or another their sojourning was done in relationship to the land which they claimed for an inheritance.

Deuteronomic ethics. The Deuteronomist and his

followers encouraged Israelites to be hospitable and kind to the stranger (gēr) (Dt. 10:18-19; Jer. 7:6; Zech. 7:10; Mal. 3:5) and see to it that he received justice, remembering that Israelites themselves had once been strangers in Egypt (Dt. 23:8; 24:17-18; 27:19). The stranger was classed together with widows and orphans who needed special attention, but Jews in NT times, at least, did not feel kindly to most non-Jews who were residents of Palestine.

People of the land. The sojourners or strangers were not confused with the "people of the land" ('ammē ha'areṣ) after the time of Nehemiah. When upper class Babylonian Jews returned to reestablish the land, they found in Palestine the descendants of the local Palestinian Jews who had not been taken into captivity. The reason they had been left behind was that they were not leaders, and they had no ability to organize a revolution. There was an obvious class difference between the Babylonian Jews and the Palestinian Jews whom the former called "the people of the land," probably comparing them insultingly to the pagan Canaanites that occupied the land before Joshua's conquest.

Even though the Babylonian Jews insulted the Palestinian Jews, they did not reject them from the land. They admitted that these Palestinian Jews had a right to be there. They were not confused with "sojourners" or "strangers."

Sojourners in NT Times. In NT times there was a strong anti-sojourner movement. Jews wanted Palestine for themselves alone, and there were many sojourners there. When Herod rebuilt Samaria and named it Sebaste after Caesar, he settled 6,000 colonists in the city. These were probably foreigners, because this was one of the few cities that did not cooperate in the anti-Roman rebellion while Archaelaus was trying to obtain control of Palestine (BJ I.403; II.69). At that time Gaza, Gadara, and Hippos were known as Greek cities (BJ II.97). Herod had built for the Greeks in Caesarea non-Jewish statues and temples. Greeks in that city were numerous enough to demand and obtain from Nero control of the city (BJ II.266-267, 284). As the war was breaking out between Rome and the Jews, bands of Jews attacked the Syrian cities of Philadelphia, Sebonitis, Gerasa, Pella, and Scythopolis, and they burned both Sebaste and Ascalon to the ground. They also razed Gaza and Anthedon (BJ II.458-460). These

settlements of foreigners in Palestine helped to keep
down any type of rebellion against Rome, so they also
provided a group of Roman sympathizers which Jewish
nationalists resented. When it became clear that the
Jews were going to fight Rome to the finish, it seemed
necessary at the outset to reduce these internal sabo-
teurs, the sojourners of the land. The sojourners,
then, were unwanted non-Jewish residents in Palestine.
The so-called "dwellers on the earth" in the Book of
Revelation were also people whom the author disliked.
This is only one of the reasons for thinking that those
who have been called "dwellers on the earth" were
really "sojourners on the land." The following analysis will support this possibility.

Saints and sojourners. At the hour of testing, the
sojourners of the land would be punished, but the Lord
would keep those who had kept his word. On those who
were not sojourners the Lord would write his new name
and the name of the new Jerusalem which comes down from
heaven (Rev. 3:7-12). When the fifth seal was opened,
and the seer saw under the altar the souls of those who
had been slaughtered because of their witness to the
word of God, he cried out, asking God how long it would
be before God avenged those sojourners on the land,
implying that these were the ones responsible for the
deaths of the martyrs (6:9-10). Following the type of
the exodus plagues, four angels blew their trumpets,
after which four different plagues fell from heaven.
Then the eagle flew in the middle of heaven, crying
out, "Woe, woe to the sojourners on the land, because
of the rest of the trumpet blasts which the three
angels are about to sound" (8:13). The two witnesses,
who were identified both with Elijah and Elisha and
also the two olive trees that symbolized the high
priest and the king, were killed, and their bodies were
left unburied in the streets of Jerusalem for three
days. During that time, the sojourners of the land rejoiced at their death and held celebrations, because
the witnesses had previously tortured these sojourners.
From the view point of the seer, the two witnesses were
God's chosen messiahs, and the sojourners were some of
his enemies (11:1-11). Following the typology of Dan
7, a beast came up out of the sea who epitomized all
four beasts in Daniel. This new antitype of Antiochus
Epiphanes was given authority for forty-two months (or
three and a half years), during which time he spoke
blasphemies and made war against the saints. This
beast had authority over every tribe, people, tongue,

and nation. He was also worshipped by the sojourners
of the land. These sojourners, like all the tribes,
peoples, languages, and nations under the beast's
authority, were the ones whose names were not written
in the Book of Life. There followed another subordinate
beast, who apparently acted as an agent of the first
beast. It exercised the authority of the first beast
and made the land and its sojourners worship the first
beast. Its great signs deceived the sojourners of the
land into making an image of the first beast. Those,
then, who would not worship the image of the beast,
namely the non-sojourners, would be slain (13:1-15).
The sojourners here were set in contrast to those who
would not worship the beast. Therefore, they did not
comprise all those inhabitants of the earth. In this
typological narrative, the first beast was probably
Rome, and the second beast who worked under Rome's
authority, probably represented some of the Herods who
ruled Palestine in behalf of Rome. They instituted
Roman policies, erected Roman temples and statues, and
enforced Roman law on Jews in Palestine. They evidently had the cooperation of a group of non-Jews who lived
in Palestine as sojourners.

The RSV rendered Rev. 14:6 as "those who dwell on
earth," even though it literally means "those who are
seated" either on earth or on the land. The translators
were correct, however, in recognizing that the group
involved was the same group as those others who dwelled,
either on the earth or on the land. In this case the
sojourners were classed again with every nation, tribe,
language, and people (except the Jews) as the recipients
of an eternal gospel which commanded them to fear God
and give him glory. This would happen just before the
new Babylon fell (14:6-8, 12). This means all Gentiles
in foreign countries, as well as those in Palestine,
would be forced to accept the God of the Jews and submit to his decrees. Although they had put their confidence in Rome, Rome would fall as Babylon had fallen
before.

In a vision the seer was shown the great harlot
(Rome), with whom the kings of the earth had committed
adultery and with whose wine of adultery the sojourners
of the land became intoxicated (17:1-2). These sojourners were cast in an unfavorable light. They were
those who were aligned with all other nations, peoples,
tongues, and tribes. They gave allegiance to Rome,
worshipping its image and becoming intoxicated with its

192

association. They opposed the messianic movements that originated in Jerusalem. They were responsible for the deaths of the martyrs, and when the day of God's visitation came, they would be punished along with the rest of the Gentiles who lived outside of the land.

<u>Palestine and the Apocalypse</u>. When this group of people whom the seer disliked is understood as a group of sojourners on the land of Palestine rather than a general group consisting of all the inhabitants of the earth, it becomes more obvious that the promised land is the central geographical unit in the Book of Revelation. The one who had authority to open the seals of the scroll was the Lion from the tribe of Judah of the root of David (5:5)--obviously someone from Palestine. After the Lamb had opened the sixth seal, there were so many plagues that great leaders fled and hid in caves and rocks of the mountains (of which there are many in Palestine) out of their fear of the Lamb's anger. Since the Lamb was situated at Jerusalem, the geography seems to have been designated against Palestinian background (6:12-17). Crowds of people were expected to gather before the Lamb on his throne with palm branches, Jewish nationalistic symbols (7:9-10). That the Lamb was located at Jerusalem is evident from the claim that the 144,000 would be gathered together with him on Mount Zion (14:7). The bride of the Lamb was to be the holy city, the new Jerusalem (21:9-27). In that city, as in Ezekiel's vision of Jerusalem, was a stream of water with fruit trees on either side. There also was to be the throne of God and of the Lamb (22:1-5). The two messianic witnesses were to have been active and to have been killed in the great city-- apparently Jerusalem (11:7-8).

The northern border of the promised land was believed for many years to have been the river Euphrates.[7] It was probably on this basis that the seer visualized four angels released from the river Euphrates (9:13-14). The antitype of the Egyptian plagues were expected to include drying up the river Euphrates, so that the kings of the East could come to Israel's assistance. This was probably an anticipated miracle to expedite the military support of the Parthians in opposing Rome (16:1-14, esp. 12).

Following the harvest and winepress metaphor of which Joel's prophecy is the prototype, the seer visualized a great battle at the valley of Jehoshaphat in

the Kidron valley, just opposite the temple area of
Jerusalem (14:14-20). This would also recur in the
same place after the millennium was over. Then Satan
would lead all nations together for battle, according
to the same type. The nations would surround the beloved city (of Jerusalem) where the camp of the saints
was gathered (20:7-9). Immediately following this
battle, there would be a judgment, apparently right
there at Jerusalem (20:11-15). When the seventh angel
poured out its vial, there would be terrible natural
catastrophes, and the great city would be divided into
three parts, the cities of the nations would fall, and
God would remember great Babylon for punishment (16:17-
19). This may reflect the events at the beginning of
A.D. 70, when Jerusalem was divided into three parts,
each part governed by a different pretending, zealotish
messiah--John, Simon, or Eleazar. At that time there
were wars in many parts of the world, and Rome was engaged in another civil war (BJ V.21). This would follow the sixth angel who poured out its vial just before
the great battle at Mount Megiddo, an important fortification at the end of the Carmel range in Palestine
(16:12-16).

Cosmic influences. Apart from Palestinian geographical
sites in the Book of Revelation were only those of
typological significance, such as Sodom or Egypt, along
with the enemy nation, Rome, who was represented by
terms like "beast," "dragon," and "harlot." To be sure,
there was a great deal of mythological activity described in relationship to heaven, but even this was
patterned after Jerusalem, the temple, and the ministers
who functioned there. The angels were like heavenly
priests and Levites, and the heavenly temple fixtures,
such as the throne and the tent were prototypes of those
in Jerusalem.[8] Natural and supernatural heavenly activity of cosmic proportions did not preclude earthly
events of local significance. When the sun stood still
for Joshua, he won a battle that was important for con-
quering the land. The stars in their courses fought
against Sisera so Deborah and Barak could win the battle. When the Reed sea miraculously opened up, the
Israelites escaped from Egypt. Also in the Book of
Revelation, angels poured out vials of curses, and blew
trumpets. There were earthquakes, and fire fell from
heaven, but the end result desired was that Rome would
be defeated, Jews would be liberated to rule at least
Palestine and possibly the whole Roman world under the
leadership of their own messianic king from the Davidic

line. When all of this happened, the Jewish merchants
who dealt with Rome would weep, and God would punish
those sojourners of the land who had supported Rome
against Jewish nationalistic efforts.

Conclusions

Although the Greek expressions, which the RSV
translated to mean the inhabitants of the whole earth,
can hypothetically bear that meaning from the purely
linguistic point of view, there are several reasons why
that meaning does not satisfy the contexts in Revelation
in which the term occurs: 1) The group in question was
clearly not a general group including all humankind;
2) the group was not associated with the whole world,
geographically; and 3) the members were always hated by
the author of Revelation, who was not a complete mis-
anthropist. These same problems do not occur when the
members of the group are considered "sojourners in the
land," which is an equally valid translation from a
purely etymological point of view. Contextually, "sojourners of the land" is a much more satisfactory
translation, because there were sojourners in Palestine
who were hated by nationalistic Jews of NT times. They
constituted only a small portion of humankind, and they
were closely related to problems of Jews in the promised
land in NT times. For these reasons it is more satisfactory to call this group "sojourners of the land"
than "inhabitants of the earth."

FOOTNOTES
1. R.H. Charles, A Critical and Exegetical Commentary on the Revelation of St. John; Edinburgh: 1963, I, loc cit.
2. Ibid., p. 289.
3. Ibid., p. 290. S. Brown, "'The Hour of Trial' (Rev. 3:10),"
JBL 85 (1966), 309, held that the phrase "upon the entire earth"
(3:10) precluded the possibility that the inhabitants referred to
only those in Palestine. But just because the test was to come upon all the Roman world (tēs oikoumenēs holēs) does not mean the
dwellers who would be tested at that time were the only ones to be
punished or that they inhabited the whole world, as Brown thought.
Brown argued that the expression must be translated "the inhabitants of the earth," but it could not mean all human beings without exception (pp. 311-2). Therefore they must refer only to the
enemies of the church. Brown clearly saw that the dwellers were enemies of the faithful and not all the inhabitants, but his deduction from this that the dwellers must not be only Palestinians
does not follow. F. Duesterdeich, Critical and Exegetical Handbook
of the Revelation of John tr. H.E. Jacobs; Winona Lake, 1883, 1979,

rendered the passages to mean inhabitants of the earth, although
he once held that it meant the unbelieving inhabitants (p. 173),
and at another place it meant the inhabitants of Jerusalem who
represented all the inhabitants of the earth (p. 319).
4.   Charles, ICC I:90, 175.
5.   So C. Dos Santos, An Expanded Hebrew Index for the Hatch-Red-
path Concordance to the Septuagint; Jerusalem: n.d., p. 87.
6.   J.M. Ford, Revelation; Garden City: 1975, p. xxxvii, rendered
the passage, "those who are enthroned on the earth." She translated the other passages as those who dwelled on the earth. Brown,
"Trial," thought the seer intentionally changed the verb to "seated" in the phrase "with the same conceptual content," because
this context has no pejorative moral overtones (f.n. 7, p. 309).
Brown, however, overlooked the overtones that are there. The "e-
ternal gospel" announced to these people was not good news to them.
As in Second Isaiah, the good news announced that the land was a-
bout to be restored to the Jews. That was good news to the Jews,
but not to the foreigners who lived in Palestine, as well as the
other Gentiles of every nation, tribe, language, and people (14:6).
When God acted, these would be terrified, expelled, and forced to
give God glory (11:13; 14:6-7).
7.   GWB, The Consequences of the Covenant; Leiden: 1970, pp. 91-109.
8.   GWB, To The Hebrews; Garden City: 1972, pp. 157-162.

BIBLICAL INSIGHTS FOR MODERN ISSUES

Thurman L. Coss

Once each year the bishop in our church conse-
crates ordinands for the ministry of our church. With
the solemnity and dignity appropriate to the occasion,
the bishop says "Take thou authority as an elder in the
Church to preach the Word of God, and to administer the
holy Sacraments in the congregation." Awed and inspired, these persons go forth to accept the challenge
and the sacred opportunity of being ministers for God,
perhaps blissfully unaware of some of the problems and
criticism which will confront them in the parish.
Their tasks will be rewarding but not easy. It is primarily for these persons that the following pages are
written. If I can provide a new insight or two for
their preaching, I shall be content. Professor Toombs
has already done this in his book, THE OLD TESTAMENT IN
CHRISTIAN PREACHING, but since that work was published
in 1961, some new issues have arisen which invite our
attention. I shall attempt to address some of them
here, but first a few words about the challenges and
the pitfalls of preaching the Word of God.

Quoting a poll conducted by the Roper Center at
the University of Connecticut, William Buckley proceeds
to raise the alarm about what is going on in our seminaries. From Buckley's conservative point of view,
these seminaries have become "liberal hotbeds" where
three out of four of the faculty are Democrats. If our
preachers are failing to preach the pure word of God,
the problem may begin with their professors.

According to Buckley, "there is considerable ignorance among theologians about what is going on in the
world of political and economic thought."[1] Noting the
imbalance in the distribution of food on a worldwide
basis, these professors become unbalanced in their
judgements and quickly assume that the fault for this
inequity must surely lie at the feet of the more developed nations, especially the United States, since obviously people who are hurting with hunger cannot be
held responsible for the misery which they certainly do
not enjoy.

These misguided professors believe overwhelmingly
that repressive regimes backed by the United States are
a much greater threat to the stability of the modern

197

world than communist expansionism. They pay for full
page advertisements in prominent periodicals and news-
papers decrying the nuclear arms race (sentimentally
unaware that given the sinful nature of human beings
there are times when such weapons are essential). Ap-
palled by what they regard as excessive spending on
defense when entitlement programs for the poor are being cut, these teachers can be counted on to vote for
the likes of McGovern and Carter.

Buckley does hold out some hope in the midst of
this depressing turn of events. Professors do care
very much about deprived persons. Their problem is
muddleheadedness not compassion. Their possible salvation? They do believe in God, and God is "merciful
toward the invincibly ignorant." Unfortunately, these
theologians do pass along their ignorance to their students who tend to perpetuate their errors in the pul-
pits of our land.

If it were only Buckley and his conservative colleagues on the right chiding us theologians and preachers, we might be cowed into retreating into the safety
of our dogmatic rubrics, content to stimulate a little
intellectual thought about theology, but careful to
avoid taking sides when economic, social, and political
matters come up for discussion. We could concentrate
on comforting affirmations of God's love and forgive-
ness, while refraining from pronouncements about reform in areas where we are untutored, or at least
tutored badly.

The pesky theologians, however, will not allow us
to escape criticism in this matter. Speaking on behalf
of liberation for black people, James H. Cone says,
that Black Power means "complete emancipation of black
people from white oppression by whatever means black
people deem necessary."2 And Letty Russell refers to
the cri de coeur of the oppressed everywhere, but in
her case especially women, who have not been permitted
to realize their full dignity as human beings.3 Is
there no respite from these persons who throw Camus in
our face, telling us that "it is better to die on one's
feet than to live on one's knees"?

There are some, of course, who recommend simplis-
tically that the answers to all of our dilemmas are to
be found in the Bible. A little investigation reveals
that what this quite often means is that we should be

against abortions, homosexuals, ERA, and for prayer in public schools where by law teachers will be required to teach Creationism along with evolution. These same persons are not quite as quick to tell us what to do with a Bible that commands death for all non-virgins, and for all those taken in adultery. Anyone who follows the latest polls knows how such behavior would decimate the populations of both schools and churches, not to mention the fact that adherence to the biblical injunctions at these points is now quite illegal in some countries. And most of us would abhor the thought that God could be party to sending out two she bears to tear and mutilate forty-two little boys who made the mistake of jeering the bald pate of a holy man of God.

Karl Barth offers a corrective for such glib solutions to the ills of our world when he says,

> The Bible is an embarrassment in the school and foreign to it. How shall we find in the life and teaching of Jesus something to "do" in "practical life"? Is it not as if he wished to say to us at every step "What interest have I in your 'practical life'? I have little to do with that. Follow after me or let me go my way!"[4]

So much for the Bible as a quick and easy guide to solutions for the moral, political, and social problems of our age. Called by Amos to let justice roll down like the waters, we are left on our own to find out how to get justice in El Salvador and South Africa and in our own country.

Buckley makes an obvious point. Theological expertise and political acumen do not necessarily go together. The bishop's ordination to preach the Word of God ought not become an easy license for pontifications about matters where we are inadequately trained.

There is one last disturbing thought before we try to provide biblical insights for modern issues, a thought which comes from the Radical Theology ("Death of God" theologians) of the sixties. Writing for this group, William Hamilton says, "I do not see how preaching, worship, prayer, ordination, the sacraments can be taken seriously by the radical theologian."[5] To make very clear the theological position of this group of thinkers, Hamilton goes on to say, "We are not talking about the absence of the experience of God, but about the experience of the absence of God."[6] For Hamilton, the time has come to proclaim the death of God (Requiem aeternam deo) even as he observes that Christian atheists (!) are waiting and searching for a language and a style "by which we might be enabled to stand before him once again, delighting in his presence."[7]

Have we become so clever in our mythmaking that we have explained away the mystery that was once God? Is it perhaps absurd to proclaim the sovereignty of God in the face of seemingly meaningless suffering? Does the Incarnation tell Christians all they need to know about the purpose of human existence? Can we, indeed, proclaim the death of God?

By this time, the complexities of being a pastor and proclaiming the Word are becoming embarrassingly clear. We are called to effect justice, but woefully ignorant of the complexities of the ills of our time. Liberation Theology calls us to act now. Radical Theology warns us of the futility of our traditional preaching. Feminists want us to make our language more inclusive, and ecologists want us to preserve creation. The Moral Majority suggests that the answers are in the Bible. We cannot hope to solve such momentous problems in one little essay, but we can address ourselves to one or two issues and make occasional suggestions about biblical insights which may be relevant for our thinking as we search for solutions.

A Case Study for Liberation Theology

The Reverend John Fife of the Southside Presbyterian Church in Tucson, Arizona, has been a leader in the movement of some forty churches in the United States to offer sanctuary to refugees from other countries who come to the United States seeking asylum. Fife reportedly arranged for the first such sanctuary in March, 1982. Two months later, a Minnesota friend of Fife met with him at the General Assembly Mission Council of the United Presbyterian Church and began a discussion which would culminate in the offering of sanctuary to Rene Hurtado (an alias used to protect his family who remains behind in El Salvador) in the St. Luke Presbyterian Church of Wayzata, Minnesota. With the cooperation of this church, I have obtained an interview with Rene, parts of which I would like to present here as evidence of the complexities of preaching the word and applying the Christian gospel to the intricate social, economic, and political problems of our day.

Q: What is your name, and how long have you lived in El Salvador?

A: My name is Rene Hurtado. I am twenty-five years of age. I have lived in El Salvador all my life, except for the last few months when I have lived briefly in Los Angeles, El Centro, Idaho, and now here in Wayzata.

Q: Why did you flee from your own country?

A: There are many reasons. I would like to tell you about them. First, it is very important for you to know that I was born of peasant parents and was very poor. Prior to entering the military service, I had received only six years of schooling. This was all the education my family could afford. We were destitute.

Q: Why did you enter the armed forces of your country?

A: For economic reasons. I thought by entering the service I would not only acquire a measure of economic security for me and for my family, but would also be able to pursue my education further. I did, in fact, receive two more years of schooling, but it was nothing in comparison to what I had hoped to achieve. I remained in the army for six and one-half years during which time I served as a parachutist, a military policeman, and in army intelligence. I really thought in those days that by serving in the military I could help my people and also improve my own financial situation.

Q: Were you able to achieve these goals, and if not, why not?

A: No, I was not able to achieve these goals. To my surprise, the military police served to dehumanize the populace instead of promoting its welfare. I found myself becoming dehumanized as I served. I began to lose sight of the laws of morality, as did the others who served with me. In such an atmosphere, a person begins to turn into an animal. At first, I was very young and susceptible to all the new ideas presented to me in the military, but when this force, which was supposedly set up to protect the people, began to kill and torture the peasants, I began to question the policies.

Q: Can you tell me more about this alleged mistreatment of the peasants by the military?

A: Yes, I can. I have seen the soldiers gouge out the eyes of their victims. I have seen them cut out tongues and cut off genitalia even before they killed the people. Even I was commanded to cut off the head of a little child who was already dead. I refused to obey this order, and this was the beginning of a process which ended in my being discharged from the service. My superiors interpreted my refusal to obey this order as a sign that I was a guerrilla sympathizer, and some of my fellow soldiers taunted me with the remark that I should find refuge with nuns so that I would not have to see such things.

Q: And all of this has something to do with your wanting to flee from El Salvador?

A: Yes, I could no longer believe that all of the peasants and church people we were killing were really communists as I had been told. I began to read my Bible, and I began to doubt that all of the students, priests, and poor people were really communists, and even if they were, is this sufficient reason for killing them? The answer I gave to myself was, "No!"

Q: If the military is as inhumane as you suggest, why, given the opportunity, did so many people vote for Roberto D'Aubuisson in the last general election?

A: I am lacking information on this point, but I do know that the very president of the electoral commission admitted that there was fraud. I also think that in part this election was planned with aid from the Department of State of your own country with the purpose of legitimizing the Christian Democratic Party which your country supports. It is also true that opposition candidates feared for their lives if they really attempted to run against the government approved slate of officers, and the common people feared death if they failed to vote for the government slate. These elections should have been more believable.

Q: Who killed Archbishop Romero?

A: I do not know who actually carried out the act, but I know who gave the order.   Roberto D'Aubuisson. The order was given because in these later times, the Catholic Church has, on the whole, taken a clear stand for the peasants, the poor, the hungry, the sick, and the undereducated.   Since the government oligarchy clearly favors the rich minority, there was felt a need to kill such a courageous and outspoken critic of government policies as Archbishop Romero.

Q: How much arable land is controlled by the peasants?

A: Our country is a small country of about eight thousand square miles.   Eighty percent of this land is controlled by perhaps fourteen families, at most thirty families.   This means that more than 5,000,000 people must eke out an existence on only twenty percent of the arable land.   To do this, peasants must work long hours on unproductive hillsides to grow their crops.   The redistribution of the land is a very great need in our country.   The poverty is so great that our people are faced with the alternative of either dying of hunger and disease or fighting.   In such circumstances I think it is permissible to fight rather than to die.   This is why I could no longer be a part of the military which conveniently called all of these people communists in order to have an excuse for killing them whenever it chose to do so.   If Christ were here, whose side would he have been on?

Q: You say that the present day Catholic Church has gained the enmity of the right wing and certain factions within the government because of its sympathy for the poor.   Has the church always taken this stand?

A: No!   In earlier days the Church took the opposite side.   The Church aligned itself with the rich and the landowners.   Portions of the Church still side with the wealthy, but on the whole the church, especially the local priests, are on the side of the poor.   In the earlier days, the Church taught us that we should become reconciled to our poverty, because God had ordained that some people should be rich while others are poor.   The Church had taught us to believe that our rewards would come in heaven when there would be justice and equality for all, but now a time of renewal has come to the Church, and the Church is helping the poor in their struggle against the rich.

Q: What can our country best do to help your
people? How do you feel about our military aid to your
government? Do you favor negotiations between the guerrillas and the government?

A: Your country should quit interfering. Period!
El Salvador is an independent country. The United
Nations charter says that every nation should have self
determination. When our laws are unjust, our people
have the right to revolution. The kind of help your
country is giving perpetuates the internal problems of
our country. You should leave our country alone, without help to any side. Then we shall see whom the people
really support. We would welcome economic assistance
in the form of food and medical care for our people.
Ten percent of our children are born suffering from
malnutrition and five percent die before they get to be
one year old. We could use help here.

Yes, I do favor negotiations, but they must be
negotiations without preconditions attached. The present government is imposing conditions which are totally
unacceptable to the guerrillas. These guerrillas, who
are about seventy percent Christian, have often proposed
dialogue, but the government fears free discussion and
democracy lest the cherished predominance of the few
come into question.

Q: What do you see for your own future?

A: I would like to return to my own country and
help my people, but this, of course, cannot happen unless there is a radical change in the government. I
have asked for asylum twice in your country. Both times
I have been turned down because your government claims
that I have no evidence that I would be persecuted if I
returned to El Salvador. [The interviewer would note
that it is precisely at this moment when our own country
has granted political asylum to Hu Na, China's top rank-
ing tennis player, under the assumption that Hu Na would
be persecuted if she returned to her homeland!]

Q: One last question: Why have the murderers of
the four church women not been brought to justice?

A: Those who are directing the investigation do
not find proofs and evidence. This is not because the
evidence is not readily available, but if the available
evidence were brought to light it would certainly

implicate high officials in the present government and in the military. Of course, the evidence will not be collected. [And here the interviewer notes that Judge Luis Alonso Melara in El Salvador has just ruled that the testimony of one of the five national guardsmen implicated in these murders is inadmissable in the trial of the other four. The resolution of the December, 1980 murders seems at least as remote now as ever. A group of lawyers from our own country, visiting in El Salvador, has characterized this action as indicative of the "shocking pattern of official indifference" in a judicial system which has become a "shambles".]8

Problems of the Case Study

The problems arising from this case study are legion. As far as Rene Hurtado is concerned, we could question both his understanding and his motivation. Can a relatively young man of limited academic training be relied upon to understand and report accurately the complex issues involved in the political, economic, and social turmoil of his own country? Rene may be sincere and well intentioned, but not fully aware of the threat of communist infiltration into his own country. Critics might even suggest that our young defector is clever enough to fabricate a tale designed to win for himself political sanctuary and economic security in the United States. Beyond these possible doubts, there are even greater problems.

Is it wise to break the established laws of the land? Socrates preferred to die rather than defy the laws of Athens. No less a person than Archbishop John Roach, President of the National Conference of Catholic Bishops has reportedly urged the churches in his own archdiocese not to provide sanctuary for those who may be illegal aliens. Archbishop Roach's reasoning apparently is that the good achieved by such civil disobedience cannot outweigh the possible dangers of engendering disrespect for the duly established laws of the land. We would not want to live in a nation where everyone felt free to break the law whenever his or her conscience so dictated, or would we? One person may argue that to attack the law is to attack the core of order, while another can argue that the breaking of certain laws becomes a sign of compassion and an effective witness against legislation which, in fact, deprives persons of their human rights.

There are certainly practical concerns as well as theoretical questions involved in the granting of sanctuary. Is the granting of sanctuary by the church really a punishable offense under our laws? Some would say that such behavior is a felony for which a fine of $2,000 and/or five years imprisonment can be meted out. If this should happen, who suffers the consequences? Who pays the fine? Who goes to prison? The pastor? The chief administrator of the guilty church? Where is the line of demarcation between political partisanship and commendable Christian concern for human rights? Should we work from within the system to reform the laws or take the more dramatic action of breaking the laws in order to demonstrate their inherent inability to guarantee the true rights and freedoms of our people? An attorney once observed that due process under the law may not be anything more than alcohol on the edge of the guillotine if the laws themselves are unfair.

Recent polls indicate quite clearly that on the whole the lay persons in our churches do not want their churches to become involved in the granting of sanctuary to aliens. When I, myself, chose to speak out about the wisdom of U.S. intervention in Nicaragua and cited the case of Rene Hurtado as an example of an action taken by one church to show its concern for human dignity in Central America, at least one layperson was troubled enough and courageous enough to come to me and make sure that I had no intention of advocating a similar plan of action for our own congregation. Still, in the case of the St. Luke Presbyterian Church in Wayzata, Minnesota, the vote of the lay people was overwhelmingly in favor of granting sanctuary to Rene.

Of course, there is always the argument that we should seek to convert individuals as the necessary and proper prerequisite for changing structures and societies. If we can first transform the hearts of human beings, we can easily bring about the desired transformation of oppressive regimes. How effective are laws if the people are not motivated from within to support them?

The other side of this argument is that human nature being what it is we are in desperate need of legal restraints to protect us from one another until such time as this inner transformation of spirit is accomplished. The truth may be that we need to promote simultaneously both the prophetic emphasis upon right

inner spirit with the priestly emphasis upon correct
outer form.

The Stance of the United States Government

Moving beyond the simple case of one refugee seeking asylum in our country, we can take a look at the
official policy of our country in Central America.
Oversimplified, this policy seems to be that communism
poses the most dangerous threat in our world today.
Since the communists are using the unrest in Central
America to gain a new foothold on our continent, we
must oppose them in every possible manner. The guerrillas in El Salvador are communist inspired and led.
They are being supplied weapons by Cuba and indirectly
by the Soviets. Knowing that communism is avowedly
expansionist, we must stop this threat immediately. We
are concerned about the human rights abuses of the present government and are striving to bring about reform,
but this evil is inconsequential when compared to the
threat of a guerrilla takeover with the consequent
establishment of another communist regime at our own
backdoor. We must not allow communists to shoot their
way into power only to spread their revolution to
neighboring countries in Central America.

In support of this position, evidence can also be
brought forth to show that guerrilla fighters have been
known to kidnap innocent persons and carry them away
for indoctrination. Guerrillas have also employed
scorched earth policies of their own and have, at times,
tortured and killed their adversaries either real or
imagined. And some of their military support clearly
does come from other communist nations. Even the guerrilla claim to an abject poverty which threatens their
very lives, can scarcely condone their own excesses.

There are times when outsiders are tempted to
throw up their hands in despair at these people who
seem so violent in their treatment of one another.
Juan Vasquez, writing in the Los Angeles Times, has
said that terror is what El Salvador is all about.
What we must all be concerned about is that our present
support for the established regime in El Salvador may
be nothing less than support for terrorism on the right
in order to oppose terrorism on the left, and if this
is the case to wonder if the realities warrant our present policy.

Liberation Theology

Liberation theology appears to be a Latin American phenomenon which has grown out of the abject poverty of the people. As early as the late 1950's, priests like Marcos Gregory McGrath, who is now the Archbishop of Panama, began suggesting to the poor, the hungry, and the dispossessed in Chile that they could organize and improve their whole standard of living. Not only could they do this, but it was their Christian obligation to do so. They had a God given right to food, shelter, and clothing. They had a right to the basic material necessities for a reasonable human existence. In accordance with the United Nations Declaration of Social Rights, they also had a right to expect gainful employment as an expression of their own human dignity and usefulness. God had never ordained that some persons are preordained to poverty and near slavery, as even the Church had taught in an earlier time. On the contrary, God had built into each and every person a dignity which must be respected by everyone. It was wrong for the church to favor the rich and the landed when the poor existed in such wretched conditions that their essential humanity was in danger. These poor had a right to education, to health care, to an appreciation of their own music and art. They should resist, peaceably, anyone who tried to deprive them of these rights.

Going beyond these material concerns, Father McGrath and other priests, encouraged these disenfranchised people that they had not only a right, but a responsibility to become involved in the political processes of their country. They must assume responsibility for fashioning the laws and electing the persons who would be governing them. They had a right to challenge the church, if that church discriminated against them in favor of the wealthy.

The movement toward a theology of liberation moved slowly at first, attracting interest among young students in the universities who came to be concerned about the inequities which even they from their privileged positions could see existed between the rich and the poor. Vatican II tended to reenforce the social sensitivities of these students, and by the 1970's the movement had emerged from the campuses to the poor people themselves who by this time were slowly becoming aware of their own rights and dignity, and their Christian obligation to work for their own economic, political, and social redemption. Many priests have favored the peaceful resolution of outstanding grievances, but liberation theology has gone one step farther and suggested that regrettable as it is violent revolution can be condoned if it is the only remaining hope for the liberation of the dispossessed.

Encouraged by both student concerns for the poor and by Vatican II, the bishops of Latin America convened in 1968 at Medellin, Columbia to address themselves in a formal way to the plight of a people who seemed to be suffering egregiously from injustices systemic to the kind of government, society, and even church in which they were trying to exist. One author[9] has even suggested that the Medellin Documents became the "Magna Carta of Latin America's new socially conscious church." The dangers of such an involvement have become painfully clear in the murder of four church women in El Salvador and in the gunning down of Archbishop Romero who apparently once said to the ruling oligarchs, "Woe unto you, because tomorrow you will cry. It is better to take off your rings in time before they cut off your hands." Independent of European theology, there has arisen in Latin America a theology rooted in the miseries of the people which seems to be working effectively to ameliorate the oppressive conditions of the poor.

Biblical Insights for Liberation Theology

In our interview, Rene says that his own consciousness was raised by the reading of the scriptures. As an example of passages which prompted him to sense that the policies of his own country, as exemplified in the behavior of the armed forces, were contrary to the best interests of his own people, he read the following passage:

> Woe to those who call evil good and good evil,
> who put darkness for light and light for
> darkness, who put bitter for sweet and sweet
> for bitter![10]

Rene went ahead to say that the Bible is full of such good things. One does not always know how to interpret the Bible, but it would appear that the Bible used rightly could help the people. I prayed to God to help me, promising God that I would dedicate myself to the

study of scriptures, and to the search for justice.
Rene's final observation with respect to the role of
the scriptures was this: If it is communistic to oppose the injustices I have experienced in my own
country, then the Bible is a communist book.

Perhaps Rene can find comfort in the biblical
teaching about sanctuary and cities of refuge. In its
most primitive form the Code of the Covenant (Exodus
20:22-23:33) includes legislation to protect those
responsible for unpremeditated manslaughter. If it is
simply by accident that one person kills another, the
Code says that there shall be a "place" (Ex. 21:13)
where the guilty one can go for refuge. There is a
safe sanctuary for the unintentional killer, probably
at the altars of shrines dedicated to Yahweh prior to
the era of centralized cult worship in Jerusalem.

When Adonijah's attempt to succeed David as king
is thwarted by David's command that Solomon shall be
his successor to the throne, Adonijah fears for his
life and seeks refuge by seizing the horns of the altar.
Solomon agrees not to slay Adonijah if Adonijah promises
loyalty to the king, which Adonijah does.

Rene may or may not have killed anyone, but he has
clearly run afoul of his government and has sought sanctuary in St. Luke Presbyterian Church. The Old Testament does describe Cities of Refuge where persons
guilty of involuntary manslaughter may flee for refuge.
As long as they remain in these cities, they are protected by law from the avenger. The humane considerations of such legislation may encourage modern churches
to provide sanctuary for refugees seeking asylum.

One of the eschatological hopes of the Bible is
found in the passage of scripture which reads,

> the blind will receive their sight and the
> lame walk, lepers are cleansed and the deaf
> hear, and the dead are raised up, and the
> poor have good news preached to them.[11]

Born into a Paradise, fallen human nature longs for a
new Zion in an oasis of flowing waters and growing
plants, in a New Jerusalem where God will be with the
people and there will be no more crying nor death.
Crippling diseases will be gone. Warfare will be ended.
The animosities of nature will be pacified and the wolf

shall dwell with the lamb. When these things happen
we shall know that the Kingdom of God has come among us.

The fact is that we wait like a woman in travail
for the coming of such an age. Christians may be right
in believing that the kingdom dawned in the life of
Christ, but even they will grant that the consummation
is yet to come. As they wait for the consummation,
they pray longingly with Jesus, "Thy kingdom come, thy
will be done on earth as it is in heaven." This long-
ing for peace with justice, wholeness of life, recognition of human dignity, and respect for human rights
permeates Liberation Theology. The oppressed want freedom and liberty not only as human beings but because
they are convinced that their hopes are grounded in the
very intent of God. Frederick Herzog puts it this way:
"If we do not turn our theological attention to the oppressed, we will never understand the Gospel."[12]

The biblical proof texts for a theology of liberation are numerous and obvious. The cry of the prophet
Amos to "let justice roll down like the waters, and
righteousness like an everflowing stream," has already
been noted. It would also be appropriate to note that
it was this very same prophet who condemned the Israelites because they were willing to sell the righteous
for silver and the needy for a pair of shoes. Amos
cried out in anguish because these supposedly faithful
members of God's own covenanted community could "trample
the head of the poor into the dust of the earth, and
turn aside the way of the afflicted."[13] At such a moment it is also appropriate to remember Jesus' words,
"Truly I say to you, as you did it to one of the least
of these my brethren, you did it to me."[14] To care for
the naked and the sick, the hungry and the strangers,
is to do the will of God and to be one with Christ in
will and intention.

Any discussion of biblical insights for liberation
theology will of necessity take into account the biblical book of Exodus. Brevard Childs[15] has said "there
would be no better place in Scripture on which to test
the theological legitimacy of a 'theology of liberation'
than the book of Exodus." Certainly Judaism has long
proclaimed the Passover festival described in Exodus as
a celebration of freedom and liberty for an oppressed
and enslaved people. God looks upon the Hebrews in
Egypt and says "I have seen the affliction of my people
who are in Egypt, and have heard their cry because of

their taskmasters; I know their sufferings, and I have
come down to deliver them out of that land to a good
and broad land, a land flowing with milk and honey."16
The affectional involvement of God with these oppressed
people may be instructive for those of us who wish to
help free the oppressed. Here the Lord sees, hears,
and knows the suffering of the people. As the existen-
tialist might suggest, there is little room here for
the spectator stance; there is need for passional involvement. When God says, "let my people go," we understand that God is willing to act in history to deliver
a people in bondage into freedom in a new land.

Other biblical texts come readily to mind as we
consider the challenge to religious people to become
involved in a liberating theology.17 In The Old Testament we read from the Holiness Code that "you shall
love your neighbor as yourself," and in The New Testament we are taught that the Good Samaritan was the
friend because he showed mercy to the man in need. The
Golden Rule in its various forms obviously encourages a
kind of reciprocity that would go far to eliminate injustices and inequities if observed by all. The New
Testament version has Jesus saying, "So whatever you
wish that men would do to you, do so to them; for this
is the law and the prophets."

But perhaps the most appropriate biblical text of
all for liberation theology is that found in Isaiah
where the author says,

> The Spirit of the Lord God is upon me,
>   because the Lord has anointed me
> to bring good tidings to the afflicted;
>   he has sent me to bind up the broken-
>   hearted,
> to proclaim liberty to the captives
>   and the opening of the prison to those
>   who are bound;

Speaking of this beautiful passage, Professor James
Muilenburg has said, "A poem such as this is not of an
age but for all time."18 Christians are bound to view
the person of Christ as the example of one involved in
Liberation Theology because the above poetry comes
again from the mouth of Jesus:

> The Spirit of the Lord is upon me,
>   because he has anointed me to preach good

news to the poor. He has sent me to
proclaim release to the captives and
recovering of sight to the blind, to
set at liberty those who are oppressed,
to proclaim the acceptable year of the
Lord.[19]

Proponents of Liberation Theology see Jesus Christ
as Bonhoeffer's man for others, one called by God both
to herald salvation and to mediate it. The empowering
Spirit of the Lord rests upon the servant-like figure
enabling him to offer both physical and spiritual
liberation to those who are afflicted. The challenge
for the Christian is clear. We are called in suffering
love to identify with others through suffering love to
the end that freedom and liberty, health and wholeness
come to all of God's people.

Some Criticisms of Liberation Theology

Walter Benjamin, who insists that he is no mere
knee-jerk capitalist, has written recently about a trip
to Eastern Europe. Concerned about what he observes to
be a somewhat unfair indictment of capitalism by some
liberation theologians, Benjamin says, "...the near
silence of liberation theology regarding Eastern Europe
reveals ethical astigmatism."[20] Benjamin's point seems
to be that the facile assumption that capitalism is
guilty because it has failed to produce the utopia envisioned by the disenfranchised is unfair. Communism
and socialism have also failed, and do not offer any
better hope for liberation than the capitalism we know
in our own country. Benjamin says that he did not find
a "communism with a human face," but rather found vibra-
tions of depression, resignation, alienation, anger,
and suspicion. Communism and socialism are every bit
as exploitive of human beings and nature as capitalism.
From Benjamin's point of view, the re-introduction of
the profit motive along with private ownership might
encourage Eastern Europeans to recover their mystical,
primordial, "I-Thou" relationship with the soil.

An even less inhibited defense of capitalism is
advanced by Michael Novak who argues that capitalism,
rightly understood, can wear a Christian face.[21] Novak
thinks that capitalism can produce both wealth and
virtue, in a manner consistent with and supportive of
the original intent of the Creator. This does not mean

that there will be equality of results for everyone in
this ideal capitalistic system. God never had that intention. In our human freedom we can create disparities
not of God's choosing, but of our willing. God may
also let us suffer the consequences of some of our
choices.

From the perspective of the hungry and the dispossessed, there may be very little interest in the speculations of either Benjamin or Novak. They want practical theology not theory. Rightly or wrongly they think
their oppression results from the system which prevails
and they want reform. They may well believe that both
capitalism and socialism are devils to be exorcized immediately, in a peaceable manner if possible, but if
not, with revolution. They are weary of waiting for
the new age when the leopard will lie down amicably
with the kid.

The Rights of Women

The Equal Rights Amendment (ERA) has failed, at
least temporarily. Polls indicate that a clear majority
of the people in the United States favor the ERA movement, but in spite of widespread support the proposal
for a constitutional amendment has stalled for the moment. Just why our people opposed a formal move to
guarantee that women should not be discriminated against
simply because of their sex is not clear. What is clear
is that the attempt to secure such a guarantee will continue until feminists and their sympathizers succeed in
winning official acknowledgement for their rights.

There seems little doubt that our conditioning and
our habitual manner of thinking may be inimical, at
least unconsciously, to the interests of women. When
we hear the word "doctor" many of us automatically think
male, just as we in this country think male when we
hear the expressions "day laborer" or "heavy equipment
operator." Within the church, divisions have already
taken place because some church members favor the ordination of women while others, like Pope Paul, have resisted such ordination with adamant resolve.

Many women wish to abolish these stereotypes.
They want to be equal to seek the employment and professions of their choice. They want to be free. They
want full recognition of their human dignity, and the

ability to select a vocation on the basis of ability and interest rather than on a basis of sex. Like their oppressed sisters and brothers in Third World countries, they are convinced that men cannot be truly free until women's rights are secure.

Unfortunately, the Bible cannot be regarded as the best of proof texts for this movement. There is an unmistakable patriarchal context for the biblical stories. To be sure, the Apostle Paul can say that there is neither Jew nor Greek, slave nor free, male nor female, for those who are in Christ Jesus. And we all know Sarah, Miriam, Deborah, Ruth and Judith. In the New Testament, women were the first to witness the resurrection, and Priscilla is actively involved in the mission of the emerging Christian Church. But the fact remains that the clear and predominant orientation of the Bible is masculine.

The occasional references to the wise woman of Tekoa and the historical fiction of Esther, and even the Catholic Church's centuries old emphasis upon Mary as the Mother of God cannot dim the biblical predilections for male heroes. Huldah notwithstanding, the great prophetic figures of the Old Testament are Amos, Hosea, Isaiah, Micah, Jeremiah, and Ezekiel. The twelve apostles are also male. Jesus is male, and even the Hebrew designation for God, 'Elohim, is male. It is a patriarchal setting with Abraham, Isaac, and Jacob. Moses leads the Hebrew people out of Egypt and David is the time honored king. Daniel and three friends courageously defy a foreign culture, Job questions the way of God, and narrow Jonah discovers that the earth is round when he tries to flee from God only to be confronted by the Eternal Presence.

Douglas Knight has said, "...the Old Testament retains a largely disparaging ethic concerning the status and rights of women. Women were under all the obligations of the law but shared in few of the social and religious prerogatives."[22] Even Phyllis Trible who is one of the foremost scholars attempting to liberate the feminine nuances of scripture admits that "Hebrew grammar employs masculine pronouns for God." Her feeling about all of this is worth quoting in full:

> Though grammatical gender decides '
> neither sexuality nor theology, these
> distinctions are difficult, if not impossible,

to maintain in our hearing and understanding. Consequently, masculine pronouns reinforce a male image of God, an image that obscures, even obliterates female metaphors for deity. The affect is detrimental for faith and its participants. I avoid pronouns for deity; an occasional resulting awkwardness in style is a small price to pay for a valuable theological statement. As yet, however, I do not know how to resolve the dilemma posed by grammatical gender for deity in the scriptures themselves, since translation must answer to both grammatical accuracy and interpretive validity. Illumination on this issue is a pressing need in contemporary hermeneutics.[23]

The old saw about our surprise upon arrival in heaven and discovering upon sight of God that she is black and speaks Spanish is not very humorous for those who are sensitive to the kind of language we are using in our worship. Virginia Ramey Mollenkott, who is a member of the National Council of Churches' inclusive language Lectionary Committee, admits that her child-hood God was indeed too small. He was rich, white, and old. Through no fault of her own, her deity embodied classism, racism, ageism, and sexism.[24] For all who may think her concerns here trivial, Mollenkott suggests that they subject themselves to a full length service of worship where all references to the deity are female, and the sisterhood of women is mentioned constantly.

The attempts to avoid sexist language are not always entirely successful. An example of this fact can be found in the printed schedule of events and worship program for the Minnesota statewide rally of some 6,000 United Methodists in October, 1981. The leaders of this UM gathering, as it was called, obviously decided to eliminate the sexist language from the hymns which would be sung on this occasion. Here, in part, is their edited version of Martin Luther's EIN' FESTE BURG:

> A mighty fortress is our God,
> A bulwark never failing;
> Our helper God amid the flood
>
> Of mortal ills prevailing;
> For still our ancient foes

Doth seek to work us woe;
Their craft and power are great,
And, armed with cruel hate,
On earth is not their equal.

Did we in our own strength confide,
Our striving would be losing,
Were not the right one on our side,
The one of God's own choosing;
Dost ask who that may be?
Christ Jesus, it is he;
Lord Saboath, his name,
From age to age the same,
And he must win the battle.

And though this world, with devils filled,
Should threaten to undo us,
We will not fear, for God hath willed
The truth to triumph through us;
The Prince of Darkness grim,
We tremble not for him;
His rage we can endure,
For lo, his doom is sure;
One little word shall fell him.

I have underlined the edited words so that the reader
can discern easily the intent of those who wish to
eliminate sexist language from our worship. In the
first stanza, the word God replaces the masculine pronoun he, and the ancient foe, which for Luther was
probably the devil, is made to read foes so that their
craft replaces his craft. In the second stanza it is
no longer the right man who is on our side, but the
right one, and in the third stanza it is the truth
rather than his truth which will triumph through us.
Curiously enough, the editors do allow the Prince of
Darkness to remain a him in this same stanza.

Those interested in using non-sexist language in
worship readily admit that there are inconsistencies in
their efforts and occasional awkward results, but they
are thoroughly convinced that the end justifies the
means even if the means remain imperfect. They do not
hesitate to rewrite the words of the original authors,
and they are convinced that given time they can overcome the fears of those in the churches who really do
not want to change the time hallowed words. The long
range goal will be to make all the language of worship,
indeed all language, inclusive language. Only time

217

will tell how successful these attempts to change the language which has become habitual with us will be.

Curiously enough, the theological basis for an improved relationship between the sexes may come from none other than the oft maligned passage in Ephesians (5:21-33) where feminists have chafed at Paul's seemingly male chauvinistic attitudes. Markus Barth[25] interprets Paul to say that if we truly "fear" Christ (a word which Barth prefers to the "reverence" of the RSV) that we shall have a love relationship with Christ which will affect our family relationships as well. We shall gladly be subject to one another because it is the very nature of true love to put others first in our considerations, just as the holy love of God in Christ puts us first at the cross. In this sense, fear can mean appreciation and respect for a loving relationship which has the power to overcome all other obstacles. Whether Barth is right or wrong in his interpretation of Ephesians, there seems little doubt that it is precisely this kind of Christian respect for one another that will erase the inequities and injustices which do in fact exist between the sexes at the present moment.

A Theological Postscript

The very fact that there is a felt need for Liberation Theology suggests that there are interpersonal and social problems which must be addressed, and these problems may reflect some flaws in our human nature. A student once asked one of my colleagues if he believed in Original Sin. My colleague retorted, "Of course! I believe that we are very original in the way we sin." This declaration may simply reaffirm the biblical observation that

> All we like sheep have gone astray;
> we have turned every one to his own way;[26]

or the Apostle Paul's statement that we, too, may die in alienation from our God because we all sin (Romans 5:12). I certainly find myself much more drawn to the Niebuhrian notion that self idolization will soon reveal to us the emptiness of trying to derive infinite meaning from finite objects, than to the blusterings of a Wayne Dyer who is trying to tell us how to be a "No-Limit" person. There is no doubt in my mind that we must continue to proclaim the gospel of grace as the real hope for our personal and social salvation. A rabbi and I once prepared a brief program for radio broadcast in which we discussed the biblical view of human nature. After I had accentuated those biblical passages which spoke positively about human nature, the rabbi, who had escaped the holocaust, reminded me that "The LORD saw that the wickedness of man was great in the earth, and that every imagination of the thoughts of his heart was only evil continually."[27] The rabbi knew whereof he spoke.

Our task, however, is not desperate. We have been created in the image of God and bear within us that homing device which tugs on our souls like an unseen kite pulling at its tether. In our Christian tradition we do affirm that God has affirmed creation even to the point of becoming flesh in Jesus Christ. If the fullness of God is pleased to dwell with us in our human condition, then the holy resources for our redemption are never far from us. We ought not to wish for an escape from history into eternity, but rather believe that through our own response to grace we can reform not only our own lives but the very injustices and inequalities which plague our common humanity.

Being a prophet is a lonely chore. Jeremiah rebelled against his own mission and we may well do the same. We, too, want to be liked. We do not like to become the laughingstock. Moreover, we admit freely that there are intricacies to our political, social and economic malaise which simply confuse us. The answers are not sure. We have introduced so much chaos into God's ordered creation that we have almost lost sight of both the Garden and the New Jerusalem, but guided by the Spirit we may yet proclaim the saving Word of God.

Our dignity is grounded in creation so we must affirm it for ourselves and for all other people. I am not yet willing to ask my own congregation to offer sanctuary to anyone seeking asylum, but speaking personally, I am willing to affirm the right of St. Luke Presbyterian church to do what they have done. It may be that the courageous witness of our religious communities can change political policies and point toward the peace of the kingdom.

FOOTNOTES

1. William F. Buckley, Jr., "Meanwhile, in the Seminaries," Santa Monica Evening Outlook (15 July 82), 6.
2. James H. Cone, Black Theology and Black Power; NY: Seabury, 1969, p. 6.
3. Letty M. Russell, Human Liberation in a Feminine Perspective - A Theology; Philadelphia: Westminster, 1974, p. 17.
4. Karl Barth, The Word of God and Word of Man; NY: Harper, 1957, p. 38.
5. Thomas J. A. Altizer and William Hamilton, Radical Theology and the Death of God; Indianapolis: Bobbs Merrill, 1966, p. 7.
6. Ibid., p. 28.
7. Ibid., p. 41.
8. The Christian Century (CC) (6 Ap 83), 304f.
9. Penny Lernoux, "Talking Back to the Pharaoh," Notre Dame Magazine (Dec 82), 26-8.
10. Isaiah 5:20.
11. Matthew 11:5.
12. Frederick Herzog, Liberation Theology; NY: Seabury, 1972, p. viii.
13. Amos 5:24; 2:6.
14. Mt. 25:40.
15. Brevard Childs, Introduction to the Old Testament as Scripture; Philadelphia: Fortress, 1979, p. 178.
16. Exodus 3:7, 8.
17. Leviticus 19:18; Luke 10:29-37; Mat. 7:12; Is. 61:1.
18. The Interpreter's Bible V:708.
19. Lu. 4:18.
20. Walter Benjamin, "Liberation Theology: European Hopelessness Exposes Latin Hoax," Christianity Today (5 Mar 82), 21.
21. Kenneth L. Woodward, "A Cheer for Capitalism," Newsweek (17 May 82), 97.
22. Doublas Knight, "Old Testament Ethics," CC (20 Jan 82), 57.
23. Phyllis Trible, God and the Rhetoric of Sexuality; Philadelphia: Fortress, 1978, p. 23, n. 5.
24. Virginia Ramey Mollenkott, "Feminine Images of God in the Bible," Circuit Rider (12 June 82), 12.
25. Markus Barth, Ephesians 4-6 (Anchor Bible), 667. I am indebted to Dr. Thorne Wittstruck for calling Barth's work to my attention.
26. Is. 53:6a.
27. Genesis 6:5.

THE LIST OF SEVEN PEOPLES IN CANAAN: A FRESH ANALYSIS

Kevin G. O'Connell, S.J.

Introduction

It is a pleasure to dedicate this venture in "textual archaeology" to my dear friend and colleague, Dr. Lawrence E. Toombs.[1] I first met Larry in the field at Tell el-Hesi in 1971, when he was serving as senior archaeologist and I came as a young post-doctoral volunteer for my first (and, I thought, only) archaeological experience. I was bitten by the archaeological bug, however, and succumbed to an invitation in 1973 to return as administrative director (and subsequently as series editor and director of publications). My fate was sealed! Henceforth both Tell el-Hesi and Larry Toombs were to be an important part of my life. I count it a gift and a privilege to have been able to work closely with Larry (and our sorely missed late colleague, Dr. D. Glenn Rose) on many aspects of archaeological organization, excavation, and publication. Since Larry's teaching and research range widely over the fields of archaeology and biblical study, I thought it particularly appropriate to contribute this analysis of surviving textual evidence and reconstruction of lost antecedents, to the present volume in his honor.

The State of the Question

In 1979, Tomoo Ishida published a study entitled "The Structure and Historical Implications of the Lists of Pre-Israelite Nations."[2] He found twenty-seven (actually twenty-eight) instances of the list in the MT,[3] ranging from twelve names twice (in parallel texts)[4] and ten names once[5] to just two names four (or five) times.[6] There were eight names once,[7] seven names three times,[8] six names eleven times,[9] five names four times,[10] and three names once.[11] These totals were based exclusively on the present MT. To diagram the lists conveniently in tables, Ishida adopted the following abbreviations for the seven most common names: C (Canaanite), H (Hittite), A (Amorite), P (Perizzite), G (Girgashite), V (Hivite), and J (Jebusite). Any additional names were written out as necessary.

The preponderance of the six-name list (normally with the same names, although in different sequences) made it appear to be an independent category.[12] However, Ishida argued that two instances of the six-name list should be put under other categories[13] and that all three seven-name lists[14] and two of the five-name lists[15] should be added to form a single category of fourteen "six-name lists with variations."[16] The remaining thirteen (or fourteen) lists -- approximately half of the total -- were then grouped under four further categories: four (or five) "lists of representative nations";[17] four "geographical lists";[18] "the list found in the Table of Nations";[19] and three "lists found in later sources."[20] As will be argued below, these divisions arbitrarily mask the underlying pattern that finds expression in all the lists (with the possible exception of the so-called "two-name" lists).

In his Table II,[21] Ishida arranged the occurrences of the six-name list according to the order of the first three names (while the last three names generally appeared in the sequence P V J). In his opinion, the earliest form of the list was C A H P V J. The first name, Canaanite (כנעני), would have signified not only the ethnic group dwelling by the sea coast and in the Jordan valley, but also the entire population of Palestine.[22] A variation of this form (A C H P V J) would have reflected a change, probably after the rise of the Israelite monarchy, in which Canaanite had been replaced as a generic term for the whole population of Pre-Israelite Palestine by Amorite (אמרי), originally a name for the inhabitants of the western mountains. In yet other forms of the lists (C H A P V J and H A C P V J), Hittite (חתי) would have moved from being a designation for the small community of Hittite origin in southern Palestine or the small Syrian kingdoms which had succeeded the Hittite Empire after 1200 B.C. to serving as a new term for the nations that had inhabited the land prior to the Israelite settlement.[23] The most important shift, for Ishida, was from Canaanite to Hittite as the initial name in the lists.[24]

From his analyses, which I have partially summarized, Ishida arrived at the following conclusions:[25]

> a) From the period of the settlement down to the establishment of David's Empire, the Israelites considered the indigenous population as composite. This recognition was expressed first in the "geographical lists" as well as in the "lists of representative nations". . . .
> b) Both the geographical lists and the lists of representative nations served as proto-

types for the six-name lists and provided them with their general framework, when they were compiled in the days of Solomon as an expression of the legitimation of the Israelite seizure of the Promised Land from the indigenous nations. After that, the first formula of the six-name lists, "C A H P V J", underwent several modifications, corresponding to the shift in implication of the terms Canaanites, Amorites and Hittites, up to the time of the compilation of the Book of Deuteronomy. . . .

c) The fact that the second formula of the six-name lists, "C H A P V J", was employed by the authors in later times suggests that it was accepted as the quasi-canonical formula of the lists of nations in biblical traditions.

d) Besides the lists in the main stream of development . . . , other lists were composed as modifications of the basic patterns or formulae, such as the five- or seven-name lists or the lists in the Table of Nations and Gn 15.

A Fresh Analysis

While Ishida has made a number of creative observations, his entire analysis is seriously weakened by the unaccountable failure to look critically at *all* the primary textual evidence (and not just the MT) for the various occurrences of the lists of pre-Israelite peoples before drawing conclusions as to structure and historical development. In particular, he should have investigated the evidence for each instance of the list in LXX (and its variants), SP (for Pentateuch), and (where extant) Qumran fragments. The present report summarizes the results of such an investigation, begun before I had come across Ishida's article and carried further after I had worked through it. Chart One presents the textual evidence in tabular form, supplementing Ishida's symbols for the seven most common names with lower-case letters for the names which appear only occasionally. The entire code is given at the beginning and end of the chart.[26]

One conclusion of the analysis, argued in what follows, is that G (גרשי, Girgashite), although omitted more frequently, nonetheless belongs with the other six names as an integral part of an original seven-name

list. This list of seven peoples (explicitly described
as such in Dt. 7:1), always using gentilic singular
forms (preceded by the definite article) in Hebrew, but
frequently translated by plural forms in LXX and versions, occurs more or less completely twenty-three times
in the Biblical text, four times as part of a more extended list,[27] once in conjunction with a single added
name in all witnesses,[28] and eighteen times without
added names in all or most witnesses.[29] There are also
five instances in which two names from the list occur
together,[30] but it is not clear that these constitute
examples of the list in the strict sense. For this reason they are entered in Chart One at the end, separated
from the more obviously genuine occurrences of the list,
and are omitted from the following discussion (see Note
76 below).

     While the seven-name list is vulnerable to multiple
haplographies, misspellings, and displacements (often
due to careless replacement of words dropped by haplography), as well as to deliberate alteration, it has remained remarkably constant in all its occurrences, as
the extensive entries in Chart One will show. The fourteen additional names found in Gen. 10:15-18 // 1 Chr.
1:13-16 (six names),[31] Gen. 15:19-21 (LXX vv. 19-20,
four names),[32] Ezra (Esdr. B) 9:1 (three names),[33] and
Num. 13:29 (LXX v. 30, one name)[34] are all different
from each other and from both the name that occurs in
some LXX mss for Josh. 11:3 (as well as in a single different ms for Josh. 9:1 and Josh. 12:8)[35] and the name
found in one LXX ms for Neh. 9:8 (Esdr. B 19:8).[36]
Using the same upper-case letters as Ishida for the sev-
en names that occur regularly in the lists, and lower-
case letters for the sixteen additional names, Chart One
outlines divergences within the main Hebrew and Greek
witnesses for each occurrence of the list.[37]

     Several observations are in order: (1) MT is far
more likely to omit one or more names in the list than
are either SP or LXX. MT has all seven names only three
times.[38] The most common MT omission is G. It alone is
omitted ten times,[39] and together with other names it is
omitted six more times.[40] The omission of G alone is
shared by some or all LXX witnesses five times.[41] LXX
agrees with MT on the omission of C G once and of G V
once.[42] In Ex. 23:28, where MT omits A P G J, many LXX
witnesses omit P G J and a few others omit P G. There
are also four cases in which MT has G, but omits either

P (twice) or V (twice).[43] Nowhere do SP and/or a significant number of LXX witnesses omit any of the seven standard names against MT.[44]

(2) While MT has all seven names in only three cases,[45] it has six of the seven names some fourteen times (G is the missing name ten times, while P and V are each missing twice), five of the seven names four times (C G are missing twice, while P G and C V are each missing once), and once only three of the seven names (A P G J are all missing).[46]

(3) While many haplographies occur in the various LXX witnesses, most or all LXX witnesses have the full seven-name list eleven times (out of twenty-two occurrences[47]), three times in agreement with MT[48] and eight times against MT (seven times in the Pentateuch, where SP also has the complete list,[49] and also in Josh. 9:1). Apart from 1 Kings 9:20 (where most LXX witnesses lack vv. 15-25 and the few that have the verses also have C G against MT), Ex. 23:28 (where MT's omissions from the list are more extensive than those of any LXX witnesses and where only SP and a few LXX witnesses have all seven names), and Num. 13:29 (LXX v. 30, where LXX and SP agree with MT on the omission of P G, but have V against MT), many or all LXX witnesses agree with MT on the omission of one or two names from the list nine times.[50] The LXX omissions are P twice,[51] G three times,[52] V twice,[53] C G once,[54] and G V once.[55] Many LXX witnesses also agree with MT on the omission of P G J once.[56]

(4) SP evidence is possible only for the twelve Pentateuchal occurrences of the list. In Gen. 10:15-18 and Dt. 7:1, SP agrees with both MT and LXX on the order and content of the list (and all omit P in Gen. 10). In Num. 13:29 (LXX v. 30), SP and LXX agree with MT on the omission of P G, but both have V against MT. In the other nine cases, SP supplies the name(s) missing in MT, five times otherwise agreeing with MT on the order of the list[57] and four times also exhibiting a different sequence of names from MT.[58]

Apart from the expanded lists of Gen. 10 // 1 Chr. 1 and Gen. 15, where the standard names occur in the sequences C H J A G V and H P A C G [V] J, respectively, MT and SP have the following six agreements on sequence (names only in SP are in brackets):

Ex. 3:8.	C	H	A	P	[G]	V	J
Ex. 3:17.	C	H	A	P	[G]	V	J
Ex. 13:5.	C	H	A	[P]	[G]	V	J
Ex. 33:2.	C	A	H	[G]	P	V	J
Num. 13:29.	H	[V]	J	A	C
Dt. 7:1.	H	G	A	C	P	V	J

When SP and MT sequences differ (four times),[59] SP always has the sequence C A H G P V J, and LXX witnesses either agree with MT against SP or are closer to MT than to SP. In Ex. 33:2, LXX witnesses which share the MT sequence all add G to that sequence at different places than SP does. In other words, SP has a single sequence for the list five out of eleven times,[60] and it is a sequence peculiar to SP. It is more likely that this sequence arose secondarily in SP than that it alone preserves unchanged the list's presumed original standard sequence.

(5) While no single sequence of names emerges convincingly from the evidence presented in Chart One, it is clear that three of the names C H A P are normally found in some order in the first three positions and that two of the names G V J are usually found in some order in the last two positions. There is a clear preference for V J to be in the last two positions; C occurs about as often as either H or A in the first position; and there is a clear tendency for H to follow in second position after either C or A. Given the frequent omission of G by MT, it is difficult to draw any conclusions about preferred sequence in the center of the list. The sequence C H A P G V J (or G P for P G) appears to have been generally preferred more often in the tradition, but its universal originality cannot be demonstrated with any precision. Wherever that sequence is one of the alternatives supported by any textual evidence, however, it should probably be given preference in translation.

(6) While the frequent absence of G, Girgashite (הגרגשי), from MT remains puzzling, there is no reason to deny its place within what appears to have been an originally standard list of seven gentilic names.[61] Given the repetitious quality of names linked by the conjunc-

tion "and," all beginning with the definite article and all ending with the same gentilic -$\hat{\imath}$ ($\cdot_{\overline{\cdot}}$), it is not surprising that individual names were frequently left out (by haplography) and sometimes restored to different positions within the sequence.

What emerges with clarity from Chart One is the basic consistency of the sequential pattern and its surprising resistance to the insertion of new names. Apart from the parallel lists of Gen. 10:15-18 // 1 Chr. 1:13-16, no "new" name appears in more than one occurrence of the list.[62] That attests to the closed, formulaic character of the original seven-name list.

(7) Within the Pentateuch, the list appears within Yahwist ("J") materials three to five times,[63] in "D" materials some five times,[64] and in other "old" materials twice.[65] Within the Deuteronomistic History, it occurs five times in Joshua,[66] once in Judges (in an editorial summary),[67] and once in 1 Kings (in an editorial summary about the reign of Solomon).[68] The occurrences in 1-2 Chr.[69] are dependent on Gen. 10[70] and 1 Kings 9:20, respectively, while those in Ezra and Nehemiah[71] are consciously drawing on the preserved Pentateuchal traditions.

Conclusion

This list of seven peoples in Canaan seems to have been very deeply rooted in the tradition and to reflect experiences of the settlement (or at least of the premonarchical period). Like the stereotyped descriptions, "a good and broad land" and "a land flowing with milk and honey,"[72] this list became a symbol to be repeated often in referring to the territory which had been provided by Yahweh for his people. Its use is anachronistic in all Pentateuchal texts that describe Canaan from the perspective of the period before the settlement. While the list may well have come into existence prior to the time of the Judges, in a context and for a purpose that we cannot as yet discover, it probably only took its firm place within the people's traditions when the ancient stories were told and retold, expanded and polished, in praise of Yahweh and to preserve the memory of what the people Israel had experienced. This had almost certainly taken place before the Yahwist drew the stories and story-cycles into a new literary epic. By then the list was already fixed formula and symbol.

This is shown especially by the fact that *only seven names* figure repeatedly in the many occurrences of the list. Any other name that joins the list does so once, or at best twice in parallel citations, but in general the boundaries of the seven-name set were clearly regarded as fixed and closed.[73] For this reason, the Girgashites -- recurring so often and yet not well attested elsewhere -- can only be understood as an integral part of the set of names from the beginning. Otherwise there would be no reason for their name to be added so often and in so many different positions, while other additions are never repeated.

Subsequent changes in the list's content or sequence were for the most part, not deliberate, but the result of errors and inadequate recorrection within the process of scribal transmission.[74] In a few instances, the seven-name list was itself used as the basis for more extended lists,[75] but these are special cases that need not be discussed further here.[76]

FOOTNOTES

1. The initial research for this article was done in 1980-81 at the Albright Institute of Archaeological Research in Jerusalem, where I was in residence as Annual Professor (first term) and Research Associate with the support of a one-semester sabbatical from Weston School of Theology and a Grant-in-Aid from the American Council of Learned Societies. The project grew out of my primary research that year for a commentary on Exodus. A preliminary report on the seven-peoples list was included in my presentation about my year's work on Exodus at the Albright Institute on 28 May 1981, and a more developed analysis was presented at the annual meeting of the Eastern Great Lakes Biblical Society in Coraopolis, PA, 16 April 1982. I have profited from the comments and questions of several persons who heard either talk or who read various drafts of the article since then, but the final responsibility for the analysis and conclusions presented here is my own.
2. *Bib.* 60 (1979), 461-90.
3. *Ibid.*, Table I on pp. 461-62; the two instances in Jud. 1:4-5 are counted as a single example by Ishida, but I have chosen to count each instance separately. This divergence has no bearing on the analyses presented here.
4. Gen. 10:15-18 // 1 Chr. 1:13-16.
5. Gen. 15:19-21.
6. Gen. 13:7; 34:30; Josh. 5:1; Jud. 1:4, 5 (see Note 3 above).
7. Ezra 9:1.
8. Dt. 7:1; Josh. 3:10; 24:11.
9. Ex. 3:8, 17; 23:23; 33:2; 34:11; Dt. 20:17; Josh. 9:1; 11:3;

12:8; Jud. 3:5; Neh. 9:8.
10. Ex 13:5; Num. 13:29; 1 Kings 9:20; 2 Chr. 8:7.
11. Ex 23:28.
12. Of the seven most common names, ten six-name lists lack only
G, while Neh. 9:8 lacks only V; see Note 9 for all eleven six-name
lists.
13. Josh. 11:3 (one of the four "geographical lists"--see Note 18)
and Neh. 9:8 (one of the three "lists found in later sources"--see
Note 20).
14. Dt. 7:1; Josh. 3:10; 24:11.
15. Ex. 13:5; 1 Kings 9:20.
16. *Ibid.*, p. 464 and Table II on p. 471.
17. The three (actually four) two-name lists that are identical
(Gen. 13:7; 34:30; the two occurrences in Jud. 1:4-5) and the
three-name list (Ex. 23:28) which he regards as different examples
of building blocks leading to the earliest formula for six-name
lists; cf. *ibid.*, pp. 478-81.
18. Gen. 15:19-21; Num. 13:29; Josh. 5:1; 11:3; cf. *ibid.*, pp.
481-85 and Table III on p. 481. Ishida argues that these lists all
arrange the nations in one or another geographical sequence.
19. Gen. 10:15-18 // 1 Chr. 1:13-16; cf. *ibid.*, pp. 485-87.
20. Ezra 9:1; Neh. 9:8; 2 Chr. 8:7; cf. *ibid.*, pp. 487-89 and
Table IV on p. 487. Ishida argues that these three lists were all
composed according to the intermediate pattern for six-name lists
in which H has moved from third to second position, immediately
after C (see quote from p. 470 in Note 24 below).
21. *Ibid.*, p. 471.
22. Throughout this summary of Ishida's position, the term "Palestine" is used in the anachronistic way that he employs it.
23. Cf. *ibid.*, pp. 465-70, esp. p. 470.
24. "The order of the lists is determined by the promotion of the
Hittites from the third position to the second and then the first,
and the demotion of the Canaanites from the first to the third.
The lists in which the Amorites occupy the first position are to be
subordinated to the scheme determined by the order of the Hittites
and the Canaanites." *Ibid.*, p. 470.
25. *Ibid.*, pp. 489-90.
26. The Masoretic Text (MT) has been cited from *Biblia Hebraica
Stuttgartensia*, eds. K. Elliger and W. Rudolph; Stuttgart: Deutsche
Bibelstiftung, c. 1967/77. The Septuagint (LXX) and its versions
and variants have been cited from the various fascicles of the
Greater Cambridge Septuagint (*The Old Testament in Greek*, eds. A. E.
Brooke, N. McLean, and H. St. John Thackeray; London: Cambridge
University Press, 1906-40), and the symbols of that edition have
been retained. Where appropriate, additional variants have been
drawn from available volumes of the Göttingen critical edition (J.
W. Wevers, ed., *Genesis* [1974], *Numeri* [1982], *Deuteronomium* [1977];
Göttingen: Vandenhoeck & Ruprecht), and the symbols of that edition
have been used for its mss groupings. The Samaritan Pentateuch (SP)
has been cited from *Der Hebräische Pentateuch der Samaritaner*, ed.
A. von Gall; Berlin: Alfred Töpelmann Verlag, 1966 (photomechanical

reprint of the 1918 Giessen edition), and the symbols of that edition have been retained. (The notations "LXX's" & "SP's" indicate that LXX or SP witnesses are cited on the authority of the respective critical editions.) The reading cited from 4Q paleo Ex^m for Ex. 34:11 was verified on the photograph, transcription, and collation graciously made available to me by the late Monsignor Patrick W. Skehan. His draft manuscript on that and other Qumran documents in paleo-Hebrew script is being prepared for publication by Professor Eugene C. Ulrich of Notre Dame University.

27. Gen. 10:15-18 // 1 Chr. 1:13-16; Gen. 15:19-21 (LXX vv. 19-20); Ezra (Esdr. B) 9:1. All witnesses omit P in Gen. 10:15-18 // 1 Chr. 1:13-16; almost all witnesses omit G V in Ezra (Esdr. B) 9:1, but V is restored in LXX's y; MT and one major strand of LXX witnesses omit V in Gen. 15:19-21 (LXX vv. 19-20).

28. Num. 13:29 (LXX v. 30); no witness exhibits more than four or five of the standard names here (all omit P G, MT & LXX's 𝔅 Arab also omit V, LXX's 128 ℭ also omit J).

29. Ex. 3:8, 17; 13:5; 23:23, 28; 33:2; 34:11; Dt. 7:1; 20:17; Josh 3:10; 9:1; 11:3 (some LXX mss add χορραιοι here, as does one ms in Josh. 9:1; 12:8); 12:8; 24:11; Jud. 3:5; 1 Kings 9:20 // 2 Chr. 8:7; Neh. 9:8 (Esdr. B 19:8, one LXX ms adds χαλδαιοι here).

30. Gen. 13:7; 34:30; Josh. 5:1; Jud. 1:4, 5.

31. (a): צידן; b: ערקי; c: סיני; d: ארודי; e: צמרי; f: חמתי. As indicated in the code to the chart, parentheses around the symbol for a name indicate that the Hebrew singular proper name has replaced the expected gentilic.

32. g: קיני; h: קנזי; i: קדמני; j: רפאים (this is the only name to appear as plural in Hebrew).

33. n: עמני; o: מאבי; p: מצרי.

34. (k): עמלק. Once again, the parentheses indicate that the Hebrew singular proper name has replaced the expected gentilic.

35. m: χορραιοι (= חורי*).

36. q: χαλδαιοι (= כשׂדי*).

37. LXX evidence is given in great detail, but insignificant variants have occasionally been omitted. In Gen. 10 // 1 Chr. 1 the list has been incorporated into a genealogy of Canaan, and so the name כנען occurs instead of the gentilic כנעני in Hebrew (and the corresponding χανααν appears in Greek), while the name חת is used in place of the gentilic חתי in Hebrew (but not in Greek). Parentheses are used with the symbols C and H in Chart One to call attention to this difference when it occurs; they are similarly used with the lower-case symbols a (representing Sidon, Canaan's firstborn) and k (for Amelek) in Gen. 10:15 // 1 Chr. 1:13 and Num. 13:29 (LXX v. 30), respectively. No attempt has been made to indicate the occasional presence of added phrases or other non-list materials in Gen. 10:15-18 // 1 Chr. 1:13-16, in Num. 13:29 (LXX v. 30), in Josh. 5:1 (at end of chart) and 11:3, or in some Greek witnesses for Ex. 23:28. Qualitative differences between various Greek equivalents for any one Hebrew gentilic have not been noted, even when they coexist as doublets within the same witness (e.g., in LXX's dpt for Josh. 12:8).

38. Dt. 7:1; Josh 3:10; 24:11.
39. Ex. 3:8, 17; 23:23; 33:2; 34:11; Dt. 20:17; Josh. 9:1; 11:3; 12:8; Jud. 3:5.
40. Ex. 13:5 (with P); 23:28 (with A P J); Num. 13:29 (LXX v. 30, with P V); 1 Kings 9:20 // 2 Chr. 8:7 (with C); Ezra (Esdr. B) 9:1 (with V).
41. Dt. 20:17 (B*k); Josh. 9:1 (A-cod𝔖); 11:3 (all); 12:8 (many); Jud. 3:5 (most).
42. 2 Chr. 8:7 (C G); Ezra (Esdr. B) 9:1 (G V). LXX originally may have agreed with MT on the omission of C G in 1 Kings 9:20 (parallel to 2 Chr. 8:7) as well, but vv. 15-25 are missing from almost all LXX witnesses (and Ax𝔄𝔖 presumably represent a secondary revision).
43. P in Gen. 10:15-18 // 1 Chr. 1:13-16 (also omitted by LXX both times and by SP in Gen. 10); V in Gen. 15:19-21 (LXX vv. 19-20, also omitted by one major LXX strand) and Neh. 9:8 (Esdr. B 19:8, also omitted by most LXX witnesses).
44. In Ex. 33:2 LXX's Bqu omit C against MT, SP, and all other LXX witnesses, however; cf. other omissions in LXX's k, 77, and 𝔈ᶠ.
45. Dt. 7:1; Josh. 3:10; 24:11.
46. See the right-hand column of Chart One for details.
47. LXX lacks 1 Kings 9:15-25 (except for Ax𝔄𝔖, which have all seven names against MT's five names in v. 20).
48. Dt. 7:1; Josh. 3:10; 24:11.
49. Ex. 3:8, 17; 13:5; 23:23; 33:2; 34:11; Dt. 20:17 (LXX's B*k agree with MT in omitting G).
50. Gen. 10:15-18 // 1 Chr. 1:13-16; Gen. 15:19-21 (LXX vv. 19-20); Josh. 11:3; 12:8; Jud. 3:5; 2 Chr. 8:7; Ezra (Esdr. B) 9:1; Neh. 9:8 (Esdr. B 19:8). The omission is shared also by SP in Gen. 10:15-18, but not in Gen. 15:19-21.
51. Gen. 10:15-18 // 1 Chr. 1:13-16.
52. Josh. 11:3; 12:8; Jud. 3:5.
53. Gen. 15:19-21 (LXX vv. 19-20); Neh. 9:8 (Esdr. B 19:8).
54. 2 Chr. 8:7.
55. Ezra (Esdr. B) 9:1.
56. Ez. 23:28, where MT also omits A.
57. LXX shares the same order in Gen. 15:19-21 (LXX vv. 19-20); LXX agrees with the MT order in Ex. 3:8, but most LXX witnesses insert the missing name in a different position from SP; many LXX witnesses agree with SP in Ex. 3:17, but others have a different sequence from SP and MT; and in both Ex. 13:5 and Ex. 33:2 there are various sequences in the LXX witnesses, but none agree with SP.
58. Ex. 23:23, 28; 34:11; Dt. 20:17. Each time most or all LXX witnesses retain the MT sequence against SP, even though the missing names may be variously inserted.
59. Ex. 23:23, 28; 34:11; Dt. 20:17; see also SP for Ex. 33:2.
60. Ex. 23:23, 28; 33:2; 34:11; Dt. 20:17.
61. If Girgashite were not an original part of the list, it would be difficult to account for its frequent presence in all witnesses or its insertion in LXX and SP against MT, especially since the name is otherwise unattested in MT. Apart from the four instances

of expanded lists (Gen. 10:15-18 // 1 Chr. 1:13-16; Gen. 15:19-21 [LXX vv. 19-20]; Ezra [Esdr. B] 9:1), the list always contains seven names or less. (A very few LXX witnesses have an eighth name or doublet in Ex. 33:2 [r*^{vid}]; 34:11 [128]; Josh. 12:8 [k, pt]; Neh. 9:8 [Esdr. B 19:8][b]--but these are all late, secondary corruptions that "prove the rule.") Apart from the exception given below in Note 62 and the six names that occur twice in the parallel texts of Gen. 10:15-18 and 1 Chr. 1:13-16, no new name is inserted into more than one occurrence of the list. This cannot be accidental. Girgashite, and only Girgashite, was felt to "belong" with the other six names in the standard list. If its original position in the list was fifth or fourth (out of seven), that might have caused it to be omitted accidentally far more often than the preceding or final names. Be that as it may, the name Girgashite is missing from *all* witnesses to the list--exclusive of the two-name occurrences which are probably not pertinent--only four times: Num. 13:29 (LXX v. 30); Josh. 11:3; 2 Chr. 8:7; Ezra (Esdr. B) 9:1. This is in marked contrast with other new names, which were added only once or twice, either secondarily or for very specific reasons. (For reflections on the appropriateness of seven names-- rather than six--in the list, see Note 73 below.)

62. The transfer of m (χορραιοι) from various LXX witnesses for Josh. 11:3 to LXX's k for Josh. 9:1 and 12:8 is obviously a secondary, inner-Greek phenomenon (especially since LXX's k lacks m in Josh. 11:3).

63. Gen. 10:15-18; 15:19-21 (possibly "E"); Ex 3:8, 17; Num. 13:29 (perhaps a secondary insertion).

64. Ex. 13:5; 33:2; 34:11; Dt. 7:1; 20:17.

65. Ex. 23:23, 28.

66. Josh. 3:10; 9:1; 11:3; 12:8; 24:11.

67. Jud. 3:5.

68. 1 Kings 9:20.

69. 1 Chr. 1:13-16; 2 Chr. 8:7.

70. Vv. 15-18.

71. Ezra 9:1; Neh. 9:8.

72. Ex. 3:8 and *passim*.

73. In a recent article which he kindly called to my attention ("The Foreign Nations - Israel's 'Nine Bows,'" *Bulletin of the Egyptological Seminar* 3 [1981], 113-24, esp. 120-23), Walter Wifall discusses Egyptian patterns that may provide Middle Kingdom analogies for a seven-name list of foreign peoples. He notes that the Egyptian "Nine Bows" stood for nine peoples who may have represented "the submission of the whole world to the Pharaoh" (p. 120). When lists of such peoples began to appear in the Middle Kingdom, they named seven foreign peoples and apparently presupposed (or sometimes explicitly mentioned) the Two Lands of Upper and Lower Egypt as the other two "Bows." Later, in the 18th and 19th dynasties, all nine peoples mentioned were foreign enemies, not friends or peaceful neighbors. He suggests that the various Egyptian lists might provide analogies for eight- and nine-name lists of geographical areas or peoples that occur in Pss. 68 and 83 and in various

prophetic oracles against foreign nations. Almost in passing (p. 122), he also suggests that several Hexateuchal instances of "a stereotyped list of six or seven foreign nations in Exod 23:23, 33:2, 34:11, and Josh 24:11"--all of which he attributes to the Elohist--may reflect a similar list of "Bows" in Syria-Palestine (in which, as in Middle Kingdom Egyptian lists, the two peoples of one's own land--here Israel and Judah--are left unmentioned, and seven foreign nations or peoples are detailed). While this is not the place to critique Wifall's argument, it is significant that the standard seven-name list established in this article would be more suitable for his analogy than a six-name one (see also his comment about the problem of six-name lists in Dt. and Josh. on p. 123).
74. The many variants in LXX witnesses for most instances of the list provide ample illustration of the frequency with which such errors and recorrections were made; see the entries in Chart One.
75. Gen. 10:15-18 // 1 Chr. 1:13-16; Gen. 15:19-21 (LXX vv. 19-20); Num. 13:29 (LXX v. 30); Ezra (Esdr. B) 9:1.
76. A brief observation needs to be made about the so-called "two-name lists": The two names C and P occur together four times, twice in "J" materials (Gen. 13:7; 34:30) and twice in Jud. 1:4-5, to refer in summary fashion to the same early inhabitants of the land that are described more extensively in the seven-name list. Similarly the names A and C in Josh. 5:1 refer to groupings of Israel's opponents at the time of the initial passage across the Jordan under Joshua's leadership. It is not at all clear whether these examples reflect usages older than the seven-name list (so Ishida), or whether they are secondary usages dependent on that list. Neither assessment need stand in contradiction to the analysis developed in this article.

CHART ONE. EVIDENCE FOR THE LIST OF SEVEN PEOPLES (MT, SP, & VARIOUS LXX WITNESSES)
****

CODE. C = כְּנַעֲנִי, (C) = כְּנַעַן, H = הַחִתִּי, (H) = חֵת, A = הָאֱמֹרִי, P = הַפְּרִזִּי, G = הַגִּרְגָּשִׁי, V = הַחִוִּי, J = הַיְבוּסִי;

(a) = אֶרֶץ, b = עֲמֹרָה, c = צִידֹן, d = הָעַרְקִי, e = הָאַרְוָדִי, f = הַחֲמָתִי, g = הַקַּדְמֹנִי, h = הַקְּנִזִּי, i = הַקֵּינִי,

j = רְפָאִים, (k) = עֲמָלֵק, m = χορραῖοι (= הַחֹרִי*), n = הַעַוִּים, o = הַצִּנְעָנִי, p = הַצְּמָרִי, q = χαλδαιοι (= כַּשְׂדִּים*).

Parentheses around a symbol indicate that a singular name replaces the usual gentilic form. (a)–f are in Gen 10:15–18 // 1 Chron 1:13–16; g–j are in Gen 15:19–21 (LXX vv. 19–20); (k) is in Num 13:29 (LXX v. 30); m is in Josh 9:1; 11:3; 12:8; n–p are in Ezra (Esdr B) 9:1; q is in Neh 9:8 (Esdr B 19:8).

NOTE. The five instances of only two names from the list (Gen 13:7; 34:30; Josh 5:1; Judg 1:4, 5) are listed separately, because it is not clear that they are examples of the list at all.

Gen 10:15–18.

(C)	(a)	(H)	J	A	G	V	b	c	d	e	f	MT, SP	All omit P
(C)	(a)		H	J	A	G	V	b	c	d	e	f	LXX
(C)	(a)		H	J	A	G	V	b	c	f	LXX's 413-cII	LXX's 413-cII also omit d e
(C)	(a)		H	J	A	V	G	b	c	d	e	f	LXX's k
(C)	(a)		H	J	G	V	b	c	A	d	e	f	LXX's 128
(C)	(a)		H	J	G	c	A	d	e	f	LXX's C''-128 (includes ej)	LXX's C''-128 also omit V b

Gen 15:19–21 (LXX vv. 19–20).

g h i H P j A C G J   MT, LXX's Ma(+ V post A a^{b?})bd(om H P j A)efimorwxc2a?lw(om i)Œ   MT & one major LXX strand omit V; LXX's d also omits H P j A and lw also omits i

g h i H P j A C G V J   SP, LXX's ℭ^c

g h i H P j A C V G J   LXX's (A)Dghjlnp(om H P)q(om i H P) s(+ i H P post P)tu(om i H P)vyℜᵖ   LXX's A begins at v. 20; LXX's p omits H P, qu omit i H P, and s inserts a second i H P after P

234

Ex 3:8.

C H A P V J	MT
C H A P G V J	SP, LXX's Bmn𝔈ᶜ
C H A P V G J	LXX's AFMac-eghj-lo-rt-c₂A𝔈f𝔏rₛ(G *sub* ⊤)
C H A P V J G	LXX's b
C H V P A G J	LXX's is
C H V J	LXX's f

MT omits G

LXX's 𝔖 has G under ⊤

LXX's f omits A P G

Ex 3:17.

C H A P V J	MT
C H A P G V J	SP, LXX's BAaoqrux𝔄𝔖(G *sub* ⊤)
C H A G P V J	LXX's bw
C H A P J G V	LXX's n
C H V A P G J	LXX's FMdeghjlptya₂b₂c₂𝔈𝔛
C H V P A G J	LXX's fis
C H V A G P J	LXX's vz

MT omits G

LXX's 𝔖 has G under ⊤

Ex 13:5.

C H A V J	MT
C H A V G V J	SP
C H A V J G P	LXX's AFMa-ceghjlmv-z𝔈𝔖(G P *sub* ⊤)
C H A V J P G	LXX's kA
C H A P J V G	LXX's dpta₂b₂𝔛
C H V G A P J	LXX's Bfioqrs
C H V A J G P	LXX's n𝔏ᶻ(*om* P)
C H P V A G J	LXX's 71

MT omits P G

LXX's 𝔖 has G P under ⊤

LXX's 𝔏ᶻ omits P

Ex 23:23.

A H P C V J
A H P C G V J
A H P C G V V
A P C G V J
C A H G P V J

MT, LXX's 1𝕮ᵐ(*om* V)
LXX's BAFMa-jm-pru-xza₂b₂𝔄𝔘𝔈𝔖
LXX's k(*om* V)q(*om* V)s
LXX's t(*om* P)𝓛ᵛ
SP

MT & LXX's 1 omit G; LXX's 𝕮ᵐ omits G V

LXX's kq omit V J and s omits J
LXX's t omits H P and 𝓛ᵛ omits H

Ex 23:28.

V C H
A V C H
A V C H J
A V C H P G J
A H V C
A H C V
C A H G P V J
C A H

MT
LXX's BAFa-cfhiklmoruwxa₂b₂𝔄𝔖
LXX's Mdpt
LXX's egjnsvz 18(*om* G)𝔈
LXX's 𝔈
LXX's 𝓛ᵛ
SP(*om* P 𝔄𝔈*[*i.l.s.m.*])
LXX's 𝕮ᵐ

MT omits A P G J
Many LXX witnesses omit P G J
LXX's Mdpt omit P G
LXX's 18 omits G
LXX's 𝔈𝓛ᵛ omit G P J

SP's 𝔄𝔈* omit P
LXX's 𝕮ᵐ omits G P V J

Ex 33:2.

C A H P V J
C A H P V J
C A H P V G J
C A H G P V J
A H P V J C G
A H P G V J C

A H P V G J C
A H P G V J J
A C H P V G J

MT
LXX's AFMdlpta₂b₂𝔄𝔈𝔈(*om* J 𝔈ᶠ)𝔖(G *sub* ÷)
LXX's ck(*om* J)m
SP
LXX's egjnsvxz 77ᵛⁱᵈ(*om* C G)𝓛ʳᶻ
LXX's ahor𝕮ᵐ(+ C *inter* G *et* V *in* r*ᵛⁱᵈ)

LXX's fi
LXX's Bqu (+ C *post* V *in* ᵇᵃᵇmg)
LXX's bwy(G V *pro* V G)

MT omits G
LXX's 𝔈ᶠ omits J and 𝔖 has G under ÷
LXX's k omits J

LXX's 77 omits C G
LXX's r* apparently inserts another C
   between G and V

LXX's Bqu omit C (restored in ᵇᵃᵇ mg)

236

Ex 34:11.

A C H P V J J   MT

A C H P V G J   LXX's AFMabc(*om* P G J)dhklm(*om* C)oprtuwxya₂b₂ AꞦ𝒞ᵐ(*om* J)Ɇ(*om* G)𝔖(G *sub* ÷)

MT omits G

LXX's c omits P G J, m omits C, 𝒞ᵐ omits J, Ɇ omits G, and 𝔖 has G under ÷

A C H P V J G   LXX's egjnsvz𝓛ʳ

A C P H V G J   LXX's Bq 128(+ P *ad fin*)

LXX's 128 adds a second P at end

A C P H V J G   LXX's fi

A H P C V J   LXX's 𝓛ʷ

LXX's 𝓛ʷ omits G

C A H G P V J   SP

    J G [4Q paleo Exᵐ(only G preserved, but space demands reconstruction in 5th position in 7-name list)

Num 13:29 (LXX v. 30).

(k) H J A C   MT, LXX's ℬ Arab

(k) H V J A C   SP, LXX(V *sub* ÷ *in* 𝔊𝔖)

MT & LXX's ℬ Arab omit P G V

SP & LXX omit P G; LXX's 𝔊𝔖 have V under ÷

(k) H A V J C   LXX's Ɇ

(k) H V A C   LXX's 128 𝒞

LXX's Ɇ omits P G

LXX's 128 𝒞 omit P G J

Deut 7:1.

H G A C P V J   MT, SP, LXX(*om* A   s: *om* C Ɇᵐ: *om* V Cyr)

LXX's s omits A, Ɇᵐ omits C, and Cyr omits V

H A G C P V J   LXX's B* 392

A H P J C V G   LXX's 𝓛

H A C P G V J   LXX's 𝔑ᶜ

H A C P V J G   LXX's 381

Deut 20:17.

H A C P V J
H A C P V J G

MT, LXX's B*k
LXX's AFMⓈabçẹ(om P V)fij(om P V)lmoqrsvwyzb₂
  Aᵈwℤℭr𝔖ᵐ vid(G sub ÷)

MT & LXX's B*k omit G
LXX's ej omit P V and 𝔖ᵐ has G under ÷

H A C P V G J
H A P C V G J
H A P V G J
C A H G P V J

LXX's Bab ᵐgNgn(om J)a₂ℤlv
LXX's x
LXX's d(om J)pt
SP

LXX's n omits J

LXX's pt omit C and d omits C J

Josh 3:10.

C H V P G A J
C H P V A G J
C H P V A J G
C H V P A G J
C H P V G A J

MT, LXX's Aabdhlm(om H)optyb₂A(H C pro C H A-codd)𝔖ᵐ vid
LXX's BM(om V)Ncefjqrsuvzℤℭᵗ(V pro J)
LXX's gnwℤ(om H ℤᶠ)ℭʳ
LXX's Fia₂
LXX's kx

LXX's m omits H

LXX's M omits V and ℭᵗ has a second V for J

LXX's ℤᶠ omits H

Josh 9:1.

H A C P V J

MT, LXX's A-codⓈ(+ G inter V et J in 𝔖ᵐ mg)

MT & LXX's A-codⓈ omit G, but it is added in 6th position in margin of 𝔖ᵐ (cf. ℭʳ Or-Lat)

H A G C P V J
H A C P V G J
H A C P V m J
H C P V A G J
H C V A G J P

LXX's AFMNⓈa-dlm(om A)oprtxya₂b₂A-ed
LXX's ℭʳ Or-lat
LXX's k (cf. Josh 11:3; 12:8)
LXX's Befhijqsuvzℭᵗℤ
LXX's gn(om A G J)w

LXX's m omits A

LXX's k replaces G with m

LXX's n omits A G J

Josh 11:3.

C A H P J V MT, LXX's A(C *pro* A *in* A*, *corr in* A^a)FGNϑab ciklmoxya₂(*om* C)b₂𝔄𝔖 Or-lat — All omit G; LXX's a₂ also omits C and A* has a second C for A

C m A H P J V LXX's efjs(*om* C)z — LXX's K(apparently) and defgjnpstvwz

C m A J H P V LXX's v — 18(apparently) 𝔏^r add m, sw𝔏^r also

C m A V J P H LXX's K^*vid* gnw(*om* C) 18^*vid* 𝔏^r(*om* C) — omit C, and dpt also omit J V P (cf.

C m A H LXX's dpt — LXX's k for Josh 9:1; 12:8)

C A V J P H LXX's Bhqru(*om* C)Æ — LXX's u also omits C

C A V P J H LXX's Cᵗ

C A P V J H LXX's Cᶜ

Josh 12:8.

H A C P V J MT, LXX's BAFGNϑab(*om* H b'b*)c(*om* C)hi(*om* P V i*)lqruxya₂Æ(J V *pro* V J)𝔏^r𝔖(+ G *in fine* 𝔖^m mg) — MT & many LXX witnesses omit G; LXX's b'b* also omit H, c also omits C, i* also omits P V, and 𝔖^m adds G at end in margin

H A C P V J G LXX's Kgnw(*om* P V)Cᵗ (cf. 𝔖^m mg) — LXX's w omits P V

H A C P G V J LXX's m(C A *pro* A C)ob₂𝔄(V G *pro* G V)

H G A C P V J LXX's ejsvz 16 236

m A H C P P G V J LXX's k (cf. Josh 9:1; 11:3) — LXX's k adds m

C H A C P V G J LXX's d(*om* G J)pt — LXX's dpt have C twice, but d also omits G J

Josh 24:11.

A P C H G V J MT, LXX's Aϑabc(G H *pro* H G)iluxya₂(V G *pro* G V)b₂𝔖

A C P V J H G LXX's BMNho-rtAÆ

A C P V H J G LXX's d-fjkmsvz

A P C V H J G LXX's gnw𝔏^r

239

Judg 3:5.

C H A P V J	MT, LXX's BAMNa-cefh-koq-sux-a₂$\mathfrak{C}^t\mathfrak{E}\mathfrak{L}^r\mathfrak{S}$
C H A P V J G	LXX's glnwÅ
C H A P V G J	LXX's b₂
C H A V P J G	LXX's dptv
H C A P V J	LXX's m

MT & most LXX witnesses omit G

LXX's m omits G

1 Kings 9:20.

A H P V J	MT (*vacat* LXX)
A H P C V J G	LXX's Ax$\mathfrak{S}$(C *et* G *sub* ÷)
A H P V C J G	LXX's Å(*om* G Å-cod)

MT omits C G; LXX lacks vv. 15-25

$\mathfrak{S}$ has C and G under ÷

LXX's Å-cod omits G

1 Chron 1:13-16.

(C) (a) (H)	J A G V b c d e f	MT	
(C) (a)	H	J A G V b c d e f	LXX's ANa-e(*om* V e*)fijmn p(J *pro* b)q(*om* d e)tyze₂ Å(C *pro* H)

All omit P (cf. // Gen 10:15-18)
LXX's Bghc₂ lack vv. 11-16 (vv. 11-23 and 13-16 are under ⁕ in LXX's cn and i, respectively); LXX's e* omits V, p has a second J for b, q omits d e, and Å has C for H

2 Chron 8:7.

H A P V J	MT, LXX

All omit C G

Ezra (Esdr B) 9:1.

C H P J n o p A	MT, LXX's BANc-ehjlmpqtwÅ
C H P J A p n o	LXX's be₂
C H V P J A p n o	LXX's y
C H P J n A p	LXX's n

MT & almost all LXX witnesses omit G V

LXX's y omits only G

Neh 9:8 (Esdr B 19:8).

C H A P J G	MT, LXX's BASc-ej-lnpqtwₓ	MT & most LXX witnesses omit V
C H A P J G V	LXX's ye₂	
q C H A P J G V	LXX's b	LXX's b adds q
C H A P V J G	LXX's h	

Gen 13:7.

C P   MT, SP, LXX   All lack H A G V J

Gen 34:30.

C P   MT, SP, LXX   All lack H A G V J

Josh 5:1.

A C   MT, LXX (φοινικης *loco* χαναναιων *pro* ʾⁿⁿⁿ)   All lack H P G V J

Judg 1:4.

C P   MT, LXX   All lack H A G V J

Judg 1:5.

C P   MT, LXX   All lack H A G V J

CODE. C = כנען, (C) = כנעני, H = חתי, (H) = חת, A = אמרי, P = פרזי, G = גרגשי, V = חוי, J = יבוסי;
(a) = צידן, b = עמרה, c = סדם, d = אדמה, e = אדמי, f = חמת, g = ערקי, h = ארודי, i = צמרי,
j = מאנזב, (k) = עמלק, m = χομμαιοι (=), n = , o = עמלק, p = מאכתי, q = χαλδαιοι, q = χαλδαιοι .

MISOGYNY IN THE OLD TESTAMENT

Morgan L. Phillips

Over the past decade a fresh critical perspective
on the biblical materials has been generated by feminist commentators. This perspective has sensitized
many of us to one of the most negative characteristics
of the Bible: its denigration of women. This article
will not defend this denigration nor deny its existence.
It will question the appropriateness of charging the
Old Testament with sex discrimination, anti-feminism,
and misogyny.

There is a gamut of feminist opinion on the extent
of the Bible's anti-feminist bias. Judith Ochshorn[1]
summarizes these opinions in the following passage from
her recent book:

> Since the current revival of feminism, so
> much has been written in the last decade
> about women and the Judeo-Christian tradition
> that it is now possible to isolate a number
> of the major positions. Some have rejected
> Western religions outright as a part of the
> patriarchal oppression of women. At the
> other extreme are those who see the vision
> of parts of the Old and New Testaments as
> originally benign, egalitarian, even feminist,
> but later distorted, either by translations
> that masculinized more sexually inclusive
> imagery, or by attitudinal changes in the
> Bible rooted in sociological necessities,
> or by moral decadance. In between these
> two positions are those who, for example,
> believe that despite the patriarchal social
> structure of ancient Israel, or the "domestic
> code" of the New Testament, which restricted
> or subordinated women because of the secular
> conflict between order and freedom, women
> either were as highly honored as men in
> their separate-but-equal roles as mothers
> or shared with men a spiritual equality in
> Christ.[2]

Two moderate views with which we shall be concerned in
the following pages are represented by Phyllis Trible
and Phyllis Bird.

Discrimination against women was inherent
in the socio-religious organization of
Israel. It was a function of the system.
And though this systematic discrimination
need not be represented as a plot to
subjugate women - and thereby liberate the
male ego - the system did enforce and
perpetuate the dependence of women and an
image of the female as inferior to the
male.[3]

Feminism is my concluding illustration of
involvement between the world and the Bible.
By feminism I do not mean a narrow focus
upon women, but rather a critique of culture
in light of misogyny. This critique affects
the issues of race and class, psychology,
ecology, and human sexuality. For some
people today the Bible supports female
slavery and male dominance in culture,
while for others it offers freedom from
sexism. Central in the discussions are
such passages as the creation accounts in
Genesis, certain laws in Leviticus, Song
of Songs, the wisdom literature, various
Gospel stories about Jesus and the powerless
and particular admonitions of Paul and his
successors. Out of these materials a
biblical hermeneutics of feminism is
emerging.[4]

These two quotations represent reasonable, sup-
portable claims with respect to Scripture. Dr. Bird
recognizes that the Bible is a collection of materials
reflecting the limitations and relativities of a human
culture, and that it is unreasonable to blame those
materials for being unable to transcend those limitations. She widely renounces theories of conspiracy.
She recognizes the need to see the discriminatory materials in the wider context of the "socioreligious organization of Israel."

Ms. Trible recognizes that there is some ambiguity
in the overall "position" of the Bible with regard to
sexism; she recognizes that in asking the feminist
question one assumes certain hermeneutical principles
which must themselves be critically evaluated.

A third and less irenic perspective is represented

by Judith Ochshorn in the stimulating study cited
above. Her thesis is that misogyny is indigenous to
the monotheistic religion of Israel, in contrast to the
sexual equalitarianism of the polytheistic religions
belonging to Israel's neighbors. It is not possible
to evaluate her interpretations of Ancient Near Eastern
texts here, but her understanding of the biblical materials will be challenged at some points.

One finds in all three of these feminists commentators a sound, scientific approach to the question of
women and the Bible, and with most of their insights
the current author must agree. Why, then, the need for
this article?

There are certain rhetorical elements in the two
quotations cited above which illustrate a basic problem
in addressing a biblical text with a contemporary issue-
related question. "Discrimination against women,"
"image of the female as inferior to the male," "critique of culture in the light of misogyny." These
rhetorical elements when applied to the Bible are anachronistic, and their use, however much divorced from
simplistic claims of male conspiracy, carries the connotation of modern attitudes into the ancient perspective. This article will attempt to introduce into the
valuable analysis of the feminists cited above a caution and a wider perspective than their work acknowledges.

One must distinguish between the paradigm or
Weltanschauung which lies behind the biblical materials
under discussion, and the logical implications of those
materials when viewed in isolation. It is not difficult
to find examples of sex discrimination in the laws of
the Old Testament. This is particularly true in matters
of sexual behavior i.e., adultery, loss of virginity
before marriage, rape. One can make a seemingly invin-
cible case for gross discrimination, for blatant misogyny. It cannot be disputed that if separated from a
world view, a religious world view and not merely a
sociological context, these particular elements are unjust to women.

But within the religious world view of ancient
Israel the "misogynous" texts of the Old Testament cannot be properly evaluated in such modern categories.
Evaluative statements involving "misogyny," "discrimination against," "inferiority of females" are true

criticisms if one is responding to attempts on the part
of contemporary religionists to import these ideas into
a modern Weltanschauung. They do not belong there because they clash with other elements of that modern
world view which contradict them. They do however belong in the world view of the society which produced
the biblical materials where they form a logical and
consistent whole with other elements of the total
Weltanschauung.

One cannot, for example, judge the laws of purification within the priestly Weltanschauung in the same
way that one must judge these same laws when they become contemporary attitudes towards the female body.
One must understand the priestly attitude toward blood
and ritual purity before one can properly evaluate the
attitude toward menstruation in the priestly law code.
"Understanding" does not mean a condescending nod
toward the scientific ignorance of ancient priests; it
means an empathetic comprehension of the survival value
of these attitudes and regulations, as this value is
confirmed by the Weltanschauung of the priests and
their society.

The term "survival value" here does not mean the
survival of a set of social values designed to perpetuate the power of the ruling group, though such perpetu-
ation may well be the by-product of survival. The
reference is to the physical survival of the group in
terms of its understanding of what constitutes the necessary conditions of survival. Its understanding may
be quite different from that of a modern society, and
may therefore appear to be irrelevant or counterproduc-
tive to us. But our evaluation of any ancient materials must begin from the perspective of those who produced them.

At least two critical responses could be made to
the above argument. One could say that regardless of
the original meaning or contextual significance of
alledgedly sexist elements in the Bible, the logical
implication and subsequent influence of these elements
has been and continues to be prejudicial to women. One
could also say that the reservation toward applying
contemporary categories of judgement upon elements of
the biblical text merely pushes the process back (or
ahead?) one step. If it is the Weltanschauung which
validates and gives meaning to these elements which we
can isolate and label "sexist," then it must be the

Weltanschauung itself that is sexist. We have simply
succeeded in widening the scope of feminist critique
rather than qualifying it. The first response is easy
to meet. "Logical implication" is in the eye of the
beholder. Logic itself derives its authority and definition from the Weltanschauung of the logicians and
their disciples. Buddhist logic is not Ayer's logic.
Logicians are ignored on many crucial existential
questions by most people. The priests of Israel are
not responsible for what future generations have made
of their statements, and this is certainly the case if
the significance of the statement is very different
within the context of the Weltanschauung than it is
outside of that context.

The second response is not so easy to refute. If
women are denied access to certain social resources,
if they are denied redress of wrongs or if certain
rights which we consider basic are denied them, what
difference does it make if this comes about because of
an intentional devaluation of the sex, or because of a
different intention which nevertheless has the side
effect of reducing the status of women to an inferior
one vis-a-vis males? In one sense, it makes no difference. When confronted with the Weltanschauung of
ancient Israel, we will reject it on several grounds.
First, it conflicts with our perceptions of reality,
our experience of the world, which of course does not
originate with us but is based on our assimilation of
a paradigm of reality different from that of biblical
society -- let us call this paradigm the scientific
one. We have assimilated the scientific paradigm and
the fact that this paradigm like all others is relative
to culture does not change the fact that it is ours, as
much a part of us as the sensory apparatus and rational
ability by means of which we apprehend and comprehend
the world. The paradigm is subjective and relative,
but it is also objective in that our perceptions and
reason confirm it. That such confirmation is due, at
least in part, to the fact that we have assimilated
the scientific paradigm as a cultural value does not
destroy its objectivity. The fact merely illustrates
that subjectivity and objectivity cannot be separated,
save for purposes of abstract discussion.

We may reject the biblical paradigm because it
conflicts with our experience of the world and our best
understanding of what that experience implies. We may
reject that paradigm on moral grounds. We may find the

division of humanity into the righteous and the sinful
based on adherence or nonadherence to a specific code
of behavior to be unjust, contradicting the dynamics
of the human situation to which we are all subject. We
may reject it on religious grounds, because it is based
on a view of revelation which absolutizes certain modes
of communication between humanity and God, or because
many of its images of God are unacceptable.

We cannot avoid evaluating the biblical
Weltanschauung in terms of our own. But such evaluation is not to be confused with anachronistic judgements about the nature and intentions of the biblical
materials in their historical context. Critical evaluation does not preclude a hermeneutic by which we can
profitably engage the biblical materials and address
our existential questions to them. Anachronistic
judgement obscures the meaning of the text, and prevents
us from finding the authentic human values preserved
therein. In what follows we shall illustrate this
point by comparing examples of feminist hermeneutic
with a more holistic approach.

We turn now to Old Testament materials concerning
creation and law. The selection is not arbitrary. The
creation traditions contain aetiologies of the origin
of humanity and male/female roles. Such aetiologies
purport to reveal the ontological status of their subject matter - the essence of male/female humanity. The
laws are important because as laws they reflect the
values of a society directly. They are the values of
record in any given society. If anything as abstract
as a society has a will, that will is experienced in
the society's laws.

The juxtaposition of creation tradition and legal
material is based on a third point. To speak of a
Weltanschauung may give rise to the misconception that
there is one single viewpoint that characterizes the
entire Old Testament. This is clearly not so. There
are many viewpoints in the Old Testament as every careful reader of the material knows, but these viewpoints
have some fundamental things in common, and these fund-
amentals are what we call here the biblical
Weltanschauung. The center of this Weltanschauung is
justice, the concept of an overarching order that unites
the physical with the social and moral, and which determines the outcome of our behavior.

The creation traditions give us the origin and thus the essential nature of this order, while the legal materials define this order in detail, i.e., what human beings must do to conform to the divinely ordained order. This overall concept of justice is essential for the biblical Weltanschauung because it contains the hub of its theology -- the image of God and the divine-human relationship. It provides the authority of the social order, and is the key to Israel's understanding of her survival, not only in the cultural sense but in the bare physical sense as well.

If justice -- the proper ordering of reality -- is not sustained by God and humanity, then the creation returns to chaos and of course human life is not possible. It is no startling insight to point out that in the biblical Weltanschauung, the realm of social organization, religious and moral choices, and the physical environment, are interlocked in a way that they are not and cannot be in a contemporary western Weltanschauung. When David sins against God by taking a census, the sin may be atoned for by a natural disaster striking the community. When innocent blood is spilled and there is no proper atonement, the ground itself is cursed and will not yield its fruit. A ritual act may disrupt or restore the social order, and an immoral one may cause the physical environment to malfunction. Reality is one, and my division into realms for the sake of comparing Weltanschauung is of course totally foreign to the Bible. It is here contended that we must keep this biblical monism in mind when we evaluate the biblical Weltanschauung based upon it and the morally loaded concepts of such things as sex and race, which are a part of that Weltanschauung.

Ochshorn correctly points out that the God of the Old Testament is consistently portrayed as a "god of righteousness, compassion, justice, and, to a lesser extent, omnipotence and omniscience."[5] She then goes on to conclude from a survey of Old Testament narratives involving women "either that God does behave capriciously in respect to women, or that his passion for righteousness does not extend to women as fully as to men."[6]

If justice is defined as equality, if natural human rights are an assumed fact, then Ochshorn's criticism is correct. But the biblical concept of justice is based on an understanding of the interplay between a given natural, social, and moral order supported by what seemed within the ancient experience to be the self evident facts of life. Our judgement of the biblical materials ought to be made in the light of that interplay. We have inherited the concept of justice from the Bible. We must and have refined the concept to accord with what appears to us to be self evident facts of human existence. It is at the point of the demands of justice that we maintain the biblical image of God and by which we judge the Bible itself. Out of the biblical demand and our response comes our own superior concept of what the justice of God entails for human life. This should not blind us to the fact that ancient Israel sought with equal fidelity to live by that same justice and by her understanding did so.

It is incorrect to say as Ochshorn does that women received less justice than men. The status of women is just in the context of the biblical Weltanschauung. Needless to say, that same status would be unjust in the context of our own Weltanschauung. The contemporary relevance of biblical justice lies not in its substantive rules but in its understanding that there is relationship between morality and the quality of human life.

The creation traditions have been thoroughly treated by feminist commentators and their observations need not be repeated. The usual procedure is to compare the P tradition, especially the creation of human beings, with that of J, and to note that the P story begins with a non-sexist concept of humanity -- man is humankind, made in the image of God and divided into male/female who together receive the divine commission. The commission has three parts: be fruitful and multiply, fill the earth and subdue it, have dominion over all animal life. Phyllis Trible points out that the uniqueness of humankind is expressed in the following features of this part of the narrative: humankind alone is made in the divine image, is separated into male/female, is addressed by God directly, is given dominion. She further notes that in contrast to the J story humankind is composed of an original unity of male/female, and sexual differentiation is not hierarchial. Trible draws the conclusion from all of this that sex role differences play no part in God's creation of humankind, and that therefore the P writer leaves us free of any constraining definitions of masculine-feminine. She writes:

The human creation poeticized in this verse
is not delineated by sexual relationships,
roles, characteristics, attitudes, or emo-
tions. To be sure, the content itself
identifies two responsibilities for humankind,
procreation and dominion over the earth, but
it does not differentiate between the sexes
in assigning this work. Since the first of
these responsibilities, procreation, parallels the divine command given to the fish
of the sea and the birds of the heavens, who
are not themselves explicitly designated
male and female, the use of the phrase "male
and female" in 1:27 does not itself signify
the potential for human fertility but rather
indicates, along with other items, the
uniqueness of humankind in creation. Thus,
in relation to the context, this phrase is
not in the Liturgy to define the specific
sexual functions of man and woman in pro-
creating. On the other hand, a definite
link does exist between the phrase "male
and female" and the responsibility to have
dominion over the earth, since both of these
descriptions manifest the uniqueness of
humankind.[7]

If I have understood Ms. Trible correctly, she
wishes to demonstrate that P avoids creating men and
women into roles shaped by the need to fulfill the
divine commission. The link between the creation of
humankind as male and female, and the divine commission,
is not that this commission can best be carried out by
a division of labor of the type J provides us. According to Trible P avoids sex roles based on the necessity
of carrying out the divine commission, and thus allows
us maximum freedom in defining masculine/feminine.

Trible continues her ironic interpretation of these
oft criticized traditions in her analysis of J. I shall
not repeat her very helpful discussion of Genesis 2 & 3,
but only indicate that she finds the J treatment of the
creation of woman to be one which stresses the equality
of woman, if not her superiority in the temptation narrative, rather than her inferiority as is often argued.
Only after the fall is woman subordinated to man in the
J tradition. Only when we reach the point where the
man is to rule over the woman is there a sexist ordering
of life. This rule takes effect when the man names the

251

woman, an act which according to Trible "chillingly echoes the vocabulary of domination over the animals in episode three" and which reduces the woman to the status of an animal.

> The act itself faults the man for corrupting one flesh of equality, for asserting power over the woman, and for violating the companion corresponding to him.[8]

Trible therefore sees a sharp break in the creation traditions -- prior to the alienation of the first disobedience, man and woman were one -- ontologically in P and ontically in J. There was differentiation but no discriminatory distinction. Sexism belongs to the Fall. Since we are not talking about actual events, this statement means that P & J wish to assert that God's original intention for humanity was a male/female personhood without defined role differences. Such differences are the product of a divine curse and male ego -- a distortion of creation itself.

One may be happy with the concept of such a humanity, but it is doubtful this picture accurately represents P or J. On the contrary P & J see role differentiation as an essential part of the divine intention, and while there is a break between Gen. 2 & 3, it is not the watershed which either Trible or others, i.e., St. Paul, would make it.

Ms. Trible sees P's divine commission consisting of two parts -- procreation and dominion. There is a third element, however -- to subdue. Humankind must multiply, subdue the earth and dominate all life in the earth. The images are not pleasant. To subdue is cabash; the term is brutal and used with regard to people it means either to rape or to enslave. With regard to land it means to conquer. Here it is used in relation to an unpopulated earth -- so the connotation is conquer. This is consistent with the concept of radah -- to have dominion. A survey of places in which the term appears shows it carries a connotation of oppression and abuse. Those who hate you shall dominate; the master dominates the slave; the officer dominates the forced labor group. Israel shall dominate the alien; the unworthy shepards have dominated Israel; the king shall dominate his enemies; the Israelite shall be redeemed from bondage to the stranger so that the stranger will not dominate him. P sees humanity

252

and God united to master a recalcitrant nature. The
means required for this is a social order based on the
procreation power of humanity. The procreative function is essential if this order is to exist and its existence is essential if humanity itself is to survive.
Subjugation and domination are predicated upon procreation. This fact prepares us for the importance that P
(and others) place upon the sexual role consigned to
woman, an importance which is reflected in the legal
codes. Since the divine purpose in creating humankind,
and the survival of humankind, depend upon this subjug-
gation and domination it is no wonder that the process
of procreation is carefully guarded in legal regulations which these same circles have preserved. While
the P creation tradition stresses the God-humanity
axis, the J tradition is concerned with, among other
things, the specific ordering of male/female roles
necessary to carry out the domination of humanity over
nature. At this point one might object that we are
treating the two traditions as though they were one.
One can assume that P, as the final redactor of the
Pentateuch, was familiar with the material he was
redacting. Although his tradition was formed prior to
its integration into the Pentateuch, P was obviously
able to edit his material to achieve some synchroniza-
tion, if not a total harmonization, with what lay before him. Of course we cannot simply assume that J
knew P's material, but surely it was not the exclusive
idea of the priests that humanity was commissioned by
God to dominate nature, i.e., to utilize the natural
resources of the environment according to the divine
will and direction. The concept is rooted in an agricultural, labor intensive society and in its general
import would have been familiar to J.

Trible argues that the materials in Gen. 3:16ff
are not meant to define the appropriate sexual roles of
male and female, but are meant to underscore the curse
-- tilling the soil and bearing children are not pre-
scriptions for the fulfillment of two sexually distinct
humanities, but are the accursed consequences of disobedience (p. 133). Trible has failed here to mark a
distinction between what is considered to be the appropriate role for each human and the existential conditions under which that role shall be fulfilled. Bearing children and tilling the soil are the prescribed
conditions of human creation. This is clear from what
J writes about humans before the Fall. Man is created
originally to till the garden (2:15), and the union of

the man and the woman implies that procreation is expected. It is not childbirth and desire for the man which is the curse, but the pain. It is not labor in the earth which is the curse, but the recalcitrance of the soil which is the actual recipient of the curse rather than man himself. Distinct sex roles are not the result of sin. This result is the anguished conditions of fulfilling these roles.

Trible sees the rule of man over woman stated here as part of the alienation belonging to the human situation. From the viewpoint of the contemporary world this is certainly true. But in the biblical world view it is a natural and logical result of the concept of justice. Humanity is charged in the "P" story with the maintenance of the divinely created order, which requires human control of nature. Such control is implicit in the "J" story- man tills and keeps the garden. This control is indicated by the harsh term radah. The "J" story serves to develop this concept of order by indicating that within the human sphere there is a structure of order based on sexual role definition, a structure which the "P" redactor must have seen as a compliment to his own understanding of humanity's domination of nature.

To be fruitful and multiply the woman must be willing to bear, and to subdue the earth man must be willing to work a recalcitrant field. To ensure this order, man will rule over woman. The term used here is mashal, a term much less harsh and reductive than radah. Mashal signifies the rule of king who secures the proper structure of his kingdom. It is the establishment of a just reign, one in accordance with the rule of God. Thus the sun and the moon rule over their respective spheres, the spheres whose orderly movements determine the celebration of the cult and preserve the sacred times. God rules over Israel and nature. The wise rules over his spirit. God's rule prevents the return of chaos. His rule is revealed in His salvation deeds. Mashal means to keep things in their proper place, to insure justice. Thus man rules over woman to insure the proper ordering of the human sphere.

In the modern world such an arrangement is no longer consistent with the world view which our knowledge and experience dictates. To attempt to implement such an arrangement is to violate the rationality of our own perceptions of reality, which does not mean that such violation is not possible or even probable. That such an arrangement was rational in the context of the biblical world view does not mean that woman was inferior or that there was a plot to subjugate her to purely male needs.

In a labor intensive society the continuing production of a labor force is essential to survival. The biblical materials are primarily concerned with survival. The religion of Israel is among other things a survival mechanism. It is a system of behaviors designed to preserve the life sustaining order of the environment. This aspect is often overlooked or undervalued because we are accustomed to viewing religion as a private matter, as an area of individual conscience concerned with private values, or as an ideological facade for our social/political concerns. In the ancient world the cult and its associated values had survival value. To violate a taboo or fail to conform to the divinely ordained pattern was to risk the destruction of the world as a life sustaining network of forces.

The biblical Weltanschauung demanded that the active male force, which appeared to be the stronger, the dynamic element of society and of nature, be the organizing force of human society. As man tilled the soil and brought forth its fruit, so he must bring forth from woman the humanity to continue the process. As the soil was created to be productive, to be the passive recipient of the seed and of the male activity of cultivation, so woman was created to be the passive recipient of her husband's impregnating power. It follows from this that man must rule over, i.e., set in her proper place, in her role, the woman, just as he does for the soil and just as God does for him. It is a logical hierarchy, as consistent with the rationality of the ancient worldview as it is inconsistent with the rationality of ours.

Both Trible and Ochshorn make much of the fact that it is the male who calls the name of the female in the creation story of "J". They interpret this as an assertion of male power over the very being of the female. The argument turns on the widely acknowledged connection in the Semitic world between name and object. The name is an expression of the essence of what or who is named, and thus has a tangible relation with that essence. Thus man is responsible for the secondary status of woman in society and in the "natural" ordering of things.

It is a mistake to assume that the connection of name with essence means that the name confers the essence. The man names only after God has conferred with nature of what is being named. The giving of the name is not an act of creation but of recognition. It is not man who determines the nature of the beasts or the function of woman. He merely recognizes and suitably acknowledges what has already been determined. The power of male over female is not as blatant or as absolute as the feminists believe it to be.

The paradigm of role, order, survival explains the laws which we commonly designate as discriminatory. There are eight areas in the legal codes where one can easily claim sex discrimination. These are cases involving rape, divorce, virginity, the ordeal of jealousy, inheritance, purification, vows, and redemption from the sanctuary. In the first three types of cases the woman clearly bears the onus of maintaining a special sexual status. The virgin who is raped must marry her attacker. The betrothed virgin who falsely claims rape is guilty of adultery and dies with her partner. The betrothed virgin who is raped is innocent. In the first case the woman is "compensated" with a divorce proof marriage; while this practice would clearly be brutal in a contemporary setting, it may well have appeared humane in a society in which male protection was made essential by physical as well as social conditions. In the second case male and female suffer equally. Divorce is in the hands of the male, which is consistent with the male ordering principle discussed above. The emphasis on virginity -- the bride must be a virgin and proof must be available if the bridegroom disputes the fact after the wedding night -- is clearly rooted in fundamental misconceptions of the power of virgin soil to nourish the seed, and a fear of mixing different seeds. Ancient taboos and magic practices are more likely explanations for these laws than male ego concerns. This is consistent with the significance of procreation and the female role therein. It is not surprising that the most blatantly discriminatory laws -- from our point of view -- involve sexual relationships. Such relationships are the basis of humanity's fulfillment of the divine commission, and of physical survival in a labor intensive society.

The remaining cases are all found in the P codes of Numbers and Leviticus. The laws of inheritance favor the male heir. A daughter may inherit in the absence of sons, and a widow apparently does not inherit under any circumstances (perhaps she has her dowry or a claim on her children?). This discrimination is based on the desire to avoid alienation of land from the tribe, which is in turn based on the ownership of that land by God and His distribution of that land among the tribes. The Providental ordering of things requires the 12 tribe structure, the divine right to distribute the land, and safeguards to ensure each tribe and clan participates in this distribution in perpetuity. The female who inherits must marry within the tribe, and the reluctance to permit inheritance by a widow who is no longer a member of the tribe may be traced to fear of land alienation rather than to a pervasive sense of female inferiority.

The law pertaining to the ordeal of jealousy shows a strong bias against the woman. The jealous husband may require his wife to drink a magic potion -- the water of bitterness made of water mixed with dust from the sanctuary floor, which the woman drinks before the priest, while holding a cereal offering and taking an oath. If she is guilty she shall swell, if innocent, "she shall be free and conceive children." The point is clear. The spirit of jealousy which comes upon the husband is a divinely appointed safeguard for the sexual purity of the wife, which is essential for producing children free from the taint of a violated taboo. The discrimination here is not based on the woman's inferiority but on what is perceived as necessary in preserving her vital social and human function -- a function which adultery subverts in this Weltanschauung. It is a discrimination which does not create female inferiority as long as the procreative role remains vital and the view that adultery counters this role is realistic. In a contemporary setting where these factors do not hold such discrimination would obviously be sexist.

Redemption from the sanctuary involves discrimination in the price to be paid for a male and a female child when they are bought back from the sanctuary after having been dedicated to sanctuary service, i.e., Samuel. A higher valuation is placed on the male than the female. The discrimination here is two fold -- age and sex. The male in the prime of life (20-60 yrs.)

has the highest valuation. This is clearly based on
the productivity potential of the adult male which is
superior to that of any other person in a labor intensive society. Such valuations reflect what the sanctuary could expect to realize from the work of this
person, and is no more or less sexist than a modern
court awarding damages to a family who has lost a wage
earner based on the potential earning power of that
wage earner.

The laws pertaining to women's vows gives the
father of an unmarried woman and the husband of a married one the right to annul her vow. One must consider
two things here. The male, who is charged by God with
the responsibility of preserving the divine order, is
responsible to protect that order from any rash vow
which could bind the woman and her family to a bad
course of action. The rash vow is seen as a frequent
danger in the Hebrew world. Secondly, the law is word-
ed with the intention of protecting the woman from arbitrary actions on the part of the male. The man must
cancel the vow immediately upon hearing it. He may not
use the threat of cancellation to harass the woman, and
if he does cancel it he bears responsibility for the
unfulfilled oath, not the woman who is then guiltless.
The dynamic here is obviously the power of the oath and
the results of its violation. Since the male in the
divine scheme of things bears primary responsibility
before God for the world order, he must bear the onus
for the results of the oath taken by the woman who is
part of his responsibility. The law stems naturally
from the hierarchial principle of order essential to
the biblical Weltanschauung.

The priestly laws of purification are often invoked as proof that women were regarded as inferior in
Israelite society. They are unclean in certain situations -- menstruation, child birth -- which are unique
to women, and therefore such uncleanness implies the
inferior status of the female function and a defect in
women's physical makeup. Unclean is assumed to imply
immoral, sinful, dirty, inferior. It is here contended
that this is not the case. Unclean is a sui generis
category which cannot be translated into the categories
of sinfulness, immorality, unhygenic, or inferiority.
It is a category which was obviously very important in
the biblical Weltanschauung, certainly in the world of
the priests, but which has no analogue in ours.

The following things render one unclean: certain
dead animals and dead humans, body discharges, childbirth, skin disease, sin, and the ashes of the red
heifer. This list makes clear that uncleanness includes sin, but is not identical with it. One can be
rendered unclean by bodily functions which are not
themselves condemned in any way, and by things which
are in themselves considered holy. There is therefore
no connotation of inferiority here. Menstruating women
are unclean, as are men who have nocturnal emissions.
The mystery of the blood, fraught with magic power and
having a powerful holiness about it creates the taboo
of the menstruating woman, not any desire to label her
weak, inferior, or unhygenic. The mystery of childbirth, involving the transition from one realm to another, a rite de passage of enormous power, creates the
taboo of the new mother. These taboos are attempts to
safeguard the essential process of procreation and
birth, which involve contact with the forbidden power
of the blood. It is of course often pointed out that
the woman must undergo a longer time of purification
for her bodily emission than the man for his, and that
the time required for purification in the case of a
female birth is twice as long as the case for a male
birth. This is due to the greater power of female
fertility and the greater taboo associated with blood
than with any other emission. The greater taboo applies to the woman because her situation brings her into closer contact with a holy power which inexplicably
erupts into the profane and constitutes a threat to
the order of things. To say that this is a rationali-
zation masking a desire to keep woman in a weak and
ineffectual position is to misunderstand the realism of
this taboo in the context of the priestly Weltanschauung.

That which renders unclean is not necessarily itself unclean. This is illustrated in the matter of the
red heifer. In order to make the water of impurity,
which sprinkled upon a person cleanses that person from
defiling contact with the dead, one slaughters a perfect
red heifer outside the camp. The heifer is burned completely. The ashes are collected, and when mixed with
water makes the mixture which cleanses when sprinkled
on the unclean person. The presiding priest and the
person who gathers the ashes to bring them back to the
sanctuary are both rendered unclean by this procedure.
That which makes clean, also makes unclean. The sacred
makes unclean, as in later rabbinic thought the sacred
books defile the hands. One cannot assume that

259

uncleanness, or the power to render unclean, means inferiority or immorality or sinfulness. Blood which
renders unclean is also the effective agent in atoning
for sin. The proper ordering of the world requires
the proper relationship of the sacred to the profane
and this requirement, fundamental to the biblical
Weltanschauung implicit in the Pentateuch, is behind
the hierarchial ordering of human society and the basic
distinction between the roles of men and women as they
appear in these materials.

Conclusion

It is not surprising that we are tempted to label
the Old Testament misogynous, and to dispute on that
basis the claim that the God of Hebrew scripture is
just. But if we are to maintain a fruitful theological
engagement with the biblical tradition, we must seek
the significance of these materials within their original Weltanschauung. We cannot accept Israel's substantive understanding of justice because it is rooted
in a world view alien in many ways to our own. We cannot adopt into our perspective Israel's understanding
of the world order, in which her definition of justice
is rooted. But we can affirm with her the formal understanding of justice as the conformity to a divinely
created order which is experienced in concrete principles of moral behavior. We can preserve biblical
thoughts, even if we cannot preserve the whole perspective of biblical culture.

Such a position does not apologize for readings of
the Bible which lead to oppression. It ought to be
clear that one cannot arbitrarily import into a contemporary Weltanschauung elements from an ancient one.
When this is attempted there are contradictions between
the imported elements and those integral to the modern
Weltanschauung. At the same time the imported elements
lose their original meaning and take on a meaning they
did not have in their original context. This is the
true injustice.

FOOTNOTES

1. Judith Ochshorn, <u>The Female Experience and the Nature of the Divine</u>; Bloomington: University of Indiana Press, 1981.
2. <u>Ibid</u>., p. 13.
3. Phyllis Bird, "Images of Women in the Old Testament," p. 50 in <u>Religion and Sexism</u> ed. Rosemary Radforth Reuther; NY: Simon and Schuster, 1974.
4. Phyllis Trible, <u>God and the Rhetoric of Sexuality</u>; Philadelphia: Fortress Press, 1978, p. 7.
5. Ochshorn, <u>op</u>. <u>cit</u>., p. 141.
6. <u>Ibid</u>., p. 154.
7. <u>Ibid</u>., p. 19.
8. Trible, <u>op</u>. <u>cit</u>., p. 133.

WISDOM AND HUMANISM

John Priest

"The heavens are the LORD'S heavens, but the
earth he has given to the sons of men"
(Ps. 115:16)

In one of his earliest publications Professor
Toombs addressed the question of "Old Testament
Theology and the Wisdom Literature."[1] In the article
he proposed that wisdom materials can be integrated
into Old Testament theology by analogy to the Law,
which he argues "takes its religious significance, not
from its content, but from its context" (194). He
notes that while law, cult, and covenant arise out of a
historical context, "Wisdom, on the other hand, takes
its rise in individual experience, and speaks again to
individual experience... But recognition that the contexts of wisdom and covenant are thus radically different does not preclude the possibility that both wisdom
and covenant came into those contexts in fundamentally
the same way; as a mighty act of God in response to
human need and human insufficiency" (196).

A central support of his thesis comes from an
exegesis of Pro. 2:1-5, hinging upon the final verse of
the passage.[2] The teacher, having called his son to
the most arduous pursuit of wisdom and understanding,
concludes, "then you will understand the fear of YHWH
and find the knowledge of God." Toombs comments, "It
appears that the search for wisdom, demanding as it is,
does not lead directly to wisdom, but to God. It
brings not a sense of achievement, but of reverence"
(194). In the article, however, he also notes that
much of Proverbs "has a definite 'humanistic' cast,
speaking as man to man, and evoking no specific religious principles" (194). Thus, upon the occasion of
this volume honoring him, I propose to reflect upon the
issues he raised, wisdom, theology, and humanism, in
light of the extensive wisdom research which has been
done since his publication.

That research has been both extensive and intensive. There is no need to review its history since
excellent surveys, with copious bibliography, are readily available.[3] As with any burgeoning enterprise,
however, wisdom research has not only proposed new solutions and proposals but also has raised new problems

and reassessed old ones from a fresh perspective. The most significant of these, in my judgment, relate to the scope of wisdom in the canonical materials and the location of wisdom in the broader context of the religion of the biblical community. Both of these bear directly on the subject of this article, wisdom and humanism.

For a long time the study of Old Testament wisdom was limited to the canonical books of Proverbs, Job, Ecclesiastes, a few Psalms, and the deutero-canonical books of Sirach and the Wisdom of Solomon. Now, as is well known, the situation is entirely changed. It is claimed that wisdom may be found in most of the prophets, narratives such as the Joseph Story and the so-called Succession Narrative, Deuteronomy, Daniel, the Primeval History, Esther, and even certain cultic materials.[4] This expansion has led Roland Murphy to remark that the question now would be "Where has Old Testament wisdom failed to appear?"[5] The proliferation of canonical material claimed to fall within the orbit of wisdom leads to a methodological morass and has, with considerable justification, been sharply criticized.[6] Nevertheless, that such claims could seriously be made raises a significant question which we shall address in the concluding section of this paper.

The problem of finding an appropriate place for wisdom in an overall survey of Old Testament religion and theology has long been recognized,[7] and quite divergent proposals have been made. Some have maintained that wisdom, in its original formulation at least, represents an aberrant block and cannot be integrated into Yahwism.[8] Perhaps the most prevalent view of an older generation, a view still maintained with considerable diversities of nuance, was that of a rather straightforward development in wisdom from an earlier Israelite secular wisdom to wisdom brought under the way of Yahwistic piety and finally "nationalized" by its equation with the revealed Law.[9] A significant modification of this position asserts that even the earlier apparently secular outlook was itself religious though not Yahwistic and that the movement is not from the secular to the religious but from the general religious to the specific Yahwistic.[10] Further, it has been persuasively argued that wisdom from the beginning was implicitly Yahwistic and only became more explicitly so in its development.[11] This requires adopting of a definition of Yahwism broader than is commonly made,

and in this connection Toombs decades ago made a remarkably prescient comment, "as long as Old Testament theology is represented exclusively in terms of the history, institutions and cultus of the Hebrew people, it
will exclude the wisdom literature by definition."[12]
Finally, from the earliest period to the present there
have been scholars who seek to resolve the problem by
simply recognizing that there are divergent strands of
tradition embedded in the wisdom material, some essentially secularistic which must be brought under the
purview of religious wisdom in order for the whole to
become a viable part of the religious outlook of the
Old Testament.[13]

A good case can be made for the view that wisdom,
in some instances at least, seems to stand outside the
central traditions of the Old Testament. Much of the
material shows no overt interest in Torah, salvation
history, election or covenant. This fact simply must
be recognized and taken seriously, but as I shall suggest below, I believe that it can be explained in a
manner which can account for its inclusion in a genuine
Israelite framework. Similarly, while the view which
holds that all wisdom was secular in the beginning and
only gradually took on the religious overtones now de-
tected in the collections ought to be rejected, studies
which continue to call attention to some religious development continue to remain valuable in many exegetical
contexts.[14] Assertion that all wisdom was from the outset implicitly Yahwistic seems more problematical, but
the implications inherent in that view are of considerable consequence for the proposal to be made in the
concluding section of this article.

Despite the insights which each of the above proposals may contribute to our understanding of rich fullness of wisdom, none of them seems to do full justice
to all of the evidence, and the thesis of divergent
strands remains the best explanation congruent with the
texts themselves. No single wisdom doctrine is to be
found. There were sages, from the earliest period
which can be reconstructed, who were informed by
Yahwism, and so they taught. There were sages apparently informed by a broader religious outlook, and so they
taught. But there were sages who taught without either
explicit or implicit reference to religion in general
or to Yahwism in particular.

If the above conclusion be allowed, at least for

purposes of further discussion, an interesting question emerges. Did the collectors of diverse wisdom traditions simply collect, without comment, differing points of view, or can we detect traces of tension, conflict, or inner dialectic alluding to a recognition of the inherent diversity of the materials? The biblical evidence utilized in the following discussion will be limited primarily to material in Proverbs, the only canonical book universally agreed upon as representing wisdom. Biblical quotations from Proverbs will be noted only by chapter and verse. It seems clear that such evidence is present and we shall proceed on the basis of the lesser to the greater. Notice has often been given to the immediate juxtaposition of the sentences in 15:16f.:

> Better a little with fear of the Lord
> than great treasure and trouble with it.
> Better is a dinner of herbs where love is
> than a fatted ox and hatred with it.
> (Cf. also 17:1)

One might also call attention to the secular judgment on a lying tongue (12:19) and lying lips which are an abomination to YHWH (12:22);[15] or to the shift from simply saying that "The sacrifice of the wicked is an abomination"(21:27), to specifying that "The sacrifice of the wicked is an abomination to YHWH" (15:8).

The above examples are intended to be illustrative and by no means exhaustive. In and of themselves they could appear trivial, but a step further may be taken. It has often been said that however secularistic the sages may seem to have been, they were fully aware of "limits" imposed on human activity. "Man proposes, but God disposes."[16] However, one of the parade examples adduced in support of this conclusion warrants comparison with two other sentences.

> No wisdom, no understanding, no counsel,
> can avail against YHWH.
> The horse is made ready for the day of battle,
> but the victory belongs to YHWH.
> (21:30f.)

To this may be counterposed 20:18:

> Plans are established by counsel;
> by wise guidance wage war.

266

or 24:6

> For by wise guidance you can wage your war,
> and in abundance of counselors there is
> victory.

Still and all, the above examples could be interpreted
simply as reflecting retention of "secular" and "religious" strands without any sense of tension or conflict.
More substantive evidence, however, is at hand.

Roland Murphy has observed that "The kerygma of
wisdom can be summed up in one word: life."[17] A representative examination of "life" with respect to a
secular perspective and a religious perspective may be
illuminating. On the one hand we are told that wisdom
is a tree of life in whose right hand is long life
(3:16-18), the words of the wise are life to him who
finds them (4:22), the one who heeds instruction is on
the path to life (10:27), and the wise man's path leads
upward to life (15:24). On the other, it is the fear
of YHWH which prolongs life, (10:27), and which leads
to life (19:23). These examples imply significant tension, but a comparison of two other sentences makes the
issue explicit.

> The teaching of the wise is a fountain of
> life, that one may avoid the snares of
> death. (13:14)
> The fear of YHWH is a fountain of life,
> that one may avoid the snares of death.
> (14:27)

The source, the substance, the path to life comes
from YHWH. Do we have here similar points of view
simply expressed in divergent vocabulary, or is there a
genuine tension between a secular strand of wisdom and
a religious one?[18] An examination of what has often
been termed the "motto" of the wisdom movement may be
useful in proposing a resolution to this question.
Found in varying forms three times in Proverbs (1:7;
9:10; 15:33), in Ps. 111:10, and in Job 28:28[19] the
affirmation that the fear of YHWH is the beginning/
instruction of wisdom/knowledge is widely recognized as
providing the interpretative guide for understanding
the proverbial collection in particular and the wisdom
literature in general. Some maintain that it is a late
development marking the triumph of Yahwistic piety over
the older secular wisdom, while others affirm that,

though it might well come from a later stage in the
wisdom movement, "the later biblical editor did not
transform the tradition in kind, but developed program-
matically a religious understanding of wisdom which
was at first only implicit."[20]

It is not to be denied that combining wisdom/
knowledge with the fear of YHWH occupies a crucial role
in Proverbs. That role is by no means limited to the
three cited passages. Although the precise terminology
is not present, surely 1:29 and 2:5 must be considered
in the discussion, and with a little imagination 8:13;
10:27; 14:27; 16:6, and 19:23 may also be germane.
This would reckon ten of the fourteen occurrences of
"fear of YHWH" in Proverbs as bearing on the equation
of wisdom and Yahwistic religion. In addition, at
least one of the five verbal occurrences "fear YHWY" is
relevant:

>   Be not wise in your own eyes;
>   fear YHWH and turn from evil. (3:7)

In this connection von Rad makes, but does not
develop, an intriguing observation: "In the almost
abrupt way in which it [wisdom/knowledge = fear of YHWH]
is expressed, it gives the impression that some form of
polemic might be involved. Why the repetition of this
firm assertion that all knowledge has its point of departure in knowledge about God, that the pupil's range
of vision did not contain other ways of acquiring
knowledge which were being firmly repulsed? But nothing
specific can be said about this."[21] Something specific
may be said. Repetition of the sentence and the tenor
of the other sentences mentioned above (one ought not
omit 3:5-7, perhaps the sharpest of all, even though it
does not mention fear of YHWH directly) do give the
impression of polemic, or at least internal tension.
Further there is another passage which may be seen as
expressing the other dimension of the dialectic.

An observation by D. B. Macdonald is worth citing
at some length:[22]

>   But these protests [fear of YHWH
>   sentences] must mean that there were those
>   who asserted that Reason was not simply an
>   aid or guide, or discipline, useful for
>   carrying out the commands of Jehovah, but
>   was an ultimate of itself and in itself.

> That, besides the recorded Will of Jehovah,
> to be accepted and obeyed as Jehovah's will,
> there was a guide in life, called Reason,
> working in and through the mind of man,
> which was least of equal authority with the
> recorded Will of Jehovah and might even
> criticize that will as it was recorded.
> Ultimately this meant that man could apply
> this Reason to the understanding and
> criticism of the personality of Jehovah.

I shall refer to this somewhat problematical attempt to
establish a notion of an Absolute Reason in the concluding section of this article, but of interest here
is his positing a mode of thinking in wisdom which was
independent of YHWH and Yahwism. Particularly striking
is his exegesis of Pro. 4:1-7.

Set in the context of an instructional passage,
4:7 abruptly states:

> The beginning of wisdom is this: Get wisdom,
> and whatever you get, get insight. (RSV)

Initial reading of the sentence gives a perfectly
straightforward meaning. The first thing, or the principal thing, about wisdom is simply, "Get wisdom."
Further, one can hardly avoid seeing in the sentence a
conscious counterpoint to those sentences which have
equated the beginning, principal part, of wisdom with
the fear of YHWH. The tension, or polemic, is apparent.
The commentaries and many translations dilute or
obfuscate this obvious first impression. The text is
considered to be corrupt, confused, not very clear,
hardly possible syntactically, tautologous, interrup-
tive of the connection between verses 6 and 8, and since
it is not found in Greek texts, an intrusive addition.

There are problems with the text. The syntax is
awkward, though not so much as Toy suggested.[23] The
problem of its relation to the larger unit and the witness of the Greek are not significant, though the latter
may well be interpreted as a theological omission.
Nevertheless, if the sentence integrating wisdom with
the fear of YHWH may be read as affirmations of the
centrality of Yahwistic religion in the context of wisdom, then this verse can at the very least be read as
reflecting insistence on the humanistic dimension.
Macdonald's conclusion is altogether probable, "There

can be no doubt that the last verse [7] ... is a
deliberate protest against the subordination of Reason
to the fear of Jehovah."[24] That the verse is clear
evidence of a perspective which attributes to wisdom a
humanistic origin and basis seems beyond dispute. "Whoever set up 'The beginning of Reason is "Get Reason"'
over against 'the beginning of Reason is the Fear of
Jehovah' meant what he said."[25]

        Such a humanistic approach, indeed, need not be
irreligious, and I am not equating humanism with practical atheism which does appear in the canon. Attitudes
expressed in Job 21:14f.; Ps. 10:4; 14:1; 53:1; 73:8-11;
Isa. 5:19; Jer. 5:12f.; Zeph. 1:12; etc. which deny the
presence and activity of God are not the necessary consequences of humanism. Nor, within the wisdom tradition
itself would such a humanistic stance necessarily issue
in the bitter complaint preserved in Pro. 30:1-4.
Translation and interpretation of this piece are notori-
ously difficult and we cannot enter into an examination
of the details, but it seems most probable that the
speaker has reached a stage of total agnosticism about
understanding the ways of God in the world or even he
has finally concluded that there is no God at all.[26]
I am not here concerned with the consequences of humanism for a religious tradition, though that is worth a
detailed separate examination. The thesis thus far is
to demonstrate that within Israelite wisdom, as reflected in Proverbs at least, there was an approach to
reality, a mode of interpreting experience, which can
most properly be called humanistic. That it has been
cogently argued that all Israelite wisdom is in fact to
be understood within the framework of Yahwism challenges
that conclusion. The concluding section of this article
will examine the implications raised by the conclusion
and the challenge.

                            II.

        At this point a return to the problem of the scope
of wisdom material in the canon is appropriate. Once
the contention that study of Old Testament wisdom ought
not be limited to traditionally defined Wisdom literature was widely and seriously raised, it became necessary to utilize certain modifiers when speaking of wisdom. The broad diversity of literary forms and subject
matter now placed in the domain of wisdom led to speaking of wisdom influence, wisdom thinking, wisdom contact, or, much more broadly, an intellectual

tradition.[27]

Excessive expansion of the territorial claims for
wisdom seems to be on the wane, but, as was noted
earlier in this paper, that such claims could seriously
be made warrants attention. My conclusion is that
there was a growing awareness that there were considerable blocks of biblical material which were the result
of modes of interpreting experience that simply could
not be subsumed under the rubrics of traditional
Yahwism. Another biblical category, wisdom, lay neatly
at hand and was readily, if not always appropriately,
utilized. If designating all such material as wisdom,
whether in terms of influence, thinking, contact, tradition, etc. be deemed methodologically unsound, is there
an alternative? Can we, rather, simply speak of humanism?

When one allows for the indisputable fact that
there are diverse varieties of humanism, that there may
be theological humanists, religious humanists, and just
plain humanists, this conclusion seems best able to
account for the data. There were Israelites who assumed
that the experiences of life must be assessed and assimilated solely within the context of the human. That is
humanism. This attractive conclusion has been vigorously challenged on the grounds that it makes a distinction
between the secular and the religious which would not
have been possible in Israelite thought. An examination
of this challenge is in order.

Though the notion that such a distinction is to be
rejected figures prominently in many recent wisdom
studies, von Rad has given the most thoroughgoing exposition of the issue. In his intricate, and often con-
voluted, presentation, von Rad attempts to do justice
to two apparently contradictory impressions one receives
from reading the proverbial literature. On the one
hand, it is clear that "wisdom has to do with human understanding, that it is a particular form of human
knowledge and behaviour, is not to be disputed."[28] In
the older sentence literature, in particular, "since
the objects of this search for knowledge were of a secular kind, questions about man's daily life, systematic
reflection on them was held to be a secular occupation
about which no more needed to be said except that it
was to be pursued in an organized and careful way" (57).
This recognition might well lead to the conclusion that
a secular, humanistic wisdom is indeed present. Not so!

271

Von Rad affirms, "We hold fast to the fact that in the case of the wise man's search for knowledge, even when they expressed their results in a completely secular form, there was never any question of what we would call absolute knowledge functioning independently of their faith in Yahweh." (64) Or again, and such examples could be multiplied many times over, he concludes that while "we are unable to define from a traditio-historical point of view to what specific extent the teachers participated in Yahwism... it is not, however, open to doubt that they stood in a broad stream of Yahwistic traditions and that they drew on their knowledge and experience of these." (255)

The key to reconciling these apparent divergencies is, according to von Rad, the fact that "it can be categorically stated that for Israel there was only one world of experience and that this was apperceived by means of a perceptive apparatus in which rational perceptions and religious perceptions were not differentiated." (61) The experiences of the world were for her always divine experiences as well, and the experiences of God were for her experiences of the world." (62) His development of this thesis with respect to the coalescence of "orders" as perceived as integral to the world of sense experience and equally a part of the sages' recognition of the "orders" of Yahweh is highly suggestive but cannot be developed here.[29] What is important, for our purposes, is the contention that there is a single field of experience for Israel and that apparently divergent, secular and religious, affirmations can be held together within the contours of that univocal field.[30]

Macdonald's much earlier conclusion is germane. He agrees that Israelite thinking is not to be understood without implicit reference to Yahweh. But there is a significant difference in the conclusion which he draws. Von Rad recognizes that there may have been some tension between experiences of the world and experiences of Yahweh, but he minimizes the extent to that tension. Macdonald, on the other hand, while acknowledging that Israelite experience inevitably included Yahweh, was well aware of the depth of tension inherent in such an outlook. "Jehovah was simply a fact of experience, as each one of themselves was to every other, only he was a stupendous and overwhelming fact."[31] Von Rad's position makes it possible to include wisdom, even expressed in secular terminology, within Yahwism.

Macdonald concludes that while "certain Hebrews thought that man should limit himself to the knowledge that Jehovah himself imparts, that to seek further was impious... it is equally plain that the Hebrews very generally did seek further and entered upon paths which led to independent conclusions and even to conclusions critical of Jehovah himself." (29) However different their conclusions, von Rad and Macdonald agree that in Israelite thought Yahweh, interpreted as good, bad or indifferent, was an indispensable frame of reference.

The evidence may be interpreted in this manner, and at one time I tended so to interpret it:32

> The experiences of the noumenal, of the divine, of Yahweh if you will, were just that - experiences, in dealing with the data of the world the Hebrew, conditioned by his historical and cultural milieu, was open to a dimension of experience which he could not designate as the presence and activity of Yahweh... Yahweh was interpreted as another, albeit highly significant, datum of human experience.

I am now inclined to be more explicit and contend that there were also experiences which were interpreted without any reference to Yahweh, either as an active agent or as a hidden Absolute,33 who set limits within which all human activity and experience must finally be assessed. Exegesis of Proverbs, and many other sections of the canon, carried out without a theological a priori, leads to the inevitable conclusion, mentioned earlier, that there were Israelites who approached reality from the perspective of the human condition alone.34 There was a way of looking at life, a way of thinking, a stance which can even be called an Israelite philosophy. It should not be an occasion of surprise that so little literary remains of such a stance are to be found in the canon, though I am convinced that there is much more than is generally allowed. When one remembers that the canon was collected, preserved, edited and transmitted largely by the religious establishment, the surprise, rather, is that any remains at all.

But one can speak of a Hebrew philosophy? Macdonald, above all, has argued that there was indeed a Hebrew philosophical genius. While his final presentation of the nature of that philosophy seems abstruse

273

and unconvincing, the mode of analysis by which he came
to his notion of the existence of such a philosophy is
perceptive. He defines philosophy simply as "Reason,
that is independent thinking."[35] Somewhat more elabor-
ately he raises these questions:[36]

> For what is philosophy in its final analysis?
> Is it not thinking as clearly and rationally as we
> can, about all the sides of life as we know it;
> about ourselves and this world in which we find
> ourselves, our relation to it, our knowledge of
> it, along with our whence and whither? Is it not,
> in a word, the application of our reason to life?

Fundamental to his thesis is the conviction that
to translate ḥokmah simply as wisdom is erroneous. He
thought that often it is better to render it not as
wisdom but as Reason:[37]

> Let the English reader read in Proverbs or
> Ecclesiastes or Job and pause at every occurrence
> of the word 'wisdom.' Let him experiment putting
> 'reason' in its place -- or some cognate word,
> 'rational,' 'rationality,' to suit the construc-
> tion and he will see how often the meaning flashes
> out in new reality. Often, too, he will find that
> he has to retain the word wisdom; that is that the
> curious combination of ripened experienced and con-
> scious thinking which is meant. The two meanings
> of the word <u>hochma'</u> will thus become assured to
> him.

Such thinking, stemming from the application of
reason to experience, could include Yahweh, but it
could also operate with no reference to Yahweh at all.
Further, it is a misunderstanding to try to relate all
such thinking to wisdom, even when wisdom is modified
by such terms as contact, influence, thinking or tradition. There was in Israel a mode of interpreting experience, concentrated, to be sure in wisdom materials but
by no means limited to them, which transcended definition in terms of wisdom and which is more appropriately
to be understood as humanism. But, and this point is
to be stressed, it was an Israelite humanism. It is
this recognition which provides a possible answer to a
question raised earlier in this article. Material
which shows no overt interest in Torah, salvation history, election or covenant can be included in a genuine
Israelite framework because there were Israelites who

interpreted their experience without conscious reference
to those Yahwistic categories. Failure to allow them
to speak seriously truncates our understanding of the
multiple streams which finally coalesced to form the
biblical tradition.

The validity and utility of the foregoing interpretation would have to bear the scrutiny of detailed
exegetical studies. Even preliminary results of such
studies, already undertaken, cannot be presented here,
but they seem to indicate that evidence of this humanistic stance, sometimes in a relatively unmodified
form, sometimes embedded in a theological mold which
obscures its original nature, affords a more comprehensive ideological outlook which permits us to see more
clearly the broad and rich diversity of Israelite
thought.[38]

In a volume of this nature it may not be considered
inappropriate to conclude with remarks more personal
than are normally included in our literature. In discussing my earlier analysis of Israelite humanism,
Sibley Towner correctly noted that the article did not
"spell out in any detail the hermeneutical implications..."[39] No hermeneutical principle was involved,
the task was simply to take seriously the textual evidence. Much contemporary stress on humanistic dimensions of biblical thought, even when an overarching
Yahwism remains, seems to be designed to make a point
of contact with contemporary theological positions.[40]
Similarly, emphasis on the essentially Yahwistic nature
of apparently secular or humanistic strands in the Bible
seems designed to conserve the centrality of a comprehensive biblical theology. If there has been any
"hermeneutic" operative in this article, it is a very
simple and non-theological one. I am concerned that
the Old Testament "be placed in the midst of the human
race [where it can] show both its general humanity and
its unique character."[41] To do so is simply to do
justice to the biblical material itself and to our
understanding of it. Macdonald, as often, said it
well"[42]

> Are they [the Hebrews] an interesting people,
> a human people; are they in the language of today,
> "folks"? If we can once rid ourselves of the idea
> that they were perpetually uttering prophecies or
> singing psalms or smiting Agag before the Lord,
> and take them as they have written themselves down

in their own literature, we shall find how many
sides of common humanity they show and how full
and artistically they show those sides.

I believe they were a human people, an interesting
people, and a people whose multifaceted interpretations
of reality, when understood fully within the contexts
of Yahwism, theological and religious wisdom, secular
wisdom, and just plain humanism, may yet contribute
significantly to our multifaceted encounters.

FOOTNOTES

1. JBR 23 (1955), 193-196. Specific references are noted by parentheses in the body of the text. To reduce the number of footnotes,
this procedure will be followed throughout the article where no ambiguity may follow. It should be noted that Toombs' article was
written nearly three decades ago and the views may not represent
his present position. The issues he raised, however, have moved
more and more to the center of contemporary wisdom study.
2. R.N. Whybray, Wisdom in Proverbs (London: 1965) also emphasizes
the centrality of this passage: "here the whole literary history of
Prov. 1-9 is epitomized." 98.
3. Representative studies may be found in R.B.Y. Scott, Inter 24
(1970), 20-45; J.A. Emerton, Tradition and Interpretation ed. G.W.
Anderson (Oxford: 1979), 214-237; J.L. Crenshaw, Studies in Ancient
Israelite Wisdom (NY: 1976), 1-45.
4. See esp. Crenshaw, 9-13.
5. "The Interpretation of Old Testament Wisdom Literature," Inter
23 (1969), 290.
6. The analysis by Crenshaw, "Method in Determining Wisdom Influence Upon 'Historical' Literature," JBL 88 (1969), 129-142, remains
a highly useful programmatic statement. See also his comments in
the work cited in n. 4 above, and in Old Testament Wisdom (Atlanta: 1981), 39-41.
7. See my preliminary statement in JBR 31 (1963), 275-282; W. Zim-
merli, "The Place and Limit of Widsom in the Framework of an Old
Testament Theology," SJT 17 (1964), 146-158; Crenshaw, Studies, 22-
35. The recent study by D. Morgan, Wisdom in the Old Testament Traditions (Atlanta: 1981) warrants careful consideration.
8. E.g., H. Gese, Lehre und Wirklichkeit in der alten Weisheit (Tu-
gingen: 1958); H. Preuss, "Erwaegungen zum theologischen Ort alt-
testamentlicher Weisheitsliteratur," Ev Th 30 (1970), 393-417.
9. For representative statements of earlier scholars holding this
view see the article cited in n. 7, esp. 276f. J. Rylaarsdam, Revelation in Jewish Wisdom Literature (Chicago: 1946) presented the
most detailed exposition. Among current scholars W. McKane, Proverbs, OTL (Philadelphia: 1970) continues to maintain the position.
See my review, JBL 90 (1971), 219-222.
10. This view clearly underlies Whybray's exposition of Pro. 1-9,

Wisdom in Proverbs and seems to be the present positions of Crenshaw, Old Testament Wisdom, esp. 77, 92, and W. Brueggemann, The
Creative Word (Philadelphia: 1982), esp. 149ff. There remains, in
my judgment however, some oscillation between the secular and religious dimensions in their discussion of specific texts.
11. See R. Murphy, "Wisdom and Yahwism," No Famine in the Land ed.
J. Flanagan and A. Robinson (Missoula: 1975), 117-126. G. von Rad
gives the most extensive exposition of this view, Wisdom in Israel
tr. J. Martin (Nashville: 1972), discussed later.
12. JBR 23:195.
13. While there are considerable variations in their views, this
seems to be the position of, for example, R.B.Y. Scott and B. Gemser in their commentaries. See McKane, 10-22.
14. This applies to positions which assume a straightforward development from the secular to the religious to the Yahwistic, movement from non-Yahwistic religious to Yahwism, or the existence of
parallel strands in which the Yahwistic came to exercise a decisive
influence. Though they start from different perspectives, there is
agreement on a development in the material and that the development
was toward subordination of wisdom to Yahwism.
15. Crenshaw's comment on these two passages that "Behind such
pragmatism stood God's will." (Old Testament Wisdom 85) is a possible interpretation, but that they represent different traditions
is equally possible unless one assumes a religious a priori for
the material as a whole. That is the point at issue.
16. Common examples include 16:1,2,9,33; 19:21; 20:24; 21:30f. See
the discussion in von Rad, Wisdom.., 97-110.
17. "The Kerygma of the Book of Proverbs," Inter 20 (1966), 3-14.
The citation is from p. 9.
18. It is possible to read in Pro. 8:35 an attempt to reconcile
these differing views:
         For he who finds me (wisdom) finds life
               and obtains favor from YHWH.
but this is problematical.
19. The lexical variations between r'eshith in Pro. 1:7, Ps. 111:10
and tihilath in Pro. 15:33; d'ath in Pro. 1:7 and hokmah in all the
other passages are not significant. Nor is the issue as to interpreting r'eshith/tihilath chronologically or essentially. Even the
omission of any reference to "beginning" in Job 28:28 seems required for stylistic reasons. The overall meaning is clear: wisdom is
to be subordinated to Yahwism.
20. B. Childs, Introduction to the Old Testament as Scripture
(Philadelphia: 1979), 553.
21. Wisdom.., 67. See also B. Gemser, Sprüche Salomos HAT 16 (19-
63), 19.
22. The Hebrew Philosophical Genius (Princeton: 1936), 32f.
23. Proverbs ICC, 88.
24. Hebrew.., 34.
25. Hebrew.., 44.
26. I read the passage as a statement by a skeptic or agnostic or
atheist (vv. 1-4, the last vs a bitter parody of divine speech) and

a pious response (vv. 5-6). Whether the speaker is to be classified as a skeptical agnostic or an atheist is not clear since a precise translation of the opening words is almost impossible. For a
full discussion see the commentaries of Gemser, Ringgren, McKane
and Scott. Scott in The Way of Wisdom (NY: 1971), 165-170 and C.C.
Torrey, "Proverbs, Chapter 30," JBL 73 (1954), 93-103 provide additional suggestions. G. Sauer's Die Sprüche Agurs (Stuttgart: 1963)
provides an overview of the entire chapter, but is not particularly helpful on the point in question.
27. A perceptive summary of the differences in nuance of these
descriptions may be found in Morgan, pp. 13-29.
28. Wisdom.., 8.   The following references in parentheses are
from the same work.
29. A lengthy excursus would be in order here, but it must be reserved for another occasion. Crucial points for consideration would
be detailed examination of Koch's thesis of "act/consequence"; see
"Gibt es eub Vergeltungsdogma im Alten Testament," ZThk 52 (1955),
1-42 and von Rad's ambivalence between seeing the orders as a consequence of human perception or as seeing them in terms of prior
trust in Yahweh. (See, e.g., Wisdom.., 194   for the former and
307ff for the latter.) I think that Koch has overstated his case,
but the contention that in some circles of Israelite thought a
cause-effect relationship apart from Yahweh existed seems beyond
dispute.
30. See Creshaw's trenchant criticism of von Rad's "baptizing" wisdom, RSR 2 (1976), 6-12 and his comment, "I prefer to empahsize the
complementarity of the two approaches (Yahwism and wisdom) to reality, and to consider each appropriate." Tradition and Theology in the
Old Testament ed. D. Knight (Philadelphia: 1977), 245. Whether Crenshaw now views secularism as part of wisdom or as a way of thinking
to be distinguished from wisdom consideration is not clear to me.
31. Hebrew.., 6.
32. JAAR 36 (1968), 314f.
33. The term is Macdonald's and is integral to his development of
a genuine Hebrew philosophy.
34. J. McKenzie shortly before the "explosion" in wisdom research
reached its peak provided some perceptive observations about the
direction which might be taken. "Reflections on Wisdom," JBL 86 (19-
67), 1-9. In speaking of wisdom as an approach to reality rather
than as a formal movement he came near to the position set forth in
this article. Yet at a crucial point there remains a difference.
McKenzie commented that "both the traditionalists and their critics
agree that the human condition cannot be understood unless Yahweh
be recognized as present and active in the human condition. What
man is and can be is not understood by the exclusive consideration
of man; and here the sages part company with the secularists." (4)
I would count some of the sages among those he terms secularists.
35. Hebrew.., 2.
36. Hebrew.., 172.
37. Hebrew.., 174f. In his programmatic statement in JBL 88, Crenshaw suggested that understanding wisdom thinking in terms of hok-

mah as "a particular stance, an approach to reality" (130) would be useful. Whybray, The Intellectual Tradition of the Old Testament (Berlin: 1974), makes a similar suggestion. In his recognition of the pervasiveness of rational thought in the Old Testament (2), his acknowledgement that wisdom was available to all willing to engage in superior intelligence (54), his consciousness of the fluidity of any intellectual tradition (70), and his awareness of intellectual activities outside the tradition which he finally defines primarily on lexical grounds, he comes very close to the conclusions reached in this article. Both Crenshaw and Whybray, however, appear to reckon the methodological consequences of pursuing this avenue too problematical for controlled study.

38. In a number of papers read at professional meetings I have explored this issue in "wisdom" materials in Proberbs and Koheleth, in legal corpora, historical narrative and prophetic literature. I emphasize the proposal in this article can be only a proposal until specific examples are subjected to criticism and comment.

39. "The Renewed Authority of Old Testament Wisdom for Contemporary Faith," Canon and Authority ed. G. Coats and B. Long (Philadelphia: 1977), 132-147. The citation is on p. 139.

40. This is most obvious in a series of works by W. Brueggemann. See summary by Morgan, Wisdom.., 13-29, 150-4; Towner, 142-147.

41. Hebrew.., 6. My own view could well be summarized as an attempt designed not to secularize the sacred, but to humanize the whole.

42. Hebrew.., 217f. Von Rad comes near to an affirmation of humanism, "What was wisdom, if not Israel's attempt to unfold her humanity in the very sphere of a reality which she experienced quite specifically, that is a humanness on Israel's part?" (Wisdom..,308) but that humanism is carried out in the "shadow of Yahwism.." as the Israelite "strove to discover his humanity in the spere which had been allotted to him by God." (309)

PATRIMONY IN DEUTERONOMY 18:8-A POSSIBLE EXPLANATION

Thomas E. Ranck

Perhaps one of the joys which Dr. L. Toombs gave to his students was the spirit and adventure of investigation. Whether it was sorting potsherds or investigating the text which was before the student, Dr. Toombs always made the process exciting. To him we dedicate this article.

The subject under discussion is the text of Deuteronomy 18:8. The R.S.V. reads, "They shall have equal portions to eat, besides what he receives from the sale of his patrimony."[1] The problem rests in the latter part of the verse which is translated "besides what he receives from the sale of his patrimony." Just exactly what is meant is open to dispute and the interpretation varies greatly. This essay seeks to provide an adequate interpretation for this phrase.

Dt. 18:8 belongs to a larger unit, 18:1-8, which specifies the rights and duties of the Levites and the Levitical priests. This unit stipulates that the Levitical priests shall have no portion or inheritance with Israel. Rather, they are given certain portions of the sacrificial animal as their rightful due. Vss. 6-8 continue the thought of vss. 1-5 but the subject has changed. We are now concerned directly with the Levites. Vs. 8 indicates that the Levites are to have equal portions to eat of the sacrifices which the Levitical priests receive from the worshipper. Further, the Levites are given specific permission to retain whatever remains from the sale of his patrimony.

To illustrate the problem which is present, the New American Bible translates the passage as "He shall then receive the same portions to eat as the rest, along with his monetary offerings and heirlooms."[2] Just what constitutes an "heirloom" is open to as much speculation as the term "patrimony."

In the history of Israel, problems began to arise when certain Levites ascended to the office of priest in the central sanctuary in Jerusalem. Much of the legislation found in Deuteronomy speaks to the legitimate rights of each community. For example, what would happen when a Levite came to Jerusalem? Would he be regarded as a "second-class" citizen by the Levitical priests who functioned at the central sanctuary? The law is clear. The Levites are to have a parity with the Levitical priests when they come to the central sanctuary. There must have been an obvious tension which had developed between the communities or the law would have never come into being.

The problem seems to grow even more complex. The Levites, as a community believed that Yahweh was their "nahalah," inheritance.[3] The word "inheritance" implies many things. That the Levites were Yahweh's inheritance did not preclude the possibility of the Levites receiving an inheritance left to them by their own fathers. Exactly what it is that was left to the Levites has been the object of much conjecture. Some scholars believe that the close of 18:8 refers to the passing on of family houses within the designated Levitical cities.[4] This belief was reinforced by S. R. Driver who felt that the passage referred to either a physical property, like a domicile which belonged to the fathers, or a source of personal income distinct and separate from any allowed in the offerings received by the Levites. A distinction had been made which was important. The Levite could inherit either a piece of property, a domicile, or personal income.[5] The exact source of this income was never explicitly stated. Driver had added a new element.

The scholarly community tended to agree. Rennes, in his commentary, felt that the term patrimony didn't designate landed property but rather personal property.[6] This understanding was affirmed by Phillips. He stated that we are dealing with "an obscure clause which indicates that while a Levite might not own land, he could inherit personal property."[7] The emphasis in interpretation has moved away from the Levites owning land or having landed property to the possession of personal property inherited from one's father.

The scholarly community in France continued its investigation along slightly different lines. "La fin due v. 8 rests également obscure," states Buis and LeClerq in their commentary. "La Loi ne vise donc pas tant à assurer la subsistance des Levites qu'à maintenir leur égalité de principe, le droit de tous aux fonctions sacerdotales."[8] It would seem that the scholastic emphasis in France seemed to be shifting to an understanding of the priestly role and to stress the Levites ability to function on a par with the Levitical priests.

Hulst, in his exciting work, Old Testament Translation Problems, divided the "problem verses" into
three categories. The first group were texts which
were so corrupt that their meanings were obscure and
in their present form practically untranslatable. The
second group involved those texts which contained enough
clues from other ancient versions to allow reasonable
and "adequate exegesis." The third group contained
texts which allowed for more than one "legitimate translation of the masoretic text." Hulst categorized Dt.
18:8 as belonging to this category.[9]

> The AV, DNV and RSV are in essential agree-
> ment in translation at the close of the verse.
> The RSV renders "besides what he receives
> from the sale of his patrimony." While this
> has been the usual interpretation, Driver
> terms it as "nonsensical" (Syria 33, 1956,
> pp. 77f.). He cites the code of Hammurabi
> which carefully distinguished between a man's
> own property and the property of his father's
> house which under no circumstances could be
> sold. In Babylonian the term is makkūr bît
> abim "property derived from his father."
> Hence, here in Deuteronomy, Driver believes
> the meaning is "his patrimony shall not be
> reckoned in calculating what is due to him;
> he shall enjoy this as something
> additional."[10]

Once again the fascinating aspect of the house of the
fathers, the bt 'aboth, has made its way into the discussion. The word for house, bt, is not present in our
text. To be sure, many interpreters assumed that it
was to be understood. The problem remains. The assumption of a "physical property" such as a house is not
present in our text, either.

Cragie in his recent commentary, suggests that
Cazelles' commentary on the passage "suggests a reasonable sense for the passage.[11] Cazelles' translation of
the verse reads, "Mangeant une part égale à leur--sans
qu'on tienne compte de ses droits dur les familles
lévitiques pour les biens qu'il aurait vendus."[12]
Cazelles further comments that the latter part of the
verse is probably an addition inspired by Lev. 25:32f.
These verses refer to the understanding that the Levites
may indeed redeem houses within the Levitical cities.
"And if one of the Levites does not exercise his right

of redemption, then the house that was sold in a city
of their possession shall be released in the jubilee;
for the houses in the cities of the Levites are their
possession among the people of Israel."[13] Cazelles
continues,

> Les biens d'un lévite ne pouvaient passer
> qu'à d'autres lévites. C'est donc à l'égard
> d'une famille lévitique qu'il pouvait exercer
> le droit de rachat et de restitution qu
> jubilé. Notre texte s'oppose à ce que l'on
> évalue le montant de ce droit pour diminuer
> sa part au sanctuaire.[14]

It almost appears that we have come full circle in our
interpretation. We began with the houses of the
fathers, moved to the possible goods which the fathers
owned and again find ourselves facing the presence of
the father's domicile in the Levitical cities. The
enigma continues. We can, however, be certain that the
Levites could hold tangible personal property. The
property could be left to them in the estate of their
fathers.

While it is true that in certain instances such as
the "Code of Hammurabi" we find citations which refer
to the "bît abi," the father's house, as a clear example
of patrimony, there are yet other references which can
help our decision. In the mind of this author, a more
fruitful pursuit rests in the findings of the Royal
Archives at Mari. Many references can be found which
refer specifically to the property of the father but
which omit any mention of a house.

Examples which refer to this line of understanding
can be found in the following examples:

1. mārū ina bū (ši) a-bi-šu-nu (...) i-zu-Az-zu.
"The sons will share in their fathers property." YOS
10 41:33.[15]
2. mārū awīlī damqūtum ina E.Ḫ.I.A. a-bi-šu-nu-ma
uštallamu. "The sons of the well-to-do families will
be provided for from their own family estates." ARM 2
1:22.[16]

One would wish that there was a precise accounting of
what was involved in the estate. It could have helped
to clarify exactly what was transferred to the Levite
and what constituted his possessions. Apparently, the

Levite could sell the possessions of the father, transform them into the acceptable currency and transport this with them in their journeys throughout Judah.

The purpose of the law is apparent. It is intended to resolve the tension which was created by the traditional understanding that Yahweh was to be the "inheritance" of the Levites. This would not preclude the fact that they could own other material goods. Vs. 8 allows the Levites to own or inherit material property which had been left to them by their fathers. This inheritance belonged to them in accordance with "God's law." The issue was settled. There was not only to be parity between the Levites and the Levitical Priests; the Levites could have material possessions to sustain them. Such property could be sold to assist them in a time of need. That the Levites were Yahweh's possession went without question. Their substance came in part from what they inherited from the fathers.[17]

FOOTNOTES

1. The Bible, RSV; NY: American Bible Society, 1971, p. 168.
2. The New American Bible; NY: P. J. Kenedy, 1970, p. 235.
3. J. D. Hester, Paul's Concept of Inheritance; Edinburgh: Oliver and Boyd, 1968, p. 26.
4. C. Keil and F. Delitsch, Commentary on the Old Testament I. The Pentateuch; Grand Rapids: Eerdmans, 1975, p. 391.
5. S. R. Driver, Deuteronomy, ICC, p. 218.
6. J. Rennes, Le Deuteronome; Paris: Editions Labores et Fides, 1967, p. 90.
7. Anthony Phillips, Deuteronomy; Cambridge: University Press, 1973, p. 123.
8. Buis & LeClerq, Le Deuteronome; Paris: Libraire Le Coffre, 1963, p. 137.
9. A. R. Hulst, Old Testament Translation Problems; Leiden: E. J. Brill, 1960, p. viii.
10. Ibid., p. 15.
11. Cragie, The Book of Deuteronomy: Eerdmans, 1976, p. 259.
12. Cazelles, Le Deuteronome; Paris: Les Editions du Cerf, 1966, p. 119.
13. RSV, op. cit., p. 108.
14. Cazelles, op. cit., p. 119.
15. Assyrian Dictionary; Chicago: Oriental Institute, 1964, p.69.
16. Ibid., p. 74.
17. See also Gunneweg, Leviten und Priester; Gottingen: Vandenhoeck & Ruprecht, 1965.

THE ORIGINAL POSITION OF JOB 28

C. C. Settlemire

The textual, literary, and theological problems
presented by the Book of Job have inspired a vast
amount of scholarly discussion which concludes (sometimes legitimately and sometimes not) that various passages should be mentally excised because they are inter-
polations.[1] Although much of this effort is valid and
necessary, it is possible to conjure up a fearsome
image of the biblical scholar as a modern-day Jehoiakim
who sits before the brazier methodically slicing away
at the Book of Job, throwing unacceptable pieces into
the fire, until the "entire scroll" is consumed. This
article is an effort to save chapter twenty-eight, the
Wisdom Poem, from the fire. My interest in this chapter was inspired sixteen years ago by Professor Toombs
whose enthusiasm for Old Testament study was emulated
but never superseded by that of his students.

Chapter 28 has not been generally accepted as
authentic; a substantial number of scholars agree with
Fohrer's position that this poem is not from the author
of the discourses.[2] Another category of scholars feels
that it may have been composed by the author of the
Book of Job but inserted at a later time and therefore
is not integrally related to the original book.[3] There
are those who would retain it as authentic and theo-
logically essential in its present position with the
result that apologies worthy of the medieval scholas-
tics at their best have attempted to reconcile it with
the discussion in the cycles of discourses.[4] Finally,
there are those who would retain it as authentic and
belonging to the first "draft" of the book but out of
place in its present position as does this writer. The
third cycle of speeches in Job (chapters 22-31) has
obviously been disarranged; the regular pattern has
been broken. Zophar is not represented as speaking,
Bildad's speech is questionably short (25:1-6) and Job
defends the view of his friends (cf. 24:18-24, 26:5-14,
and 27:13-23) in his lengthy answer which is introduced
twice -- 26:1 and 27:1. Chapter 28 does not relate
well at all to that which precedes or follows it, and
it has an exalted appreciation of God's inscrutable
wisdom which is incompatible with Job's attitude at
this point in the Dialogue. Basically, there are two
reasons which are usually presented as the cause of the
difficulty: (1) an accidental error or series of

errors (which Dhorme terms an error in "pagination") occurred involving some type of physical disruption of the text[5] or (2) a later editor or series of editors have tampered with the text in order to make Job more acceptable to orthodox readers.

It is the thesis of this writer that chapter 28 is not only authentic but that it is essential to the thought of the author of the Book of Job and indeed highlights the purpose of the book as a literary unit. However, this has not been seen clearly because the chapter has been displaced from its original position following Job's repentance speech. The Wisdom Poem actually belongs after 42:6. There are three major questions brought to the forefront by the work of the scholars. "Is chapter 28 a work of the author of the Dialogue and Yahweh speeches?"[6] and "Does it belong in its present position?" If the answer to the first question is "Yes," and the answer to the second is "No," then a third question must be asked, "Where does it belong?" Furthermore, when viewed in its proper position, chapter 28 helps us to answer the ultimate question, "What is the meaning of the Book of Job?" The "answer" to Job's problem (and the problem of the wisdom movement) is presented in the twenty-eighth chapter. In the past, while attempting to focus on the purpose of the Book of Job, the wrong question has often been identified as the main concern of the book: "Why do the righteous suffer?" Driver gives a classic statement of that thinking:

> The problem with which it deals is this:
> Why do the righteous suffer? and its princi-
> pal aim is to controvert the theory, dominant
> at the time when it was written, that suffer-
> ing is a sign of the Divine displeasure, and
> presupposes sin on the part of the sufferer.[7]

The book does not "solve" the problem of suffering; its purpose is not simply to negate the theory that suffering is punishment for sin. That polemical element serves as a launching pad from which the poet is able to launch out into wider theological space and to get to the heart of Job's problem--the nature of his relationship to God.

There are numerous textual and exegetical questions raised by chapter 28 which are beyond the scope of the present essay. However, a brief synopsis of the chapter and a discussion of its content must be made before the first question is addressed: "Is chapter 28 a work of the author of the Dialogue and the Yahweh speeches?"

The first strophe, vss. 1-11, describes man's great ability to acquire the treasures in the earth by mining. Silver and gold and other secret and precious things, no matter how hard to discover and acquire, can be obtained by man. Through this Hymn to Mining the poet first brings into the highest relief the powers of man and only then moves on to the limitation of human attainment (v. 13). The mining operation in all its difficulty is described as a great accomplishment; the process is far from simple no matter what ancient mining process is being described or where these mines are located.[8] Birds fly and creatures roam in very remote areas in search of their food but have not discovered the tunnel or shaft (nātib) which is the underground path to the ore. Man overturns mountains by the root. As Fohrer states, this does not refer to the foot of of the mountain but to the "Grundfesten, auf denen die Berge ruhend gedacht sind" (cf. Dt. 32:22, "the foundations of the mountains").[9] This portrays a mighty effort requiring great skills on the part of man who even penetrates to the subterranean strata of the earth where the rivers rise.[10]

At the end of this first strophe a "refrain" appears which presents the theme of the poem and relates the seemingly irrelevant description of mining to the discussion on wisdom which follows. This rhetorical question form, which the author particularly likes (it permeates the Dialogue as well as the Yahweh Speeches), is used to tie the poem together as well as to introduce his two-fold theme which is summarized in separate verses: (1) man does not know the way to wisdom (vs. 13) but (2) God understands the way to it (vs. 23).[11] The author is highlighting the inaccessibility of wisdom in verses 13-14 and showing thereby the limits of man's ability. Man who has been able to maneuver his way into the depths of the earth has reached the limits of his knowledge. He does not know wisdom's path or place. The tone becomes more poetic: the Deep and the Sea (cf. 38:16) say that it is not in them. These personifications, which have mythological connotations, parallel those of vs. 22, 'Abaddon and māwet (death) who have heard a rumor of it.

Some scholars would eliminate verses 15-19 (or even 15-20)[12] as secondary because they have a different theme from that of the rest of the poem, that is, the incomparable worth of wisdom rather than its inaccessibility.[13] However, verses 15 through 19 are not primarily discussing the price of wisdom, but are saying that at no possible price can men acquire it. Man has taken the treasures from the earth by very intelligent and persistent efforts indeed, but the end result of his mining, the precious metals which he now holds in his hand, cannot obtain wisdom for him. This is the final blow; pride in his ability to conquer nature must surely be crushed because these products are worthless to him. Thus, this strophe builds upon the Hymn to Mining and the thought of the first strophe is advanced. To label these verses as extraneous is to miss the intended implication and to detract greatly from the brilliance of the author's carefully-structured and progressively-moving poem.

God knows the way to this wisdom (vs. 23). Verses 25-27 establish the fact wisdom came into relationship with God at the time of creation. God, creation, and wisdom are intrinsically connected, but the precise nature of that relationship is difficult to determine. The creation acts described in these verses seem to emphasize the particular care that God had taken in creation. The wind was given a weight; a precise force was regulated. The waters were meted out in just the precise measure as thkn in the piel (to measure) indicates; there is a prescribed limit for the rain. Clearly, everything has its limit or its path set very carefully by God. His control and his skill in creation are delineated in these verses. It is more a description of the nature of his activity that is presented than a description of a final product. God "saw" wisdom. This does not mean that he suddenly stumbled upon it. The usage is similar to that in the P creation story when God saw that which he had created and appraised it as good.[14]

The final verse of chapter 28 has provoked a great deal of discussion concerning its authenticity. Fohrer, Duhm, Driver and Gray, and Pope, along with many others, state that it is an addition. Weiser, Terrien, and Moller feel that it is authentic. The verse begins with a prose splice, "And he said to man," but this is necessary since the author wants to put the following words into the mouth of God. It has been argued by

Duhm (Das Buch Hiob, 137) that it is unlikely that the
poet would have stressed the inaccessibility of wisdom
for twenty-seven verses only to have his argument re-
versed.[15] Furthermore, this is the only verse in the
Old Testament that seems to equate wisdom with the fear
of the Lord (hi'ḥok°māh). However, Coss raises a good
exegetical question about the use of the Hebrew third
person, singular, feminine pronoun here: Is the writer
making wisdom identical with the fear of the Lord in
every respect, or is the fear of the Lord equal to only
one salient feature of wisdom? Does the pronoun suggest a relationship or an identity? In Dt. 10:9 and
other passages this usage does not show complete identification. Therefore, Coss interprets (and rightly so)
this verse to mean that fear is regarded in Job 28:28
as the condition for or the principal part of wisdom.[16]
Some scholars also see a different kind of wisdom spoken
of here which suggests reverent ethical and moral activity rather than a metaphysical wisdom as elsewhere in
the chapter.

It is obvious that the wisdom of God is distinct
from that of man in quality and quantity. He reserves
a great deal for himself; nevertheless, the wisdom
writers insist that God does give wisdom. Even the
wisdom that humans possess has a relationship to God--
it is under his control. Therefore, the existence of
two entirely different and unrelated types of wisdom
should not be overemphasized.[17] Verse 28 does not say
that man can attain even this ethical wisdom by his own
efforts. The tone of the chapter calls for an abandonment of human claims of wisdom; man has to be content
with mystery and unanswered questions. All he can do
is to fear God. This would be the response expected to
the Wisdom Poem even if vs. 28 were missing.[18]

The meaning of chapter 28 is that man cannot make
his way to wisdom in spite of his skill in obtaining
treasure. Wisdom is definitely at God's disposal.
This theme is vital to the author's presentation. The
Book of Job is a corrective to the wisdom school with
its easy formulas and as such is a polemic against the
wisdom of Job's friends. It calls for a positive recognition of the wisdom and transcendence of God. A relationship to this God cannot be based on wisdom formulas
and arrogant doctrines which seek to explain such deep
experiences as human suffering; nor can Job snap his
fingers and call God to task for his injustice. All
man can do is to accept the gulf between himself and

his creator at the same time he recognizes ("sees") the creator's control of wisdom as well as the creator's careful activity on behalf of his creation. The 28th chapter is the praise that echoes the author's (and Job's) understanding of this. It is the answer to the rhetorical questions of the Yahweh speeches -- questions which are not truly rhetorical; a response is required. This particular response to the Yahweh speeches appears in the Book of Job at a most awkward spot. But its content and its style are completely appropriate to the Book of Job and consideration of these will require an affirmative answer to the question, "Is chapter 28 a work of the author?"

There are those who would not retain chapter 28 as authentic because of its style, which they state is different from that of the author of the book. Terrien has a rather unique view in that he accepts the chapter as genuine because it seems to have been written by the author of the discourses of Yahweh who is probably the author of the major part of the book. Nevertheless, he states that the style of the Wisdom Poem is not the same as that of the Dialogue.[19] Steinmann notes that chapter 28 is not like the discourses; its style is more like that of the sages.[20] Driver and Gray (232) approach the subject of style from a negative stance and say that it is significant that 'dh (to pass over), slh (to value) and msk (price) which could have been used elsewhere are not used; the divine names which are most frequently used in the discourses are not present in chapter 28, and that the use of such a refrain (such as is in ch. 28) is more natural to an independent poem. A decision concerning the style of a particular passage should be based upon evidence that has been noted in exegesis and upon careful comparison of material. Unfortunately, there are few specific objections to the style of chapter 28 as authentic other than those of Driver and Gray. A number of authors simply state that the chapter is not "in the style of the author" without citing the literary basis for such a conclusion. Hopefully, it can be successfully demonstrated that the Wisdom Poem is written in the style of the author as displayed both in the Dialogue and in the Yahweh speeches.

There are several general comments which can be made initially about the style of the author of the Book of Job. These comments apply to the discourses, to the Yahweh speeches, and to the Wisdom Poem.

It has often been noted that there are more hapax legomena in the Book of Job than in any other Old Testament book. There are seventy-six hapax legomena in the Book of Job.[21] Three of these appear in chapter 28; thus the Wisdom Poem has no more of these than one could reasonably expect in a poem of its length. The author of the book seems to strive for the unusual and for the variety. Perhaps the most striking general feature of the style of the author is the richness of the vocabulary. The author uses certain words and even whole expressions which show infiltration of other Semitic tongues (Arabic, Assyrian or Babylonian, and Aramaic) and which are understood by their etymology. There are one hundred and thirty-one of these; chapter 28 has six.[22] Thus, the Wisdom Poem does not have too many of such words or expressions to be considered a product of the style of the author of Job nor is it suspect because of a lack of such words or expressions.

The author of the wisdom poem often indicates his wide vocabulary by presenting a variety of terms used as synonyms for another word. For example, he uses four terms for "gold." In 28:15, s°gor is used as a poetical expression for zāhāb sāgur and apparently refers to the excellent quality of the gold. Ketem'opir (gold of Ophir) is used in 28:16 to indicate the Egyptian designation of the land from which the gold was mined (perhaps Nubia).[23] The common word for gold zāhāb is used in 28:1. Pāz (fine gold) refers to re-fined gold whose value is being compared with that of wisdom in 28:17; it surpasses zāhāb and ketem.[24] "Pure gold" is used by the RSV to translate ketem tāhor in 28:19. This variety in expression is paralleled in 31:24 where both zāhāb and ketem are used.

The same element of style is seen in 4:10 and 11 where various phrases are used for the word "lion." The author is speaking metaphorically and referring to the roar of the 'ar°yeh and the voice of the saḥal. In 4:10b, he refers to the teeth of the "young lions," k°firim. In 4:11a, the strong lion, layis, (probably derived from the Arabic word for strong, cf. BDB 538) is mentioned and in 4:11b, a reference to the lioness, lābi', concludes the discussion. He parallels the use of these words for lion in the first Yahweh speech, 38:39, when he speaks of the lioness and then of the young lions.

The author demonstrates a wide range of knowledge.

In 18:8-10 he mentions the various traps that ensnare
the wicked: the net which catches one by the feet,
the netting stretched over a pit, the snare of the
fowler and the sammim (another one of the unique words
of which the author is fond--usually translated as
"snare"). He discusses such varied subjects as erosion
(14:18) caused by violent storms or the new growth of a
tree that seems dead (14:7-9) or the constellations
(the Bear, Orion and the Pleiades are discussed in 9:9
and paralleled in 38:31-32). Thus, it is not strange
that he exhibits in chapter 28 a knowledge of mining
techniques nor that he would use such to portray man's
ability to acquire what he wants. Although he does
not describe mining anywhere else in his book, he has
referred to it in such a manner that the discussion in
chapter 28 should not surprise the reader. In 3:21,
he speaks of those who wait for death and who "dig in
search of it more than for hidden treasures." The
author seems to be impressed with man's persistence in
his mining efforts and therefore uses that particular
persistence as a parallel to man's search for death.
It should be noted that the hiddenness of the treasures
is stressed in 3:21 as it is in 28:3, 7, 9, 11. It is
this hiddenness which then provides the parallel with
wisdom. Man's desire for gold and silver is also used
to provide a metaphor for the author in 22:25--an individual will have delight in the Almighty if He is one's
gold and one's silver.

Dhorme (clxxi) and Terrien (879-880) refer to the
Egyptian influence which has enriched the vocabulary
and thought of the author of the Book of Job. This
Egyptian flavor is seen in the Dialogue, in chapter 28
and in the Yahweh speeches. Among the Egyptian references are the skiffs of reed in 9:26, the reference in
3:14 to contented rest in ruins which kings build for
themselves (probably pyramids as suggested by Herbert
G. May and Bruce M. Metzger, eds. The Oxford Annotated
Bible with the Apocrypha, RSV (New York: Oxford U.
Press, 1973), 616, and the use of tuhot in 38:36 which
refers to the god of wisdom, Thoth, the ibis.[25]
Furthermore, many commentators think that the allusions
to mining in 28:2-6 refer to Egyptian mines in the
Sinaitic Peninsula. The poetical term in 28:10a translated as "channels," y^e'orim, refers to the branches of
the Nile. Thus, an Egyptian coloring is evident
throughout the author's work.

In addition to the richness of vocabulary and

acquaintance with a wide range of subject matter, there is another general characteristic of the author's style which is impressive. Terrien refers to what he calls the author's exquisite sense of the beauty of nature. [26] Repeatedly the author refers to various elements in nature and to animals and birds. The lion, the bird of prey, the falcon, and all living creatures are referred to in chapter 28. In 38:39, the prey of the lion is mentioned while in 38:41 reference is made to the prey of the raven. In 9:26, the author refers to the eagle swooping down on its prey. [27] In 39:5, the Yahweh speech refers to the wild ass who ranges the mountain as his pasture and in 6:5 and 11:12 the wild ass is referred to again in proverbial form. In 24:5, the term is used figuratively to describe the wicked although he is illustrating the same interest in the ass's ability to seek its food in its habitat as he displays in 39:5. In 28:7-8, 21, the author states that neither the birds nor the animals know the way to the place of understanding. This particular vein of thought seems to have been called forth as a response to 12:7 where the implication is given that the birds and beasts do know certain things about God.

The author speaks of thunderstorms and desert hurricanes (21:18; 27:21), or the constellations (9:9; 38:7), and of the thunderbolt or lightning flash (38:25b, 28:26b). The latter expression, w^{e}derek lahaziz qōlot, is a unique phrase of the author of the Book of Job; it does not appear anywhere else in the Old Testament. All agree that the marvels of God are mysterious and unfathomable: Eliphaz, 5:8-16; Job, 9:4-10; 12:9-25; Bildad, 25:2-6; 26:5-14. God's particular control over creation is seen in his binding up of the waters (26:8) and in the parallel thought of his meting them out by measure (28:25). Man has some measure of glory like God when man overturns mountains (28:9) as God overturns them (9:5). In fact, all the marvelous things that God is represented as doing in 9:8-10 sound very much like the actions of God in 28:25-27 and 38:4-11. The awareness and appreciation of nature and of creation presented in the Yahweh Speeches is certainly not without parallel in the Wisdom Poem or the Dialogue.

In addition to the above general elements of style discernible in the Dialogue, the Yahweh Speeches, and chapter 28, there are also some rather specific stylistic elements which appear in all three sections of the

Book of Job.[28] Such peculiarities of style are numerous enough to make an array of evidence for the common authorship of the Wisdom Poem, the Dialogue, and the Yahweh Speeches.

One of the most noticeable peculiarities of style is the extensive use of the rhetorical question. This style is noticeable in the Yahweh Speeches where there are 54 rhetorical questions (excluding those in 40:13-14) and in the Dialogue where there are 163 rhetorical questions. Driver and Gray think that the use of a refrain in chapter 28 points to the independent nature of the poem.[29] The refrain is given in rhetorical question form in 28:12 and 28:20 which surely belongs to the style of the author. Furthermore, the use of a refrain in question form appears elsewhere in the author's work. In 38:19a the author asks, "Where is the way to the dwelling place of light?" and in 38:24a he asks, "Where is the way to the place where the light is distributed?" In 39:19, he asks, "Where is the place of darkness"--in exactly the same form in which he asks in 28:12b, 20b, "Where is the place of understanding?" There seems to be no basis for thinking that the refrain of chapter 28 points to an independent work.

A very interesting element of the author's style is his personalization of various elements or animals by representing them as speaking. In 28:14 both the Deep and the Sea speak. In 28:22, Abaddon and Death speak. In 28:35, the lightnings are represented as saying, "here we are." The horse shows his readiness for battle by saying "Aha" where he hears the trumpet (38:25). In 8:18, "his place" says, "I have never seen you." In 3:3, Job curses the day of his birth in a manner which is reminiscent of Jer. 20:14-15. Unlike the passage in Jeremiah, however, the author of Job represents the night of his birth as saying, "A man-child is conceived" (3:3b). Thus, the author has put his personal stamp on an idea probably borrowed from Jeremiah. This stylistic element, which is present in the Dialogue, the Yahweh Speeches, and in the Wisdom Poem, is a literary device which is seldom found in the Old Testament.

The author of the Book of Job seems to be particularly fond of unexpressed subjects: in 27:2-3, the lack of a clear subject has caused difficulty for translators and exegetes. "Man" is used as the subject in most translations of 28:3, 9-11 although the subject is unexpressed in the Hebrew text. In 15:20-33, the wicked man is the subject, although after an initial indication of the subject, the passage progresses for 13 verses without expressing the specific subject again; one has to be content with "he."[30] The lack of an expressed subject in 28:3, 9-11 is another indication that the author of the Dialogue also wrote the wisdom chapter. Furthermore, the use of 'enos ("man") in 28:13 is not at all unusual (cf. 7:1 and 14:9) even though the author also uses 'adam frequently as a subject.

There are several unusual constructions which appear in Chapter 28 and which also appear in the dialogue. In 28:18 the author makes use of implicit accusatives: ra'mot w^{e}gabis (coral and crystal) are implicit accusatives of yizzaker. This is the same kind of construction that appears in 22:9. In 10:21, and in 3:5, the author uses two words in sequence in order to emphasize darkness ("deep darkness"). In 20:26, he uses "utter darkness." In 28:3 he uses ul^{e}kol-tak^{e}lit to emphasize darkness.

Finally, let us look at the specific evidence offered as objections to considering the Wisdom Poem as belonging to the style of the author. Driver and Gray note that chapter 28 avoids the divine names regularly used in the dialogue: 'lwh, 'l, and sdy.[31] Furthermore, the divine name, 'adonay, appears only in 28:28 (many manuscripts read yhwh)[32] and Driver and Gray point to this as though this evidence should be used to deny the authenticity of chapter 28 (245). It is difficult to follow their logic at this point since they view verse 28 as an addition to chapter 28. Therefore, if 28:1-27 is by an entirely different hand than 28:28, the use of any word which appears in verse 28 should not be considered in discussing the style of the author of chapter 28. If, however, this verse is a quotation then no elements of the author's style in general or vocabulary in particular should be expected to occur here even though the author was the one responsible for including this quotation at the end of the poem. The use of the divine name, 'elohim, in chapter 28 would only be crucial in the question of authenticity if this name were not used elsewhere in the book. 'Elohim (28:23) is used elsewhere but the author does not use it freely.[33] In fact, it is reserved for special usage --when the great power or ability of God is stressed and when he intends to refer to God in both members of

297

a verse which exhibits synonymous parallelism (5:8 and 20:29).

The argument that 'dh (vs. 8), slh (vs. 16) and msk (vs. 18) might have been used elsewhere but aren't is even less conclusive. Perhaps their point could have been made more clearly if they had indicated where these particular words could have been used. None of the usual words for price appear anywhere outside of chapter 28 in the Book of Job so that the use of m^e chir in 28:15 seems valid. The verb, 'dh (pass over or tread), is one of many Aramaisms with which the text of Job abounds. The author's need for a synonym is sufficient to explain its use here. The author does seem to prefer drk (which he has also used in 28:8) in other instances when he means "tread."; but there is no other stich where a parallel word for drk would be needed. The same is true for slh in vs. 16. A verb corresponding to its meaning is simply not needed elsewhere. There is no other context in which a verb meaning "to value" is used or required.

It is hoped that the above discussion has helped to build a convincing case for the common style of the Wisdom Poem, the Dialogue, and the Yahweh Speeches. If chapter 28 need not be eliminated on the basis of style but can be retained as the work of the author, the next consideration must be the possible original context of the chapter. How and where does it fit into the author's scheme?

Virtually all other arguments which term chapter 28 an interpolation are based on the incongruity of its present position. What appears initially to be many arguments against viewing the chapter as belonging to the original composition are not many but one: it is completely incongruous in its present situation. Logic and theology (which are not always on the same side) seem to combine forces to demand its excision. Neither its tone nor its thought can convince the reader that Job has uttered the words of this magnificent poem and then gone on with his laments and protestations in chapters 29-31.

Harold Knight has written an enlightening article dealing with the contribution of the Book of Job to Hebrew theology in which he states that Job feels crushed by the majesty of a transcendent God whom he can't bring down to his level, a God who is impenetrable

to man's insight and understanding. What was needed
was new revelation from the living God who makes a
dynamic approach to men. This revelation is given in
the theophany, but the operation of the divine provi-
dence and wisdom must remain a mystery to man since it
surpasses the range of his mind and is insoluble in
terms of a rational theodicy.[34] In chapter 28 Job recognizes and affirms the inaccessibility of God's wisdom.
One must be careful not to view Job from a purely philosophical plane, however; his suffering and terrible distress surely stem from a real-life experience. The wisdom school and traditional religion have not been able
to answer the agonizing question of his crisis--just
where does God stand in relation to his life. As Blank
has said, "The author of Job has learned that man is
more complicated and God less transparent than the
teachers of proverbs and their complacent clients assumed."[35] Job 28 fits into the purpose of the book as
Job's expression of his understanding of and acceptance
of God's incomprehensible wisdom. It is Job's full submission; but Job isn't ready to submit yet if we believe
him to be sincere in the discourse in chapter 27.

The non-relevance of chapter 28 to chapter 27 or
to chapter 29 tells us that no explanation can satis-
factorily justify its present position. Its appearance
at this particular place and coming from the mouth of
Job at this time would reduce the rest of the book into
an illogical and unnecessary farce. The original
author, whose masterful architectural design complete
with prose framework and a precisely planned structure
of discourses commands our deepest respect, would surely
not have placed the Wisdom Poem here.[36] However, the
intensity of Job's lament in the third cycle, particularly the extensive oaths of innocence and the final
defiant challenge (31:35-37) perhaps prompted an editor
to remove the "end piece" and place it in the third cycle to lighten the discussion as well as to compensate
for missing material. Since 42:2-6 can stand alone as
a conclusion to the book and since only in the wisdom
chapter does Job speak truly positively of God elsewhere, this is the only possible piece that would serve
such a purpose. As the doxologies were put into the
Book of Amos to relieve the somber tone, so chapter 28
was moved to the third cycle to relieve the strained
tone of the speeches of Job. The bitterness expressed
by Job in 27:2ff and the egotistical self-righteousness
of chapter 29ff must have caused the editors great difficulty. The reintroduction of Job's speech in chapter

29 indicates an arbitrary insertion; but perhaps the editors only looked to the end of the original poetry for the needed insertion.37

It is really one of the objections to the inclusion of the 28th chapter that points to the direction of the true Heimat of the chapter. Critics say that chapter 28 "spoils" the effect of the Yahweh speeches and thus makes them "superfluous," "extraneous," and even "nugatory"! But if chapter 28 cannot precede the Yahweh speeches without spoiling their effect, is it not possible that the original position of the Wisdom Poem was somewhere following the Yahweh Speeches?

As R. A. F. MacKenzie has said concerning the problems of the Book of Job: "Every year brings its quota of contributions to the discussion, and though it is becoming increasingly difficult to suggest novel interpretations, yet the old ones can always be supported by new arguments."38 The proposal that chapter 28 belongs after Job's repentance speech (42:2-6) is not a new idea. In 1931 Szczygiel stated that position: "es gehört nach 42:6 als weitere Ausfuhrung der rückhaltlosen Hingabe Jobs an Gott."39 However, in the limited space available in a commentary, Szczygiel was unable to present much evidence for his position. According to Tur-Sinai, the main aim of chapter 28, which is to teach that man is to trust God's wisdom and is not supposed to understand the order of the world, looks in the direction of the answer which the book of Job gives to its primary question. The purpose of the questions in Yahweh's discourse is to lead to the answer that man cannot find wisdom. Thus, Tur-Sinai thinks that chapter 28 is the final answer to Job's doubts. Chapter 28 expresses the idea at which the questions in the Yahweh speeches are aimed. However, in a rather startling conclusion to this discussion, Tur-Sinai states that

> while recognising that this portion forms the conclusion of the book and God's final answer to Job's doubts, and that it bears the mark of the same author as the remainder of the poem, we must realize that it represents a version of a literary composition on the subject of wisdom which was not primarily intended for this book and which, as will be gathered from v. 28, was formerly connected with the story of the Creation and of Adam.40

300

It is the contention of this essay, however, that chapter 28 is Job's final speech and that it was composed by the author for this book and was an integral part of the first version.

It has often been noted that chapter 28 has "affinities" with the Yahweh Speeches. These "affinities" are relatively obvious, e.g., the similar vocabulary and subject matter and the similarity in spirit which Fine mentions.[41] But what is the precise relationship between chapter 28 and the Yahweh Speeches? Are there valid reasons for suggesting that chapter 28 follows rather than precedes those speeches and therefore does not spoil their effect but indeed echoes their thought?

It seems to this writer that the dependency of chapter 28 on the Yahweh Speeches is indicated by the unique manner in which the ideas presented in those speeches are echoed in the song of praise in chapter 28. Furthermore, the command used by the author indicates that such a response will be forthcoming; "I will question you, and you shall declare to me" indicates that an answer is expected (cf. 38:3 and 40:7) which will declare quite clearly that Job has understood the reason for the questions asked of him in the Yahweh Speeches. Chapter 28 affirms that the knowledge and understanding which Job does not have indeed is accessible only to God who "understands" (28:23) the way to it. The irony of the questions in 38:16-18 highlights Job's lack of wisdom. Does he know where the gates of death or the path to the home of the place of darkness or even the sources of the sea are located? There are many entities whose place or home Job does not know (cf. 38:19). It is God who comprehends it all. Does Job realize that God is in charge of the rain and the lightning (38:25-28, 34-38)? Indeed he now does as 28:25-26 affirms. Chapter 28 has the tone of an answering response to the questions of chapters 38 and 39.

Chapter 28 begins by giving man his due and showing at what point he can manipulate his world. "Have you entered into the sources of the sea?" (38:16) and "Have you seen the gates of deep darkness?" (38:17). Chapter 28 answers by saying that, as a matter of fact, man has made his way to the sources of the rivers in his skillful search for treasures and he has entered into the very depths of darkness (28:3). Like God, he has even bound up these sources (28:11); man was not around when Yahweh laid the foundation of the earth

301

(38:4) but man has penetrated to the very foundation of the mountains (28:9). True, it is God who has cleft a channel for the torrents of rain (38:25) but man has made some channels of his own (28:10) nevertheless. Thus, the first strophe takes note of Yahweh's ironic questioning and presents the positive side of man's achievements; but this only serves to make the expose of man's limitations more pointed in 28:13. Man does not know the way to wisdom in spite of these intimations of greatness.

The purpose of chapter 28 is to praise God who is the sovereign Lord who sees everything under the heavens and who "established wisdom" and "declared it" when he performed the acts of creation listed in 28:25-26. The poem has built up to the crescendo that is the final strophe. Wisdom is in the exclusive control of God and has been from the very beginning of creation. The author intended to proclaim the great care and precision that has been put into creation--the same care and precision which characterized God's initial appraisal of wisdom.42 In view of this, man is surely now at the point where he can acknowledge God's wisdom and revere him. The right of such a God to rule with absolute sovereignty should surely be recognized by the reader and the carefulness of God's creative activity should be enough to instill confidence and trust in such a God.

The emphasis in chapter 38 and 39 is not simply on God's creation but on the carefully ordered creation. Nothing has been left to chance; everything has its precise place and its limit. In instance after instance this idea is expounded. Not only was the creation a series of endeavors carried out with precision, but God continues to control it with responsibility. The unique phraseology of 38:25b is repeated in 28:26b: God has made a way for the lightning of the thunder. He has even sent rain to the desert (38:26-27). The Wisdom Poem extols God's decree for the rain; he has meted it out by measure (28:25-26). It is the recognition of this care as well as God's sovereignty that Job is called upon to recognize and which he then does recognize in the Wisdom Poem. The author has led us to expect such a response from Job. Job's previous reference to God's control of creation have suggested that God is quite arbitrary in his use of power, e.g., it is either too dry or it pours (12:15): In fact, for Job, all of God's power seems to be quite arbitrary if not

whimsical. Job's problem could be resolved only by
recognizing the wisdom and care with which God rules
his world. Job does this, not only by his "confession"
in 42:2-6 but by his praise of God in chapter 28.

A position after the first Yahweh Speech is not
possible for the original position of chapter 28. Job
has answered in 40:4 that he is not ready to respond.
Yahweh's ironic tone increased in 40:8-9. Some critics
have rejected the authenticity of the Yahweh Speeches
because they take no note of the dialogue. However,
40:8-9 does take note of the dialogue--at least it
takes note of Job's part in the dialogue. Job has no
right to demand a <u>rib</u>. In 40:10-14, the ironic tone
builds to its highest pitch and Job's submission and
repudiation of his contention with God follows. If, as
seems most likely, the portrait of Behemoth and
Leviathan is secondary, then the confession of Job originally began immediately after 40:14. Job despises and
rejects his former attitude and utterances; gone is the
desire to bring God into court. He can now express his
changed view. Only here can the 28th chapter be spoken
by Job. He is ready to praise God and accept his own
limitations.

The position following Job's confession may be the
logical and literarily appropriate place for this chapter but that does not provide proof that it really did
stand there originally. H. H. Rowley (226) states that
"there is no evidence that it ever stood there." Although there is not enough evidence to establish the
thesis beyond question, the later, interpolated Elihu
speeches strongly suggest that their author is familiar
with both the Yahweh Speeches and chapter 28 and that
these were closely related in the text which he had
before him. In 36:24, he tells Job <u>to remember to extol
God's work</u>; then he goes on to discuss the rain and the
thunder and lightning in a manner which suggests that
he knows that these were referred to in the Wisdom Poem
at the end of the book. Obviously, however, Job has
not yet engaged in this extolling and so chapter 28 did
not originally appear before the Elihu speeches. But
Elihu has peeked at the ending of the book and knows
that Job does extol God's creation later. He seems to
have been aware of the connection between wisdom and
creation that is made in chapter 28:

> Hear this, O Job;
>   stop and consider the wondrous works of

God.
> Do you know how God lays his command upon
>   them, and causes the lightning of his
>   cloud to shine?
> Do you know the balancings of the clouds,
>   the wondrous works of him who is perfect
>   in knowledge. (37:14-16)

The initial ki has been somewhat of a problem for those who view chapter 28 as an independent poem. This conjunction is usually translated as "for"; "it provides the justification of a foregoing pronouncement, or somehow serves as a link between phrases or passages."[43] As Rowley admits, this seems to imply that it originally had a preceding context.[44] Some translate the particle as "surely" (RSV) since it does not seem to relate to what precedes it and some simply omit it (cf. Pope, 197). Others have suggested that the refrain once preceded it (Duhm, Peake) or perhaps some other part of the dialogue or some strophe now lost originally stood before 28:1. However, following Job's repentance speech in which he admits that he has uttered things he has not understood (40:2-6) ki can serve as the casual link which leads Job into an explanation of his new understanding of God's wisdom which is expressed in chapter 28. In that context "for" is not a problem; indeed, it should be expected to appear.

In addition, verse 28 gives us a literary cue that chapter 28 originally belonged between the end of the poetry and the prose epilogue.[45] This verse not only directs our attention to the fear of the Lord as the attitude which the author saw as the answer to Job's problem and Job's proper response at this point, but it also provides a transition to the epilogue and brings us back to the original story. Verse 28 reminds us of the "blameless and upright man who fears God and turns away from evil" (2:8). Verse 28 of chapter 28 had the Job of the prologue in mind.[46] The discussion has come around full circle to the original concern, "Does Job fear God for nought?" Verse 28 has all the characteristic marks of a formula from the wisdom school; it is quoted here by Job because this is the recognition of the proper relationship to God, a relationship which acknowledges his sovereignty and wisdom. The Job of the discourse now "fears" God as did the Job of the prologue; but the Job of the discourse has a new understanding of that required reverence--it is to be a thorough acceptance of and confidence in the wisdom of

God's created order and the sovereignty of God's provi-
dential care.[47] God cannot be put on trial and required
to answer questions about his justice. Job should now
understand that there are questions that cannot be answered since obviously he cannot give satisfactory answers to Yahweh's questions. The reverential fear of
the Lord is the only response appropriate to Job in his
continuing relationship to God and it is Job's relationship to God which is the central concern of the book.

Since the purpose of chapter 28 is to praise God,
the question must be raised as to whether or not a song
of praise is legitimate after the confession in 42:2-6.
If the literary evidence points to this as the original
position of the Wisdom Poem, is there a precedent in
the forms of other literature for such a positioning?

The Book of Job is not close enough in structure
or content to other Ancient Near Eastern literature for
any dependency of one upon the other to be claimed.
But the presence of certain similarities must cause a
recognition of common elements that wisdom writers consciously shared. "I Will Praise the Lord of Wisdom"
is a monologue rather than a dialogue, but the handling
of a problem very similar to Job's is remarkably like
the manner in which the author of Job dealt with his
problem. The problem of suffering is more basic to the
discussion in "I Will Praise the Lord of Wisdom" but
the sufferer has a deeper problem -- he cannot know the
ways of the gods and he does not know how to maintain a
good relationship to a god who seems to be arbitrary
and unjust.

> Oh that I only knew that these things are
> well pleasing to a god!
> What is good in one's sight is evil for a god.
> What is bad in one's own mind is good for his
> god.
> Who can understand the counsel of the gods in
> the midst of heaven?
> The plan of a god is deep waters, who can
> comprehend it?
> Where has befuddled mankind ever learned
> what a god's conduct is?[48]

Although he is not actually named in this piece of
Babylonian wisdom, it is obviously Marduk's hand that
is heavy upon the sufferer (who is presented as a model
of piety). Marduk's wrath is then appeased and tablet

four of the work includes a hymn of praise. However, there is some difficulty in establishing exactly what tablet four included. In ANET (437), Robert Pfeiffer has concluded that the Assur and Sultantepe fragments are part of the text as has H. C. Rawlinson who published the original text in A Selection from the Inscriptions of Assyria and Babylonia, Vol V (London: 1884).49 The Assur and Sultantepe manuscripts contain a hymn of praise from lines 52 onward (ANET 437) and this hymn of praise is presented after the sufferer acknowledges his salvation both with words and with offerings.

There are of course many differences between this work and the Book of Job, but it is significant that it is Marduk's appearance that has provided the sufferer with the "solution" to this problem. All that the sufferer can do is to give thanks and to praise. He does not ask "Why?" and no answer is presented that attempts to explain the cause of his suffering.

It is unfortunate that we do not know more about Israel's acquaintance with the literature of Zoroastrianism as well as more about the author (the time and setting in which he wrote) of the Book of Job. The well-versed author of the Book of Job may have been acquainted with the Gathas, but that is a conjecture.50 A relationship between Zarathustrian theology and Jewish theology at least after the exile has long been recognized. In one of the Gathas there are elements and traces of the same forms found in the Book of Job. The Gathic hymns are often concerned with the creation, with the origin of evil, and with the nature of Ahura and his powers. He is extolled as the creator who has established and ordered everything with wisdom along with the aid of his Holy Spirit.51 This is expressed in detail in the second Gatha, Ushtavaiti, which contains 4 sections--Yasna 43-46. The development of thought and the elements of form in this Gatha parallel the development and some of the formal elements of the Book of Job.

Yasna presents a doctrine of rewards and punishments52 which promises blessings in reward for pious deeds and "evil for the evil" (43:5). The righteousness and bounteousness of the deity are stressed (especially in verses 4-6); Zarathustra awaits that obedient reverence which will help him as he propagates the faith (43:12). Yasna 44 entreats Ahura to speak to him and to reveal himself; the author would like to know how to serve him. In 44, the rhetorical question style, which extends from verse one to the very last verse, directs queries to Ahura concerning his creation:

> Who gave the (recurring) sun and stars their
>   (undeviating) way?
> Who established that whereby the moon waxes,
>   and whereby she wanes, save Thee?
> These things, O Great Creator! would I know,
>   and others likewise still.
> This I ask Thee, O Ahura! tell me aright,
>   who from beneath has sustained the earth
>   and the clouds that they do not fall?
> Who made the waters and the plants?
> Who to the wind has yoked on the storm-clouds,
>   the swift and fleetest two?
> Who, O Great Creator! is the inspirer of the
>   good thoughts (within our souls)?
> This I ask Thee, O Ahura! tell me aright:
>   who, as a skillful artisan has made the
>   lights and the darkness?
> Who (spread) the Auroras, the noontides and
>   midnight, monitors to discerning (man),
>   duty's true (guides)?"[53]

Thus, it is Ahura who has fixed the "way" of the stars and sun; they are not on a random course. As in the Yahweh Speeches in Job, the atmospheric phenomena (clouds and winds) receive special note. The skillful artisan who has made the lights and the darkness is extolled. The moral order is also stressed; the author cannot distinguish the wicked and the Demon-of-the-Lie without Ahura's help (cf. Job 40:10-14).

In Yasna 45 a powerful adversary has just been crushed. There is a brief admonition to ponder Ahura's revelation and then the author turns to the praise of Ahura Mazda the creator of all (of whom he says in 45:6, "Let Him exhort me through His wisdom which is ever the best"). The author followed his own advice apparently and pondered the revelation of Ahura for he says in 45:8:

> Him in our hymns of homage and of praise
>   would I faithfully serve, for now with
>   (mine) eye, I see Him clearly,
> Lord of the good spirit, of word, and action,
>   I knowing through my Righteousness Him

307

who is Ahura Mazda.
And to Him (not here alone, but) in His home
of song,
His praise we shall bear.[54]

Yasna 46 has a cry from the depths--a lament over the
afflictions and discouragement suffered by the author.

This combination of elements--the use of the rhetorical question in extolling the deity's careful creation, that statement that the god's wisdom is the
best, the notice of a first-hand revelation by the eye
which is followed immediately by a song of praise, and
the presentation of a lament about affliction--is quite
like the themes and elements of form presented in the
Book of Job. There is much that is dissimilar; no
dependency can be claimed. All that can be said legitimately is that a mixture of elements such as are present in the Book of Job is not unique in the literature
of about the 6th century B.C.

The Wisdom Poem does not appear to have any relation to the structure of the Book of Job.[55] If the answer to the question, "Where does chapter 28 belong?",
is that it originally stood after the confession of
Job, then it is necessary to demonstrate that this poem
fits into the basic pattern or form of the book and is
essential to it in that position. In what pattern in
Hebrew literature can a song of praise be an element as
well as statements of lament, a theophany, and a declaration of repentance and trust? It is the thesis of
Westermann that the dialogue in Job is a dramatization
of the lament.[56] According to Westermann (cf. 25) the
basic framework is provided by the laments in chapters
3 and 29-31 although expressions of lament also appear
elsewhere. The lament proper is spoken by Job while
the friends give the only expression of trust (Westermann, 11-12). The answer of God appears in the Book of
Job at the precise point where one expects the answer
of God (Heilsorakel) in a lament psalm (Westermann, 83).
Since the book is a lament, however, he suggests that
it does not belong to wisdom literature and that chapter 28 is not part of the lament structure; it is a
pure wisdom piece (104). However, chapter 28 cannot be
so easily excluded from the individual lament form.
We need to look rather closely at the characteristics
of this form.

It is the view of Hans Schmidt that in many of the

individual laments in the psalms which portray the
righteousness of the sufferer and affirm his innocence
that the enemies are those who are involved in the
legal accusation of the suppliant. The accused was
brought before the priests and the case presented to
Yahweh who would somehow give a verdict. The enemies
are the false accusers; however, they have not caused
the problem -- Yahweh has.57 If the Book of Job is a
literary adaptation of the lament form, that view would
explain the presence of rib terminology in Job's
speeches. Harvey Guthrie notes that within the lament
proper of the individual lament, the focus shifts among
three objects of attention: the lamenter's suffering
and his innocence, the enemies, and God who is directly
or indirectly accused of not having cared for the suppliant. The motive behind the accusations of God's
negligence is to shame him into action. Thus, some
laments remind God that the suppliant's condition has
become an occasion of mockery (cf. Ps. 42:9-10).58 Job
most certainly attempts to shame God into action.

Included in many of the individual laments is a
vow of praise (Lobgelubde). In some psalms where it
appears to be missing it is present in a different form
(17:15; 31:7) or it has been transformed into a report
(Ps. 73:28) or an exhortation (Pss. 27:14; 31:24) or
into a future condition (43:4).59 This vow, declares
Westermann (72), corresponds to the praise of God rather
than to thanks: "it is a witness to an understanding
of existence in which man does not yet stand alone."
The vow indicates that the lamenter has been heard by
God and therefore has been changed or transformed himself. This change is often indicated by a "now" or
"but now," e.g., Ps. 20:6: "Now I know that the Lord
will help." The confession of trust usually precedes
the vow of praise and indicates that a transition is
about to be made from one mode of speech (lamentation)
to another (praise) which is being promised in the
vow.60 In the book of Job, such a profession of trust
follows the Yahweh Speeches. Job says, "I know that
thou canst do all things, and that no purpose of thine
can be thwarted" (42:2).

A final element in many of the individual laments
is an expression of praise or song of thanksgiving.
These differ from the usual expressions of confidence
that are quite often intermingled with the lamentation.
The entire psalm takes on a different character; "within these psalms something decisive has occurred,

something which changes what is being said here."61
This abrupt and decisive change of mood is the result
of a conviction that God has heard the worshipper.
Something has happened to give him this assurance.
Gunkel suggests a <u>priesterliche Heilsorakel</u>.62 With
the exception of Ps. 12, cultic oracles do not appear
in the individual laments, but there are prophetic imi-
tations of such oracles. After Jeremiah's lament in
15:15-18, an oracle appears in 15:19-21 which gives
Yahweh's answer to Jeremiah in terms both of rebuke and
assurance (cf. 11:21-23 and 12:5-6). The lament form
in Jeremiah is quite broken--indicating not only
Jeremiah's free use of it but also its separation from
the cult.63

If the secondary nature of the Elihu speeches is
acknowledged, then the answer of God (the Yahweh
Speeches) follows Job's oath of purgation and final
challenge to God to answer him in chapter 31. It was
at such a point in the temple pattern that the theophany
occurred or the oracle of God was given by the priest
or cult prophet. The answer of Yahweh appears at the
same point in the structure of the Book of Job. The
tone of Yahweh in these speeches reflects the legal setting that Schmidt suggests, "Shall a faultfinder contend
with the Almighty?" The theophany answers Job but not
on Job's terms. Following his profession of trust in
42:2, Job echoes the Yahweh Speeches (42:3-4) indicating
that the theophany has brought about his change of mind.
In Job 42:5-6, there is no verb stating that Job "will
sing" the praises of God. However, as has been noted
the vow can appear in a different form and it does so
in Job 42:5-6. These verses do not present an explicit
vow of praise, yet they are tantamount to such. Job
admits that he had formerly misunderstood. Thus, one
expects a presentation of his new understanding--some
definition of what he now "sees." Therefore, a song of
praise which presents in didactic fashion what the suppliant has learned is prepared for by the repentance of
Job which may be understood as an implied vow of praise.

After the profession of trust and repentance speech
(vow) in 42:2-6, the Wisdom Poem serves the function of
the song of praise (thanksgiving) of the individual lament pattern. In the psalms, the reason for the following song of thanksgiving is presented as the first element in the song or else the whole song of thanks provides the motivation to respond by praising God. The
reason for offering praise or thanksgiving is usually

introduced by the particle ki. The wording of this
motivation can be quite general; it may be a reference
to God's goodness or the wonders of nature. The psalm-
ist proclaims that God has acted but does not describe
the specific action.[64] Nevertheless, there is a relationship between the worshipper's experience and the
praise that he utters. If chapter 28 is viewed as having its original position after 42:6, the troublesome
introductory particle provides the reason for the presence of the song of praise (cf. Ps. 22:24, 28:6b and
31:21b). Job has undergone a change of attitude and
repents of his former words for he now understands, and
thus praises, God's wisdom which is contrasted to man's.
Exegetes have noted the absence of motivation for the
change of mood in chapter 28 in its present position in
the dialogue. However, in its original position after
42:6, the encounter with Yahweh has provided this. In
the psalms, the reason for praise is sometimes explicit
and personal and sometimes quite general as in Ps.
22:28: "For dominion belongs to the Lord, and he rules
over the nations." It is such general, non-personal
praise which composes the wisdom poem in Job. Job does
not say that Yahweh has shown him evidences of his wisdom. Job praises him in general terms for his understanding and for his work (Job 28:23-27) and implies
that this is far superior to man's understanding and
ability for man can find treasure but not wisdom.

One of the reasons that the final verse of chapter
28 is suspected of being unauthentic is because of its
didactic element. However, didactic elements are integral elements in thanksgiving songs and usually appear at the end of the songs of thanksgiving in individual laments. Ps. 31:23 concludes the song of thanksgiving begun in 31:21 and consists of a pure didactic
speech which includes what appears to be a proverb in
quotation. "Love the Lord, all you his saints! The
Lord preserves the faithful, but abundantly requites
him who acts haughtily." The didactic element is simply
part of the pattern.

Thus, rather than speaking against its authenticity, the form of chapter 28--a song of praise declaring
God's sole possession of wisdom--presents an argument
for its authenticity and speaks for its original position after 42:6 when it is recognized that the Book of
Job is patterned after the individual lament structure.
The author has chosen his literary pattern deliberately
even though he varies it by using a dialogue form as

well. The lament is the best means of expressing the intensity of Job's problem--his estrangement from God.

The Book of Job shows that in the Israel of the author's day a crisis had arisen in regard to wisdom. The wisdom view of life as expressed by Job's friends in the dialogue is one that Job (and the author) cannot accept; the book must be understood as a polemic against the views of the friends who do not speak "rightly" about God. Job's passionate plea for God to answer him demonstrates the presence of a serious problem in Israel's religious life. Religious faith suffered from the inversion of the doctrine of rewards and punishments. Difficulty arose when misfortune came to be seen as the outward sign of inward wickedness and sin. The truly wise man could see that this neat system of balances was not always a true measurement of the individual's religious life. But this was only the beginning of the problem. If God's justice could not be depended upon, then what relationship could one have with God?

The author's solution to Job's problem is presented in the poetical material that follows the Dialogue. The Yahweh Speeches, the confession, and chapter 28 are vital for the theology of the Book of Job. Job had questioned God and exalted his own knowledge. The friends were confident of their wisdom also. It is this attitude--that of confidence in one's own ability to arrive at a solution of the human dilemma--that is the core of the difficulty. Job is confident that if he could just take God to court, he could argue his way out of his problem. The Yahweh Speeches shift the whole problem to another plane and provide an answer which lays a completely different foundation for Job's relationship to God. In his confession, Job renounces his former attitude, and in chapter 28, he proclaims his newly found understanding. Job's encounter with the Lord teaches him that wisdom is knowledge of God gained through direct communion with him; it is not merely insights and answers. God is no longer impenetrable to Job's sight, but he is not to be questioned nor is his wisdom to be put at man's disposal. Job must fear God "for nought." The individual must accept the fact that God alone knows the way to wisdom; the individual can only "fear" God who will impart what he wills to impart.

The importance of the Wisdom Poem for our understanding of the meaning of the Book of Job depends then upon its content and its position. By its position after the Yahweh Speeches, Job is demonstrating in chapter 28 that wisdom has been given to him by God through the encounter with God. Thus, the greatest possible significance is given to the theophany by the demonstration in the Wisdom Poem of Job's new awareness. The man who fears God as he should speaks like this. The reader is not left to guess what effect the theophany had on Job's thinking. Job does not have the great wisdom of God, but he has a new comprehension which is a gift of God who has acted on his behalf. Job's problem has been solved.

FOOTNOTES

1. Robert Polzin says "Few books in the Old Testament have discrepancy and contradicition so central to their make-up as the book of Job. Many scholars have solved the problems these contradictions entail by employing a process of subtraction, that is by eliminating 'What-Does-Not-Fit'." Biblical Structuralism: Method and Subjectivity in the Study of Ancient Texts; Missoula: Scholars, 1977, p. 57.
2. Georg Fohrer, Das Buch Hiob, KAT; Gutersloh: Mohn, 1963, p. 392. Bernhard Duhm's discussion is short but definitive. Nothing can connect ch. 28 to the book of Job! Das Buch Hiob, KHC; Freiburg: Mohr, 1897, pp. vii-viii.
3. Robert Gordis supposes it was preserved with the other writings of the poet by admirers and included by a copyist. The Book of Job; NY: Jewish Theological Seminary, 1978, p. 298.
4. Robert Laurin suggests the author borrowed the poem from Israel's hymnody which explains its structural and stylistic differences with the dialogues. See later for his argument that its present position is integral to the author's theological argument. "The Theological Structure of Job," ZAW 84 (1972), 87.
5. R. Tournay notes Lefevre's hypothesis on errors in copying and on the basis of the size of stichs into which a psalter from Qumran is divided, has rearranged the third cycle according to what he sees as the actual length of columns. This seems quite hypothetical. He assumes the scroll on which Job was originally written was like the Qumran scrolls on whose measurements he based his findings. By reconstructing the third cycle by the measurements of the stichs, he presents a case for retaining ch. 28 as authentic to the original scroll. "L'Ordre Primitif des Chp. 24-28 de Job," RB 64 (1957), 321-334. Cf. E. Dhorme, A Commentary on the Book of Job tr. H. Knight; London: Nelson, 1967.
6. The Yahweh speeches with the probable exception of 40:15-24 and 41:12-34 are surely authentic. Note the absence of the questions used consistently in Yahweh's speaking elsewhere. Gordis says the purpose of the Yahweh speeches "is not the glorification of nature but the vindication of nature's God; the transcendental side of the question is presented." The Book of God and Man; Chicago: University of Chicago, 1966. R.A.F. McKenzie says the Yahweh speeches are im-

peratively called for: "Job repeatedly desires or demands, expects or predicts, that God may or will eventually answer him." The author is not showing Job vainly wishing that God would speak; rather, he is allowing him to stake his religious existence on it. It seems unlikely that there would be no answer; if the author's purpose were cynical and meant to show that Job's faith was vainly expressed, one would expect a statement that God did not answer. "The Purpose of the Yahweh Speeches in the Book of Job," Bib 40 (1959), 47.

7. S.R. Driver, An Introduction to the Literature of the Old Testament; NY: Scribner's, 1902, p. 409.

8. Vs. 4 is especially difficult to understand. A rich variety of emendations are proposed. See Fohrer, p. 390; Dhorme, p. 401; Driver and Gray, p. 192. The lack of a clear subject and of detailed knowledge of ancient mining causes any translation of this verse to be only a proposal.

9. Das Buch Hiob, p. 391.

10. Dhorme, A Commentary.., p. 406. M. Pope reports the term mbk nhrm of the Ugaritic myths is identical in meaning and virtually identical in form with the hitherto unique expression mibbeke neharot. He says that in the Ugaritic texts, this is one of the regular designations of the watery abode of the god El. Job, Anchor Bible; Garden City: Doubleday, 1965, p. 180. C.L. Feinberg discusses all the Ugaritic passages where the construction mabbike nabarema appears. In all of them the proper translation is "the sources of the rivers.' Ugartiic Literature and the Book of Job, Ph.D. dissertation; Baltimore: Johns Hopkins, pp. 26-7.

11. Hokemah and binah are not to be understood here as different entities. "Wisdom" is meant by both terms.

12. Gustav Hölscher states that vss. 15-20 form an expansion of the original poem; the verses divert from the theme and give an "exhausting enumeration" in the repetition of the gold in 16a, 17a, and 19. Das Buch Hiob; Tubingen: Mohr, 1937, p. 65.

13. The LXX does not have vss. 14-19. However, as Gordis has noted, the LXX text of Job is at least one-sixth shorter than the Hebrew. The Alexandrine and others often paraphrased and even corrrected wording. It is quite likely that they could have omitted these verses. Job, p. 122.

14. Cf. Ecclus. 1 where the same thoughts are expressed in logical order: "The Lord Himself created it and saw it and reckoned it."

15. Duhm, p.137.

16. Thurmond Coss, The Fear of the Lord in Hebrew Wisdom, Ph.D. dissertation; Madison: Drew, 1957, p. 182.

17. Terrien suggested Job 28:1-27 does not necessarily refer to a metaphysical, hypostatized wisdom which remains forever absolutely beyond man's reach. "Job," Interpreter's Bible(IB) 3:1105.

18. Most of the literary difficulties of vs. 28 (including 'adonay) could be resolved if it were a proverb in quotation. The form and vocabulary would then be fixed. Is a didactic element appropriate to the end of this chapter? We shall return to that question.

19. Terrien, "Job," IB 3:1099-1100.

20. J. Steinmann, Le Lévre de Job; Paris: Cerf, 1955, p. 230.

21. This is according to the broadest definition of <u>hapax logomen-</u>
<u>on</u> and not that of Harold Cohen whose excellent study defines it as
"any biblical word whose root occurs in but one context" and thereby identifies the functional uniqueness of those words he terms
<u>hapax logomena</u>. <u>Biblical Hapax Logomena in the Light of the Akka-</u>
<u>dian and Ugaritic</u>; Missoula: Scholars, 1978, pp. 6-7.
22. Dhorme, pp. clxxv-clxxvi.
23. Pope, <u>Job</u>, 3rd ed.; 1973, p. 204.
24. Dhorme, p. 409.
25. Dhorme, p. 593. Pope, p. 302.
26. Terrien, p. 892.
27. In 39:26-7, the hawk and eagle soar to lofty heights and the
eagle's keen eyes see his prey (38:29). The author seems quite impressed with the ability of these creatures to get their prey.
28. The prologue and epilogue are not considered here. The auth-
or's style was not free but subservient to the folk tale.
29. Driver and Gray, p.232.
30. There is no expressed subject in 20:6-28. In 17:6, "He has
made me a byword of the peoples" refers to God but God is not the
subject of the immediately preceeding passages.
31. Driver and Gray, p. 232.
32. R. Kittel, <u>Biblia Hebraica</u>; Stuttgart: Wurttembergische Bibel-
anstalt Stuttgart, 1961, p. 1136.
33. '1wh, '1, sdy are used rather freely - 90 times in all.
34. Harold Knight, "Job (Considered as a Contribution to Hebrew
Theology)," <u>Scottish Journal of Theology</u> 9 (1956), 63-76.
35. S.H. Blank, "Wisdom," IDB 4:858.
36. The Wisdom Poem is certainly not integrated into Job. Critics
refer to its "independence" since it does not refer to Job's suffering nor to the discussion. This is also only an argument against
its present position. If it is a response to Yahweh's speeches, it
<u>should not</u> refer to Job's suffering or the arguments. As Hölscher
says (p. 65), the burden of its message - that wisdom and the secrets of the universe are inaccessible to man - does not comport
with Job's desire to bring God into court. God did not answer Job's
accusations nor enter a <u>rib</u> with him.
37. Zophar is sometimes credited with ch. 28 since he cannot find
"out the deep things of God (11:7) but he is interested only in the
wisdom which helps man understand his own situation, particularly
his guilt (11:6). His impassioned speech in the second cycle makes
him an unlikely candidate for such a calm, reflective poem.
38. McKenzie, pp. 435-436.
39. P. Szczygiel, <u>Das Buch Job</u>; Bonn: Hanstein, 1931, p. 20.
Denn nach 42:6 ist es nichts anderes als eine Zustimmung zur
göttlichen Belehrung und ein Beweis dafur, wie Job aus derselben
die praktische Nutzanwendung für sich zieht. Dann ist auch Gottes
Wort, dass Job 'bis zum Zuverlässigen' von Gott geredet habe (42:
7), um so verständlicher, denn gemäss K. 28 verschwindet alles,
was Welt und Leben an Gutem oder an Wundern bietet, gegenüber dem
höchsten Gut der Religion. Diese allein löst das Rätsel auch des
unschuldigen Leidens, nicht etwa durch Mitteilung einer alles

315

meisternden Wissenschaft, sondern durch die Hingabe an Gott, des-
sen Weisheit auch dann von aller Ungerechtigkeit freibleibt,
wenn sie wie im Falle Jobs prüft.
40. N.H. Tur-Sinai, The Book of Job; Jerusalem: Kiryath Sepher,
1957, pp. 394-5. Commenting on ch. 42, he suggests the chapter on
wisdom was the conclusion of God's speech and follows 42:4 (pp.
578-9).
41. H. A. Fine, "The Tradition of a Patient Job," JBL 74 (1955),31.
42. Pope, p. 206, suggests spr in the factitive stem may mean,
"count, number, evaluate." H.H. Rowley says "The general sense of
the verb is that God perfectly fathomed the nature of Wisdom." Job
The Century Bible, New Series; London: Nelson, 1970, p. 234.
43. Peter Zerafa, The Wisdom of God in the Book of Job; Rome: Her-
der, 1978, p. 137. He retains ch. 28 in its present position. However, he says ki can stand by itself to indicate an absolute beginning with a hint of stress.
44. Rowley, p. 227.
45. As noted earlier, if the proverbial nature of this verse is
accepted, there is no problem with the author's inclusion of it.
Even if it is the work of a later editor, its placement serves the
same function: to draw the necessary conclusion which ends the entire poetry section and reminds of the prose framework. Even as an
addition, the verse indicates ch. 28 is the end of the poetry.
46. Fine, p. 32.
47. Coss, p. 141, concludes "The revelation which brings Job to
his knees in repentance is a revelation which makes Job aware of
his own ignorance and presumptuousness. The lesson which Job must
learn is that man's wisdom is limited and that man oversteps his
rights when he criticizes the Lord's lack of wisdom."
48. "I will Praise the Lord of Wisdom," tr. R.H.Pfeiffer, ANET,
2nd ed.; Princeton: Princeton University Press, 1955, p. 435.
49. W.G. Lambert, Babylonian Wisdom Literature; Oxford: Clarendon,
1960, p. 15.
50. The Gathas are the oldest part of the Avesta. It is not known
when Zarathustra lived; most think he was born c. 660 B.C. but the
date ranges from 1000-600. J. Noss, Man's Religions, 4th ed.; London: Collier-Macmillan, 1969, p. 346. The Gathas were probably composed c. 600 B.C. or shortly thereafter.
51. A.V. Williams Jackson, Zoroastrian Studies; NY: Columbia, 19-
28, p. 119.
52. Yasna 43:3-5, as tr. Sacred Books of the East ed. F.M. Muller,
31, and The Zend-Avesta, 3: Oxford: Clarendon, 1887, pp. 113-4.
53. Yasna 44:3b-5 (Muller, 113-4).
54. Yasna 45:8 (Muller, 128).
55. Duncan Macdonald, The Hebrew Philosophical Genius; Princeton:
Princeton University Press, 1936, p. 41.
56. C. Westermann, Der Aufbau des Buches Hiob; Tubingen: Mohr,
1956, p. 9.
57. H. Schmidt, Das Gebet der Angeklagten im Alten Testament; Giessen: Topelmann, 1928, pp. 2ff.
58. H. Guthrie, Israel's Sacred Songs; NY: Seabury, 1966, p. 132.

59. O. Eissfeldt, <u>The Old Testament</u> tr. P. Ackroyd; NY: Harper & Row, 1965, p. 75.
60. Westermann, p. 78.
61. Ibid., p. 65.
62. H. Gunkel, J. Begrich, <u>Einleitung in die Psalmen</u>; Gottingen: Vandenhoek and Ruprecht, 1933, pp. 245-7.
63. Jeremiah has altered the lament form and filled it with new content so that the prophetic motifs have replaced liturgical phrases; the general phrases of distress have been replaced by particular phrases indicating distress caused by his vocation.
64. H. Ringgren, <u>Faith of the Psalmists</u>; Philadelphia: Fortress, 1963, pp. 81-3.

THE INITIATED

Rabbi Rav A. Soloff

The image of a child wandering in awe among majestic mountains is appropriate to express the feelings of a non-professional student reading in the fields of Assryiology, Egyptology, Archeology, Bible and related specialties in pursuit of the Habiru. But what could I do? I am bound in friendship and gratitude to Dr. Lawrence Toombs who was my teacher at Drew University when I took courses there, 1955-1958 and my advisor, when finally I submitted a thesis to receive the coveted Ph.D. in 1967. The present effort, regardless of the result, bespeaks enduring influence and inspiration imparted by a fine scholar, a truly religious teacher.

A verse in the Book of Deuteronomy suggests to me a ray of fresh light on some longstanding questions. Who were the Habiru? What relationship, if any, is there between the name "Habiru" (with its related terms, Apiru and SA.GAZ) and the name "Hebrews?" What relationship, if any, was there among the peoples designated by these names? Before citing any verses, however, I shall review some of the literature which has, for almost a century, taken two paths: 1) examining whatever sociological, political, legal, ethnic or other historical information can be found about people designated Habiru, often comparing it with information about Hebrews; 2) philological study of roots and forms that may underlie the individual names, seeking clues to the nature or identity of each group and any possible relationships among them.

"The origins of the Hebrews are as Habiru," concluded a very recent writer. "All the evidence from archaeological discoveries to date seems to point to the conclusion that, sociologically, the Hebrews were in fact Habiru, although not all Habiru were Hebrews. It could well be that the word...(Hebrew) was originally only a sociological designation, indicating status or class — in which case the words Hebrew and Habiru are synonymous. The fact that in the later Books of the Bible and in its usage in post-biblical times, the word Hebrew has been as an ethnic designation simply means that the original meaning of the word has been changed. With the eventual disappearance of the Habiru, etymological explanations of the term 'Hebrew' [found in the Bible]...were inevitable."[1]

But this is neither the beginning nor the end of the problem of the Habiru. H. H. Rowley surveyed the available texts and literature on Habiru analytically, in terms of his reconstruction of the biblical period From Joseph to Joshua, in the Schweich Lectures of the British Academy in 1948.[2] While he considered the philological equation of Habiru with the Hebrews "possible but uncertain," as he had in 1942, Rowley continued, on non-philological grounds, to assert the probability that Habiru and Hebrews are terms that overlap.[3] "In Nuzi the Habiru were socially depressed classes, but in Palestine they were habbatu, or plunderers, seeking to get possession of lands and townships," and thus the entry of the Hebrew tribes into Palestine (in the age of Jacob) is reflected in the Amarna letters.[4] He also agrees with de Vaux, "As the Hebrews of the patriarchal age led the same life as the Habiru of the cuneiform documents, so the Hebrews of the Sojourn in Egypt shared the condition of the 'Apiru of the Egyptian documents."[5]

By 1954 the problem of the Habiru had already been discussed and disputed for 65 years, Jean Bottéro informs us, when he was entrusted with the task of presenting in one place all the cuneiform and Egyptian documents which could help researchers resolve it. Bottero found the whole matter peripheral to the great issues of Assyriology, "truly more irritating than of real importance."[6] Nevertheless, he supplied a thorough discussion of the best scholarship on Habiru to that date as the more-than-twenty-page introduction to his collection of texts.

Without giving credit to each and every scholar cited, we may note that, in articles published 1888-1900, A. H. Sayce proposed Hebron and later haberîm (Hebrew for "allies" of "confederates") as possible sources for the name Habiru, but almost equally soon after the discovery of the term, C. R. Conder (1890, 1893) identified Habiru with the biblical Hebrews.[7] The character of the Habiru, however, only grew more elusive as they were identified with groups designated by the Sumerian term SA.GAZ (H. Winckler), by the Egyptian term 'pr. w (F.M.Th. Bohl, 1911; already identified with Hebrews by F. Chabas, 1862), and in various theories, by west-semitic words, often related to the name, Hebrews.[8] Beno Landsberger (1924) identified Habiru with "those who go in bands—bandits....ethnically disparate groups, sometimes used as soldiers, but

not real desert nomads." A. Jirku (also 1924) gave
Habiru an ethnic value as the name of a people. Julius
Lewy (1927) also allowed the possibility that Habiru
(immigrants, those who "crossed over" a frontier) might
form homogeneous, ethnic groups.[9]

Only a few scholars before 1939 favored the theory
that the middle, root letter of the name Hab/piru
should be read pe/fe rather than bet/vet. Against the
more common speculations about "those who crossed over"
or "confederates" from the roots avar or haver they proposed explanations like "dusty" (caravaneers) from a
root like afar. With the Ch. Virolleaud publication of
Ugaritic finds, however, more scholars, including E. G.
H. Kraeling concluded that the Akkadian must be
ḫa-pi-ri and not ḫa-bi-ri (i.e. not Hebrews), while
J. W. Jack still asserted (1940) the total identity of
Habiru and Hebrews. And some like Lewy responded that
Hurrites at Ras Shamra—Ugarit always confused b and p,
so he held to his view that Habiru were those who had
"crossed over the frontier," from a root like avar,
meaning they were strangers, immigrants.[11] Lewy's definition of Habiru is very close to what Jean Bottéro
concluded after his full treatment of "Le Probleme des
Ḥabiru." This work is still the first item cited by
the Encyclopedia Judaica (EJ) in its bibliography on
Habiru.[12]

The most recent summary discussion cited by EJ is
again "Le Probleme des Ḥapiru," this time by de Vaux.[13]
He describes the views of Bottéro and Greenberg[14] in a
single sentence. "For Bottéro, the Hapiru are princi-
pally refugees who have 'crossed' the frontier (root:
ayin-vet-resh); for Greenberg, they are especially the
uprooted, who hired themselves out in order to live
(after the Akkadian epēru, assuming a West-semitic root
ayin-pe-resh)." For his own part, de Vaux is convinced
that the authentic form of the name is almost certainly
'Apiru, related neither to drivers of asses, caravaneers
(against some Albright suggestions) nor to SA.GAZ. (at
least in the most ancient, Alishar instance). M. B.
Rowton, "The Topological Factor in the Ḥapiru Problem,"
proposes deriving this name from an Akkadian eperu and
a West-semitic afar in the sense of "men from the Territory (the wooded, wild area into which they had
escaped)," refugees and deserters from beyond the control of any Syrian city-state, but de Vaux objects because of the vast range of times and places in which
Hab/piru appear.[15] The difficulties encountered by

321

every theory that tries to derive the original name
Hab/piru from a root describing a social class, he says,
disappear when it is viewed as an ethnic term. So he
proposes it started as a name which later may have come
to designate a particular job, as "swiss" meant "con-
cierge" in 17th century French, or means "church em-
ployee," in modern French.[16]

"Habiru" in the 1973 edition of EJ is a fine summary, and Hanoch Reviv draws his own conclusions in
another article for that encyclopedia. "From all that
has been said thus far it may be assumed that the general term 'Hebrew' (meaning the Ḫabiru) was applied only
at a later stage to the tribes of Israel as a branch of
this class and thus became an ethnic designation. It
is possible that their non-Israelite neighbors, because
they regarded the ancient Hebrews as a component of the
general class of Habiru, ignored those specific features
which distinguished this small group from the other
Habiru and West Semitic elements."[17]

Since then the subject of Habiru has been discussed
by C. H. J. De Geus, reaching conclusions similar to
some noted above, but providing a uniquely broad, current set of notes.[18] Even so, I feel that my reading
leaves me, probably about a decade behind the frontiers
of professional scholarship, wondering what will yet be
published from Ebla.

From the other direction, among those asking not
what near eastern studies of the Habiru can tell us
about biblical backgrounds, but what light, the Bible
itself may cast upon Hebrews—Habiru, we have J. Weingreen's paper, "Saul and the Habiru."[19] Weingreen was
not the first to distinguish between the meanings of
"Israelite" and "Hebrew" in certain biblical texts, as
de Vaux points out.[20] Weingreen himself claims to be
applying a known device: "Julius Lewy, in an article
entitled 'Origin and signification of the biblical term
"Hebrew,"' demonstrated most convincingly that the term
'ibrim is to be taken as signifying the Habiru."[21]
Nevertheless, it appears that Weingreen did move in a
new direction, basing his restoration of an historical
episode at the time of King Saul upon words of the biblical text in which he finds reference to Habiru.

Now I come to that verse in Deuteronomy, to an
episode in the Bible which may suggest an origin for
the term Habiru = Apiru = Hebrew,[22] beside derivations

from the root ayin-bet/vet-resh in the name Ever[23] or
in the verb "to cross (a river)."[24] In Deuteronomy
29:11 the same root, in the verb-form l'ovrecha means
"to initiate you (into the covenant of YHWH)." The
writer of this verse had no problem applying the verb
to Israelites and non-Israelites alike, as we read in
the preceding verses, "all the men of Israel, your
children, your wives, even the stranger within your
camp." Indeed, those preceding verses and the following ones make clear the purpose of this initiation: to
unify the diverse ethnic and social elements gathered
about Moses (the "mixed multitude" that went with him
from Egypt, and the family of his wife, for example)
along with all of Jacob's descendants into a single,
powerful, covenant people. Without further comment
about Moses in the wilderness or about the text of
Deuteronomy, it seems inevitable that other peoples
of the ancient near east also used covenant-initiation
ceremonies to seal their mutual alliances on whatever
level, from extended family to empire. If so, and they
spoke a language closely related to that of the Bible,
those entering into, or being brought into any such
covenant-bound social unit or "nation" might properly
be called ivrim = Hebrews = Apiru = Habiru.

Is there any evidence in the Bible that the root
ayin-bet/vet-resh may mean "to initiate (into a covenant)," other than that one usage in Deuteronomy 29:11?
For the Hebrew Bible, Even-Shoshan lists 707 appearances
of this root, plus 34 instances of 'ivri (including m.,
f. and both plurals).[25] Tregelles' translation of the
Gesenuis Lexicon does not associate any of these with a
covenant ceremony except our verse.[26] Yet, when we turn
to the covenant ceremony or vision of Abram, the first
biblical personage to be called ha-ivri (Gen. 14:13),[27]
the physical image presented is that of a flaming torch
representing the deity, which avar between the divided
sacrificial animals as YHWH established a covenant with
Abram which promised him the Land (Gen. 15:17,18).[28]
We assume that each party to the covenant did the same,
so that after Abram avar (on this occasion and/or
others) he could properly be called ha-ivri.

Very early in the Abram saga we are told that
Abram "crossed over" through the land (Gen. 12:6) in
compliance with YHWH's instructions; YHWH again appeared
to Abram and promised the land to Abram's descendents;
Abram built an altar to YHWH (Gen. 12:7). The place of
Abram's act of "crossing over" through the land

(va-ya'avor), in series with divine commands and promises, concluding with Abram building an altar to "YHWH
Who appeared to him," suggests that here too, the root
ayin-bet/vet-resh is used to describe an act by which
Abram entered into a covenant with YHWH.

And the full verse which describes Abram as ha-
ivri (Gen. 14:13) presents exactly the same picture of
disparate ethnic elements unified around a covenant,
which we saw in Dt. 29:11. Gen. 14:13 tells us, after
Lot was taken captive, a fugitive who had escaped the
capture of Sodom "brought the news to Abram ha-ivri;
now he was dwelling at The Oaks of Mamre the Amorite
[who was] the brother of Eshkol and brother of Aner,
and they were ba'ale v'rit Avram ("confederates" or
"members of the covenant" of Abram). Once they had been
initiated into that covenant (ovru ba-brit?), it seems
to me that Mamre, Eshkol and Aner became ivrim along
with Abram, just as the "mixed multitude" did at Mt.
Sinai along with Moses and the Children of Israel.

The sense of "initiated" or "dedicated" for the
root ayin-bet/vet-resh appears to be required in translating another biblical usage. Gesenius translates
he-evir in some cases as, "to bring, specifically to
offer as a sacrifice, to consecrate."29 A pagan rite
of child-sacrifice is described in numerous instances
as he'evir ba-esh ("maketh...to pass through the
fire.")30 This is best understood as "to dedicate by
fire," not merely a physical description of the ritual.
Ezekiel adds gruesome details to one form of such "dedication" (16:21; 23:37) and Jeremiah 32:35 uses the
same phrase as Leviticus 18:21, to "dedicate" children
to Moloch without specifying "by fire." By way of contrast, Exodus 13:12 directs, "v'ha'avarta ('you shall
dedicate') every one that 'opens the womb' to YHWH,"
though the context in which Ezek. 20:26 refers to this
law (using the term ha'avir) does not rule out the possibility that the prophet understood such dedication,
even in the case of the Exodus rule, as a fire-offering.
Even so, however, "pass-through fire" a possible, physical description of the ritual, conveys less of the
obvious meaning of the Hebrew words than "dedicated
[the child to the deity] by fire," much as another
religion may have used that same West-semitic root to
mean "dedicated [the people to the deity, or initiated
them into a special relationship with the deity] by
covenant."

Turning to Numbers 31:23 we find an instance of
he'evir ba-esh (fire) which does not refer to child
sacrifice, but parallels he'evir ba-mayim (water).
Metal objects, we are told, which may enter the fire
(safely) ta'aviru ("you shall dedicate by" or "pass
through") fire... and whatever may not enter the fire
(safely) ta'aviru ("you shall dedicate by" or "pass
through") water. As in the instances above, I prefer
a translation of ta-aviru (from the root ayin-bet/vet-
resh) which gives the sense of "dedicated, brought into
a state of purity, related to the deity," rather than a
translation which offers only a possible, physical
description of the ritual.31

Usually the root ayin-bet/vet resh (even the verb
in a hiphil form and followed by the prefix bet/vet)
is correctly translated by "crossed over" or another
simple phrase indicating physical action. Other forms
mean "transgress," "past," "overlook," etc. But in the
few instances noted above, it seems to mean "enter into
a special relationship, be initiated, be dedicated" as
through covenant or through fire or water.

Can the biblical, proper noun ivri be related to
this special sense of "initiated?" In the Book of
Genesis, after 14:13 wherein Abram is called ha-ivri,
the term appears five times in the Joseph saga. In
39:14 Potiphar's wife calls Joseph ish ivri (an ivri
man); in 39:17 she calls him ha-eved ha-ivri (the ivri
servant); and in 41:12 Pharaoh's steward calls him
na'ar ivri (an ivri lad). It is possible to understand
ivri as an ethnic designation though this "ethnic"
origin could well be Hebrew = Habiru = Apiru, that is a
people united as covenanters rather than, as blood
relatives. It is also possible to see "ivri servant"
as a special status, different from that of an ordinary
slave, perhaps "indentured servant." In the latter
case we would take eved ivri to mean "one who was initiated into a servant-covenant." Joseph's references
to his abduction me-eretz ha-ivrim (from the land of
the ivrim, 40:15) and to Egyptian abhorance of ha-ivrim
(43:32) can be understood as referring to Hebrews =
Habiru = Apiru for the ears of his Egyptian audience
or, of his brethren who would know that Egyptians made
no special distinction among groups of Apiru, that is
between Israelite and other Apiru.

In the Book of Exodus, the law of the ivri servant
is spelled out: six years he shall serve but in the

325

seventh, he shall go free; as he entered service (alone
or married), so shall he depart; if he chooses to become a slave, never to leave his master, his master
shall bring him to ha-elohim ("God," or "the judges")
for a ritual marking him as a slave (21:2-6). This law
is repeated in Deuteronomy 15:12-18, and the prophet
Jeremiah confirmed that this law was carried out (later,
betrayed) in at least one instance (34:8-16). However,
while the original law seems to distinguish the eved
ivri as an indentured servant, it may be arguable that
Jeremiah saw all Jewish slaves as ivrim, ethnically
fellow-Hebrews, entitled to freedom after six years.
Thus, at one time eved ivri may well have designated
the servant who was initiated into a covenant of service (and therefore ivri), whereas later usage came to
regard ivri, even in the phrase eved ivri, as a synonym
for Judean or Jew.

Jonah 1:9 says, "I am an ivri and YHWH God of the
Heavens do I revere." This reflects the two facets of
our term in Exodus, one as the name of a people (1:15,
16, 19; 2:6,7,11,13) and the other as the people associated with a particular deity, later specified as YHWH
(3:18; 5:3; 7:16; and then 9:1, 15; 10:3). These uses
of the term ivri (it does not appear in Leviticus or
Numbers) fit in with and, I believe support the interpretation of Dt. 29:11 offered above: the ivrim were
those "initiated," unified as covenanters under a deity
(or deities).

All the rest of the 34 appearances of ivri in the
Hebrew Bible are in I Samuel (4:6,9; 13:3,7,19; 14:11,
21; 29:3) and they have been discussed by Weingreen who
concludes that these stories deal with non-Israelite
Habiru.[32] I would only stress the description of David
as leader of a band of ivrim, perhaps even constituting
his empire on the principle of peoples covenanted under
the deity and scepter of David.[33] Consider the list of
those who sided with David against Absolom (II Sam.
15:17-22), especially the statement of Ittai the
Gittite, "as YHWH lives and as my lord, the king lives,
only in the place where my lord, the king shall be,
whether for death or for life, there will your servant
be." (v. 21) Abram ha-ivri and his confederates in
Gen. 14:13, the people who stood at Sinai l'ovrecha
(to initiate you) into the covenant of YHWH accordingly
to Dt. 29:11 and the ivrim who made up David's band in
I Sam. 29:3 all reflect common characteristics as in
ethnically disparate folk united by a covenant with

their leader and his deity.

   The use of _ivri_ to designate one of the Habiru, a
distinct group of people who might ally themselves with
Saul or David (or with their Philistine enemies) is
argued by Weingreen, not only for the passages in I
Sam. noted above, but also for the passages dealing
with the _ivri_ servant. "Julius Lewy, in the aforementioned article,[34] makes a convincing case for regarding
the 'ebed 'ibri of Exodus XXI:2ff. and in the expanded
version of Deuteronomy XV:12-16, not as an Israelite
slave at all, but as a Habiru who entered into slavery.
He points out that, according to Leviticus XXV:39-46,
an Israelite who, because of poverty, entered into the
service of a fellow Israelite, was not to be treated as
a slave and that, in fact, the acquiring of a free-born
Israelite as a slave was expressly forbidden (v. 42)."[35]
With fear and trembling, as one who had the privilege
when yet a callow youth of sitting at the feet of the
formidable Julius Lewy, I suggest that _ivri_ servant,
meaning indentured servant, was a legal term of some
antiquity in Israel and Judah rather than a construction
of the post-Davidic period. That is, I suggest that in
this usage _ivri_ means "one who has entered into (a
servant-covenant)" rather than "one of the Habiru."

   In conclusion, consider how neatly the philological
explanation of _ivrim_ as "the initiated," those unified
by having entered into a covenant with their leader(s)
and his/their god(s), fits the sociological, historical
evidence. "From their earliest appearance...a class of
dependents....bands of warriors....Habiru military
units....Habiru units and individuals receiving protection...contracts entered into between individual Habiru
men and women and wealthy citizens....list the gods of
the Habiru....captives from Palestine-Syria, and as
slaves of the state....Their names also testify to a
varied ethnic makeup....The ease with which they absorbed everyone who wished 'to be a Habiru' (in the
language of the documents) indicates that they were not
distinguished by ethnic unity."[36] With _ivrim_ as "covenanters," the sense of "confederates" that Sayce and
Dhorme felt so necessary is supplied without resorting
to the philologically unacceptable root _haver_, and the
objection of de Vaux that a class or a mass of refugees
would hardly have their own gods is fully met without
trying to find an ethnic origin for the Habiru.

FOOTNOTES

1. Stuart A. West, "The Habiru and the Hebrews: From a Social Class to an Ethnic Group," Dor Le Dor VII, No. 3 (Spr 79), 106. West includes a brief, popular, accessible bibliography. Cf. also G. Ernest Wright in Robert G. Boling and Wright, Joshua (The Anchor Bible); Garden City: Doubleday, 1982, pp. 83-84. Michael C. Astour, "Habiru or, more Correctly, Hapiru," Supplementary Volume, The Interpreter's Dictionary of the Bible (IDB); Nashville: Abingdon, 1976, pp. 382-385. Alfred Haldar, "Habiru, Hapiru," IDB 2 (1962), 506. George E. Mendenhall, "The 'Apiru Movements in the Late Bronze Age," pp. 122-141 in his The Tenth Generation; Baltimore: Johns Hopkins Press, 1973.
2. H. H. Rowley, From Joseph to Joshua; London: Oxford, 1950.
3. Ibid., p. 56.
4. Ibid., pp. 110, 113.
5. Ibid., p. 129.
6. Jean Bottéro, "Le Problème des Ḥabiru...," Cahiers de la Société Asiatique XII (1954), V.
7. Ibid., "à la vérité plus irritant que d'une réele importance, au moins pour les assyriologues... Il s'agit seulement de savoir ce qu'étaient, en eux-mêmes et par rapport aux Hébreux de l'Ancien Testament, ces personnages qui apparaissent un peu partout dans les documents cunéiformes...."
8. Ibid., pp. VIf.
9. Ibid., pp. IXf, XIII, "le parti nationaliste composé de nomads et de gens des campagnes, qui résiste à l'influence des étrangers dans le pays." (É. Dhorme, 1908, 1909).
   "Étaient-ce des Bédouins....des nomades errants et belliqueux, dont une partie qurait pu par la suite se fixer en Canaan et devenir le peuple hébreu?" (F. M. Th. Bŏhl, 1911)
   Dhorme (1924) rejected the identification of SA.GAZ-habiru with Hebrews and returned to "confederates," as Sayce had held.
10. Ibid., pp. XIIIff, XVII, XXI.
11. Ibid., p. XXI, citing William F. Albright, Archaeology of Palestine and the Bible; NY: Penguin, 1932, pp. 206ff. Albright still held to his theory of "caravaneers" in his The Biblical Period from Abraham to Ezra; NY: Harper & Row, 1963, pp. 2, 26. Cf. also Albright's Yahweh and the Gods of Canaan; NY: Doubleday, 19-68, pp. 73-91, and "Midianite Donkey Caravans," pp. 197-205 in Translating and Understanding the Old Testament ed. Harry Thomas Frank and William L. Reed; NY: Abingdon, 1970. Cf. Robert G. Boling, Judges (Anchor Bible); Doubleday, 1975, pp. 14-15.
12. Ibid., pp. XIV, XXI.
13. "Habiru," Encyclopedia Judaica (EJ) VII (1973), 1035; Jerusalem: Keter. The full article, pp. 1033-1035 is by the editorial staff and cites sources from the 18th-12th centuries B.C.E. Bottéro, op. cit., pp. 2ff, cites texts as old as the 23rd century, but he feels certain only about those of the 19th century and later (p. 8). Bottéro continued the discussion and updated the bibliography in 1972 in his "Habiru," Reallexikon der Assyriologie IV,

fasc. 1, pp. 14-27.

14. Roland de Vaux, "Le Problème des Ḫapiru," Journal of Near Eastern Studies XXVII (1968), 221-228.

15. Moshe Greenberg, The Hab/piru; New Haven: American Oriental Society, 1955 (2nd ed. 1961).

16. de Vaux, op. cit., pp. 221f, 224.

17. Ibid., pp. 224-228.

18. Hanoch Reviv, "History," EJ VIII:575.

19. C. H. J. DeGeus, The Tribes of Israel...; Assen and Amsterdam: Van Gorcum, 1976, p. 183. "In spite of the arguments of Pohl, de Vaux and Koch, we still think a social explanation best fits the greater part of the texts. The term 'outlaw' chosen by Weippert seems serviceable to render the intention. ... That Habiru equals 'Apiru is linguistically pretty well established now."

20. J. Weingreen, "Saul and the Habiru," Papers of the Fourth World Congress of Jewish Studies I (1967), 63-66; Jerusalem: World Union of Jewish Studies, 1967.

21. Op. cit., p. 225, n. 29. Albrecht Alt, Essays on Old Testament History & Religion; Garden City: Doubleday, 1967 (original 1934), pp. 121-122, "'a Hebrew,' then, tells us as little about anyone's nationality, and as much about his legal status, as habiru in cuneiform records of the third and second millennia B.C. from Babylon, Mesopotamia, Asia Minor and Palestine; the word not only corresponds in meaning to 'ivri, but it is certainly also connected etymologically with it, although no attempt to derive the one from the other has yet been made which is not open to objections."

22. Op. cit., p. 63, n. 2 cites the Hebrew Union College Annual 28 (1957), 1ff.

23. DeGeus, op. cit., pp. 184f, especially Weippert quoted in n. 247, support this equation.

24. Eber appears in Gen. 10:21, 24, 25; 11:14, 15, 16, 17. Vs. 26 carries this genealogy down to Abram.

25. West, op. cit., p. 101, cites the Josh. 24:2-3 tradition that YHWH brought Abraham me'ever ha-nahar, making him ha-ivri.

26. Abraham Even-Shoshan, A New Concordance of the Bible; Jerusalem: Kiryath Sepher, 1980, vol. 3, book 1, pp. 1537-1545. Four proper names are also cited: Eber (n. 24 above) and har ha-averim.

27. Gesenius' Hebrew and Chaldee Lexicon to the Old Testament Scriptures; Grand Rapids, Michigan: Eerdmans, 1949 (13th printing 1978), p. 602. "(d) to enter, followed by an accus. into a gate, Mic. 2:13 (opp. to yatsa'); metaph. 'abar baberith to enter into a covenant, Deu. 29:11...."

28. Solomon Mandelkern, Concordance to the Bible, New Edition; NY: Shulsinger, 1955, p. 815. Listing verses in the order of their appearance in the Hebrew Bible makes this useful.

29. Cp. Jer. 34:18-19.

30. Gesenius, op. cit., p. 603.

31. Dt. 18:10. II Kings 16:3; 17:17; 21:6; 23:10. Ezek. 20:31. II Chr. 28:3; 33:6.

32. II Sam. 12:31, v'he'evir otam ba-malben is translated, "or assigned them to brickmaking" in The Prophets; Philadelphia: Jewish

Publication Society, 1978, p. 189. A comment on the same words in Gesenius, op. cit., p. 603, is "The idea of offering being neglected, this word (he'evir) appears to have the signification of burning, in the phrase...to cast into the brick-kiln 2 Sa. 12:31."

33. Op. cit., p. 63, "the 'ibrim of our text are the Habiru."
34. Cp. Alt, op. cit., in n. 21 above, "The Formation of the Israelite State," pp. 282ff.
35. See n. 22 above.
36. Weingreen, op. cit., p. 65.
37. "Habiru," JE VII, pp. 1033f.

THE BAPTISM OF JESUS AND THE BINDING OF ISAAC

An Analysis of Mark 1:9-11

W. R. Stegner

Introduction

New Testament scholars have not been able to
arrive at any consensus concerning the interpretation
of the story of Jesus' baptism. Older interpreters,
for example, saw the significance of the event in the
inner experience of Jesus. Accordingly, he underwent
"a deep religious experience which convinced him of his
divine mission and powers."[1] In our generation,
Jeremias has spoken of "the call which Jesus experienced
when he was baptized by John,"[2] although he acknowledges
that there is considerable difference between the call
portrayed in the gospels and that of Old Testament
prophets. Bultmann rejects any such interpretation
that involves psychologizing and further notes that
"there is also no word of commission to the person
called and no answer for him."[3]

Rather, for Bultmann, the story is not concerned
with Jesus at all, but it serves as a vehicle to tell
us about the significance of the baptism for the faith
of the early church. Thus, he classifies the story as
a "faith-legend" which originated in Hellenistic Jewish
Christian circles. For Rudolph Bultmann, the story
primarily "tells of Jesus' consecration as messiah."[4]
However, Vincent Taylor deemphasizes the messianic interpretation because, the more obvious messianic expressions are not found in the story.[5] Certainly,
Bultmann's view rests heavily on the "quote" from Psalm
2:7 which Lindars maintains "did not originally belong
to the text of the baptism."[6]

Alan Richardson has pointed to the typological
relationship between the baptism-temptation of Jesus
and that of Israel under Moses. "As Israel of old, the
'son' whom God called out of Egypt, was baptized in the
Red Sea and tempted in the Wilderness, so also God's
Son, the Messiah, is baptized and tempted...."[7] In
addition, Richardson and others have pointed to the
words of the voice from heaven as "a clear echo of
Gen. 22:12" and posited the story of the sacrifice of
Isaac as "one of the Old Testament themes which underlie

331

the Synoptic account of the baptism...."[8]

While the above sampling does not claim to be exhaustive, two observations must be made. On the one hand, the contradictory nature of some of the above views shows that they cannot all be true. On the other hand, Biblical stories frequently are many-faceted and consequently sustain a number of interpretations. The same is true of Midrashic material where the _davar acher_ is a frequent phenomenon.

However, the purpose of this paper is not so much to review the strengths and weaknesses of the above interpretations as it is to suggest another interpretation that accounts for more of the elements in Mark's story than do the other views. This paper will argue that the story of the baptism of Jesus is modeled on the rabbinic development of the Old Testament story found in Genesis 22. By rabbinic development we mean a series of exegetical traditions that continued to develop with the passage of time. Some exegetical traditions, such as the kind of symbolical interpretation which equated the term "Lebanon" (wherever it occurred in the text) with the temple or Jerusalem, continued unchanged for centuries.[9] Other exegetical traditions were changed by the addition of new elements to address the changing needs of the community. The latter seems to be the case with the exegetical traditions associated with Genesis 22. For example, one of the greatest changes introduced into the Biblical account has to do with the role of Isaac, who played an increasingly prominent part.

> In Genesis it is Abraham's faith and obedience to God's will even to the offering of his only son, the child of promise, that constitutes the whole significance of the story: Isaac is a purely passive figure. In the rabbinical literature, however, the voluntariness of the sacrifice on Isaac's part is strongly emphasized.[10]

Thus, Isaac's age and willingness to be sacrificed are emphasized in the imaginary dialogue between Isaac and Ishmael in _Midrash Rabbah_ Genesis LV. 4:

> Another version: Said Ishmael to him: 'I am more beloved than thou, since I was circumcised at the age of thirteen, but thou wast circumcised as a baby and couldst not refuse.' Isaac retorted:

'All that thou didst lend to the Holy One, blessed
be He, was three drops of blood. But lo, I am now
thirty-seven years old, yet if God desired to me
that I be slaughtered, I would not refuse.' Said
the Holy One, blessed be He, 'This is the moment!'
Straightway, GOD DID PROVE ABRAHAM.[11]

However, such changes in the tradition pose immense difficulties for comparisons with the New Testament. With what stage of the tradition are we dealing?
Here the work of Chilton and Davies has introduced some
clarity into the discussion by reserving the term Aqedah
for a relatively late stage of the tradition.

We define the Aqedah as a haggadic presentation
of the vicariously atoning sacrifice of Isaac in
which he is said, e.g., to have shed his blood
freely and/or to have been reduced to ashes.[12]

Of course, such a fully developed Aqedah tradition is
much later than the Marcan account. Rather, the Marcan
account must be compared with haggadic developments
that, so far as possible, are datable within the first
century. After such comparisons have been made, a fuller discussion of dating will be undertaken.

However, before exploring the parallels between
the Binding of Isaac and the Baptism of Jesus, two
prior considerations should be explored. The first is
the matter of the verbal echoes from the Septuagint
(LXX) version of Genesis 22 that are found in the
Marcan account and the second is the issue of the
Gattung of Mark 1:9-11.

Verbal Echoes from Genesis 22

While most interpreters say the voice from heaven
uttered a sentence composed of phrases from Psalm 2:7
and Isaiah 42:1, a number of others have pointed to the
words in Mark 1:11 (ho huios mou ho agapētos) as a
distinct verbal echo of the phrase that occurs three
times in Genesis 22:2, 12, and 17.[13]

While this phrase is crucially important for our
thesis, no one seems to have noticed that Mark's short
account of the baptism (only 53 words) contains other
significant echoes of the Septuagint version of Genesis
22. For example, both the account in Mark and the LXX

use the same introduction (kai egenēto). Also, the
verb (schizō) which has so troubled interpreters of
Mark's account is found in both. While Jesus sees the
heavens "being split," Abraham "having split" the wood
for the burnt offering, went to the place God designated. Perhaps the key verb in both accounts is the
verb (eiden) "he saw." Jesus "saw" the heavens being
split and the spirit descending. In 22:4, Abraham
"saw" the place and in verse 14 he calls the name of
the place "(The) Lord saw." Certainly, in the development of the story recorded in the Mechilta the "seeing"
of God becomes the focal point of interpretation.14
Perhaps, another echo is heard in the phrase "from the
heaven" (ek tou ouranou) in Genesis 22:11 and 15 and in
Mark 1:11 "from the heavens" (in the plural).

The cumulative effect of the verbal echoes of key
terms from Genesis 22 within the short span of Mark's
narrative of 53 words is indeed remarkable.

The Form of the Narrative

Another preliminary consideration which should
precede an examination of the similarities between the
two narratives is the matter of form. We have already
noted that Bultmann designates the story as a "faith-
legend." Perhaps with more precision Lentzen-Deis in
his exhaustive work Die Taufe Jesu nach den Synoptikern
seeks to classify the form of the passage as a "vision."
Unlike older interpreters who pointed to the absence of
distinct formal elements within the story, Lentzen-Deis
identifies the form on the basis of definite structural
or formal elements found within the story itself.15
Hence, the "opening of heaven" and the "voice from
heaven" point to the Gattung of the "Vision," and not
the Gattung of the Theophany or the Epiphany, under
which it is sometimes classified. The Gattung of the
Vision is found in the Old Testament and in "the Jewish
Literature."16

In the Targums, the Old Testament form is refined
into the related literary form of the Deute-Vision.
The Targumic Deute-Vision retains the formal elements
of the opening of heaven and the voice from heaven,
but focuses on the content of the words or the speech
given by the heavenly voice. These words from heaven
point out or inform the reader of the significance of
this moment in the life of the

person who sees the vision and hears the voice. After
analyzing the elements that constitute the form Deute-
Vision, Lentzen-Deis shows that the Markan story corresponds to the elements of this form or Gattung.[17]

Another important aspect of the discussion should
be noted. Since the Deute-Vision is found in the
Targums, a Palestinian Hintergrund is assigned to it.
Of course the Sitz im Leben would be the Synagogue.
Accordingly, the employment of the Deute-Vision for
telling the story of Jesus' baptism could take place
only in a "Jewish-Christian milieu."[18]

Parallels Between the Stories

The stage has now been set for a discussion of the
parallels between the Baptism of Jesus and the Binding
of Isaac. While such a discussion must consider the
dating of the elements of the rabbinic development of
Genesis 22 which are to be compared with the New Testament, for the sake of convenience the question of dating
will be deferred to a later section of this paper.
Nevertheless, let it be said here that only those elements which may be considered "early" or datable with
the first century of our era can legitimately be
stressed in any comparisons with New Testament materials. While not all scholars will agree that the rabbinic elements adduced in the following discussion are
first century, various scholars have argued persuasively that they are first century. Occasionally, an element from the Binding of Isaac trajectory will be considered although it is found in a late strata of the
material and cannot be demonstrated to be early. Such
elements will be duly noted as we proceed. Perhaps
they will serve to broaden the data-base for the vexed
questions of dating.

Perhaps the most significant parallel between the
Markan account and the Targumic expansion of Genesis 22
is the fact that both accounts exemplify the same form
or Gattung.[19] In describing the characteristics of the
Deute-Vision, the first passages examined are the Targums expansions of Genesis 22:10 and 14. In addition
to Genesis 22, Genesis 28:12, Genesis 3:22 and Isaiah
6:6-7 are examined. Lentzen-Deis relies primarily on
Targum "Pseudo-Jonathan" or "Jeruschalmi I," the "Frag-
menttargum" or "Jeruschalmi II," and "Neofiti." He
employs the following sigla for these three Targums:

Tg J I, Tg J II, and Tg N.

Let us now compare the formal elements (or characteristics) of the Deute-Vision in both Mark and the Targums. In Mark 1:10, the "opening of heaven" is described very simply: "And when he came up out of the water, immediately he saw the heavens opened..." According to the Targums to Genesis 22:10, as Isaac lies upon the altar, "the eyes of Isaac" behold (Tg J I uses a different verb from Tg J II and Tg N) "the angels of the height." As the object of his vision Jesus sees "the Spirit descending upon him..." In the Targums to Genesis 22:14 "the Shekinah of the Lord" is revealed to Isaac in Tg J I while in Tg J II and Tg N "the glory of the Shekinah of the Lord" is revealed.

As for the "voice from heaven," Mark simply records in 1:11 that "a voice came from heaven." At this point the Targums to Genesis 22:10 diverge. According to Tg J I "the angels of the height respond," while in Tg J II "the angels of the height come and speak to each other." According to Tg N "a voice came from heaven and said."

In Mark 1:11, the voice speaks these famous words: "Thou art my beloved Son, with thee I am well pleased." Of course, the words explain the significance of the scene and seem to be the primary focus of the Deute-Vision. In the Targums to Genesis 22:10, the wording of the passage is relatively uniform so that only the words in common will be translated and the differences between the three Targums will not be noted. "Come, see two chosen individuals (yachidain) in the world: the one sacrificing and the other being sacrificed; the one sacrificing is not hesitating and the one being sacrificed stretches forth his neck."

Equally as impressive as the fact that both accounts exemplify the same form are the similarities within the content of that form. Since the Deute-Vision is related to the Old Testament Gattung of the Vision, it is not surprising that both Isaac and Jesus see a vision. However, it is surprising that the content of the vision is so similar. We have noted that in Mark, Jesus saw "the Spirit descending upon him...," while in the Targums the content of the vision is either the "Shekinah" or "the glory of the Shekinah." Outside these three Targums the content of Isaac's vision varies with the source. Sometimes it is the angels of heaven, sometimes the Shekinah, sometimes the Holy One. However, both Lentzen-Deis and Geza Vermes argue that the revelation of the Shekinah is the oldest version of the tradition.[20] However, if this be granted, there is still another difficulty: the precise nuance to be given to the term Shekinah varies with the passage. Nevertheless, there seems to be uniform usage within certain strata of the literature as E. E. Urbach shows:

> We may sum up as follows: in Tannaitic literature the term Shekinah is used when the manifestation of the Lord and His nearness to man are spoken of.[21]

The particular nuance that the word carries for these three targums is most probably the nearness of God to his people in the temple. (This, of course, will be explained more in detail in the section dealing with dating.) Nevertheless, that the term is not far from the Tannaitic meaning of "the manifestation of the Lord and His nearness" is indicated by the presence of the term yachida in the same context, for in the targums the title yachida belongs to men who are elected by God and to the elected people of Israel.[22] Thus, in these three targums, at least, Isaac's vision of the Shekinah expresses the "manifestation" and "nearness" of God. Of course, the same is true of Mark's narrative where the Spirit (and the contents of the heavenly words) indicate the presence and nearness of God.[23]

Thus, the Holy Spirit in the Synoptic accounts functions much the same as does the Shekinah in the targumic accounts. Is it surprising then to find that in the old rabbinic texts the two terms were sometimes interchangeable?

> The two expressions are often interchanged in the old Rabbinic texts. Both are frequently used as synonyms for God and are so to be interpreted in Tannaitic texts..............
> ....
> The man who is closely united with the Shekhinah also possesses the Holy Spirit, and the one possessing the Spirit also sees the Shekhinah.[24]

In addition to the fact that the Shekinah and the Holy Spirit are sometimes interchangeable, there is an interesting similarity in the fluidity in which both terms are used in their respective stories. Luke uses

"Holy Spirit," Matthew, "Spirit of God," and Mark simply "the Spirit."[25] This fluidity in the use of terms is precisely what we would expect in a Jewish-Christian community. Also, it is precisely what we find in the various accounts of Isaac's vision! Note what McNamara says about parallel texts:

> Rabbinic texts can express the same idea in other ways. In some contexts 'the holy spirit' can be replaced by such terms as 'the Shekhinah', 'the Dibbêra' (Word) and 'Bath Qol' (Voice). In point of fact, where in one text we find 'holy spirit', in parallel texts we read one of the others, these being more or less synonymous in certain contexts.[26]

How close are the vision of the Shekinah and of the descent of the Spirit? Given the fluidity in the use of terms and given the Church's experience of the Holy Spirit, Mark seems to be saying much the same thing as the targumists were saying in their account of Isaac's vision of the Shekinah.

In addition, there are striking points of similarity between the accounts of the Binding of Isaac and between the words from heaven in Mark's account of the Baptism of Jesus. Most interpreters hold that the words from heaven are a composite quotation drawn from Psalm 2:7 and from Isaiah 42:1. Let us look at the two parts of the quotation separately, beginning with the alleged quote from Psalm 2:7.

If the words "Thou art my beloved Son" are drawn from Psalm 2:7, then two difficulties immediately arise: 1) What is the origin of the adjective "beloved"? and 2) What is the meaning of the term "Son" in this context? Since the adjective "beloved" is not found in Psalm 2:7, some recent interpreters have suggested the influence of the targumic rendering of this Psalm. However, Marshall cites the uncertain date of the targumic rendering and the similar wording in the Targum on II Sam 7:14 "where the relationship of the Messiah to God as His Son is clearly weakened." Then Marshall writes:

> It is possible, therefore, that we should return to the older suggestion that the baptismal saying shows the influence of the description of Isaac in Gen xxii. 2, 12, 16. Here the wording of LXX ho huios sou ho agapētos offers a close parallel

to the text, and is indeed closer to it than any of the various versions of Isa xlii.I, in all of which the genitive of the possessive pronoun appears twice.[27]

Accordingly, the difficulty still stands for those who argue that the words are a quote from Psalm 2:7. The other difficulty concerns the meaning of the term "Son" in this passage. Is it a messianic title and hence is it to be understood in a purely functional manner? Or is the personal relationship of Jesus to God as His Father the more basic stage of development, as Marshall, Dunn, and others have argued? Howard Marshall states that the term "Son" describes Jesus' personal relationship to God as His Father.

> It goes beyond a purely functional or messianic use of the title by the use of the qualifying adjective [agapētos] which indicates the unique relationship of Jesus to His Father. Thus the personal relationship expressed in Gen xxii becomes important for the understanding of the text.[28]

Now let us examine the view that the words "with thee I am well pleased" is a quote from Isaiah 42:1. Again, difficulties immediately present themselves. Various interpreters have derived these words from a number of sources other than Isaiah 42:1. Also, the LXX does not use the word eudokeō, which is found in Mark, but the word prosdechomai. Since the argument for Markan dependence on Isaiah 42:1 lacks cogency, the following paragraphs will argue that the rabbinic development of Genesis 22 is the source of the latter half of the words from heaven.

Perhaps the place to begin is with a definition of the key term eudokeō. While in some contexts the term may mean a person's delight in something, and in other contexts the term may mean "choice, resolve or decree"; in this context the word means "God's decree of election." Here, Jesus is the recipient of God's "elective good pleasure."[29]

We have already alluded to the fact that the idea of election is also found in our three targumic accounts in the word yachida which is applied to both Isaac and Abraham in Genesis 22:10. As in Mark, the word yachida is found among the words from heaven which interpret the meaning of the scene. Footnote 22 has already noted that the word belongs to men who are elected by God. It is assigned to Adam by Tg J I in Genesis 3:22, to Abraham and Isaac by Tg N, Tg J I, and Tg J II in Genesis 22:10 and by Tg N to Isaac in Leviticus 22:27.[30] Even more to the point is the use of the term bachar in the three targums to Leviticus 22:27. Here Isaac has been designated as a "lamb" who "has been elected/ chosen" ('imr' 'ithbaḥar). Of course, bachar is one of the terms that eudokeō is used to translate in the LXX.[31] Thus, two words for election were associated with this story from early times.

In the above paragraphs we have argued that the word eudokeō was derived from the rabbinic expansion of Genesis 22. While the argument falls short of certainty, as does every other hypothesis for the origin of the words of the heavenly voice, it has the advantage that both parts of the statement were derived from the same story. Accordingly, the messianic and servanthood motifs should not receive primary emphasis in interpretation.

In our discussion of the parallels between Mark's account and the rabbinic development of Genesis 22 only the phrase in Mark 1:10 "... like a dove" remains. How does this fit into the hypothesis? In an exhaustive treatment of Mark's ambiguous phrase hōs peristeron Leander Keck concludes that it represents kyōnah and was originally meant as an adverbial phrase specifying, not appearance, but the action of the Spirit.

The point is not a dove-like Spirit descending but the Spirit coming with dove-like descent.[32]

Nevertheless, most interpreters have failed to follow Keck's suggestion. Perhaps Lentzen-Deis represents the majority opinion in saying that the dove primarily is a symbol for Israel.[33] As a symbol for Israel, the Midrash on the Song of Songs compares the qualities of the dove to the qualities of Israel. The Midrash comments on the phrase: 'Thine eyes are as doves':

As the dove is chaste, so Israel are chaste. As the dove puts forth her neck for slaughter, so do Israel, as it says, 'For Thy sake we are killed all the day' (Ps xliv. 23). As the dove atones for iniquities, so Israel atone for the other nations...'[34]

Is there a possible bridge here to the figure of Isaac and then the story of the baptism?

The dove shares a remarkable characteristic with Isaac: they both stretch forth their neck. We have already met this characteristic in the three Targums to Genesis 22:10: "Come, see two unique individuals... the one being sacrificed stretches forth his neck." The characteristic is repeated in Midrash Rabbah Deuteronomy 9:4: "What mighty man is there like Isaac who stretched out his neck on the altar...."[35]

Note how these ideas flow together. The dove is an example or token for Israel in that it makes atonement and stretches forth the neck. Isaac stretches forth his neck on the altar as he makes atonement for Israel. Is it possible that the dove, which later was associated with Isaac,[36] had been associated with Issac in New Testament times and consequently found its way into the baptismal account?

The Theological Significance of the Two Scenes

In the preceding section we have drawn parallels between the two stories. Now let us consider the theological thrust of each.

The theological significance of the Isaac story is simply stated in Tg J II to Genesis 22:14:

> Now I pray for mercy before you, O Lord God, that when the children of Isaac come to a time of distress, You may remember on their behalf the binding of Isaac their father, and loose and forgive them their sins and deliver them from all distress, so that the generations which follow him may say: In the mountain of the Temple of the Lord, Abraham offered Isaac his son....[37]

Unfortunately, the theological significance of the Markan story cannot be stated so simply because the story is not directly interpreted. Perhaps the place to begin is with the gospel as a whole. Certainly, most scholars agree that Mark proclaims a theology of the cross as C.F.D. Moule states: "I believe, as who does not?, that there is, in Mark, a clear theologia

341

crucis."[38] In addition, the shadow of that cross falls
across most of the gospel. Indeed, if our thesis is
correct, the shadow of that cross falls across the very
first pericope that deals with Jesus! In addition,
there are two important words in the gospel that tie
the baptism to the cross. The first word is baptism
itself. In the third prediction of the passion, Jesus
asks, "Are you able to drink the cup that I drink, or
to be baptized with the baptism with which I am baptized?" (10:38). The second word, found within the
baptismal account itself, is schizo. This term is
found again significantly enough in 15:38: "And the
curtain of the temple was torn in two...." The rabbis
would recognize this at once as a Gazera Shava which is
an "analogy of expressions, that is, an analogy based
on identical or similar words occurring in two different passages of Scripture."[39] According to exegetical
practice, if one of the passages in which the word occurs is obscure, its meaning is to be ascertained from
the other passage.

Dating the Targumic Material

Dating the targumic material is a difficult task.
While the final editing of the Targums took place at
relatively late dates, passages within a given Targum
may have been written at a much earlier date. Nevertheless, the dating of targumic material is essential
for any comparative study involving the New Testament
in order to determine whether the exegetical traditions
found in the Targums could have influenced New Testament writers.

Frequently, targumic material is dated by the
presence of similar material in outside sources which
can be dated. For example, both the Targums and IV
Maccabees present the death of Isaac as that of a
martyr and both regard his death as effective and ex-
piatory (see quote No. 37 above). When Sam Williams
fixes "the composition date of IV Maccabees...at a time
antedating the period of Paul's literary activity by at
least a decade,"[40] he has shown that the exegetical
traditions incorporated in the Targums could have been
known by and used by the New Testament writers.

"Isaac's voluntary submission to sacrifice" is
another example of the possibility of dating targumic
material by the presence of similar material in outside

sources which can be dated. The first-century writers,
Philo and Josephus, and the first-century documents, IV
Maccabees and Pseudo-Philo, present a similar picture.[41]

Davies and Chilton offer another possible criterion
for dating the rabbinic traditions based on Genesis 22.
As the "trajectory" develops, the focus shifts from
Abraham to Isaac.[42] According to this criterion the
fact that Abraham's prayer sets forth the theological
significance of the scene (see above) marks this material as early.

Sometimes, external events, such as the destruction
of the temple in A.D. 70, provide help in dating passages. For example, the targumic material locates the
Binding of Isaac on the temple mount in Jerusalem. Also,
the object of Isaac's vision is either the Shekinah or
the glory of the Shekinah (which later came to dwell
within the temple building). The emphasis on such data
shows

> that the Targums have used Aqedah to prove the sole
> legitimacy of Jerusalem and its Temple as the place
> of sacrifice.
> ....
> Such assertions would make good sense in the period
> before 70 A.D., when the Jerusalem cult was direct-
> ly challenged by the Samaritans and the adherents
> of the Temple of Onias at Leontopolis, as well as
> by the Qumran Sect.[43]

Finally, in the conclusion to his article, Hayward
outlines the "basic substratum of the Targumic Aqedah"
that was in existence by the first century A.D.

> The Targums to the Pentateuch...convey the idea
> that Isaac, a grown man, in total agreement with
> Abraham, willingly consented to be bound in sacri-
> fice upon an altar on the Temple mount. They pre-
> sent Isaac as a perfect victim, and strongly empha-
> size that he is an archetypal martyr. He is the
> lamb of sacrifice, who, although not killed, is
> fully and completely offered. He has a vision of
> heaven, and his action has expiatory value. All
> future lamb sacrifices recall his Aqedah, and they
> and the site of their offering are validated by
> it....[44]

The above arguments show that portions of the targumic material may well form a bridge between Genesis

22 and the later Midrashic materials and could have been known by New Testament writers. In addition, exegetical traditions (crucial for our thesis) were known to such first-century writers as Josephus and are found in such first-century works as IV Maccabees and Pseudo-Philo.

Conclusions

In seeking to prove that the baptism of Jesus was modeled on exegetical traditions arising from the rabbinic development of Genesis 22, several conclusions have presented themselves. Keck, Lentzen-Deis, and others are probably correct in tracing the first formulation of the story to "old Palestinian Jewish Aramaic Christian circles," rather than Hellenistic circles. The delineation of the Deute-Vision, the investigation of the dove tradition, and word studies all point in this direction.

Secondly, there is probably no one correct interpretation of the story of the baptism. The story was formulated in the Palestinian church before it came to Mark. Consequently, there are probably layers of meaning in the story. This became evident in the investigation of the term "Son." Also, an Isaac-Jesus typology does not exclude an Exodus-Wilderness typology between Israel on the one hand and Jesus on the other. This is simply the rabbinic "another interpretation" and is entirely consistent with a Palestinian milieu.

Finally, the Isaac-Jesus typology must be taken more seriously than it has been in recent research. The strength of this interpretation lies in its ability to account for matters of form and content and origin. The form Deute-Vision is shared by the Markan account and the targumic accounts. The contents show striking parallels to exegetical traditions incorporated into the three Targums and also found in first-century works such as IV Maccabees and the writing of Josephus and Philo. Nearly every element of content finds parallels in the Isaac story with the possible exception of the dove motif and no one can adequately account for that. The Palestinian origin in the milieu of the synagogue is also shared. While other interpretations focus on a phrase or a possible quote from the Old Testament, the Isaac-Jesus typology is much more comprehensive in its scope.

FOOTNOTES

1. A. Richardson, <u>An Introduction to the Theology of the New Test-ment</u>; London: SCM, 1958, p. 178.
2. J. Jeremias, <u>New Testament Theology</u> Vol. 1; London: SCM, 1971, p. 56.
3. R. Bultmann, <u>History of the Synoptic Tradition</u> tr. John Marsh; NY: Harper & Row, 1963, p. 247.
4. Bultmann, <u>ibid</u>., p. 248. So also B. Lindars who says the baptism "has become the moment of revelation" of Jesus as Messiah. <u>New Testament Apologetics: The Doctrinal Significance of the Old Testament Quotations</u>; Philadelphia: Westminster, 1961, p. 146.
5. V. Taylor, <u>The Gospel According to St. Mark</u>; London: Macmillan, 1955, p. 162.
6. Lindars, <u>ibid</u>., p. 140.
7. Richardson, <u>ibid</u>., p. 150.
8. <u>Ibid</u>., p. 180.
9. G. Vermes, <u>Scripture and Tradition in Judaism</u>; Leiden: Brill, 1973, p. 36.
10. G.F. Moore, <u>Judaism in the First Centuries of the Christian Era</u>, Vol I; Cambridge: Harvard University Press, 1932, p. 539.
11. <u>Midrash Rabbah</u>, Genesis, Vol. I, tr. Rabbi Dr. H. Freedman; London: Soncino, 1977, p. 485. In another account Isaac even binds himself upon the altar. Vermes, <u>loc. cit</u>. See Sifre-Deuteronomy 32.
12. P. Davies and B. Chilton, "The Aqedah: A Revised Tradition History," <u>Catholic Biblical Quarterly</u> 40 (1978), 515.
13. Richardson, <u>op. cit</u>., p. 180 and Vermes, <u>op. cit</u>., pp. 222-223. The phrase found in Gen. 22:12 and again in 22:17 is <u>tou huiou sou tou agapētou</u>. Also H. Marshall, "Son of God or Servant of Yahweh? A Reconsideration of Mark 1:11," <u>New Testament Studies</u> 15:334.
14. <u>Mekilta de-Rabbi Ishmael</u>, Jacob Lauterbach, Vol. 1: Philadelphia: Jewish Publication Society, 1976, Pischa 7, p. 57: "<u>And When I See the Blood</u>. I see the blood of the sacrifice of Isaac. For it is said: 'And Abraham called the name of that place Adonai-jireh' (The Lord will see), etc. (Gen 22:14)."
15. F. Lentzen-Deis, <u>Die Taufe Jesu nach den Synoptikern</u>; Frankfurt Am Main: Knecht, 1970. See esp. ch. 4 & 5, pp. 97-248. See also V. Taylor, <u>The Gospel According to St. Mark</u>; London: Macmillan, 1955, p. 158. See esp. p. 80 where Taylor speaks of "stories.. with no distinctive form" and thereafter classifies the Baptism of Jesus under the form STORIES ABOUT JESUS.
16. Lentzen-Deis, <u>op. cit</u>., pp. 126-7.
17. <u>Ibid</u>., p. 279.
18. <u>Ibid</u>., p. 252. See also pp. 227 and 232.
19. <u>Ibid</u>., ch. V, pp. 195-248. While I am following him closely in the comparison of the form, the translations of Targumic material are my own. In citing Mark, I have used the RSV.
20. Lentzen-Deis, <u>op. cit</u>., p. 209. He quotes R. Le Déaut with approval on this point. Also, Vermes, <u>Scripture and Tradition in Judaism</u>, 2nd ed.; Leiden: Brill, 1973, p. 195, n. 6.
21. E.E. Urbach, <u>The Sages - Their Concepts and Beliefs</u> tr. from the Hebrew by I. Abrahams; Jerusalem: Magnes, 1975, p. 43. Also see

the discussion by A. Unterman, Encyclopedia Judaica, Vol. 14, "She-kinah,"; Jerusalem: Keter, 1971, pp. 1350ff.

22. Lentzen-Deis, op. cit., pp. 239-240.

23. J. Dunn, Jesus and the Spirit; Philadelphia: Westminster, 1975, pp. 62-67.

24. A. Marmorstein, Studies in Jewish Theology ed. J. Rabbinowitz and M. Lew; Freeport, NY: Books for Libraries, 1950, p. 131.

25. V. Taylor calls the Lukan and Matthean terms "the more Jewish terms," op. cit., p. 160. Bultmann, op. cit., p. 251, "The use of to pneuma absolutely is a decisive pointer to the conclusion that Mk 1:9-11 could not have come from the Palestinian Church." However M. McNamara, Targum and Testament: Aramaic Paraphrases of the He-brew Bible: A Light on the New Testament; Grand Rapids: Eerdmans, 1972, p. 112, disputes this: "We should note how Pseudo-Jonathan (like Paul in 2 Cor 3:17) uses the term Spirit not 'Holy Spirit' which was the usual Jewish expression."

26. McNamara, op. cit., p. 108.

27. Marshall, op. cit., p. 334. He goes on to say that the argu-ment loses its weight if the saying is not dependent on the LXX. In the above section entitled VERBAL ECHOES FROM GENESIS 22 I have argued that the story of the baptism is dependent on the LXX. P. Bretscher, "Exodus 4:22-23 and the Voice from Heaven," Journal of Biblical Literature LXXXVII (1968), 302f also argues that the case for Ps. 2:7 is weak and feels that in the original tradition the voice spoke in the third person.

28. Marshall, op. cit., p. 336. Dunn, loc. cit. Bretscher, loc.cit.

29. Schrenk, TWNT II:740ff.

30. Lentzen-Deis, op. cit., p. 232.

31. Schrenk, loc. cit. For the Targums, Lentzen-Deis, op. cit., p. 211.

32. L.E. Keck, "The Spirit and the Dove " New Testament Studies 17 (1970), 63. Of great significance for our thesis is the statement Keck makes in the concluding paragraph, p. 67: "Specifically, we ... have anchored the story in the earliest milieu in which tradi-tions of Jesus emerged - Palestinian, Aramaic-using Christianity."

33. Lentzen-Deis, op. cit., p. 270. "Die Taube bezeichnet das Heils-volk Israel." See also Greeven, peristera, TWNT VI:63-72.

34. Midrash Rabbah. Song of Songs tr. M. Simon; London: Soncino, 1939, p. 86.

35. Midrash Rabbah. Deuteronomy tr. J. Rabinowitz; London: Soncino, 1977, p. 160. This Midrash is late. This characteristic of the dove is noted in several midrashim, e.g., S. Spiegel, The Last Trial; NY: Behrman, 1979, p. 146, n. 39. "Note the dove - all other birds when they are slaughtered shudder, but the dove is not like that. On the contrary, it stretches form its neck." Found in Tanchuma, ed. Buber, Teṣawweh (II, p. 96).

36. Spiegel, loc. cit.

37. Tr. Verme, op. cit., p. 195.

38. C. Moule, The Origin of Christology; Cambridge: University Press, 1977, p. 44.

39. M. Mielzinger, Introduction to the Talmud; NY: Bloch, 1968, p.

143. For our purposes it does not matter whether the tearing of the curtain is a sign of God's judgment on the Temple or whether it is a sign that access to God is now open and visible as a result of the cross.

40. S. Williams, <u>Jesus' Death as Saving Event: The Background and Origin of a Concept</u>, Harvard Dissertations in Religion 2; Missoula: Scholars Press, 1975, p. 202. Williams argues that Paul and Hebrews <u>knew</u> IV Maccabees. See also R. Hayward, "The Present State of Research into the Targumic Account of the Sacrifice of Ksaac," <u>Journal of Jewish Studies</u> XXXII (1981), 130 and n. 22. He also dates IV Maccabees to the first century A.D.

41. Hayward, <u>op</u>. <u>cit</u>., p. 135.

42. Davies and Chilton, <u>op</u>. <u>cit</u>., p. 541.

43. Hayward, <u>op</u>. <u>cit</u>., p. 133. He goes on to argue against the position of Davies and Chilton that the Aqedah is a <u>substitute</u> for the temple and its sacrifices.

44. <u>Ibid</u>., pp. 148f.

Humans and their Deities in Babylon, Sixth Century B.C.,

or

The Answers Came from Within, Though Above and Below

Prescott H. Williams, Jr.

This inquiry into the understanding of life in the sixth century world of Babylonia began with the study of Isaiah 40-55, usually regarded as coming from that place and time. The insistent opposition of Second Isaiah to the deities of Babylon, though he names only Bel and Nabu in chapter 46, shaped the search question "How did the gods and goddesses of Babylon function in Babylonian society at that time?" Though Isaiah derides them as nonentities, his extensive attacks on them indicate that they were regarded as powerful. He describes them as dead and their images as deaf and mute, but obviously they were not so regarded by all. He describes the processes of their manufacture and saves his strongest satire for their makers. Did they not recognize them as human products? He obviously thought not. Though his barbs are directed primarily to their human makers, the images themselves are also derogated as deceptive.

While he might have attacked the institution of kingship or some other human institution as an object of trust, he directed his denunciations at the gods and their representations. Why?

The "Why?" becomes even more pointed when the careful reader notices the wide range and great variety of literary images which his god, Yahweh, is declared, imagery which evokes imaginative mental pictures of a mighty, powerful deity. His singular identity is expounded with many words and phrases which evoke images. What makes these human products so different from those which he attacks? In order to deal with this issue, it seemed important first to discover and describe how the deities of Babylon were presented to the eyes and ears of those whom he was addressing.

This essay is a brief report on the first steps taken to understand these issues. It is presented here in honor of a loyal friend, stimulating teacher, and productive scholar with the kind of attention to the evidence upon which he characteristically has always

insisted. Though the evidence is somewhat random and
limited, the attempt was made both with respect to the
limitations and with an attempt to develop empathy for
an understanding of an "alien" culture.[1]

My paradigms for this effort were provided by
Shalom Paul, George E. Mendenhall, and William F.
Albright. I have observed the cautions articulated by
A. Leo Oppenheim's, John Oates' and Shemaryahu Talmon's
insistence that Sitze im Leben are critical to every
assessment of the function(s) of literary (and, I would
add, artistic) forms.[2] I was almost deterred by the
titles given to chapters on the Neo-Babylonians by informed authors, where "epilogue" as a designation,
brevity of treatment and virtual dismissal of their
importance are found alongside "renaissance" as descriptions of Babylonian culture at the time.[3] But the
search proved too interesting to allow changing to a
more manageable question. The conclusions are, of
course, preliminary, at best intermediate.

No post-539 B.C. data will be adduced without clear
labelling and that only when earlier and later data provide a basis for interpolation of Neo-Babylonian realities. The focus is the generation preceding Cyrus'
peaceful march into the "spiritual center" of Mesopotamian life. The limited contemporary data for this
time necessitate the careful adducement of earlier data,
particularly from post-Kassite and Assyrian times and
even from the Hammurabi period so important for Semitic
traditions in Babylon. Along the way it became necessary to describe the Chaldeans, who like the Kassiste
dynasty before them, appreciated traditions and institutions more significant than their own native ones
when they took power for the brief period, 605 to 539
B.C.E.[4] This time did not even exceed the lifetime of
Nabonidus' mother, but it provides our last opportunity
to perceive the end results of millenia of pioneering
in agriculture, urbanization, language and literature.

Who were the great gods of Neo-Babylonia? The
question is of necessity cast in the plural, for the
pantheon of Babylon in all its periods was a complex of
interacting, shifting roles by those regarded as the
powers of life. The very fluidity of the amalgam provides much of its attraction as a way of accounting for
the forces at work within the scene where humans live.

It must be clearly stated that the gods were within

the universe as Babylonians construed it. Even Anu, "Sky" and remote, inhabited the middle of the three "heavens." And Ea, "Deep," was part of the natural structure. The famous "three-storied" universe propounded by Mesopotamian culture and so lasting in its effects on biblical and classical understandings included the deities. They were not conceived as acting from beyond it nor even as residing outside its limits. They were essential functionaries within it. And "it" was designed by those whose affirmation focused on "order." The gods and goddesses were the maintainers and renewers of the world's order, over against some of the offspring of Anu and Enlil ("Lord Wind") who regularly disturbed that order, especially for the humans who wrote the literature and produced the arts and crafts which provide most of our evidence.[5]

At the time we glimpse life in southern Mesopotamia, Marduk is Bel, "Lord." Though a relative latecomer with uncertain ancestry, he was legitimated by his sonship to Anu, the giver of kingship at its origin, the patron of Sumer and Uruk; Marduk is also regarded as Ea's son with particular reference to his function in magic ritual. Marduk assimilated to himself the powers and functions of many other deities: of agriculture, of war, of close-in combat, of might and counsel, of accounting, of illumination of the night, of justice, of rain, and, particularly, of the 'fixed order' (shimtu; rather than "destiny," which is misleading as a translation.)[6] His supremacy in Babylon was rivaled by Nabu in the time of the last Babylonian domain, but by 539 he was still dominant. Even Cyrus proclaimed Marduk as his sponsor in taking and restoring Marduk's city and temple to its rightful owner. In summary, this lordly figure was the prime organizer of the world humans and deities lived in. How he achieved this central role both by bargain and battle was narrated in Enuma Elish, "When the gods . . .," the Epic of Creation, as we usually call it. Each year the Akitu Festival celebrated near the spring equinox recelebrated his kingship and renewed his claims. Enuma Elish was read aloud in conjunction with ceremonies in his temple, Esagila, with the humble participation of the current human king, Marduk's "servant." The fact that the king had to be present and had an essential role to perform, otherwise the New Year festival could not happen, underlines the close identification of Marduk with kingship as the 'orderly' institution for the world's welfare.

"Aliens" like ourselves might well ask, "Who else was needed?" Marduk's claims approach monopoly. But that monistic resolution did not happen in Babylon, no matter how centralized life, worship, and power were consolidated. In Neo-Babylonian times there was a contest for supremacy between Marduk and his courtiers (rather than "priests")[7] and Nabonidus' allegiance to Nabu (older: Sin/Nanna), the moon god, Marduk's "son," and Ishtar's "father." Nabu begins to appear in royal names with Nabu-shumu-libur (1034-1027) and then with great frequency from the time of Nabonassar (747-734), the reputed founder of the Neo-Babylonian dynasty. The older name, Sin, occurs as early as Warad-Sin and Rim-Sin (1834-23 and 1822-1763) and some of their predecessors and contemporaries both in the north and the south, well in advance of Hammurabi. Contrast the earliest occurrence of Marduk in a royal name, 1173-1161 (Marduk-apla-iddina 1), and frequently thereafter. Some, at least, might perceive the growing ascendancy of Sin/Nabu over Bel-Marduk, as a return to tradition, a reform, a conservative movement. In fact, Sin occurs in names of both the old Sumerian kings (Puzur-Sin) and the first Akkadians (e.g., Naram-Sin, 2254-2218), thereafter in both north and south, whereas Marduk is found in only southern kings' names, though others beside him are regarded as Bel, e.g. Assur-bel-kala, 1074-57.

Back to Nabu, which could have been a rallying cry for his adherents and a critical comment by those loyal to Bel-Marduk. His home was Ezida in Borsippa, not far from Babylon. He was patron of scribes, sponsor of wisdom, involved in magic (with his two "fathers": Ea, Marduk); his appearance as crescent marked the beginning of the month and his phases named its parts; his illumination of the night is associated with his "fathering" of Shamash, the sun-god. As Ea's "son" he was patron of arts and crafts. He was known to enjoy hunting in the game park, as kings did. His growing popularity in the first millenium should not be surprising, since the scribes did the writing, and were strategically located to function in power and control because of their unique accomplishments.

Through Sin and Nanna, Nabu was associated with Ur and Harran; through his "father" Ea with Eridu; through his "daughter" Ishtar with Uruk, Kish, Agade, Arbela and many points north, east, south, and west(?).

Ishtar-Inanna, the most widely worshiped goddess

of the second millenium, became synonymous with "goddess." She seems to stand alone among the male deities of Neo-Babylonia as the omni-functional female power: of love, of war, of fertility; as Venus, both morning and evening star (and as such, "heraldess" of Sun and Moon and of the seasons); "Our Lady of Uruk," whose fourth millenium precinct Eanna had earlier overshadowed that of Anu himself. Her role in the Akitu festival is not clear, nor her exact relation to Tammuz (Dumuzi). Her dominance in art and the colorful, powerful portrayals of her roles will stress that though the one female deity truly important for our period, her multiple roles more than compensated for her numerical minority if appeals to her in prayers and letters are taken together with her frequent appearance on seals and royal grant stones (so-called "boundary stones," i.e. kudurru).[8]

If one were to take his orientation from the semipublic standing stones which record royal grants of land, it might be accurate to speak of a trinity of Sun, Moon, and Venus. These apparent guardians of land grants ("apparent" because the deities invoked on the accompanying inscriptions do not always coincide with the three portrayed in the upper positions on the stones themselves) and their familiar symbols: eight-pointed star: Venus; crescent, in or without circle: Nabu; and sun-disk with four points alternating with four groups of radiation lines: Shamash, appear dominant on the Kudurru. The importance of the sun-god is somewhat surprising, because some of his traditional functions as judge and regulator of weights and measures, had been assumed by other human institutions, especially in our period.

Shamash was nevertheless important and to be numbered with the greats as one of the Big Four. Sippar was his city, as also Larsa seemed to be; his older name was Utu. His importance may derive from his role as judge of both earth and heaven (and underworld?), his patronage of justice (see his commissioning of Hammurabi's code) and, perhaps surprising to us, his protectorate of the poor and under privileged. The association with both judgment, rights and the poor may be associated with his light-giving function and the heat of his "fire." His importance to an agricultural economy might have been stressed more if it were not for the fierceness of his light and heat, especially during dry times. Though he did not assume the

calendaric importance of his "father" Moon and sister
Venus, his persistence in royal names is striking:
from Hammurabi's contemporary in the north, Shamsi-Adad
I (1813-1781), Hammurabi's usurper-successor, Samsu-
iluna, through five Shamshi-Adads and down to Shamash-
shuma-ukin, successor to Esarhaddon and even on to
Shamash-eriba in Achaemenid times (482 B.C.).

To this group of four, my studies led me to add
three others, not out of necessity to have a "seven,"
though "The Seven" are the last. Ea has appeared in
several ways in the preceding. During our period of
focus Adad, the old storm god, had assimilated to himself many of Ea's functions. But it was an ambivalent
association because the storm god was reckoned both as
favorable to humans and as dangerous to them. The emphasis in Ea's characterizations had long been on his
friendship with humans, his siding with them at such
strategic times as the flood, his skill in devising
stratagems for avoiding plots against human welfare.

We have already noted the occurrence of Adad in
royal names, e.g., the five Shamshi-Adads. His forked
lightning signaled both life-giving rain (note the
association with Ea's ground water) and the fearsome
fire from heaven, so destructive of the very crops
which the rain nurtured.

Because the Neo-Babylonian dynasty was Chaldean,
for whom Aramaic seems to have been a native language,
and because other Arameans appear frequently in Babylonian history, the shepherd god, Amurru is also to be
included in our lineup. Even his name, "westerner,"
indicates his association with those non-Sumerian, non-
Akkadian Semites who played a variety of roles in the
complex history of Babylon and Assyria. Their roles
and his are hard to trace with clarity though the foot-
prints are distinctive. He appears frequently in Neo-
Babylonian times but always seems less important than
his more dominant colleagues.

Finally, and especially in those latter days of
Babylon's long career as cultural capital of Mesopotamia, we come to the Pleiades, Sibittu, the "Seven."
More about them later, in connection with divination
which we arbitrarily set apart from religion and worship, in spite of the fact that these domains constituted a unified field of power in the Babylonian universe of humans and deities.[9]

Who were the Chaldeans? They established the last
Babylonian dynasty, though they were not natives. Our
access to them is both secondary, in the written records
in which they are mentioned, and primary, in the Babylonian Chronicles and other first hand records.[10]

The Chaldeans are first mentioned ca. 878 in the
phrase "Land of Chaldea" (mat Kaldu) and in 850, when
mat Kaldi refers to the tribally ("house of . . .")
organized Chaldeans in Assyrian records. They appear
as those in southern Babylonia engaged in agriculture,
trade, and in opposing Assyrian rule. In 812 the As-
syrians exacted tribute from the "kings of Chaldea,"
and by the 8th century period of Assyrian weakness it
seems that Marduk-apla-usur and Eriba-Marduk were the
first Chaldeans to assume kingship in Babylon. Eriba-
Marduk is identified as from Bit-Yakin, one of the major
"houses" of this group, while Nabu-shuma-ishkun is from
the Dakkuru "tribe." The Neo-Babylonians regarded
Nabonassar (747-734) as the founder of their dynasty,
and he is credited in the Chronicle with having instituted the keeping of such records, so closely related
to "astronomical diaries." By Neo-Babylonian times
these had become more exact through the wedding of
mathematics and astronomical observations, exact enough
to predict celestial phenomena.

Though they shared the use of the Aramaic language
with the "Arameans" who began to appear much earlier in
the sources, the relations of these two groups ethnically and linguistically remain uncertain. Their political
relations are clearer: they often appear in Assyrian
records as allied with local temple officials in cham-
pioning anti-Assyrian sentiment. The early Arameans
(mentioned from 1150-700) seem to have located in the
lower Tigris valley and in middle Babylonia, while the
Chaldeans were farther south, in the lower, wetter
lands toward the gulf. In Assyria, Aramaic writing is
known from the 8th century and became common in the 7th,
whereas in Babylonia it begins in the 7th c. and flour-
ishes in the 6th. Oppenheim thinks that our lack of
"literature" in this language is probably due to the
use of perishable writing materials.[11] He credits the
Chaldeans with supporting the Babylonian cause against
Assyria so effectively that their activity "eventually
led, quite successfully, the liberation movement that
culminated in the rise of the Chaldean dynasty under
Nabopolassar and his son Nebuchadrezzar II."[12]

Though there was demonstrable Babylonian cultural influence on Assyria, specific Neo-Babylonian influence on the north is hard to analyze. But some generalizations about them can be offered. They were the conscious heirs of old Babylonian culture, language, and traditions, so that Nabonidus' "introduction" of "new" practices can be described as revival and return to tradition, a tradition which some regard as the civilizing influence in the complex history of Mesopotamia.[13] During the last dynasty there was an increase of family consciousness: parents offered their children as "oblates" to the temples in times of famine (although some have classified this as "selling children"), slaves were apprenticed to craftsmen and became skilled workers. There is documentary evidence for insistence upon the virginity of brides, though the general status of women seems to have diminished during this period of "gentility."[14]

There was increased emphasis upon private capital while the temple as an institution seems to have declined from its dominance in economic life. Royal land grants were made to individuals. The cities, such as huge Babylon (2,500 acres), had zones for various markets, and "cities" for craftsmen, such as tanners. Many craft groups took ancestral names and family names as their designations in order to claim status. This picture of differentiated occupations and variegated economy is partly traceable to the involvement of the Chaldeans in their southern homeland in animal husbandry, several forms of horticulture and agriculture, and international trade, for which they were strategically located near the sea. Even the city plan of Babylon reflects a non-Assyrian idea, with the separation of palace from temple and the "gates" for differing groups of artists, craftsmen, and citizens.[15]

The evidence for the Neo-Babylonian period is sparse, particularly for temple and religion.[16] The existing evidence substantiates the proposition that the Chaldeans sponsored a revival of specifically Babylonian practices over against Assyrian, e.g., the central importance of the Assyrian king as chief "priest" of Ashur and the proximity of temple and palace contrasted with the "humiliation" of the Neo-Babylonian king by the temple chief courtier during the Akitu festival, when his insignia of office were removed for a time before his kingship was "renewed." The above mentioned distance between the Babylon   palace of Nebuchadrezzar II

and the large temple complex shows a difference from
their adjacence in the Assyrian cities. While certainly not to be construed as the separation of church and
state, it was an alliance, and not a royal institution
as in Assyria. One wonders about the significance of
the introduction of coinage to Mesopotamia during
Sennacherib's reign (704-681) as a means of secularizing
commerce and trade, in which the temple had played such
a central role as one of the great organizations, along
with palace and city. Coinage standardizes values in
trade by its size, weight, and authority. This reduced
the control of temple and a god like Shamash, whose protection of the poor involved standardization of weights
and measures.[17]

The   Public   Sector: Because of the shape of our
concern, it is important to qualify the above with the
disclaimers of both Oppenheim and Oates. Oppenheim continued, even in his last essay, to insist on the "un-
knowness" of the common man in our careful, evidence-
limited descriptions of the "alien" Mesopotamian life-
story. However, he also documented many aspects of life
for the Neo-Babylonian period which seem to refer either
primarily or secondarily to the ordinary folk.[18] Oates'
discussion of Babylonian religion emphasizes the "observer" role of common people: at processionals and
festivals, in the large ziggurat complex, and before the
palace of inscriptions. To be sure many of the Chaldean
documents were intended to be buried in temples for the
private reading of the gods or whoever might discover
them in the course of time. But inscriptions and
kudduru, along with cylinder seals, provided public access of various degrees, even for the non-literate populace. The actions of the festivals, seen or heard
about, conveyed dramatic understandings of the organization of life with and by the gods.[19]

Oppenheim is correctly cautious in holding himself
and us to the evidence, literary and artistic, architectural and artifactual. But he seems to withdraw from
legitimate extrapolations from the evidence, random
though it is, probably because of his conviction, shared
by Oates, that the gap between there and here, then and
now is more than just spatial and temporal. It is a
conversation among aliens, conducted mostly by living
foreigners with dead people. This section presents my
classification of the evidence according to public access, moving from least accessible to most, in order to
observe these cautions while listening carefully to the
voices of that "dead civilization."[20]

Though the evidence of all kinds is severely limited, Oppenheim insists that the Neo-Babylonian dynasty
was the conservator of Old Babylonian and Assyrian-
Kassite culture.[21] Henri Frankfort asserts this also,
with reference to art.[22]

The royal/official and ceremonial documents were
the least available to those to whom they were not addressed and for whom they were not intended, the populace. This can be deduced from their form, material,
and location. The royal inscriptions were primarily
votives, intended for the eyes and ears of the deity
credited with the king's achievements or the deities to
whom these achievements were offered as evidence of
royal devotion. They were very much like our time cap-
sules and foundation-stone deposits, intended for another time and another realm. The Neo-Babylonians
understood this clearly, for they regularly added prayers to gods at the ends of the inscriptions.[23]

But even so, the reliefs, symbols and scenes on
the inscriptions were more accessible than texts in the
complicated cuneiform writing and little-known, even
then, language, with all its dialects, including a Neo-
Babylonian dialect detectable as early as the 7th century. While the unlettered majority might not read
such an inscription, the decor, the portraits, the
stories-in-pictures could be viewed, especially when
seen on the more public royal grant markers with familiar symbols and on the common cylinder seals used to
seal transactions of both important and unimportant
folk. The increasingly popular stamp seals which,
though smaller and offering less space for the artist,
preserved important traditional representations of god,
king, intercessor-deities, humans, animals, plants and
other familiar aspects of life in Mesopotamia.[24]

The Chronicles were not intended for the gods, but
for the current and later leaders of the nation. Their
record of atypical events on earth and in the heavens,
and their record of battles won and lost, which approach
"historical" writing, provide files for those leaders
who came after, together with a sober record of the
times when the king's absence necessitated the omission
of the all-important New Year Festival. It seems that
we now have more access to these special documents than
anyone since the time of their writing and storage.
The close relationship between these Chronicles and the
astronomical diaries underlines their importance for

observing the association of phenomena above and below with victory or defeat, success or failure of the rulers, and suggest that they ought to be closely related to the omen texts and other aspects of divination as part of the understanding of the way life was managed.[25]

There is little primary evidence as yet for divination in Neo-Babylonia. What there is leads to the assumption that this important institution continued to be influential in decision-making regarding public policy, strategies and empire-building.

The omen texts, which constitute the largest single genre of surviving "literature" from Mesopotamia, were cast in "if . . ., then . . ." form.[26] They were based on extensive, firsthand observation of natural phenomena, particularly the atypical or signal; the coincidences of such phenomena with public events good or bad formed a repository employed to predict good and bad fortune. A "bad reading" became the occasion for prescribing magical rituals of avoidance; hence, the importance of the patrons of magic, Ea and his offspring.[27] Unlike the horoscopic astrology of later times with its deterministic implications, omens were regarded as warnings, from a generally unknown source expressing itself in the universe, and not as the fixed course of events no matter what. The mathematical precision achieved in astronomy by Neo-Babylonian times gave greater weight to the omens deduced from celestial occurrences, with greatest weight attached to the unusual. So also for occurrences on earth, particularly in important environs - the sudden appearance of a malformed newborn, animal or human, the unexpected "visit" of a wild animal to the city, arriving on land or on the river - were carefully noted and then the "diviners" observed important accidents, deaths, and other problematic events.[28]

For whom? Although there seem to be some for private individuals, the important people and institutions were both more observable and more highly regarded as the signs of "order" in life. Diviners became important functionaries in the royal establishment; one even achieved kingship. Access was limited, though the events on which omens were based were generally observable. What was made of concomitant occurrences was used to serve the small coterie of influential people; and to them also were offered the means of avoiding the bad

359

and insuring the good by prescribed rituals.

The many prayers of priests and kings were addressed to the deities, with whom the continuing relationship was contractual. The self- and god-extolling poetry and prose cemented the relationship and insured the favor and sponsorship of the deities, in war and peace, in plenty and in want.[29]

All of the above were the least accessible to ordinary people. Even the well-known (to us) Epic of Creation was designed to be read to the god himself as praise during the Marduk rites of the Akitu festival. The Epic of Gilgamesh had a limited audience and should not be labelled a "national epic," unless the nation is defined as its leaders.[30]

Much more accessible to ordinary people were the scenes and figures portrayed on both temple and palace inscriptions and exteriors, on the kudurru, and on cylinder and stamp seals, so widely-used to identify possessions, documents, objects in storage or in trade. The public processionals associated with official festivals included the visible presentation of the images of the deities, as they were carefully brought from their sanctuaries out on to the roads provided for their travel. Even letters, though not readily readable in their cuneiform writing, were used for correspondence between various kinds of people; their phraseology and their wishes for welfare invoked the characteristics and powers of the important, sometimes the less important, deities. In all of these ways, greater access was provided to those not directly involved in the events or transactions which involved the deities of the official religion.

The royal land grant markers, once called "boundary stones," were used frequently in Neo-Babylonian times. Nabonidus and his son, for instance, leased land to private individuals. These large, heavy stones were set up on the land granted. While fixed in place and hard to remove, the major deities of the king were portrayed, both in figure, symbol, and inscription, as the guardians of the grant in such a way that even passerby could view them and take heed. The representation of the gods and goddess by their well-known symbols or emblems could be seen and at least partially understood by those who could not read the inscriptions. Most of them would not be aware of the fact that the deities invoked in the inscriptions were often different from those portrayed symbolically above the inscriptions. The clear representations of the gods' presence by their emblems were probably sufficient to deter violation, even if the curses invoked upon removers could not be read.

Cylinder and stamp seals are more numerous, portable, and often personal. Their greater numbers do not necessarily indicate their greater importance, but their proliferation made them widely accessible to people of many stations and occupations. They were designed to belong to people and to move with them where they went. These glyptic art forms, certainly one of the most difficult of the arts because they required reverse images, are replete with representations of the deities. Both in central scene, in border, background, foreground and, most importantly over the scenes, these figures and symbols of the deities appear on most of the seals. The artists' repertory included other motifs from nature and human life, but most numerous are those with gods and goddesses central in the repeated scenes. Their function as means of identifying participants in transactions provides access to daily life, but they cannot be studied in isolation from other data.

Public access to inscriptions, festivals, buildings, town-plans and other artifacts not necessarily intended for the public is important for our description of how life was understood in relationship to the functions of deities in the Chaldean period. Though it is safer to restrict one's statements to the "observer" status of the public, observation is a form of participation. Of course, we do not have recorded "observations" to depend on.

At the same time, Oppenheim's reminders that even the writing of tablets was only a copying exercise by a learner who did not necessarily understand the contents of the paradigmatic tablet, reminds us of the severe limits on broad understanding and knowledge of our most explicit documents. And, too, the selective presentations of modern editors of those available to us in non-cuneiform translations often constrict our access to the full range of existing data.[31]

The Function of the Gods:

But, with those caveats in mind, let us ask again,
"How did the gods and goddesses of Babylon function in
Babylonian society at that time?" In itself that is a
question which comes from outside the materials in
focus. However, it is not completely from without, if
we are right in locating Second Isaiah in 6th century
Babylon as observer-participant among the Judahite
exiles during the critical last years of the Chaldean
kingdom.

Rather than single out the members of the "board
of directors" of life then and treat them one by one,
an amalgamated description of their functions seems
both truer to actuality then and more useful in understanding now. They were seldom portrayed alone.

As we proceed it is esential to remind ourselves
of the organic relationship between deity and king,
godship and kingship, which was perennial in Babylon,
a hardy perennial. As Moortgat insists, Ancient Mesopotamia was an "integrated spiritual organism" based on
a homogeneous religious outlook on the world in which
art was a collective expression mirroring Sumerian and
Akkadian, Assyrian and Babylonian concepts of god and
king.[32]

At the same time, it is important to remember, as
Oppenheim indicates, that the gods were creations of
humans, to whom they submitted themselves as "servants"
charged with the care and feeding of these functionaries
of their multi-level universe.[33] The gods were both
part of the "order" and guardians of the "order" for
their human servants. The high gods both created and
maintained or restored the "order" of life, but not
with any clear sense of overall purpose, as W. G.
Lambert has pointed out:

> Their myth was in part a result of careful obser-
> vation of the universe. The various parts and
> aspects of it were assigned to particular
> deities.[34]

Though such a division of labor led to conflicts of
divine wills and contest for divine primacy, disorder
was checked by shimtu, often translated, "destiny,"
though preferably to be understood as the act(s) of
fixing a place in the universal society for someone, so
that

every aspect of human society was decreed by the gods. Nothing was left to be chosen by the human race as suitable and convenient for it at a particular stage of development and in a particular geographical location. The gods had decreed it all.[35]

Human duty was conforming to the regulations in the interests of a well-ordered society. This static view of human life is dateable from the events in the Epic of Creation, particularly important as a central feature of the New Year Festival in Neo-Babylonian times, where chaos had existed before "destinies were fixed." Things did change, usually by the decisions of gods in council and because humans had neglected the decrees. Divine actions were calculated to restore order to its intended sway, not to alter 'decrees' or 'order' in the light of changed conditions and relations. While the diversity of deities served this unified concept of life, even the gods themselves were involved in the "destinies," and could not flout them.[36] (Perhaps the silence about the source of omnious portents and the subjection of the deities to this "order" derive from the fading, yet still powerful Anu and Enlil of early times, who were still regarded as having set loose in the world "evil spirits" and "demons.") Clearly both gods and humans were inside the established "order," though with discrete roles within it. The intervention of the gods was "not concerned with a movement in history," but with maintenance of place, prerogatives, rights and obligations within an order whose maintenance depended upon adequate service to the gods by their human "servants."[37] Status quo ante, not a near or "far off divine event," dictated both the petitions of prayers and the affirmations of occasions for thanksgiving. Oppenheim again,

Not only does man occupy the central position in such stories [cosmological/cosmogonic compositions], he is practically their unique concern. Theogony and cosmogony are but prolegomena to human history meant primarily to establish man's nature and function in the social and moral order of the cosmos. The organizing activities of the creating deity focus in the temple and in the city, and their economic requirements, such as water, fields, and workmen. There is hardly a trace of the universal concern in the Creation story of the first chapter of Genesis that reaches from the

> luminaries in the sky to all plants and living
> beings. . . . All the luminaries of the sky
> function primarily for the sake of man; they
> establish the calendar in order to allow him to
> organize his time--and, more important, his work.
> In other words, the regularity of agricultural
> and sacral activities is the sole concern of the
> gods.38

Though Oppenheim regarded the Epic of Creation as "the
concept of a scholar-poet rather than a living tradition,"39 it reflects the primal, central, and perennial
"constitution" of Babylonia: "order." Both the gods'
origins and man's are often ascribed to Ea Enki, whose
realm was the cosmic, primeval freshwater; sometimes
their birth was attributed to the sexual union of Apsu
and Tiamat, which set up an oppositional scheme, between heaven and earth, which was basic to Mesopotamian
cosmography. Ea's peculiar role as friend to humankind
is important for understanding those related to him as
"son" or "daughter," as we will see. He was part of
the great triad: Anu-Ea-Enlil. Unlike his two part-
ners who were often at enmity with humans, witness the
formula "When Anu and Enlil . . ." in omen texts, Ea
protected, taught, and "saved" humans, as Oppenheim
observed:

> Unlike the other gods, who primarily demand
> service from man, Ea, on the mythological level
> [like Prometheus], intervenes for man again and
> again; on the legendary level, Ea repeatedly
> instructs man through his fish-shaped emissaries,
> puradu.40

His functions for humans became increasingly important
in an ominous world where order could only be re-established by magic ritual, of which he and his progeny
were patrons.

"Destinies" ought to be translated and understood
as "norms," as Lambert demonstrates: "eternal destinies were the social norms, and they were re-enacted
each year, just as Marduk was re-established each New
Year as king of the gods." In the words of Nebuchadrezzar II's inscription, "they /the gods/ decreed the
destinies of endless days and the destiny of my life."41

Increasingly in the Neo-Babylonian period the
deities were represented by their symbols: on

pedestals, standards, kudurru, seals, and in the top
pictorial register of inscriptions. Their images,
three-dimensional anthropmorphic representations, were
fashioned in special workshops by careful craftsmen.
They were imbued with life through ritual consecration
and were regarded as inseparable from the deities'
presence. If the god's image was away from the temple,
the festivals could not be celebrated until the image
returned. This centrality was almost matched by the
replicas and emblems derived from the images. The
images were fed, clothed, and cared for by courtiers
and kings; for the most part they were kept in the
cella, out of public view. But their well-known symbols
were not so restricted and played important roles in
the more public domains.

The following composite description of the chief
insignia of the major deities will proceed from the
ground line upwards, drawing together the varieties of
uses characteristic of the visual representations. In
the lower zone personal deities, mostly unidentified,
occur in company with humans. Often they are portrayed
as mediaries or intercessors who lead or assist humans,
usually royal, to approach the high god or goddess.
This is reflected also in written documents, such as
Ludlul be nemegi, where the "good man" performs his
devotions to his personal goddess, at the same time
reserving the title of "savior" for Marduk.42

Also in the lower register, and often the lowest
figures shown, are the composite animals, the shedu and
lamassu. They were evidently regarded as closer to the
human scene while they are also in the company of the
major deities: with, behind, under foot, on a leash.
Their aspect is usually unthreatening, even when they
stand guard at palaces or temples. The mud brick
reliefs of Babylon, on palace and Ishtar's gate on the
processional way from the temple, are good examples of
these traditional figures.43

These shedu and lamassu, early and late in Babylonian art, are in the company of or in proximity to the
great gods and primary goddess. They often serve as
pedestals, seats, decor on seats, steeds/mounts, or
"pets" of the dominant deities or their symbols. Though
it has been thought that these represented tamed or sub-
dued evil forces, evidence is lacking for interpreting
them as once or at any time "opponents" of the deities,
as in the subduction of chaos represented by demons.

Rather, as van Buren's careful study documents, they
represented fructifying showers of rain, assistants to
fertility deities (with whom only the "dragon" is
shown), as talismans for individual use to avoid famine,
drought, and other calamities; that is, "omens" of
abundance and blessing.[44] During the Neo-Babylonian
period some of them, e.g., winged lion, are not found,
but the dragon (of Marduk) remains and persists, sometimes serving as the "mount" of Marduk's marru (actually, blade of a spade, at right angle to handle for cultivation of soil and digging of canals) and Nabu's
wedge (the writing instrument of those to whom he was
the especial patron). There is no evidence that the
dragon was inimical to the gods or malevolent to humans.
One combination of uses is striking to this observer:
animal kneeling, with temple facade on its back, and
the symbol of the deity atop the facade. No figure for
the deity, just a symbol, a development characteristic
of the Chaldean time, as Frankfort and van Buren indicate, thus indicating some remoteness of the deity's
image from localized presence.[45]

    If the image is, as Oates and others affirm, the
"presence" of the deity, enfused with "life,"[46] and the
emblems and standards of the gods represent the deities
when they are not present, as van Buren suggests,[47]
what does the proliferation of symbols, insignia, and
standards mean when combined with a severe reduction in
portraits? Frankfort characterizes the Neo-Babylonian
cylinder and stamp seals as "elegant" but with "little
force," lacking "imagination," with "everything imaginative reduced to a minimum."[48] An example is the scene
in which a praying worshipper stands reverently in the
"prayer position" (with left hand and forearm across
the chest, right hand and forearm slightly raised, body
upright, eyes forward and face set) before, e.g., a
wedge atop a temple facade resting on a composite
animal. Such "abstractions" are also found on the
kudurru. This "calligraphic" quality which is like a
"graceful monogram" stands in strong contrast to the
force and vigor of the Assyrian tradition.[49] Some find
Kassite influence in this trend, which is found alongside muscular representations of the "naked hero" with
wild hair and often carrying a small animal, a frequent
motif in the time of our interest. Nevertheless, Neo-
Babylonian cylinder and stamp seals continue the main
themes related to the great gods, and even the "mon-
sters" lose their terrifying aspect and become ornamen-
tal.[50]

Another motif found in the lower area of the Neo-Babylonian scenes is the ziggurat as a base with the symbol of the deity at the apex.[51] This is found with the insignia of the Big Four described above, thus indicating their crucial roles in the ordering of life for gods and humans by their intermediary location at the top of the stepped pyramid of a shrine entered only by officiants. (at this point it is important to point out that this peak of the Babylon ziggurat, though surrounded by the temple wall, was visible beyond the sacred region and could be seen by many.) The stationing of the godly symbol atop the holy hill, shown on seals, on kudurru, as well as on the less public displays, may offer a correction to the opinion that the god's image was necessary to affirm its presence. van Buren points out that these emblems (shurinnu) and their names were often preceded by the cuneiform "god" identifier and that the emblems themselves were sometimes placed in the temple windows and carried in processions on standards or bases.[52] The keeper of the shurinnu was responsible directly to the monarch, as documentary evidence affirms. Juridicial oaths could be made in front of the shurinnu of Judge Shamash, and oaths were sometimes tested by whether the oath-maker could remove the symbol from its socket. Perhaps the distance between god and symbol was not that great in actual practice.[53]

Moving upward from the lower part of the scenes, we come to the figure or symbol of the deities. In presentation scenes, the deity usually sits or stands regally looking to the left, with a lesser deity, marked by a cap with fewer horns than those of the great deities, approaching leading a human/king by the hand. The great deity is always larger, more stately and sartorially grand. Sometimes his seat has an awning over it supported by lesser deities. Often his symbol is on a fairly tall stand between him/her and the approaching figures who are usually of equal size to each other but much smaller than the important goddess/god. Their stances seem static, though their faces and eyes direct the viewer's attention to the majestic "presence." The intercessor deity often raises both hands in petition, with chin slightly uplifted and eyes toward the deity being implored.[54]

The treatment of the bodies and the clothing in Neo-Babylonian times seems "naturalistic" when compared with the huge-shouldered forceful figures of Assyrian

art. However, beards in the Assyrian style continued,
as well as the dominant hair-style with a bun in the
back underneath the edge of the horned cap. Most of
the horned caps are fronted by four (or five) pairs of
bull-like horns, the points of which meet at the center
front and point upward. Of course, Ishtar is different
in bodily characteristics, though sometimes her clothing
obscures her feminine shape.55

Garments are characterized by variety, though with
realistic folds of material which add to the three-
dimensional impression of the portrait. Often the garments are covered with rosettes, possibly a decor derived from the eight-pointed star of Ishtar in combination with the "dots" of the "Seven," though, of course,
more numerous. Sometimes the circlets on deities' robes
seem more clearly derived from Shamash's four-pointed
star with sets of three wavy lines at four points equi-
distant between each pair of points, and with a knob or
circle in the center. Necklaces, necklets, wrist bands,
careful tailoring, fringed cuffs and hems add beauty and
color (?) to the costumes. There is certainly nothing
unattractive in the way the deities are dressed.
Humans' and intercessors' garments are similar, though
usually less decorated and ornate. But there is a sense
in which the humans' attire "reflects" the deities,
again underlining the anthropomorphism of godly representations and the "reverse anthropomorphism" in representing the "servants, worshippers."

Hands, and arm postures, are extremely important,
both for the way they appear and for the objects in
their grasp. Most often the deity holds the "rod and
ring," in an extended hand. The rod looks like a run-
ner's baton and the ring like that used in modern "ring
toss" games. It appears that the ring, if straightened,
would equal the length of the rod. The deity grasps
the two together with one hand (usually the left) around
the middle of the rod and around one arc of the ring.
While one early portrayal clearly shows the ring as a
loop of line connected to the rod, most representations
do not encourage a "measuring line" interpretation.
However that may be, the rod and ring, or ring alone,
are held only by great gods, never by humans or by lesser deities. Often the king before the deity looks
ready to receive them, but they are never shown as given
to the royal human. Apparently it was a symbol of truly
divine power to be shared with, but not given to even
the highest of humans, the king. Among the deities who

hold it, clasped to chest or in extended hand, are:
Marduk, Shamash, Ishtar, Assur, Adad, Nabu and Enlil,
who with Anu was reputed to have received it very early
from an ancient numen. Those who grasp this in one
hand have a lightning bolt (Adad) or another identifying characteristic implement/tool/weapon in the other.
It seems to be a shared possession among the powers in
Neo-Babylon, although there does not seem to be an example of it on a temple facade or ziggurat base, probably because it was a shared power among the great
deities.[56]

Shamash's toothed saw/sword seems to have passed
out of usage early, though his association with a lion
or bull did not, nor did his holding of a mace disappear
in the late period, when it was sometimes decorated with
seven globes on the handle. Another shared item was the
net, usually being employed to seine people whose postures and pellmell arrangement indicate their capture.[57]

As one might expect from reading the written materials from the Chaldean time, there was a "functional
triad" of heavenly deities: Moon, Sun, Venus, whose
symbols appear overhead on cylinder seals and at the
apex of both kudurru and ziggurats.

The female member of this central group, Ishtar
exhibits primarily her polemic function, together with
her involvement in determining fate by the casting of
lots. Her regalia include the bow and arrow(s) clasped
in her hand, the dagger in her belt, the quivers on her
back, various complex maces (with animal heads), scep-
ters (also with animal heads), some tripartite (similar
to the lightning fork, but distinguishable), the sickle-
sword and scimitar. She often stands with face front,
in a split skirt with the forward foot and leg on one
or two lions: an awesome figure of martial power and
conquest. Though she is reputed to be a goddess of
love, it is hard to see it in her portraits.[58]

Adad, weather-god, regularly holds his characteristic three-pronged fork in one hand, usually the left,
and a weapon, often and axe, in the other. This lightning symbol also takes a foliate form, and very often
the form of a vertical zigzag pointed at the bottom end.
There is a certain ambivalence in representing him,
undoubtedly due to the combined maleficent and benefi-
cent effects of thunderstorms: rain with lightning,
hail and floods along with the necessary water upon

which agriculture depends. For people dependent upon
the earth's productivity he brought both bountiful
crops and destructive disasters for humans, plants, and
animals.59

His lightning often appears mounted atop a ziggurat, as do Ishtar's star, Nabu's crescent, and
Shamash's disk--though usually not in a group. While
some of the deities' emblems function as hand-held,
free-standing, and mounted, Marduk's spade is not hand-
held. It does appear almost anywhere else: on a base,
in the middle zone, at the top, in the background or
foreground; some of the bases seem to be suspended in
midair.60

A dominant theme on Neo-Babylonian stamp seals is
the flowing vase. While this was earlier the distinctive symbol of Ea, whose lifegiving ground water flowed
throughout the land, in the later period many deities
seem to have been associated with this important function. The vase is often held by an unnamed, and otherwise unidentifiable deity. Its "artesian" stream flows
upward from the mouth of the vase and then down into
small vases or onto the ground line itself, sometimes
flowing out the edges of the scene. Often the fish
associated with Ea swim upward against the current.
Among the great deities who are portrayed with the vase
in Chaldean times are Adad, Marduk, et al.61

Amurru, with his distinctive "top hat" and shepherd's crook is infrequent during this period, although
his association with the Arameans and Chaldeans is
clear. Sometimes his accompanying goddess holds another
crook,62 although she is not easy to identify.

The upper zone of seal scenes and kudurru stones
include some of the same symbols as the middle zone.
Often a hand extends from above the scene into its upper area; this is interpreted as Shamash's powerful
hand, perhaps associated with oath-taking which was done
before the Sun.

The sun-disk also figures prominently in the sky
zone, on seals, kudurru, and often atop ziggurats.
Sometimes it is mounted on a shaft/post, and in its most
imaginative representation is winged and sometimes has
the broad tail of predator birds. George E. Mendenhall
has fully discussed this symbol in the chapter, "The
Mask of Yahweh," in The Tenth Generation.63 Its

association with both Assur and Shamash as battlers for the king or sponsors of the king's battles, always victorious, is clear.

Shamash is, as noted earlier, described as the son of Moon: Sin/Nabu/Nanna. The moon's typical crescent is often shown as the lower part of a full disk; this may be a by-product of the workman's incising tool, but is more likely a way of portraying the all-important phases of the moon. Commentators emphasize the calendaric relationship of Nabu-Sin, because the Babylonian calendar remained lunar, with periodic adjustments to solar movement. This observer is reminded of the persistence among agriculturalists even now of the relationship between planting and moon phases.

The crescent, alone, with disk, on staff/post, with deity within, appears both on kudurru and seals as does Nabu's companion symbol, the wedge, vertical or horizontal, and the two vertical rods usually associated with his patronage of the scribal and "wisdom" arts. Of course it appears on Neo-Babylonian ziggurats where, at latest count it was the most numerous of the symbols so ensconced.[64]

The third figure/symbol dominant in the upper zones is Ishtar's eight-pointed star, alone or on a disk, sometimes on a rod or staff/post. It occurs on kudurru, stelae and all the seal forms. Often it crowns Ishtar's multi-horned cap and ziggurats.[65] How important was Ishtar's procession as evening and morning star, especially after the application of mathematics to astronomical observations--and how important for the "heralding" of the sun and moon and, thus, of the seasons as well as the days and nights? The singularity of Ishtar as one among the mighty, the only female deity of the great powers, when there had been and later were so many other consorts, mothers, mediatrices, and matrons of various arts, crafts and basic human activities strikes this observer as worth pursuing--later.

It remains to mention briefly a group of apparent close association with Ishtar, Sibittu, "the seven" who appear in the upper zone in a cluster or scattered throughout the scenes on seals. Their usual proximity to Ishtar suggests involvement in the determining of fate by casting lots. While the seven are often given an astral interpretation as the Pleiades, perhaps by extrapolation from later horoscropic astrology--from which Babylonian omenology was far distant, as mentioned earlier--van Buren prefers to identify them as the seven pebbles used to cast lots.[66] I do not know how she knows this. But I am struck by their location in the "sky" zone of so many scenes which suggests their astral /planetary correlation. Without resolving this, let me end this section by mentioning one Neo-Babylonian seal on which the seven dots are found close to an animal and a fish, with a man at prayer among the cluster of seven small circles.[67]

How then, did the gods and goddesses of Babylon function in the human society of that time? They exercised fundamental and essential roles in a world-system designed in response to the peculiar human situation in Babylon. They were the powers to be reckoned with in politics, agriculture, weather, warfare, love, and the other basic relationships of life. Their anthropomorphic representations showed the symbols of their individual and collective powers, and these very characteristic symbols became more prominent in the art of Neo-Babylonian times, in many situations seeming to replace the figure of the deity itself. As one studies this displacement and attempts to interpret a scene in which a worshiper stands before only an emblem, with no intermediary, no visage to gaze on, no real setting to the scene, the mind moves toward identifying the symbol as "principle" or abstract "force." Yet the traditionality of the stance and the association of the emblem with a long-time wellknown deity cautions one against such a depersonalized interpretation and suggests rather a relationship between humans and the dominant deities mediated by the symbol so long found in portrayals of the powers within that world.

Within the limits of the evidence and the difficulties of correlating artistic and literary representations, it is nevertheless clear, as Oppenheim affirmed, that Mesopotamian man "constructed around himself an orderly world in which he could make rational decisions within a frame of predictable events and situations."[68] The dominant deities ruled this integrated world from within its highest zones and throughout its major divisions; collectively, they encompassed and expressed the powers which had made this world orderly, maintained its orders, and, when omens warned of disorder, were appealed to for restoration of the order. While neither they nor their human servants appear as "fixtures," their clearly-defined roles and interrelations within the established order encourage stereotyping. But this orderly world, resistant to innovation and without a clear sense of long-range purpose except natural and human fertility and welfare, was equipped to deal with the disturbing or potentially ominous by its highly developed rituals designed to address the needs of specific, if recurring, situations which threatened to disorder the natural or human scenes. It was resourceful and did encourage observation of nature in all its forms; it was creative in adapting to changes while stabilizing society through appeal to the recognized authorities, the powerful deities.

Crucial to this order was the central figure, man and his paradigmatic representative, the king. The central roles of the king within this order of which Marduk was the originator and maintainer, place kingship and king at the apex of the society where it met the collective power of the gods and goddesses. Human service to the deities was carefully prescribed and assiduously executed in order to insure the reciprocal lordly "service" of the powers on behalf of human society.

Though the limited evidence for the Neo-Babylonian period restricts our view of the last of the Babylonian dynasties and their understanding of their world, we can still glimpse the main outlines of that "alien" culture.

FOOTNOTES

1. So described in Oppenheim, Ancient Mesopotamia, rev. E. Reiner; Chicago: University of Chicago, 1977, and in Oates, Babylon; London: Thames and Hudson, 1979.
2. Paul, "Deutero-Isaiah and Cuneiform Royal Inscriptions," Ephraim A. Speiser Volume; New Haven: American Oriental Society, 1968, 180–6; Mendenhall, The Tenth Generation; Baltimore: Johns Hopkins, 1973, esp. 32–66; Albright, History, Archaeology and Christian Humanism; NY: McGraw-Hill, 1964, esp. 145–54; Talmon, "The Comparative Method..," in Supplements to Vetus Testamentum 29 (1978).
3. Oppenheim and Oates, passim, and Henri Frankfort, The Art and Architecture of the Ancient Orient; Harmondsworth: Penguin, 1954, 106–8. Cp. A. Parrot, The Arts of Assyria tr. S. Gilbert and J. Emmons; NY: Golden, 1961, 167–87, and, A. Moortgat, The Art of Ancient Mesopotamia; NY: Phaidon, 1969, esp. 158–162.
4. The chronology and spelling follows J.A.Brinkman, "Mesopotamian Chronology of the Historical Period," the Appendix in Oppenheim.
5. W.G. Lambert, "History and the Gods: A Review Article [B. Albrektson, History and the Gods..]," Orientalia 39 (1970), 171.
6. Lambert, "Destiny and Divine Intervention in Babylon and Israel,"

Oudtestamentische Studien 17 (1972), 66.

7. Oates, Babylon, 174.

8. L.W. King, Babylonian Boundary-Stones and Memorial Tablets in the British Museum; London: British Museum, 1912. Cp. Oppenheim, Ancient Mesopotamia, 286-7.

9. This survey is not comprehensive. The seven were judged dominant in Neo-Babylonian times (not without others of lesser importance) on the basis of their frequency and dominence in pictorial data.

10. See Brinkman, "Political History of Post-Kassite Babylonia (1158-722 B.C.)," Analecta Orientalia 43 (1968), esp. 260-84. Cp. Oppenheim, Ancient Mesopotamia, 153-63, and Oates, Babylon, 126-35.

11. Oppenheim, pp. 23, 162-3, 168.

12. Ibid., p. 60.

13. Ibid., p. 36.

14. Ibid., pp. 75-7, 283.

15. Ibid., pp. 81-94.

16. Ibid., pp. 171-83, "Why a 'Mesopotamian Religion' Should not be written." But cp. 183-94, "The Care and Feeding of the Gods." Oates echoes this caution, Babylon, 170-80.

17. Oppenheim, p. 87.

18. Oppenheim, "Man and Nature in Mesopotamian Civilization," The Dictionary of Scientific Biography XV, Supplement 1, 634-66, esp. 634-53.

19. Oates, Babylon, 176-7.

20. See n. 1.

21. Oppenheim, Ancient Mesopotamia, 36, 65ff, 158.

22. Frankfort, Art and Architecture, 106.

23. Oppenheim, Ancient Mesopotamia, 149, 232, 279, and, A.K. Grayson Assyrian and Babylonian Chronicles in Texts from Cuneiform Sources; Locust Valley, NY: Augustin, 1975, 3,4, and 11.

24. Frankfort, Cylinder Seals: A Documentary Essay on the Art and Religion of the Ancient Near East; London: Gregg reprint, 1965 (original 1939). E.D. van Buren,"The Symbols of the Gods in Mesopotamian Art," Analecta Orientalia 23 (1945). E. Porada, Corpus of Ancient Near Eastern Series in North American Collections; NY: Pantheon, 1948.

25. Grayson, Chronicles, 10-14, 138.

26. Oppenheim, Ancient Mesopotamia, 213-223, 308.

27. Oates, Babylon, 178-180.

28. Grayson, Chronicles, 138.

29. Oppenheim, Ancient Mesopotamia, 149.

30. Ibid., pp. 232, 255.

31. Ibid., pp. 228-48, 392.

32. Moortgat, Art, ix.

33. Oppenheim, Ancient Mesopotamia, 183-198.

34. Lambert, "Destiny," 65.

35. Ibid., p. 67.

36. Ibid., p. 69.

37. Ibid., p. 71.

38. Oppenheim, "Man and Nature," 641.

39. Oppenheim, Ancient Mesopotamia, 232.

40. Oppenheim, "Man and Nature," 641.
41. Lambert, "History," 174.
42. Oppenheim, Ancient Mesopotamia, 272; tr. R.D. Biggs, "Ludlul Bēl Nēmēqi, 'I Will Praise the Lord of Wisdom'," 569-601 in J.B. Pritchard, ed., Ancient Near Eastern Texts; Princeton: Princeton University Press, 1969.
43. Oates, Babylon, 176-7; van Buren, "The Dragon in Ancient Mesopotamia," Orientalia 1:1-18, 45.
44. van Buren, "Dragon," 4, 45.
45. Frankfort, Cylinder Seals, 218; van Buren, "Symbols," 1-10.
46. Oates, Babylon, 174-5.
47. van Buren, "Symbols," 7.
48. Frankfort, Cylinder Seals, 218.
49. Frankfort, Art and Architecture, 5, 217.
50. van Buren, "Dragon," 40.
51. van Buren, "Symbols," 51-2.
52. Ibid., p. 2.
53. Ibid., p. 162.
54. Pritchard, Ancient Near East in Pictures; Princeton: Princeton University Press, 1969, Nos. 687, 688, 692, 697 with references.
55. Porada, Seals, Nos. 724-811.
56. van Buren, "The Rod and the Ring," Archiv Orientalia 17 (1949), 434-450, Nos. 1-12, and ANEP No. 537.
57. van Buren, "Symbols," 11-12, 179.
58. Ibid., pp. 72-85.
59. Ibid., pp. 67-8.
60. Ibid., pp. 14-18.
61. Ibid., pp. 124-33.
62. Ibid., pp. 142-4.
63. Mendenhall, Tenth Generation, 32-66.
64. van Buren, "Symbols," 60-67.
65. Ibid., pp. 82-5.
66. Ibid., pp. 74-82.
67. Ibid., pp. 80-1.
68. Oppenheim, "Man and Nature," 634.

Section

C

THEOLOGY

CONSCIENCE AND AUTHORITY

A CONTRIBUTION TO ECUMENICAL DIALOGUE

Norman Young

Drew Theological School in the nineteen-fifties was anything but a sectarian Methodist institution, yet even the open-ness to other churches and other faiths we experienced there hardly led us to anticipate the extent of ecumenical advances of the last two decades. Certainly I never dreamed that ten years after graduation I would be teaching theology with a Jesuit colleague to men and women preparing for the ministries of Anglican, Catholic, Congregational, Methodist and Presbyterian churches in Australia. Nor did I anticipate the scope of the dialogue with other churches that Roman Catholics have initiated since Vatican II. My involvement with this dialogue, both at national and international levels,[1] has led me to recognize that sometimes the differences between us show only the tip of the proverbial iceberg; much more often, however, I've discovered that they are ramparts built on very shaky foundations indeed. Dig below the surface and the walls of division are likely to come tumbling down.

Since leaving Drew I have worked more in theology than in biblical studies, but I have returned again and again to the Old Testament largely because Larry Toombs (along with John Paterson and Bernhard Anderson) introduced me to it in such a way that its varied imagery has remained utterly compelling and its themes inescapable. And although my knowledge of archaeology is rudimentary and my experience on the field non-existent, perhaps my concern to probe beneath the surface of theological structures and ecumenical wastelands shows that our interests are not entirely alien. In any event, it is only from this process of theological sifting that I have anything to offer that may, however inadequately, express my regard for Larry Toombs as a scholar and teacher, and my gratitude to him for his guidance and friendship.

So to the issue of conscience and authority. To extend the archaeological imagery a little further, even a first sounding shows that there is more than one stratum of ecumenical contention to be uncovered, if not undermined. On the surface, Catholics and Protestants have traditionally been seen to be profoundly divided on the role that conscience is thought to play in moral decision-making. How do I decide what I ought to do? Protestants are supposed to reply, "follow your conscience," Catholics, "heed the voice of authority." So widespread and ingrained has this type-casting been that the World Methodist/Roman Catholic Commission[2] rightly concluded that "the nexus between conscience and authority has often been seen less as a relationship than as a Protestant/Catholic antithesis."[3] But it does not take much reflection on how Protestants and Catholics actually live in the world to conclude that this antithesis is overdrawn. Imagine a Catholic nurtured in the faith by committed parents, prepared for confirmation by catechesis, enjoined to make a good confession and to live in the world as a good Catholic not being aware of the duty to obey conscience! That is about as likely as a Protestant brought up in a God-fearing bible-reading, Church-going family, hearing a Calvinist preacher week by week or going regularly to Methodist prayer meetings not being aware of standing under authority. As the Commission concluded, in rather more measured tones, "that authority is a service of the Gospel, that the assent of faith is free or nothing, that the one witnesses to the other no Catholic will deny: that Christian conscience is formed within the life of the Church, which is life in the Spirit, no Methodist will dispute."[4]

That helps to clear away the rubble of a false antithesis, but has not thereby established whether there is any substantial common ground below the surface. This I propose to do by reflecting on aspects of the theology of John Wesley, noting some points of convergence with John Henry Newman. In the process a more deepseated area of difference comes to light, which in turn may be worked through to still more substantial basis for agreement.

Faith and works.

We can go a long way toward claiming common ground by rediscovering the integral relationship between faith and works, expressing this in a way that retains the priority of faith without relegating works to the status of optional, and the essential place of works in salvation without implying salvation by works.

This rediscovery depends upon beginning with what

Christians have always seen as having priority -- the
grace of God. The significance of this starting-point,
however, was easily lost among the slogans of Reforma-
tion and Counter-reformation, with Reformers tending to
gild the lily of God's grace by over-emphasizing the
helplessness of man in his totally fallen state, and
with Catholics countering with an over-stress on the
natural righteousness of man.[5] What began as an over-
emphasis could, and in the heat of controversy, frequently did degenerate into something worse -- quietism
and antinomianism on the one side and salvation by
meritorious works on the other. To affirm the priority
of the grace of God, however, is to recognize that his
saving initiative goes before the response both of
faith and of works. As he enables us to come to faith,
so God also empowers that faith to come to full flower
in love whose fruit is good works. In his introduction
to the thought of John Wesley, Albert Outler makes it
clear why those who heed Wesley's call to spread scrip-
tural holiness are impelled thereby to engage issues of
practical and moral judgements. At the same time we
are given fair warning that the issue of authority already looms on the horizon:

> Faith is the primary reality in Christian
> experience but not its totality. It is,
> Wesley urged, a means -- a necessary means --
> to a still higher end: "Faith is only the
> handmaid of love..." The goal of the
> Christian life is holiness, "the fullness of
> the faith." This means the consecration of
> the whole self to God and to the neighbor in
> love. This, in turn, involves a process of
> corporate discipline and effort, guided by
> the motive of "devotion," by which he meant
> the delivering up of one's whole life to
> God.[6]

So it is from the standpoint of love that Wesley
discerns the unity of grace, faith and works. The
gracious initiative of God for our salvation is embodied
in Jesus Christ; this love of God, seized hold of in
faith, calls forth our response of love -- love to God
and neighbour; love for neighbour must be manifest as
working in the world for his good.

> By faith, taken in its more particular
> meaning for a confidence in a pardoning God,
> we establish his law in our hearts...for

> there is no motive which so powerfully
> inclines us to love God as the sense of the
> love of God in Christ...and from this princi-
> ple of grateful love to God arises love to
> our brother also...Now this love to man,
> grounded on faith and love to God "worketh
> no ill" to our "neighbour." It continually
> incites us to do good as we have time and
> opportunity; to do good in every possible
> kind and in every possible degree, to all
> men.[7]

Such a view would be widely shared by Catholics and
Protestants alike, but with whatever care we may peg
out this claim to common ground, does it remain a theological plot with no vein of genuine ecumenical promise
in it? Is it any more than an enticing mire that
buries our hopes unless we can agree on what it is to
love the neighbour, or, more fundamentally, on how we
decide what it is so to love? Which brings us back to
conscience and authority, for it is precisely the balance of one to the other in the overall picture of
moral decision-making that has traditionally separated
Protestant and Catholic.

Wesley, on conscience.

I hope that my view, that conscience and authority
are no more antithetical than faith and works, has already been foreshadowed. Certainly Wesley would never
have defined his position over against Rome by opting
for individual conscience rather than for more objective forms of authority as the guide to Christian
obedience. Those who have charged him with "enthusiasm" (both in his own lifetime and in ours) because of
this supposed identification of religion with private
experience have been wide of the mark, as we shall see.
He did, of course, emphasize the importance of conscience, defining it as

> that faculty whereby we are at once conscious
> of our own thoughts, words and actions; and
> of their merit and demerit, of their being
> both good and bad, and, consequently, deserv-
> ing either praise or censure.[8]

While not maintaining that it gives us detailed instruction about what course of action to follow in every

given circumstance, he does claim that everyone posses-
ses the capacity to know that there is a difference
between good and evil, and, in general terms, to grasp
broad moral principles; for instance, that it is good
to honour parents and to do right to others as we would
have them do to us.[9]

Conscience, rather than shedding light on everything we should do, makes sure that we know when we
have turned away from the light that we do have. Using
another metaphor, this time from the law court, he says
that conscience has a three-fold office: as a witness,
"testifying to what we have done in thought or word or
action"; as a judge, "passing sentence on what we have
done, that it is good or evil"; it also "in some sense
executes the sentence by occasioning a degree of compla-
cency in him that does well and uneasiness in him that
does evil."[10]

In his sermon On Conscience Wesley strikes three
additional notes which have considerable bearing on our
later discussion. First is his insistence that while
this faculty is universal it is not strictly speaking
"natural," at least not in the sense of belonging to
ordinary human endowments. It is a supernatural gift
of God -- "not nature but the Son of God which enlight-
eneth every man that cometh into the world."[11] Second
is his view of conscience in Christian perspective.
Those without faith are, as we have seen, aware of the
faculty of conscience, but the Christian discerns it as
a means by which the Spirit of God reveals "the real
quality of our thoughts, words and actions," enabling
us to know the extent to which these are in conformity
with the will of God. Third is his concern to keep
the conscience sensitive to the word of God -- not that
conscience communicates a private word that bypasses
the means of grace but that it enables us to feel the
force, to get the point of the written word. By the
assistance of the grace of God, conscience brings us
under that rule which is to direct us in every particular, "none other than the written word of God."[13] That
conscience does not stand alone to provide privileged
and untestable knowledge of God's will is clear even in
a passage in which Wesley calls most vigorously for
obedience to conscience:

> If you desire to have your conscience always
> quick to discern, and faithful to accuse or
> excuse you, be sure to obey it at all events;

continually listen to its admonitions and
steadily follow them. Whatever it directs
you to do, according to the word of God, do;
however grievous to flesh and blood. Whatever it forbids, if the prohibition be
grounded on the word of God, see that you do
it not; however pleasing it may be to flesh
and blood.[14]

Natural Law and the Ethics of Revelation.

My own limited reading of classical and contemporary Catholic writing on conscience suggests that there
are significant points of agreement here. Certainly
Wesley's views were consistent with those of many of
the Fathers; with Origen, for example, who held that
conscience is the Spirit which is found in the soul as
"tutor, companion and guide" and whose function is both
to advise on the best course of action and to rebuke
and chastise one for sin;[15] with Jerome, who set the
conscience as an eagle above reason, spirit and desire;[16] and with Albertus Magnus and Bonaventura, both
of whom affirmed that conscience is a faculty that produces in the soul an inclination toward moral goodness,
while disagreeing about whether this was done by aiding
the reason to grasp the principles of moral law
(Albertus) or by mobilizing the will to act for the
good (Bonaventura). By contending that conscience is
not a separate faculty but a reasoning act in which
knowledge is applied to conduct, Thomas Aquinas represented a different point of view, but the form that
such application takes finds an echo in Wesley's sermon
-- to testify as to what has been done, to incite us
toward the good and to accuse us when we have done
wrong.[17] And both men were convinced that this capacity is directly the gift of God, for Thomas

> the light of natural reason whereby we
> distinguish good and evil, which is the
> function of natural law, is nothing else
> but the impress upon us of the divine light
> itself.[18]

A Catholic commentator on this passage from Aquinas
follows up with the conclusion, "conscience is simply
the extension or application of this natural law to a
particular act."[19]

Now this is just the point at which we strike a stratum of much more fundamental disagreement than the superficial "Protestants follow conscience, Catholics the authority of the Church." Natural law as the basis for moral obligation was roundly dismissed by the Reformers. They denied that the rational creature, as image of God, participates in the eternal law and shares in a finite way God's own judgement of good and evil. Impossible, they declared, because the image of God in man was destroyed in the fall, or so distorted that no natural capacity to discern the will of God in and for his creation remains. In our own time this conclusion gained fresh endorsement from Barth's celebrated denial of any analogia entis between Creator and creature, and from others who have also advocated a theology based on the revelation of God centered on his unprecedented initiative in Jesus Christ. Such an initiative is held to remain a scandal to reason and can be apprehended only in faith. This theological approach demands that Christian ethics too must have its starting-point in the same revelation. Only then as reason is enlightened by faith can it work on the data of this revelation-event, and that must be reason's primary source, not any structure of natural law.

This layer of disagreement has long resisted attempts to circumvent it. Yet despite its long-standing nature as a barrier and its neo-orthodox reinforcement, I believe a way through to an underlying level of agreement is charted by soundings provided by Wesley's theology. These soundings have seldom been examined in ecumenical discussion, but there is evidence that Newman in his time and some Catholic theologians in ours draw similar conclusions, and this has wider implications when we note that Wesley began his probings on ground he fully shared with the Reformers -- a thoroughgoing conviction about the extent and effects of original sin.[20] According to Wesley, original sin is the state of rebellion of all creatures against the Creator, a state into which all have fallen, leading us to pride and idolatory:

> Man was created looking directly to God, as
> his last end; but having fallen into sin,
> he fell off from God, and turned into him-
> self. Now, this infers a total apostasy
> and universal corruption in man; for where
> the last end is changed, there can be no
> real goodness. And this is the case of

all men in their natural state: they seek not God, but themselves...Here is a three-fold cord not easily broken -- a blind mind, a perverse will, disordered affections.21

So far, then, Wesley stands squarely in the tradition of Luther and Calvin, and of Augustine before them all. His distinctive contribution, however, stemmed from his practice of never speaking of the depravity in man brought about by evil without at the same time affirming the grace of God that overcomes evil and restores wholeness. It was Wesley's understanding of this prevenient grace that enabled him to refute the dreaded logic of predestination which argued that since no man is free to respond in faith, and not all are saved, it follows that God saves whom he will by selectively apportioning saving grace. True, said Wesley, in the state of nature none of us is free to opt for faith, but none of us is now in a mere state of nature. Because of God's act in Jesus Christ grace is given that restores lost freedom, and that prevenient grace gives man the capacity to accept or reject the redeeming grace that enables him to follow the path of salvation. Why then are not all saved? Not because of any decree of God that they should die, but because they will not be saved.22

This understanding of the prevenient grace of God, "free in all and for all," is by no means alien to Catholic theology. It finds recent and influential expression in the thought of Karl Rahner who uses the phrase "supernatural existential" to refer to this universal offer of grace to all people. "Existential" because it is a real possibility given to the existence of everyone, "supernatural" because although never lacking in the existential situation, it does not belong as natural but comes as God's gift:

> Even prior to justification by sanctifying grace, whether this is conferred sacramentally or outside the sacraments, man already stands under the universal, infralapsarian salvific will of God which comprises within its scope original sin and personal sin. Man is redeemed, and is permanently the object of God's saving care and offer of grace...This situation, "objective justification" in contradistinction to its subjective application by sanctification, is all-inclusive and

386

inescapably prior to man's free action...
As an objective consequence of God's
universal salvific will, it of course super-
venes through grace upon man's essence as
"nature," but in the real order is never
lacking to it... That man is really affected
by the permanent offer of grace is not something which happens only now and again. It
is a permanent and inescapable human situation. This state of affairs can be briefly
labelled "supernatural existential," to
prevent its being overlooked. It means that
man as he really exists is always and ineluc-
tably more than mere "nature" in the theological sense.[23]

It has long been recognized that this understanding of grace allows those who hold it to stand in the
tradition of the Reformers without having to endorse
their predestinarian view of salvation. We have not
seen as clearly that the same recognition, that no-one
is now in a mere state of nature, also overcomes a
major objection to "natural law" theory -- that the
fall has so hardened our hearts and blinded our eyes
that we cannot know when we have contravened the orderly
purpose that the Creator has built into his creation.
Not so, says Wesley:

Allowing that all the souls of men are dead
in sin by nature this excuses none, seeing
that there is no man, unless he has quenched
the Spirit, that is wholly void of the grace
of God. No man is entirely destitute of what
is vulgarly called natural conscience. But
this is not natural: it is more properly
termed, preventing grace...Every one, unless
he be one of the small number whose conscience
is seared with a hot iron, feels more or less
uneasy when he acts contrary to the light of
his own conscience.[24]

This is not to say that Wesley, by substituting conscience for natural reason, was maintaining that the
natural law of God is fully accessible to everyone.
That view of the natural law which affirms such con-
gruence between human beings and God's purpose embodied
in the natural world that full knowledge of this will
is open to all, Wesley does not support. To know what
is the will of God rather than just sensing unease when

we have contravened it comes only when, in faith, we
accept the saving grace of God. Then the image is
restored. Our reason is healed and our moral nature
renewed. Through the intercession of his Son, God
gives us the Holy Spirit "to renew us both 'in knowledge,' in his natural image...and also in his moral
image, viz. 'righteousness and true holiness.'"[25]

For my part, I agree that no-one is so in tune
with the ordered creation that the natural law is fully
accessible to reason unaided by faith. I'm not sure
that it is fully accessible even when aided by faith,
but the purpose of God for his creation does come into
sharper focus from the perspective of the incarnation.
Nevertheless that there is such a purpose built into
the ordered creation and that our lives are diminished
or enhanced as we contravene or fulfill that purpose I
firmly believe and see that as the soundest basis for
Christian ethics. That aspect of natural law theory
at least seems to me to be essential unless we are to
live under an arbitrary God whose moral demands are
unrelated to the fulfillment of human nature within the
context of a creation that is "good," i.e., as God intended, having its own being and integrity. My conclusions here depend upon my understanding of what it is
to believe, from the standpoint of Christian faith, in
God as creator.[26] I have been so struck by the parallel conclusion, at least on this issue, of the contemporary Catholic author Gerard Hughes, and by what I
hear as clear echoes of Wesley, that I quote at some
length:

> If we can see no connection between our human
> fulfillment and the obligation under which
> God places us, then we would have no ground
> for believing that our God was a moral God
> at all...Even if one were to accept that the
> effect of original sin was totally to blind
> our minds to our true nature and destiny we
> would have to remember that precisely because
> Christ dies for all men we are not left sim-
> ply with our unaided sinful minds when we
> consider morality. The grace of Christ is
> offered to us...Revelation commends itself
> to us in part because it does harmonize with
> our moral aspirations present antecedently.
> I conclude, then, that the Christian theo-
> logian must hold not that man has the ability
> to understand morality independently of God's

grace, but of his coming to believe in
Christ on the basis of God's revelation.[27]

It therefore seems to me that natural law theory need
constitute no great divide between Catholics and
Protestants if we recognize on the one hand that natural law morality is not "ungraced" at all but a morality in which God and his grace are already involved,
and on the other, that the "ethics of revelation" do
not negate but are consistent with the created order
within which God brings human nature to its fulfillment.

Newman on Conscience.

Ecumenical discussions of soteriology invoke the
thought of Wesley because it has been observed more
than once that he combines a Protestant doctrine of sin
with a Catholic view of grace. I have been suggesting
that this same combination should be invoked in trying
to settle long-standing disputes in the area of moral
theology as well. I am encouraged in this because I
hear Catholic scholars speaking from their tradition
saying the same things about natural law and grace that
I want to say from the Wesleyan tradition. I am more
encouraged still when I discover that this is not an
accident of my hearing or even of the tone of twentieth-
century dialogue. Already in the writing of John Henry
Newman there was a view of conscience substantially the
same as Wesley's.

This is not the only point of similarity, of
course. Both men set out to reform the Church of
England. Just a century after Wesley preached, at St.
Mary's Oxford, his sermon Salvation by Faith that
marked a new departure for him, Newman preached from
the same pulpit the sermons that ushered in the Trac-
tarian Movement. More ironical is the fact that in
neither case could both man and reforming movement
remain within the Church of their birth -- Wesley
stayed, Methodism did not; Anglo-Catholics stayed,
Newman did not. And like Wesley, Newman was opposed to
an attitude dignified by the term "religious" that allowed one to believe pretty much what one liked, and
to put that belief into action. Wesley called it "speculative latitudinarianism,"[28] Newman "liberalism in
religion"; these days it is known as doing your own
thing. Newman opposed it with all the might of his

389

considerable intellect, appealing, as Wesley had done
before him, to men of reason.[29] Believing that the old
deductive theological systems had lost their authority
in an age dominated by the scientific method based on
experience and experiment, Newman set out to demonstrate
that the same level of certainty could be achieved in
the field of religion as of science, and by the same
empirical method.[30]

      In his A Grammar of Assent he set out the procedure
by which we come to knowledge in ordinary human affairs.
Beginning with sensory perceptions of the world around
us we order these into unified impressions of things,
and form hypotheses about what they are and how they are
related to other things. To hold such an hypothesis or
proposition is to give it notional assent. Real assent
becomes possible only when "the particular subjects of
the proposition are viewed in the concrete, and represent experiences, [for] without experience, assent is
not real."[31] When, by testing out in experience, notion and reality are recognized as one,[32] assent becomes
real and certitude follows. Applying the same method
to the field of religion, Newman asks: "Can I attain
to any more vivid assent to the Being of God than that
which is given merely to the notions of the intellect?
...Can I believe as if I saw?"[33] He answers in the
affirmative, drawing a parallel between the process of
physical perception outlined above and spiritual perception. God cannot be seen, but then neither can the
world, directly. What we have is the evidence of our
senses, which provides certitude only after a process
of testing and assent. But what in coming to know God
counts as evidence in the way that sensory phenomena
count in knowing the world? That, according to Newman,
is the role of conscience:

            We may, by means of induction from particular
            experience of conscience, have as good war-
            rant for concluding the ubiquitous presence
            of one Supreme Master as we have, from paral-
            lel experience of sense, for assenting to
            the fact of a multiform and vast world,
            material and mental.[34]

It is, of course, possible to offer alternative explanations for the existence of conscience, as Newman was
well aware, and in one of his Parochial Sermons he set
out to refute one of the most persistent of these --
that sensations of conscience are no more than guilt-

feelings induced by an education that includes awe of
Scripture. This he does by meeting the objectors on
their own ground. They claim to trust their own sight
and reason rather than the word of their ministers who
tell them that Scripture comes from God. Very well,
argues Newman, let them then trust something that is
just as much their own as their reason, namely their
own conscience.35 That sanction of conduct can be
adequately accounted for only by assuming the existence
of a Superior Being.

This, however, remains only an assumption, no matter how well-founded. In Newman's terminology it remains "notional." According to his own experimental
method, certainty follows only when the notion is put
to the test and confirmed in experience. So Newman
insists that when we live life believing that there is
a God, the events of life will confirm our faith.

> When men begin all their works with the
> thought of God...they will find that every-
> thing that happens tends to confirm them in
> the truths about Him which live in their
> imagination. They are brought into his
> presence as that of a living person.36

It is obedience to the voice of conscience, Newman concluded, that leads us to certain recognition of the
author of that voice. At the same time he was well
aware of the limitations of conscience. It cannot
stand alone in giving us knowledge of who God is or of
what he requires of us. In his novel Callista he has
the heroine of the same name say to Polermo (representing the liberals of Newman's time),

> I feel myself in God's presence. He says to
> me "Do this: don't do that." You may tell
> me that this dictate is a new law of my na-
> ture, as to joy or grieve. I cannot under-
> stand this. No, it is the echo of a person
> speaking to me...You will say, "Who is He?
> Has he ever told you anything about Himself?"
> Alas, No! the more's the pity.37

It is not possible then to move from the experience of
conscience to the fullness of the knowledge of God.
We are left acknowledging a divine speaker who can be
loved or feared, but no more than this.38 But not only
is the knowledge of God that comes from conscience

limited, its indications of what he wills are weak and unreliable as well. In a graphic passage Newman acknowledges that

> the sense of right and wrong is so delicate,
> so fitful, so easily puzzled, obscured, perverted, so subtle in its argumentative
> methods, so impressible by education, so
> biased by pride and passion, so unsteady in
> its course, that, in the struggle for existence amid the various exercises and triumphs
> of the human intellect, this sense is at once
> the highest of all teachers, yet the least
> luminous; and the Church, the Pope and the
> Hierarchy are, in the Divine purpose the
> supply of an urgent demand.[39]

Authority and Moral Judgement.

We have already noted that in his sermon On Conscience Wesley too acknowledged an "urgent demand" to inform and strengthen the conscience; not, it is true, with Church, Pope and Hierarchy (although with two of these he had no quarrel in principle!), but with the written word of God. Those who have written Wesley off for having identified religion with a "real or supposed experience"[40] will not be inclined to reconsider on the basis of this appeal to Scripture if Scripture itself is interpreted only by individual experience. It is therefore important to affirm that for Wesley and those who follow him Scripture and experience are not alone in informing conscience. The authority under which Wesley stood and which he enjoined upon the people called Methodists was a "four-element compound of interdependent norms,"[41] namely Scripture, Tradition, Reason, and Experience.

"Interdependent" is the right word, for every attempt to establish the claim that any one of these makes upon us already involves the others. In the reading and hearing of Scripture, for example, Wesley insists that reason is to be used, and he employed all the scholarly methods of biblical interpretation available to him at the time. Wherever possible, he insisted, the plain meaning of the text is to be preferred, with due reference to the original languages, and one text is to be compared with, and understood in the light of, another. The meaning of the text, however, is not

thereby exhausted; the tradition of the Church draws
out the meaning and clarifies the doctrine implied
therein, but all of this comes alive only when appropriated by faith and experienced for oneself. Then and
only then can we know that the word of salvation proclaimed in Scripture, interpreted by tradition and expounded by reason is a word spoken to us with power to
heal and save. In the same way, tradition, reason and
experience can all be shown to enhance, depend upon
and stand under the judgement of the others. Nevertheless the prior authority of Scripture is never in question; Scripture read with reason, interpreted through
tradition and appropriated in experience to be sure,
but Scripture so read, interpreted and appropriated remained the touchstone for faith and practice, or, in
other words, for doctrine and moral judgements. In the
very document in which he insists that the distinguish-
ing marks of a Methodist are not opinions, words, actions or emphases but "having the love of God shed
abroad in his heart by the Holy Spirit given unto him"
Wesley affirmed "we believe the written word of God to
be the only sufficient rule of both faith and practice."[42]

One could wish that he had not continued, "and
herein we are fundamentally distinguished from those of
the Romish Church,"[43] but we need to acknowledge that
he did, if only to emphasize that in line with Wesley's
own criteria, he must not be allowed to speak the last
word. For was that a fundamental distinction then,
and is it now?

It was if we hold Wesley to the more restrictive
way of applying this rule of faith and practice, viz.
that nothing is acceptable unless enjoined in Scripture.
This method he did follow especially when engaged in
polemical writing.[44] Nevertheless it is clear that he
was also prepared to adopt a more expansive method of
interpretation which allowed, although did not insist
upon as essential, what is not forbidden in Scripture.
So, for example, Wesley acknowledged that there was no
ground in the New Testament for a national church[45] and
did not claim that the liturgy of the Church of England
was prescribed in Scripture, yet he remained a priest
of that Church, believing her doctrines and loving her
liturgy. Again, while asserting that the three-fold
order of ministry is described in Scripture and generally obtained in the apostolic era, he did not insist
that no other order was possible. The norm of reason

is clearly in evidence as he argued that if the three-fold order of ministry were essential to a Christian Church, "what must become of all the foreign Reformed Churches? It would follow that they are no parts of the Church of Christ -- a consequence full of shocking absurdity."46 Had Wesley been prepared to test the development of doctrine and church order within the Roman Catholic Church with the same expansive rather than restrictive application of the rule of faith, and moderated by the same testimony of reason, then he would not have seen the distinction between himself and those of "Romish persuasion" to have been so fundamental.

Nor is it so fundamental now. Those who follow Wesley at his best as it were, with the expansive application of the rule of faith, can certainly recognize the authority of the hierarchy and the primacy of Peter as a legitimate development within the Church Catholic without necessarily acknowledging the way the Pope's authority is interpreted and exercised within the Roman Catholic Church. That difficulties remain in this area is acknowledged in all the dialogues in which the Catholic Church is currently engaged and perhaps we can do no better at this point than to affirm that the difficulty is sometimes couched in terms that are too stark. Nevertheless I am struck by the importance of a comment made to me by a Catholic colleague in the United Faculty of Theology in Melbourne, that despite the obvious differences, the Protestant emphasis on Scripture as "the only sufficient rule of faith and practice" and the decree on papal infallibility at least have this in common -- the concern to protect the genuine Gospel, guarding it against manipulation by those who claim ultimate authority for their own individual religious convictions, at the same time providing a check against distortion by the structured community itself.

This brings to light yet another core of agreement, that what both Protestants and Catholics need to guard against is an eroding of moral responsibility by the enticing authoritarianism of fundamentalism -- biblical fundamentalism on the one hand, ecclesiastical fundamentalism on the other. But to dig around the issues involved in all that will have to wait for another occasion.

FOOTNOTES

1. In Australia, as a member of the Methodist/Roman Catholic dialogue, now the Uniting Church/Roman Catholic dialogue; and as a member of the World Methodist/Roman Catholic Joint Commission.
2. The Commission has been meeting since 1967, and makes major reports to parent bodies every five years. The latest series began in 1982.
3. "The Holy Spirit, Christian Experience and Authority." Report of the Joint Commission between the Roman Catholic Church and the World Methodist Council, Nov 79, 2.5.
4. Ibid.
5. It is interesting to note that in the first two sessions of the Council of Trent opinion seemed to favor the view that the extreme statements should be countered by affirming the prevenient grace of God that has overcome that depravity. This was largely overlooked, however, in the later formulations.
6. Albert Outler, ed., John Wesley; NY: Oxford, 1964, p. 28.
7. John Wesley, "The Law established by Faith, Discourse II," pp. 229-30 in Outler, op. cit.
8. Sermon, "On Conscience," p. 178 in The Works of the Rev. John Wesley, vol. VII; London: John Mason, 1856.
9. Ibid.
10. Ibid.
11. Ibid., p. 179.
12. Ibid.
13. Ibid., p. 181.
14. Ibid., italics mine.
15. Setting out what were later called the legislative and judicial functions of conscience.
16. Using Ezekiel's imagery of man, lion and ox, and seeing these representing reason, spirit and desire with the eagle of conscience set above all.
17. Eric D'Arcy, Conscience and its Right to Freedom; London: Sheed & Ward, 1961, p. 48.
18. Summa Theologica I-II, q.91, a.2. Cited by J.V. Dolan, p. 11 in Conscience: Its Freedom and Limitations ed W.C. Bier; NY: Fordham Press, 1971.
19. Dolan, op. cit.
20. This, he insisted, was one of the essential doctrines. "A denial of original sin contradicts one of the main purposes of the Gospel, which is to humble vain man and to ascribe to God's free grace, not to man's free will, the whole of his salvation." Works IX:409.
21. Ibid., pp. 435-6.
22. Works VII:364.
23. Karl Rahner, "Existence," pp. 494-5 in Encyclopedia of Theology ed. K. Rahner; London: Burns & Oates, 1975.
24. Works VI:485.
25. Ibid., p. 209.
26. N.J. Young, Creator, Creation and Faith; London: Collins, 1976.

27. G.J. Hughes, <u>Authority in Morals</u>; London: Heythrop, 1978, pp. 5, 7.

28. Wesley has been accused of this himself, but nothing could be further from the truth. While ready to offer his hand to those who disagreed with him on non-essentials, he insisted that "a Catholic Spirit is not speculative latitudinarianism: this is the spawn of hell not the offspring of heaven...observe this, you who know not what spirit you are of: who call yourselves men of a catholic spirit, only because you are of muddy understanding... go, first, and learn the first elements of the Gospel of Christ, and then you shall learn to be of a truly Catholic Spirit." <u>Works</u> V:472.

29. See, for example, Wesley's "Earnest Appeal to men of Reason and Religion" and "A Further Appeal..." <u>Works</u> VIII.

30. Although Wesley wrote no extended epistemology as Newman did, it is clear that he held an empiricist view of knowledge. See, for example, his favorable remarks on Locke's <u>Essay on Human Knowledge</u> in <u>Works</u> XIII:429.

31. J.H. Newman, <u>A Grammar of Assent</u>; NY: Longmans Green, 1891, p. 237.

32. The capacity to recognize a faculty Newman attributes to what he called the "illative sense."

33. Newman, <u>op. cit.</u>, pp. 102-3.

34. <u>Ibid.</u>, p. 63.

35. Newman, <u>Parochial Sermons</u> I; NY: Appleton, 1893, p. 201.

36. Newman, <u>A Grammar...</u>, p. 117.

37. Newman, <u>Callista: A Sketch of the Third Century</u>; London: Burns & Oates, 1876, p. 244.

38. In reflecting on the early days of "Crisis Theology," Barth acknowledged that the extreme expression of the otherness of God led to the same situation. Only the rediscovery of a Christological starting-point enabled him to fill the awareness <u>that</u> God is with the knowledge of <u>who</u> he is. Contrast, for example, Barth's sermon, "The Righteousness of God" given in 1916 (<u>The Word of God and the Word of Man</u>; NY: Harper, 1957) with <u>The Humanity of God</u>; London: Collins, 1961.

39. <u>Difficulties of an Anglican</u>; London: Longmans Green, 1903. Vol. II:253.

40. Ronald Knox, <u>Enthusiasm</u>; NY: Oxford, 1950, p. 547.

41. An Interim Report of the Theological Study Commission on Doctrine and Doctrinal Standards, United Methodist Church, USA. As Albert Outler, Chair of that commission, has pointed out, Wesley himself suggested this listing of authorities. In the Preface to the third edition of his <u>Works</u> he presents his thoughts in the hope that they are "agreeable to Scripture, reason and Christian antiquity."

42. Wesley, "The Character of a Methodist." <u>Works</u> VIII:326.

43. <u>Ibid.</u>

44. When, for example, he criticizes the Bull of Pius IV for "adding to the book of life" with seven sacraments, transubstantiation, purgatory.." <u>Works</u> I:209; or maintains that Holy Writ does not establish the Bishop of Rome as Christ's Vicar on earth. <u>Works</u> X:133.

45. Minutes, 1747. Cited in Colin Williams, John Wesley's Theology Today; London: Epworth, p. 222.
46. Ibid.

Jeffrey A. Blakely is currently a doctoral student in the Oriental Studies Department at the University of Pennsylvania. His undergraduate work was at Oberlin with the late Tom Frank. He has a Master's from the University of Wisconsin (Madison campus) and a Master's from WLU where he studied with Larry Toombs. His doctoral research is on the Iron Age pottery of Tell el-Hesi. He is co-author with L.E. Toombs of The Tell el-Hesi Field Manual.

Roger S. Boraas is Professor of Religion in the Department of Philosophy and Religion of Upsala College in East Orange, NJ. He is a graduate of Gustavus Adolphus, Augustana and Drew, and has done graduate work at Union and Oberlin, and post-doctoral study at the University of London Institute of Archaeology. He was on the staff of the Shechem Expedition, Director of the excavation of Rujm el Malfuf (North), Chief Archaeologist for the Hesban Expedition and is currently in that positon for the Khirbet Iskander excavations. Among his many publications, he was co-author of the preliminary reports of the Hesban excavations (Andrews University Monographs).

George Wesley Buchanan is Professor of New Testament at Wesley Theological Seminary in Washington, D.C. A graduate of Simpson, Garrett, Northwestern and Drew, he holds the Litt.D. from Simpson and has studied at HUC-JIR, Hebrew University, HUCBAS, Goettingen, Germany, and Claremont, CA. The author of numerous articles and books, his latest volume is Jesus, The King and His Kingdom.

Joseph A. Callaway is semi-retired from his Senior Professorship of Old Testament and Archaeology at Southern Baptist Theological Seminary in Louisville, KY. He is the Director of the Expedition to Ai and has excavated at Raddana, Bethel, Shechem, and Jerusalem (with Kenyon). Among his numerous publications is The Early Bronze Age Sanctuary at Ai. He is currently President of the AIAR.

Edward F. Campbell, Jr., is Professor of Old Testament at McCormick Theological Seminary in Chicago, IL. He is a graduate of Johns Hopkins University and has held a number of offices in the ASOR. He is Acting Director of the Shechem Expedition and coordinator of the final publications for that excavation.

Thurman L. Coss is Pastor of Rosemount (MN) United Methodist Church after teaching at California Western (U.S. International) and Hamline. He is a graduate of Notre Dame, Oberlin and Drew. The author of numerous articles and reviews, his book on the Dead Sea Scrolls is titled Secrets from the Caves.

Valerie M. Fargo is the Project Director of the Joint Archaeological Expedition to Tell el-Hesi and the assistant to the director of the Oriental Institute at the University of Chicago. Besides Hesi, she has excavated in Sicily, Cyprus and Iran.

Lawrence T. Geraty is Professor of Archaeology and the History of Antiquity and Director of the Institute of Archaeology at Andrews University in Berrien Springs, MI. A doctoral graduate of Harvard, he is active in Jordan as Vice President of the American Center of Oriental Research in Amman. He is also Director of the Andrews Expedition to Tell Hesban and general editor of the final publication of the excavations.

Colin L. House was born in Mackay, Queensland, Australia. The son of a minister, he became a minister himself, serving congregations in his home State. A graduate of Avondale College in Australia and Andrews University in Michigan, he is now a doctoral student in archaeology at Andrews.

Burton MacDonald is Associate Professor in the Department of Theology at St. Francis Xavier University, Antigonish, Nova Scotia, Canada. He is a graduate of St. Francis Xavier University, the University of Ottawa, and the Catholic University of America. He is the Director of the Wadi el-Hasa Archaeological Survey and has participated in various projects in the Near East.

Kevin G. O'Connell, S.J., is Chair and Associate Professor of the Department of Religious Studies, John Carroll University, Cleveland, Ohio. He has extensive experience on the Tell el-Hesi excavations where among other roles he has served as administrative director. He is currently general editor of the Hesi reports.

Morgan L. Phillips is with the Department of Religion in Ohio Wesleyan University, Delaware, Ohio.

John Priest has both the B.D. ('55) and Ph.D. ('60) from Drew where he studied with L.E. Toombs and John Paterson. He has taught at Ohio Wesleyan, Hartford Seminary, and since 1968, Florida State University where he is currently Professor of Religion. He was President of the AAR in 1967 and Executive Director and Treasurer 1975-8. He has published in the JBL, JNES, JBR, JAAR and elsewhere.

Thomas E. Ranck is the Director of the Honors Program for Loyola University in Chicago.

C.C. Settlemire is a Professor in the History Department of Slippery Rock University (Slippery Rock, PA) and has served as Chair of the Department for the past five years.

Rav A. Soloff graduated from the University of Cincinnati in 1947, the HUC-JIR in '51 and earned his Ph.D. at Drew in '67. In 1976, after receiving an Honorary D.D. from his rabbinic alma mater, he came to Johnstown, PA to serve the Beth Sholom Congregation. He is co-author of Jewish Life, Your Siddur, and Torataynu (2 vol) - a series for teaching biblical Hebrew using texts from Jewish practice, prayerbooks and the Pentateuch.

William Richard "Dick" Stegner is Professor of New Testament at Garrett-Evangelical Theological Seminary in Evanston, IL. His doctorate is from Drew. He cites L.E. Toombs as his mentor in Hebrew and for his dissertation. He has done post-doctoral work at Tantur (Bethlehem) and Hebrew University, and HUC (Cincinnati). He has specialized in Christian origins and the Jewish background of Christianity.

James F. Strange is Dean of the College of Arts and Letters and Professor of Religious Studies at the University of South Florida in Tampa. His Ph.D. is from Drew. He has been Montgomery Fellow and NEH Fellow at the AIAR 1970-1 and '80. Since 1970, he has served as Associate Director of the Joint Expedition to Khirbet Shema, Israel and of its successor, the Meiron Excavation Project. Most recently he has directed the Survey of Lower Galilee (1981) and excavations at Sepphoris (1982). His books include Ancient Synagogue Excavations at Khirbet Shema, Israel (1976, with E.M. Meyers and A.T. Kraabel); Excavations at Ancient Meiron (1981, with E.M. and C.L. Meyers), and Archaeology, the Rabbis, and Early Palestinian Christianity (1981, with E.M. Meyers).

Henry O. "Hank" Thompson received his Ph.D. from Drew in '64 and was on the staffs of the Shechem (1960-8) and Hesban ('68-73) expeditions. He was Director (71-2) and Visiting Professor (72-3) of ACOR in Amman. He has published in both popular and scholarly journals in addition to editing and co-editing, authoring and co-authoring several books. His doctoral dissertation, Mekal, The God of Beth-shan, was published by Brill in 1971. L.E. Toombs chaired his dissertation committee, and served as dissertation advisor.

Prescott H. Williams, Jr., is Professor of Old Testament Languages and Archaeology at Austin Presbyterian Seminary and Instructor in Biblical Studies at the University of Texas at Austin. He was Dean of the Faculty at the Seminary for 10 years and Acting President and President for 6 years. He was Shechem Fellow and Acting Annual Professor at ASOR in Jerusalem in 1964 and Annual Professor at ACOR in Amman in 1983-4. He has participated in several archaeological activities in the Near East. He is a graduate of Wheaton, Princeton, and Johns Hopkins and has published a number of articles in various journals.

Norman Young is Professor of Systematic Theology at Queen's College, University of Melbourne, and Principal of the Uniting Church Theological College in that city. A Methodist minister prior to the union of Methodist, Presbyterian and Congregational Churches in Australia in 1977, he was President of the Conference in that year, and for a decade before was convener of the commission preparing for union. He was the second Australian to study at Drew University and received his B.D. (summa cum laude) and Ph.D. degrees there in the 1950s. He has published works on the theology of Rudolf Bultmann and on the doctrine of creation.

ACKNOWLEDGEMENTS: Permission to publish and/or reprint materials is gratefully acknowledged - The Joint Expedition to Caesarea Maritima (Blakely article), The Joint Archaeological Expedition to Ai (Callaway article), The Joint Expedition to Shechem (Campbell article), L.E. Toombs (Fargo article), The Wadi el-Hasa Archaeological Survey (MacDonald article), L.T. Geraty (Thompson article), and R. K. Taylor (Frontispiece).